"In the tradition of Callie House, Queen Mother Moore, and other foremothers, Women With A Vision organizes with the belief that caring for the people is inseparable from speaking truth to power. That is why this grassroots New Orleans group of Black women has won policy fights that others thought impossible. This book shows us how the history of Black women's resistance continues to birth new movements for structural change."

—Mary Frances Berry, Geraldine Segal Professor of American Social Thought, History, and Africana Studies at the University of Pennsylvania

"Unapologetically rooted in experiences and visions of Black women and trans people living at the intersections of multiple interlocking oppressions, drawing on thirty-five years of fierce Black feminist resistance to abandonment of Black HIV-affected women, the war on drugs, and criminalization of sexual and reproductive autonomy, and consistently centering Black women's dignity, self-determination, and cultures of care, *Fire Dreams* illuminates what Black feminism in action looks like and shines essential light from the South on the path forward in this moment."

—Andrea J. Ritchie, cofounder of Interrupting Criminalization and coauthor of *No More Police: A Case for Abolition*

"What are the possibilities for all of us, if we liberate poor Black women, cisgender and trans, in the Deep South? *Fire Dreams,* which documents the history of the work of Women With A Vision, shows how one organization in New Orleans has shouted this question to the world, with its bold model of organizing, policy advocacy, and service provision, using a Black feminist praxis for the women whose power is most often ignored and rarely channeled toward radical change."

—Kenyon Farrow, writer, activist, and contributor to *Healing Justice Lineages: Dreaming at the Crossroads of Liberation, Collective Care, and Safety*

"We are all indebted to the minds, hearts, and work of Women With A Vision. They've lovingly and forcefully led our collective movement to build deeper relationships and create more expansive visions. They've shifted power so that they could demand accountability for the people and the communities that need WWAV's *Fire Dreams* to be reality."

—Kassandra Frederique, Executive Director of the Drug Policy Alliance

"WWWWAVD (What Would Women With A Vision Do?) has been a constant question and guiding principle throughout my life as an activist. WWAV has taught us all what it means to center the health, rights, safety, and self-determination of people in drug-using and sex worker communities, and to unwaveringly use the power of harm reduction to free us all. Their story is inspiring, it is incredible, and it is necessary for anyone working toward liberation."

—Cyndee Clay, Executive Director of HIPS (Honoring Individual Power & Strength)

"*Fire Dreams* captures the essence of Women With A Vision brilliantly—beautifully resilient, perfectly intersectional, and Black community–centered. The history, struggle, and sacrifice are Herstory that all of us should celebrate."

—Heidi Williamson, Principal Creative and RJ Advocate, Hummingbird Black Creative

"What would our world look like if Black women, queer and trans people of color, sex workers, and drug users had everything they needed to survive, to thrive? Women With A Vision answers this question through radical acceptance, love, and transformation, and by guiding so many of us to stay and fight back. Through all the floods and fires, WWAV's ethic of Black Feminist community building has been the force that has led our repair and restoration."

—R. Cielo Cruz, writer, cultural organizer, Racial Justice facilitator, former WWAV board member, former sex worker, longtime New Orleans local

"A community of practice that has been coming together to learn and serve our people for nearly forty years, with a track record of meeting needs and saving lives. What an honor it is to follow the leadership of Deon Haywood and the Women With A Vision family."

—Ash-Lee Woodard Henderson, Co-Executive Director, Highlander Research and Education Center

FIRE DREAMS

FIRE
DREAMS

MAKING BLACK FEMINIST LIBERATION IN THE SOUTH

Laura McTighe,
with Women With A Vision

FOREWORD BY DEON HAYWOOD

DUKE UNIVERSITY PRESS
Durham and London
2024

© 2024 DUKE UNIVERSITY PRESS

All rights reserved

Printed in the United States of America on acid-free paper ∞

Project Editor: Livia Tenzer

Designed by A. Mattson Gallagher

Typeset in Garamond Premier Pro and Futura Std by
Westchester Publishing Services

Library of Congress Cataloging-in-Publication Data

Names: McTighe, Laura, [date] author. | Haywood, Deon, writer
of foreword. | Women With A Vision (Non-profit organization :
New Orleans, Louisiana), author.

Title: Fire dreams : making black feminist liberation in the
South / Laura McTighe, with Women With A Vision ; foreword
by Deon Haywood.

Description: Durham : Duke University Press, 2024. | Includes
bibliographical references and index.

Identifiers: LCCN 2023014911 (print)

LCCN 2023014912 (ebook)

ISBN 9781478025542 (paperback)

ISBN 9781478020806 (hardcover)

ISBN 9781478027690 (ebook)

Subjects: LCSH: Women With A Vision (Non-profit organization :
New Orleans, Louisiana) | African American feminists—
Southern States. | Women social reformers—Southern States. |
Social problems—Southern States. | African American women
political activists—Southern States. | Womanism—Southern
States. | Feminism—Southern States. | Racism—Study and
teaching—United States. | Southern States—Race relations. |
BISAC: SOCIAL SCIENCE / Ethnic Studies / American /
African American & Black Studies | RELIGION / General

Classification: LCC HQ1438.S63 M385 2024 (print) | LCC
HQ1438.S63 (ebook) | DDC 305.420975—dc23/eng/20230830

LC record available at https://lccn.loc.gov/2023014911

LC ebook record available at https://lccn.loc.gov/2023014912

Cover art: Carla Jay Harris, *Of the Wind,* 2021. Photography,
digital painting, and acrylic on paper, 44 × 57 in. Courtesy of
the artist and Luis De Jesus Los Angeles.

for
Bunny,
Jaliyah,
Earlneishka,
and all the other Young Women With A Vision
who will carry this work forward ever

CONTENTS

FOREWORD   xiii
Deon Haywood

Acknowledgments   xvii

INTRODUCTION   I
BORN IN FLAMES

1   **FRONT PORCH STRATEGY**   29

2   **DOING THE WORK**   52

3   **WE SPOKE OUR TRUTHS**   95

4   **WORKING WITH FIRE**   132

5   **THE GROUNDS**   172

EPILOGUE   210
FORWARD EVER

Notes   225
Born in Flames Living Archive   265
Bibliography   277
Index   307

FOREWORD

May 2023

In the spring of 2012, during a planning session, a facilitator asked us what would happen if Women With A Vision (WWAV) ceased to exist. No one in the room could truly answer the question. Instead, we replied, "The work will continue to get done, no matter what." Little did we know, weeks later, on May 24, 2012, someone would try to burn our offices, our work, and all that we stand for to the ground. And yet, we're still here. More than a decade after the attack, WWAV is working in community to stay the course and fight the fight. You can't look at WWAV's work and not know that it's important to the moment we're living through.

It's been just under a year since the US Supreme Court issued the *Dobbs* decision on June 24, 2022, triggering a total abortion ban in Louisiana. That day, all of us at WWAV felt weary but not surprised. We knew this was coming. We had been fighting it for years. However, in the months since that decision, the unrelenting attacks on so many rights that our ancestors fought and gave their lives for—the attacks on Black and Brown people, Indigenous people, women and birthing people, transgender people, and queer people—these attacks have taken a toll on us all. Now is the time to get back to basics, to the methods we have always used to free us. We need space to share our greatest fears and to come up with our own solutions. We need to help each other open the windows and doors of our imaginations to envision the futures of our dreams, and we need to honor the ways that we are already working to build those futures in real time. Most of all, we need to revisit our history to move forward. Who's gonna keep us safe? WE ARE.

As an organization, WWAV has survived the very tactics of white supremacist terror and dispossession that are everywhere right now. None of these tactics are new, even if they feel like they're happening on a whole other level. Terror is always reactionary. White supremacists see our power, they see us—Black folks, Brown folks, queer folks—living our full lives, and they're grasping at the straws of the old world to try to stop the new one we are building.

WWAV was born out of necessity and in the long history of Black women coming together to make what their communities needed to survive. The arson attack on our offices happened just two months after we successfully led the NO Justice fight to remove hundreds of mostly poor, Black, and LGBTQ+ folks from the Louisiana sex offender registry for engaging in survival sex work. We are here because our community stepped in and stood with us, and that is precisely what we need to do for each other now.

The question that propelled our foremothers to action in the depths of the AIDS crisis is the same one that drove our work to fight criminalization in the wake of Hurricane Katrina, and it is the same one that guides our work now to build an intersectional approach to reproductive justice in the South today: *What are we willing to do?*

Every day, we honor our community's refusal to bow to white supremacy. Fire means something, especially in the South. Just as terrorists, too cowardly to show their faces, set crosses ablaze under the cover of night in an attempt not only to violently interrupt radical freedom work but also to warn others who might dare to refuse to bow in the face of oppression, our attackers aimed to punish us for daring to fight for our own liberation. Ours is not a story of resilience. Black people have had to be resilient for too long. And the powers that be are too quick to label us "resilient" while refusing to question why our lives require such resilience. Ours is a story of refusal. We refused to stop fighting for the rights and dignity of sex workers, drug users, poor Black and Brown women, and LGBTQ+ people. And that's exactly what we'll continue to do.

Our attackers thought the flames would put an end to WWAV's work. They were wrong. Those flames, meant to destroy us, birthed new dreams. This book is our story of why. This book shows how something created from need, in community, became powerful. In the eleven years since the arson attack and the thirty-five years since WWAV was founded, our work has only expanded. WWAV has been so successful because people see themselves in WWAV. We come from these communities. We know sex work. We know homelessness. We know single motherhood. We know how to listen to our people. We have always been willing to do and say the things that other people were afraid to. Our people's lives depend on it. We have also been kept out of spaces because people were afraid of what we'd say—and we went back anyway. We understand that our freedom is tied to everyone else's freedom.

There is a place for all of us in this fight. We need to be everywhere—to start in New Orleans, to work across the South, to move nationally and globally. The challenges we face every day are everywhere issues. Our whole world is on fire. We need to move quickly and in unison to stop the destruction that is happening. We must also remember that fire can be a powerful force for rebirth. The future is ours to create. We can already see the embers of a new world glowing all around us, sparking new dreams and new realities.

So I'll ask you again: *What are we willing to do? How far are we willing to go?*

Please stand with us as we forge a path to freedom. The work will continue to get done, no matter what.

In solidarity,
Deon Haywood
Executive Director
Women With A Vision

ACKNOWLEDGMENTS

This book is a gift. It is an offering of love.

It is first and foremost an offering for every person who has ever touched or been touched by the work of Women With A Vision (WWAV). Everything we are is because of *you*: the people who have trusted us to be in community with you and to make the impossible possible each and every day. May this book honor our hard-won survival work and the dreams we have turned into reality through it all. May it also serve as a testament to what it means to truly commit to community and to one another.

This book is also an offering to WWAV's foremothers, Catherine Haywood and Danita Muse: to the original women and the vision they made reality. As Catherine's mother and Deon's grandmother, Mildred Farlough Gray, always said, "If you are who you say you are, then be who you say you are." Our foremothers took these words to heart. In the early days, they never kept a record of the truths they were making, because they were so busy doing the work. Too much has been taken from WWAV over the last thirty-five years. This is a story that a whole lot of people wish did not exist and worked *hard* to erase. May this book serve as a form of reparations. May it return to our foremothers what has always been theirs. May it also be a portal for bringing that healing to generations past and generations future.

We make this offering with gratitude to so many. As abolitionist organizer and educator Mariame Kaba teaches us, "Everything worthwhile is done with other people." We give thanks to the movements that have held us down and to the friends, family, comrades, and mentors who have nurtured us in this work.

Our work started at the intersections of harm reduction, HIV prevention justice, queer liberation, and sex workers' rights. Today we are proud to call Orisha Bowers, Tracie Gardner, Deborah Small, Cyndee Clay, Shira Hassan, Dázon Dixon Diallo, Naina Khanna, Venita Ray, Waheedah Shabazz-El, Laura Thomas, Kenyon Farrow, Allen Kwabena Frimpong, Catherine Hanssens, Brook Kelly-Green, Terry McGovern, and so many others our movement family. The unapologetic work you grow in the world every day is the ground that makes ours possible. Being enmeshed in these movements also sharpened the focus of our organizing for reproductive justice, abolition feminism, and drug policy. We honor Loretta Ross, Byllye Avery, Monica Simpson, Paris Hatcher, Jasmine Burnett, Marcela Howell, Andrea Ritchie, Mariame Kaba, Ruth Wilson Gilmore, Beth Richie, Laura Whitehorn, Andrea James, Victoria Law, Charlene Carruthers, Mary Hooks, Kay Whitlock, Kassandra Frederique, Asha Bandele, Roz Lee, Nakeisha Lewis, and more as our coteachers and codreamers. Each of you has helped to link our movements' work together under ever-expanding visions for liberation. And to Kimberley Hinton and Heidi Williamson, we thank you for your DC friendship, mentorship, deep thoughts, and ideas. You have been Deon's steadiest touchstones for Black women seeing each other and strategizing in ways that are achievable.

We also hold close to all of our movement family here in New Orleans and across the South: Ashley Shelton and the Power Coalition for Equity and Justice; Latona Giwa and the Birthmark Doula Collective; Ashley Hill Hamilton, "The Uptown Doula"; Ursula Price; the New Orleans Workers' Center for Racial Justice; Mama Jennifer and the Community Book Center; Norris Henderson and the Voice of the Experienced (VOTE); Sade Dumas; the Orleans Parish Prison Reform Coalition (OPPRC); Wendi Cooper; Milan Sherry; the House of Tulip; Shana M. griffin; R. Cielo Cruz; Wes Ware; Jordan Flaherty; S. Mandisa Moore-O'Neal and the Center for HIV Law and Policy; Aesha Rasheed, Wendi Moore-O'Neal, and Southerners On New Ground (SONG); Steph Guilloud and Project South; Nsombi Lambright; Valencia Robinson; Ash-Lee Woodard Henderson and the Highlander Research and Education Center; and so many more. Through our work with you, we know, as historian Robin D. G. Kelley put it, that "the reason why the South is so repressive is because it's the most radical place in North America." We commit again and again with you to building the world we need in real time. And to Eddie Burke, we will continue to honor your spirit and the legacy you have trusted us to carry forward each and every day.

In the immediate aftermath of the 2012 arson attack on our offices, WWAV was able to continue because of the support of all these movement partners and more. To the members of the NO Justice Project legal team—Andrea Ritchie, Alexis Agathocleous, Bill Quigley, Davida Finger, Sunita Patel, Nikki Thanos, David Rudovsky, Jonathan Feinberg, and Seth Kreimer—who filed a new class action lawsuit just one month after the fire to secure the removal of more than eight hundred people from the Louisiana sex offender registry, we offer thanks for your unwavering commitment to the freedom dreams of our people. To every person who organized a fundraiser or donated to our work; to the foundations who stood by us and resourced us more deeply; to First Grace United Methodist Church, who provided us with our first safe haven after the fire; and to the people who have depended on us for harm reduction supplies and gave us sometimes the only pennies they had so the work would continue to get done: you showed us again and again what solidarity built through care feels like and looks like in revolutionary praxis.

As we began our research as survival in the wake of the fire, we were blessed to be held in scholarly community by Courtney Bender, Josef Sorett, John Jackson Jr., Elizabeth Castelli, Mary Frances Berry, Melinda Chateauvert, Micol Seigel, Jenna Lloyd, Sarah Haley, Dan Berger, Lydia Pelot-Hobbs, Lila Abu-Lughod, Farah Griffin, Sam Roberts, and Angela Zito, among others. Thank you for consistently honoring with us the wisdom of both the academically based and community-trained scholars who give our work shape and meaning. We also want to offer special thanks to Courtney, Josef, John, and Elizabeth: you committed to so much more than reading and nurturing the pages of writing produced through this research (which you did, and then some!); you also cared for each of us and for the work itself and helped this project have wings. And to Mary, our teacher in all of this work and more, thank you. To have you call us when you see something move and say "I know that was you" is the biggest gift possible.

We received vital support from the Institute for Religion, Culture, and Public Life at Columbia University, the Wenner-Gren Foundation for Anthropological Research, and the Institute for Citizens and Scholars to get our foundational research off the ground; from Florida State University's College of Arts and Sciences and Department of Religion to see *Fire Dreams* to publication; and from the Henry Luce Foundation to bring the Born in Flames Living Archive into the world.

So many more people have made contributions to us and to this work so that it would continue. To Laura's parents, Sue and Art, for knowing that WWAV is family and for making our family yours. To Ashley Wennerstrom, Tara Thierry, Olivia Ford, Camille Roane, Terranisha Hiley, Pascal Emmer, Danielle Sered, asmara tesfaye rogoza, Jules Netherland, Anand Venkat-krishnan, Shireen Hamza, Yesenia Barragan, Mark Bray, Lucia O'Barr, Sarah Chiddy, Hakim Ali, the Reverend Doris Green, Kimberly Wallace-Hutson, Khweze Mkhize, Suzie Ferguson, Alexis Wells-Oghoghomeh, Vaughn Booker, Samira Mehta, Matt Harris, Elayne Oliphant, and Daniel Vaca for always providing soft places to land and for searching with us for the tools to reimagine and remake our world. To our New Orleans crew, Anisa Parks, Erica Williams, Kim Seals, Rhonda Broussard, Shelley Stiaes, and Dimitri Blutcher, for love and friendship and more. And to Kali Handel-man, our friend, editor, and confidant: thank you for never losing faith in or sight of the possibility of what this work could and would become. To say that we are here because of you is no overstatement.

When a project is nurtured for as many years as this one, the webs of care continue to multiply. To Megan Raschig for the years of covisioning the otherwise anthropology that we at WWAV and you at the Colectiva de Mujeres were creating, and to all of our cotravelers in this journey, including Deborah Thomas, Lisa Stevenson, Aditi D. Surie von Czechowski, Savannah Shange, Roseann Liu, Talisa Feliciano, Celina de Sá, and karen g. williams. In our hands, the otherwise came alive as a deeply enduring, liberatory project. To Yana Stainova for the possibilities we were able to grow by method making in concert between our New Orleans world and your Venezuelan one. And to Judith Weisenfeld for the gift that *New World A-Coming: Black Religion and Racial Identity during the Great Migration* has been for us and so many, and for the community of religio-racial study built with Matthew Cressler, Jamil Drake, Megan Goodwin, and Sylvester Johnson. We first spoke our concept "theory on the ground" into being as part of this collective. Each of you helped to sharpen the offering we make now.

Thank you to the entire community at the Dartmouth Society of Fellows for making space for this work to rest and grow in interdisciplinary conver-sation. To our dear scholar-comrades Bethany Moreton, Pamela Voekel, and Yui Hashimoto: the week of WWAV colearning we were able to host for Dartmouth students and Upper Valley organizers was our first glimmer of all the audiences that this book could and would need to speak to; it is also our model for taking the show on the road now that it is in print. And to Zahra Ayubi, Tish Lopez, Jason MacLeod, Mary Coffey, Asma Elhuni, Treva Ellison, Nathalie Batraville, Derek Woods, Becky Clark, and so many others who sustained us in this time: thank you for joining us in writing and speaking and living this work in the world.

We are grateful for the academic spaces we were invited into and those we were able to make through the American Studies Association, the American Academy of Religion, the American Anthropological Association, the Association of American Geographers, and the American Public Health Association. Thank you also to the members of the Black Religious Studies Working Group at Princeton University for your careful readings that shaped the ways in which we now center our collective authorship as one of the core interventions of this book. Thanks to the members of the Dartmouth Feminism Inquiry Seminar for your guidance on making early versions of chapter 2 into what it has become. And to the members of the American Religious History and Religion, Ethics, and Philosophy colloquia at Florida State University, especially John Corrigan, Michael McVicar, Sonia Hazard, Martin Kavka, John Kelsay, Barney Twiss, Aline Kalbian, and Matt Day, thank you for engaging so deeply with the possibilities held in chapter 3.

We have likewise been nurtured, challenged, and enlivened by public-facing spaces of study and struggle, including the International Drug Policy Reform Conference, the International Harm Reduction Conference, the Southern Harm Reduction Conference, the United States Conference on HIV/AIDS, the International AIDS Conference, the Collective Power for Reproductive Justice Conference (formerly Civil Liberties and Public Policy), Creating Change, the INCITE! Color of Violence Conference, Facing Race: A National Conference, the Allied Media Conference, and the Southern Movement Assembly, as well as those spaces built and maintained by our movement family at In Our Own Voices, SisterSong, Desiree Alliance, Positive Women's Network—USA, SisterLove, Black Feminist Future, the In Our Names Network, Critical Resistance, and Interrupting Criminalization, among others.

These many overlapping academic and movement spaces were our pathway to meeting Elizabeth Ault, our editor at Duke University Press. Elizabeth, we thank you for your steadfast commitment to this project and to us as authors at every stage. You heard in this work the challenge and offering it would be for scholarship and practice otherwise, and you ensured that it was put into the hands of reviewers who united with these aims and would nurture it to shine as brightly as possible. To that end, we also want to thank our reviewers for your deep and generous engagements with our work. Your reports showed us what is possible when *Fire Dreams* is not only engaged on its own terms but also used as the toolkit we hope it will be. To the entire (unionized!) team at Duke, to our designer A. Mattson Gallagher, and to our indexer Josh Rutner, we are so grateful for all that you have done to ensure that this work is alive on the page as it enters the world. And to Livia Tenzer, our project editor, you have been an unparalleled advocate over the last year. Thank you for steering this book through the production process with such care and understanding for all that it holds.

As this book has continued to take shape, the young organizers and students we have met have provided us with some of the steadiest visions for what *Fire Dreams* can and will do in the world. To Gabriela Rosario, Lauren Dominguez, Hannah Mandatta, Lydia Moss, Devin Burns, Rebekah Gordon, Sam McLoughlin, and Sam Davis for hearing the calls that this work makes and sharing its histories with the communities you hold close. And to our dear scholar-friends Erin Runions, Nikia Robert, LaToya Eaves, and to so many more of you whom we have already named throughout these acknowledgments, thank you for welcoming us into the communities you have built with your students and for nurturing all that we have made together. We also offer our continued appreciation to Sean King, whose first day as a Mount Holyoke student intern at WWAV was the day after the arson attack. Thank you for sticking with us and for giving so fully of yourself to build our emergency communications network in the fire's wake. It has been a thing of beauty to bear witness to the organizer you have become.

Last, we extend our deep gratitude to our Tallahassee community, especially Kristin Dowell, Peggy Wright-Cleveland, Michael Franklin, Dan Luedtke, Malia Bruker, Dave Rodriguez, Anasa Hicks, Eli Wilkins-Malloy, Ilana Goldman, Jeannine Murray-Román, Jorge Luis Hernández, and Hannah Schwadron, who made way for the whole Haywood family to evacuate in the wake of Hurricane Ida. We know that mutual aid is present in every crisis, and we learned in new ways just how deeply Tallahassee is committed to holding us down and caring for the worlds we make together.

Love is this offering and love is also sewn through its pages. To vk, you are the surprise that Laura waited a lifetime to find. You turned your home into a writer's retreat to see this book to completion, and you celebrated each and every step, big and small, on the way to its publication. Most importantly, you opened yourself and your heart to the relationships that ground this work, knowing that caring for Laura meant caring for the people she loves, and making ways for all of us to become part of your life and world.

And to Rowan Bell, sweet sun baby: you are the dream that Laura dared to imagine for herself, one that she and vk worked hard to make a reality. We all reminded her, repeatedly, that what is hers was already here. And you were. You are also all of ours. You grew inside of Laura during the very months that *Fire Dreams* moved through final review and into production. Your light illuminates every single word of this text. Together, we commit to building a much better world for you to make your own.

Our intention is to claim all the beautiful things in 2024.

This book will enter the world as the year begins. As we continue to grow the Black feminist geography charted in these pages, we do so with anticipation for the conversations that *Fire Dreams* will animate, the new activists and scholars it will mobilize, and the long-standing networks it will help to bring into tighter formation. This is the promise through which we continue to fight for all the good things that this world must be. And so we know that the love offering of this book is most especially for Bailey "Bunny" Haywood, Jaliyah Davis, Earlneishka Johnson, and all of the Young Women With A Vision members. Your generation will carry this work forward. We cannot begin to imagine the truths you will write in the course of making your own fire dreams. But we know they will be beautiful to behold. *Forward Ever.*

INTRODUCTION
BORN IN FLAMES

Sometimes people try to destroy you, precisely because they recognize your power—not because they don't see it, but because they see it and they don't want it to exist.

—bell hooks, *Reel to Real*

It was a Thursday evening, late in May 2012. Memorial Day weekend was upon us, bringing with it the New Orleans double feature of the annual Greek Fest and the Money Wasters Social Aid and Pleasure Club Second Line. Women With A Vision (WWAV) was just coming off an unprecedented victory for sex work decriminalization and abolition feminism, and we were all taking a moment to rest and to celebrate before beginning the next steps in our organizing work. Earlier that day, WWAV's executive director Deon Haywood and her wife and WWAV's director of research evaluation, Shaquita Borden, welcomed their friend and WWAV's resident writer and board member Laura McTighe to New Orleans for the summer. The three of us—Deon, Shaquita, and Laura—were now watching a horror film at home with a few others, alternating between mocking the film and plotting our summer WWAV organizing. Together, we wanted to create an oral history archive and toolkit to show how this decades-old Black feminist organization had been able to fight back against the destabilization of Black New Orleanians' worlds through predatory policing after Hurricane Katrina—and *win*.

Mid-conversation, Deon's cell phone rang. As she picked up the call, Shaquita and Laura turned their attention back to the movie. Shaquita pressed pause when she heard the tone in Deon's voice shift. "Women With A Vision is on fire. WOMEN WITH A VISION IS ON FIRE!" Deon waved her hand emphatically, motioning us toward the door. En route to WWAV's offices on North Norman C. Francis Parkway,[1] she started a telephone tree to get word to WWAV's cofounders, her mother Catherine Haywood and friend Danita Muse; board members Rosana Cruz and Shana M. griffin;[2] her best friends, Shelley Stiaes, Erica Williams, and Dimitri Blutcher; and her children, Cynthia and Brandon. When we arrived, about half of that community was standing on the sidewalk. The air was thick with humidity and smoke. Sirens wailed on a shrill loop. Red lights rolled across the front of the building. Yellow hoses snaked in through the front door. First responders flowed in and out of the fire truck, up and down the steps, in and out of the flames raging in the office.

When the police finally came to speak to Deon, they pulled her away from us and forced her to go inside the office alone, without anyone with her for support. She was shaken when she came back. It felt like she had been gone for hours. In vivid detail, she recounted what she had borne witness to. First, the arsonists had whittled the dead bolt off the back door. Then they moved through the space, setting small fires in the meditation alcove, singeing the faces off Black women in posters, and tossing out the window into the alleyway below all the awards WWAV had received from leaders in movements for sex workers' rights, ending mass criminalization, HIV prevention justice, reproductive justice, racial justice, human rights, LGBTQ rights, women's health, and more. In the outreach office, they stacked WWAV's educational breast models three-high, covered them in accelerant, and ignited a blaze strong enough to melt the blades off the ceiling fan fifteen feet overhead. Decades of participant files, harm reduction supplies, and outreach materials were reduced to ashes. It was a vile act of white supremacist terror intended to exterminate WWAV's efforts once and for all. It took years before Deon publicly recounted the violence of that night: "They refused to let anyone walk in with me, so I experienced that trauma alone. Having to stand in each room at that moment. Normally, they let people go the next day, but we went the same night when it was still *hot* and smoky."[3]

We went back together the next afternoon. The smoke had only cleared slightly. The pain of walking through that charred rubble was gut-wrenching. It conjured the terror of the Ku Klux Klan burning crosses and the firebombing of Black homes, churches, and political organizations. The arson attack could have harmed or killed members of the WWAV community. Deon fielded a call from a detective who said he had a few leads in the case: "We talked to witnesses and everybody seems to say the same thing. There was a white male running from the scene of the fire, coming from the alley of your building." We could hear Deon reply, "So do you know who it is?" Her face turned. She told us as soon as she got off the phone what he had answered: "No, what I want to know is which one of the women who work for you is fucking a white man? Cuz see, what we think is, *somebody*—it could be somebody is mad at them. Or it could be one of these crackheads y'all helping." Deon shook her head in refusal: "There are moments like this that remind us how you're criminalized in more ways than the media will ever show you."[4]

Unraveling the Racial Capitalism Playbook

The arson attack on WWAV was never investigated. We knew it would not be as soon as Deon spoke with the detective who blamed WWAV for the violence we survived. That accusation was from the same playbook as the attack itself: ISOLATE people from necessary social services; BLAME them for the abuse they survive; CRIMINALIZE them for their survival; DESTA-BILIZE their communities; ERASE them from the city of their birth; and then TAKE their land.[5] WWAV theorizes these operations of racial capitalism in our daily lives and worlds as the "racial capitalism playbook."[6] And we refuse that playbook with our very existence. Importantly, this playbook has a history that extends much deeper than our neoliberal present. It was first fashioned by the settlers and planters who made the Crescent City through colonial rule and chattel slavery, and it has been refined and perfected in response to the constant rebellion and fugitivity of Native Americans, Africans, Afro-Creoles, and African Americans.[7] WWAV, too, is the afterlife of this history of struggle.[8] And, like our ancestors, everything about WWAV, past, present, and future, flies in the face of the racial capitalism playbook.

In 1989, a collective of Black women operating out of an RV in Central City New Orleans set out to address the HIV epidemic in their community. They called themselves "Women With A Vision." The so-called war on drugs had already been raging for nearly two decades, and the impacts of these criminalization policies were deadly. Our foremothers were on a mission to improve the lives of Black women, their families, and their communities by addressing the social conditions that hinder their health and well-being. To make that vision a reality, they used street outreach, health education, mutual aid, community-engaged research, relentless advocacy, and any other tool they could put to liberatory ends. Their work was slow and patient and present, grounded always in a love for their people. By building relationships, our foremothers stood in solidarity with the very people most criminalized in our current order. In community, they celebrated the strategies that people crafted to survive and make ends meet in a world that was hell-bent on erasing them. They spoke these truths together, and they spoke them in the local, national, and international halls of power where our current order was produced and reproduced. There, they worked tirelessly to identify, reclaim, and redistribute the resources that have been steadily siphoned from their people's hands. In so doing, they *made space* for their community to belong to one another and to the land of their ancestors. And they were damn good at doing it.

After Hurricane Katrina, WWAV worked to dial back the disaster-accelerated consolidation and expansion of the racial capitalism playbook. While white developers and legislators unabashedly imagined how the storm could be used as a "clean sheet to start again," WWAV steadily organized in counterpurpose to the punitive policies that were being enacted to permanently erase Black people from the city of their birth.[9] We fought back against each layer of the isolate-blame-criminalize-destabilize-erase-take racial capitalism playbook; we did so by refusing the violence of our present and building the world we needed. WWAV *made space* for our community to belong to one another, to grieve together, to heal in concert, and to nurture our visions for a New Orleans "otherwise."[10] The arsonists who set fire to WWAV tried to *take that space*. What they could not take were the relationships that produced that space, which were always already rooted in this land.

In the wake of the arson attack, with nearly all material traces of WWAV's decades of work destroyed, research became a form of survival.[11] To ensure that WWAV could and would continue, we had to reframe and fight the official narratives of the fire as a singular event instigated by someone within WWAV's own network, which were rapidly being disseminated by police and city officials alike. Between the reality of WWAV's grassroots organizing and the labor exerted to suppress, invisibilize, and exterminate it, there was a vast terrain to map. To do so, we had to become "undisciplined"; the work we were doing required new theories and methods of research.[12] When we centered WWAV's own expertise and the knowledge our community was producing about the fire, we could see clearly that this was no isolated attack. Nor was it merely an attack on a singular organization at a single moment in time. Reckoning with the full extent of the erasure being willed against WWAV was physically, historically, and epistemologically rigorous work. The territory of WWAV's knowledge about the attack extended most immediately into the disaster that post-Katrina recovery efforts had wrought for Black New Orleanians. But it also stretched deeper—into the recesses of WWAV's own organizational past amid the targeted criminalization of drug users and sex workers, and the government's willful neglect of structural HIV vulnerability in Black communities. And it reached deeper still to the generations upon generations of Black women who had seen their own work to realize healing justice for their communities eviscerated through the same tactics of white supremacist terror.[13] We stitched the coordinates of these histories together deliberately and without compromise. *Fire Dreams* is our collective, collaborative reckoning with these pasts and the ways in which they press on WWAV's present. These are the grounds on which our research began.

Dreaming with Our Eyes Wide Open

As a contribution to the world, *Fire Dreams* is a social movement ethnography and an ethnography of Black feminist thought. But it is not simply a book to be read. It is a toolkit for, in Walter Rodney's words, "making knowledge to serve the liberation of our communities";[14] it is also a call to revolutionize that knowledge into praxis in order to build the world otherwise. The work held in these pages has been guided by three iterative and relational questions:

1 What is so threatening about Black women's leadership?
2 What would it look like to tell the history of Black women's organizing in the South so that WWAV's work had a place in it that could not be erased?
3 How would telling this history with WWAV firmly located within it change the way that we understand American history and leverage our pasts toward more livable futures?

Answering these questions is liberation work. We ask that you, our readers, hear—indeed, speak with us—WWAV's history in and through the stories of generations of southern Black feminist organizers. We also call you into the work of ensuring that these deeply enduring resistant visions for living and thriving otherwise—these *fire dreams*—can take place and have a space, that they can root and stay rooted.

In undertaking this project, we take inspiration from scholar-comrades like Mary Frances Berry, Andrea Ritchie, Mariame Kaba, Barbara Ransby, Cathy Cohen, Sarah Haley, Dayo Gore, and Emily Thuma, each of whom braids together social history and Black feminist thought to illuminate Black women's major contributions to theory and activism.[15] Like theirs, ours is not a traditional social movement study, organized by chronology or campaign theme; it is an intellectual history of the present, a story of our collective, a practice of our vision for liberation, a workbook for change. In *Fire Dreams*, we place emphasis on the persistence of WWAV's Black feminist ideas, relationships, and methods for doing the work. That is because we lead with *why* questions, not *how* questions, to recall one of Robin D. G. Kelley's famous analytics. For Kelley, *how* questions tend to reify traditional expectations of what counts as political—voting in elections, lobbying elected officials, participating in grassroots social movements—whereas *why* questions expose the paradox of engaging with political institutions and processes that traditionally have not proven to be attentive to the concerns of poor and working-class Black people.[16]

For all of us at WWAV, the most important question after the fire was not *how*, but *why* will we recover? Answer: "The work will continue to get done, no matter what." Saying this requires us to hold both the imperative of WWAV's liberatory vision and the weight of our willed repression. Long before Hurricane Katrina, policies of systematic divestment and forced removal dressed up in a whitewashed, teleological language of "development, improvement, and progress" were already conspiring to erase the very forms of Black and Indigenous life that had built the city now called New Orleans.[17] The disaster that followed the levee breaches in August 2005 was *man*-made through interlocking systems of white supremacy, patriarchy, and bigotry, just like the fire that burned WWAV down.[18] Legislators and developers alike have branded it the "new" New Orleans. That divestment, and its acceleration, has been built through the violent destabilization of long-standing Black New Orleanian worlds, through the dismemberment and disappearance of entire communities. Today, the city bears little resemblance to the streets our foremothers once walked. So many of our people have been displaced through organized abandonment, gentrification, and racist violence, separated from the traditions and knowledge keepers who held our communities together for generations. That is why we know that in order to free ourselves we have to *dream*, as Kelley's mother taught him, with our eyes wide open. The two eyes at the center of our heads will never let us forget the violence that surrounds us. But we can also learn "to live through our third eyes, to see life as possibility . . . to imagine a world free of patriarchy, a world where gender and sexual relations could be reconstructed . . . to see the poetic and prophetic in the richness of our daily lives . . . to visualize a more expansive, fluid, 'cosmos-politan' definition of blackness, to teach us that we are not merely inheritors of a culture but its makers."[19] And to do so with our hearts afire.

"Fire dreams" are quite literally *born in flames*. But more than that, they are the creative and life-giving sparks amid the ashes of our violent pasts and presents, in and through which new and more livable futures are rising. This sense of the double nature of fire—and the deliberate (re)claiming of it as a creative force (that is, to contest *fire* with *fire*)—rests on knowledge that WWAV produced immediately after the arson attack: "Fire has long been a tool of terror in the South," Deon explained at one of the first postfire community fundraisers organized for WWAV in New Orleans, "but it can also be a powerful force for rebirth." As a creative and life-giving force, *FIRE* has many inflections in WWAV's lexicon. There is the cyclical power of the phoenix rising from the ashes, the unifying speech of the fire of Pentecost, the galvanizing spark of James Baldwin's *The Fire Next Time*, and the *Words of Fire* through which Beverly Guy-Sheftall connects centuries of Black feminist thought. *DREAMS* honor what is being created. Dreams are the stuff of prophets and of everyday folk. They would almost seem like nonsense if they did not materialize again and again. They are the visions of what life could be that Kelley shows us have been passed down for generations, the windows and doors through which Angela Davis imagines that social realities can become malleable and transformable across vast expanses of time and space, and the science fiction that Walidah Imarisha and adrienne maree brown remind us that all organizing is.[20] Fire dreams are how we make the world otherwise. And WWAV has been stoking them and blowing on them to ignite change every day since our founding.

WWAV History Is Movement History

Over the last thirty-five years, the small but mighty crew behind WWAV has become a force to be reckoned with. Today, WWAV's full-time staff of twelve supports eight distinct program areas, thousands of participants locally, and hundreds of thousands of movement comrades nationally and internationally. In the early days, we were an all-volunteer operation that ran on donations. Our first office was a closet in one of our foremothers' homes, and our work was largely done after business hours. The spark that set our work into motion was "a meeting at the crossroads," which showed our foremothers just how deeply and intimately tied their vision was to the change that was rising nationally, indeed, globally.[21]

As the story goes, Danita Muse and Catherine Haywood locked eyes across a crowded New Orleans Health Department conference room at the height of the HIV/AIDS epidemic. At the time, Catherine, or "Lady" as she is more often called, was working for the Children's Pediatric AIDS Program on a project focused on increasing access to HIV testing among people who inject drugs. Danita was working for the Office of Substance Abuse (now the Office of Behavioral Health) and running groups with people struggling with addiction. HIV would soon become a leading cause of death for Black women between the ages of twenty and forty-four, and it has remained so ever since.[22] That lethal fact was far from inevitable. Violent narratives (of "welfare queens" and "crack babies," of whole communities as vectors of disease, of HIV as divine punishment) greased the wheels of the racial capitalism playbook. Both Catherine and Danita further witnessed how the largely white-led early public health responses extended the lethal racism of these narratives by emphasizing individual behaviors and assigning hierarchies to which communities deserved saving.[23] Gay bars in the French Quarter were the cornerstone of the city's condom distribution programs. *No one* was reaching out to poor Black people in the city's housing projects, which had the highest documented incidence of HIV transmission in the city. It was a classic move from the isolate-blame-criminalize-destabilize-erase-take racial capitalism playbook. The next time a meeting was called by the Office of Public Health, both Catherine and Danita were in attendance. This time, they ensured that their Uptown neighborhoods were on the outreach list, including the St. Thomas, Magnolia, Melpomene, and Calliope Projects.

Catherine always says, "You have to build a relationship." Relationships are what make all of WWAV's work possible. During their first years of work, our foremothers' relationships grew exponentially, stretching through the city's underground latticework of safe havens by and for drug user and sex worker communities. Gradually, this presence in relationship and in community enabled our foremothers to start producing their own knowledge about precisely how the logics of systemic poverty and targeted criminalization were driving HIV vulnerability and a whole host of other health issues. Simply put, the problem was not individual behaviors; it was racial capitalism. After their first five years of work on the ground in New Orleans, Danita and Catherine started searching for other people who were working in community like they were. That search landed them in a just-forming national harm reduction movement being created by drug user communities. At its core, harm reduction is a philosophy about meeting people "where they're at" and transforming the conditions in which harm arises, along with reducing the harm itself. Putting that philosophy into practice was world-building work. Alongside national and international movement leaders, Catherine and Danita built and refined models for community health and liberation rooted in a structural analysis of racial capitalism. They did so by being in relationship with the very people whom service providers and government agencies could only see as problems to be managed. And they spoke that analysis and practiced those models wherever they went, funding be damned.

In 2006, in the wake of Hurricane Katrina, it was WWAV's ongoing presence in and solidarity with drug user and sex worker communities that made our organization the destination for those who had been able to return to New Orleans after the storm. Catherine and Danita asked Deon if she would be willing to step out of her role as WWAV paid staff and assume the role of executive director, so that the organization had more stability in these uncertain times. Then, one by one, people started showing up at WWAV with photo IDs that read "SEX OFFENDER" in red block letters. Deon, Catherine, and Danita figured out that the police were booking people arrested for street-based sex work under the felony-level "crime against nature by solicitation" (CANS) statute, instead of (or sometimes *in addition to*) the state's misdemeanor prostitution charge. That policing was targeted. Ninety-seven percent of people with CANS convictions were cisgender and transgender women; 80 percent of people were Black.[24] A single CANS conviction mandated registration as a sex offender for fifteen years. Upon a second conviction, a person would be classified as an aggravated sex offender and mandated to register for the rest of their life. The statute thus, when capacitated through decades of punitive criminalization policies, was in effect a strategy of permanent banishment. It was another classic move from the racial capitalism playbook.

Under Deon's leadership, and with her wife Shaquita at her side, WWAV decided to fight back using the same theories and methods that had guided our foremothers since the organization's founding. The knowledge of people with CANS convictions led each and every step of the process. When recounting the everyday toll of being on the sex offender registry, one woman snapped, "There is NO justice in Louisiana!" Her words became the organizing call moving forward; WWAV deliberately used the all-caps "NO" as both a shout and a shorthand for New Orleans in forming the NO Justice Project. Just like Catherine and Danita had done back in the late 1980s and early 1990s, Deon and Shaquita assembled a trusted group of movement comrades—local organizers, civil rights attorneys, and national activists (like Laura) to bring a community-led challenge of the statute. The campaign against CANS roared through the city, through the state legislature, and through the federal courts. On March 29, 2012, the tireless efforts of the NO Justice legal team secured a federal judicial ruling against the statute, thereby facilitating the removal of more than eight hundred cisgender and transgender women from the state's sex offender registry. Immediately after this victory, we worked with members of the legal team to furiously write and publish our own press releases, op-eds, and policy briefs on the NO Justice Project through mainstream and independent media, just as we had been doing throughout the organizing process.[25] In late May, we came together to launch an oral history project to document the theories, methods, stories, and new forms of knowledge that we produced with our partners during the NO Justice Project—to offer with love the tools and lessons of what our Black feminist organizing looked like in practice. Then, on the evening of May 24, 2012, the erasure of our people, which we had been working to combat since Hurricane Katrina, hit intimately and painfully close. That was the night when WWAV's offices were firebombed and destroyed by still unknown arsonists.

Despite the fatal intent of the arsonists, WWAV's work *did* continue. We continued, like we always have, by linking our intimate community care work on the ground to the national and international movements of which we are a part. Deon and Shaquita went on the road for months, naming this white supremacist terror in every social movement space and gathering they could reach. Locally, in New Orleans, we also launched a sex worker organizing program, which built on Black feminist and abolition feminist visions for a world free from all forms of violence, including surveillance, policing, and punishment.[26] The program brought people diverted from court into an intentional community of support and political transformation, so that they could, in the program's name, *Emerge*. It took four years of this deliberate, hard-won survival work to make space for ourselves again. In the fall of 2016, WWAV stepped into our first home since the arson attack, a space that embodied our deepest hopes "to be able to live and thrive, and not just survive."[27] The front porch of that home provided us all a place to rest and restore. Slowly, it also became the grounds for speaking the next phases of WWAV's work into being. And it held us all as we gathered the stories of WWAV's three and a half decades of work into this offering as *Fire Dreams*.

The Tricycle Effect

This is the terrain in and through which we have produced this undisciplined, collective, collaborative ethnography. WWAV history is movement history. The spaces that first brought us into relationship as coauthors further underline this truth. Laura and Deon met in May 2008 at a national gathering at the intersections of HIV and mass criminalization: UNSHACKLE (Uniting a Network on Sentencing and HIV/AIDS with Community Knowledge Leading our Efforts). Laura had been invited by her longtime comrade Waheedah Shabazz-El, a cofounder of Positive Women's Network–USA. Laura and Waheedah met in 2003, just days after Waheedah's release from jail, while Laura was doing community outreach around the health care crisis in the Philadelphia jails. The two had been working together as organizers, writers, and cothinkers ever since.[28] The UNSHACKLE convening, for Waheedah, was taking the ground-up analysis of HIV and the carceral state that she and Laura had built alongside AIDS prison activists to the next level: recognizing that people with HIV are disproportionately affected by criminalization *because* mass criminalization is a structural driver of the domestic AIDS epidemic.[29] Deon had been invited through similarly intimate and insistent means. Shana M. griffin, a cofounder of the INCITE! Women, Gender Non-Conforming, and Trans people of Color Against Violence New Orleans chapter, a cofounder of the New Orleans Women's Health Clinic, a cofounder of the Women's Health & Justice Initiative, and a board member at WWAV, pitched the meeting to Deon as a chance to share the theories and methods that WWAV had been growing in New Orleans for twenty years by that point; she also believed that these national relationships would be essential for ensuring WWAV's survival after the storm. Shana, in turn, had been invited by Kenyon Farrow, the former field director for the New Orleans office of the prison abolitionist organization Critical Resistance. Kenyon was also the coordinator of the UNSHACKLE convening, holding the delicate line between prison abolitionist organizers and the more reformist-minded prison health care folks. He had recruited Laura to write one of the "Think Pieces" to frame discussion.

Laura and Deon still laugh about being placed in a small group and figuring out quickly that neither of them really liked people all that much, but they really liked each other. After the meeting, Laura was hired by the UNSHACKLE convening organizers, the Community HIV/AIDS Mobilization Project, to turn the collective conversations into an organizing toolkit.[30] She first piloted the toolkit in September 2008 at the tenth anniversary gathering of Critical Resistance in Oakland with Kenyon and Waheedah, and then presented it again in October at the annual United States Conference on HIV/AIDS in Fort Lauderdale, Florida. She and Deon reconnected at both meetings. At the Fort Lauderdale conference, Deon pulled her aside in the hallway so they could talk. There, Deon recounted the story of the first time someone showed her their sex offender photo ID card. Deon asked Laura to think about how many times she had to show her ID in the course of a day and paused. That method for sharing knowledge about the everyday terror that CANS criminalization wrought in the lives of Black women, queer people, gender-nonconforming people, and transgender people would become the foundational outreach strategy of the NO Justice Project.

In 2009, Deon invited Laura to New Orleans to facilitate the coalition meeting that launched WWAV's local organizing against the CANS statute. At the time, Laura was working full-time as the field organizer and project director for UNSHACKLE. She made a commitment to return to New Orleans every other month. In between visits, she and Deon connected by phone: Deon would talk, and Laura would type. Deon used this method to apprentice Laura to WWAV's decades-honed Black feminist theory, relationships, and methods for doing the work. Laura then took what they talked about, wrote it up, shared it with Deon for review, revised it, and put it up on WWAV's website and out through the organization's virtual networks. That cemented Laura's role not simply as a movement partner and accomplice, but as a member of the WWAV crew. And with each trip she made back to New Orleans, the chosen family bonds growing among herself, Deon, and Shaquita also deepened.

This method for producing knowledge in service of liberation was one that Deon, Shaquita, and Laura further refined in person as the three-part "tricycle effect." Deon gave our trio the name "tricycle" one day in the thick of WWAV's NO Justice Project when we were refining WWAV's framing language to describe the crippling terror that Black women, queer people, gender-nonconforming people, and transgender people were navigating daily in the wake of Hurricane Katrina, and to underline their will to imagine and build otherwise. The tricycle effect was the steady layering of our brains and hearts in three-part harmony: forward-facing, practice-oriented Black feminist theory (Deon), with a biting intersectional public health analysis (Shaquita), built through multimodal methods of storytelling (Laura). It was also an affirmation of the power of the bond we shared: that affective force, built through love and joy, that was capable of breaking through and unraveling the racial capitalism playbook.[31]

In the wake of the fire, we turned our NO Justice tricycle effect into a full-on emergency communications response system to keep the arson attack in the national and international media. We also started to ask the three questions that drive this book. As the summer of 2012 ended, we talked in earnest about how to design a collaborative research project to answer these questions. In 2013, we launched the "Born in Flames" oral history project to rebuild the archive of WWAV's pre-arson work; in 2014, we launched the ethnographic arm of the project to track the organization's persistence since the fire; and in 2015, Laura moved to New Orleans to begin eighteen months of dedicated research and organizing with WWAV.[32] Since that time—through this amalgamation of oral history, collective storytelling, archival tracing, and doing the work—we have been moving in partnership to document (and reconstruct) the theories and methods that have guided WWAV's work for three decades. This book unfolds in the intimacy of these relationships.

Relationships as Method

Relationships are everything at WWAV. All our work grows from and is accountable to the power we know and share by being in deep, committed relationship with one another. This power is what Audre Lorde understood as the erotic, and recognizing it is what she believed could give us "the energy to pursue genuine change within our world."[33] Relationships connect us with our truest knowledge about the operation of racial capitalism in our daily political lives—they also connect us with our most creative visions for contesting it.

That is because, to quote Mariame Kaba, "Everything worthwhile is done with other people."[34] Her words underline a core principle shared by all who dare to imagine beyond the violence of our present, to dream with our eyes wide open, to share in the power of the erotic. WWAV's work shines so brightly precisely *because* we do it together. Or, as Gloria Anzaldúa taught us, "We don't want to be stars, but parts of constellations."[35]

This organizing truth is also our research method. *Fire Dreams* is a story that has been stitched through time, in space, through pictures and porch talks, in the context of our relationships as comrades, friends, and family, both born and chosen. The relationships that anchor this book are those among WWAV's cofounders, Catherine and Danita; WWAV's current leadership, Deon and Shaquita; and WWAV's resident writer and board member, Laura. We have been joined by myriad others who have cycled in and out of staff positions at WWAV (many of whom readers will meet during the porch talk that grounds chapter 1), participant roles (for example, within the Emerge program profiled in chapter 4), and the national and international movements of which we are a part. *WE* are one.[36] The point of speaking in the collective "we" is not to erase the differences of labor but rather to emphasize the practice of solidarity that undergirds this work, which flows from and is accountable to Black women's leadership.[37] There are also points in the text when we choose to step out of that "we" and speak about ourselves in third-person singular or plural, as you have already seen. We do this because rendering these differences visible and thus differently actionable is also part of our methodology and our work.

Our processes for turning ideas into theory, into practice, and into text are as living as the relationships in which we do this work.[38] At any given time, every member of the WWAV crew has their role. We learn these roles by stepping fully into our power and using our gifts in service of the knowledge we are making together, in community. As one of the writers in the crew, Laura's role has most often been to commit the WWAV vision and practice to paper, working closely with Deon and the rest of the WWAV leadership to refine the message that is shared, and talking through drafts and dreams on the front porch, as we will show in the stories that ground each chapter. The labor of writing is inseparable from the organizing and theorizing that we are writing about. We have struggled with how to represent these complex processes of collaboration and world-making in a byline for academic publications; "with WWAV" is our attempt to signal the breadth of WWAV's multitudes as a living, breathing organization, founded and led by Black women in the South, which has also been dynamically shaped by the people doing the labor of turning its vision into practice. We use the preposition "with" here, as we do in all our published work, in the spirit of Mariame Kaba and Shira Hassan in *Fumbling towards Repair*, who distinguish "with," which signifies active, engaging copartnership, from terms that signal top-down, dependent, or disengaged forms of relationships, like "for" or "not."[39] The story we tell in these pages is a story written *with* WWAV. And it is also a story shared *with* you, our readers.

Research as Survival

This praxis of relationships as method has guided our research since the fire. With nearly all material traces of WWAV's decades of work destroyed, we held on to what could not be extinguished: our stories. There was the story of WWAV's founding across that crowded health department conference table, and that of the methodical process through which our foremothers figured out how to do community outreach. And the stories shared on front porches or at home health parties organized by community gatekeepers. There were the stories of going to little holes-in-the-wall in Texas to teach service providers about doing community outreach, and those of the researchers who contracted with the WWAV foremothers to gather data on drug use and sex work and then stole the methods that WWAV used to get that data. And there were those of fighting the local government officials who kept trying to take away necessary supports from our community, and those of bringing a grassroots challenge against the state of Louisiana and *winning*. These stories were alive in the intimacies of our work on the ground, and they stretched deep into the histories of the long Black feminist freedom struggle in the US South and up through the national and international movements steadily rising around us.

Telling these stories together was life-giving. Doing so built a shared understanding throughout the WWAV network of what really happened. And that truth underscored a second: why telling the stories matters. These two truths drove our work to collect every life-giving ember we could into the Born in Flames Living Archive, which now fills this book.[40] That work started in the immediate aftermath of the arson attack, as we gathered what photographs, posters, and documents had survived the fire, most of which had been kept safe in the homes and private collections of our foremothers. In the summer of 2013, we began documenting the individual life histories of the people who had shaped and been shaped by WWAV's decades of work. That summer we also started to document WWAV's work to build shared analysis with our communities through collective storytelling, most often on front porches. Our life history interview list included the founding WWAV collective members; all the people who had interned or volunteered with WWAV over the years; our current staff; the New Orleans community members who always had our backs (and those who did not); the organizers who moved the vision forward in their own ways, locally, nationally, and internationally; and anyone else these people said we needed to talk to. Our interview format was intentionally open-ended and expansive. We decided to ask each person we interviewed about the whole of their lives and work, not just the portions that explicitly related to WWAV, so that we could be present in our archive building as fully and complexly as WWAV has always been in community. Recording porch talks, community listening sessions, panel presentations, and other collective storytelling sessions further enabled us to document the methods through which WWAV had long turned everyday knowledge about the intimate and structural conditions that produce violence into a shared analysis of racial capitalism and a plan for coordinated action.

Building this living archive, thus, has been a relational art of listening to stories and also between them. We began from and proceeded through a critical hapticality: "The feel that what is to come is here."[41] Through the act of telling stories, we learned to appreciate the persistence of WWAV's more than three decades of Black feminist theory, relationships, and methods for doing the work. But we were also struck again and again by how profoundly *new* every facet of the work our foremothers pioneered was. In relationship, in space, in time, WWAV was building an otherwise analysis of our social world—not as empty-able, domesticate-able, or dispossess-able, but rather as deeply and radically connective.[42] The WWAV foremothers worked intimately and deliberately, moving among communities that had been banished or abandoned by our current order, so that they could nurture the connections that give life and sever those that kill.[43] Their work materialized in the shadows, beyond the glaring light of surveillance that willed the destruction of their communities, and through liberatory spatial practices of community building that kept them rooted in the land. On our own front porches, WWAV's life-giving, creative labors could be sustained and protected. There, our foremothers crafted vibrant worlds and shared histories—*fire dreams*—that held the potential for upending our current order's fatal logics. As we cared for their stories together in the fire's wake, our research as survival began to crystallize into a counter-playbook for living and thriving otherwise.

Theory on the Ground

To imagine, much less to create, the world anew is profoundly rigorous work. The fire dreams that we elucidate in this book grow from our shared analysis of the lethal violence that racial capitalism has long wrought in our communities; they also embody the knowledge we have produced about Black feminist persistence in the Gulf Coast landscape and our methods for transforming that knowledge into praxis. To emphasize the sustained grass-roots labor it takes to get these fire dreams going, we sometimes use the more descriptive term "theory on the ground"—theory developed in the midst of lived struggle, which carries forward the deeply enduring resistant visions of generations past and grows them in and through the geographies of the present, toward new and more possible futures.[44] But let us be clear: WWAV's fire dreams are not *data* that need to be theorized (which is why we do not use the term "grounded theory"[45]); they are *theory*. In approaching WWAV's theory on the ground in this way, we are drawing on a long lineage of Black feminist scholarship that epistemologically privileges the everyday knowledge people most affected produce about the systems of violence governing their lives, and that commits to an engaged research praxis of justice and transformation.[46] We are also answering calls that reverberate throughout the academy and on the ground for decentering scholarly claims to legitimate knowledge production, and engaging the theoretical precision and world-transforming visions of grassroots theorists' work and ways of knowing.

Saying this is an affirmation of our responsibility to one another and to this work. It is also a critique of how normative research ethics emphasize and perpetuate the harmful myth of "objectivity" as the ideal research position. Our theory on the ground exposes how demands for detachment and omniscience in research extend each step of the racial capitalism playbook: ISOLATE yourself from the people you "study"; BLAME them for the violence they survive by turning them into data; CRIMINALIZE them by attaching their lives and choices to academic theories that were only ever meant to oppress them (which are often also used to make laws that criminalize them); DESTABILIZE the knowledge they produce about their own lives and liberation; ERASE the communities in which this knowledge is grown and made actionable; and then TAKE their theorizing and pass it off as your own. In operationalizing this critique into a counter-playbook for liberatory study and struggle, we have worked strongly in the lineage of Black feminist and abolitionist thinkers who have taught us that telling the stories about what we witness, theorize, envision, and practice is the most rigorous kind of knowledge we can make.[47] It is, because our lives depend on it. This critique also has palpable and material effects when it is smuggled into the space of academic inquiry. We might think of it as an epistemological and ontological match. WWAV's theory on the ground, like the fire dreams it ignites, transforms the territory of our texts. The goal is not to describe what is; it is to offer the theory and method needed to build together what must be.

By being in relationship at WWAV, we have learned a very different way of analyzing, and in turn transforming, our world. Too often when studies try to describe the contours of what we call the racial capitalism playbook, they end up "descriptively rehears[ing] anti-black violence" and extending its logics in the process.[48] Our current order profits from a perception that systems of white supremacist dispossession are totalizing, othering, debasing, isolating, eviscerating, and abstracting. What is obscured from view are the hands—the *intimacies*—through which this totalizing, debasing, isolating, and eviscerating abstraction happens.[49] What also becomes unfathomable are the otherwise possibilities that are always smoldering around us.[50] Human life is deeply and radically connective—in the clutch of an arresting officer's hand, in the cut of a judge's tongue, in the grimace of a store clerk, in the pressing of two fingers together to strike a match and set an organization's lifetime of work ablaze; and also in the scarce resources shared within community after a tragic attack, in the cascades of laughter that fill the darkest of institutions, in the interstitial expanses on which stories from the day are turned into plans for coordinated action.[51] Telling stories, sharing our theory on the ground, brought these intimacies into focus. It also bent time and space. Together, we could feel how generations of southern Black feminist organizers were already pressing on our present, demanding justice.[52]

After the fire, everyone at WWAV consistently spoke about how the arson attack underlined the long racist history of fire being used in the South to destroy Black geographies and the traditions they keep. And we also emphasized fire's transgressive history in Black women's abolitionist organizing, from the plantation economy to Jim Crow modernity to the present day.[53] By rising from the ashes—that is, by literally resurrecting ourselves on this contested land—WWAV would not only ensure that our work continued, we would also carry forward the stories of this southern Black feminist tradition. These deep and enduring histories of struggle were anything but past; they also conjured futures that were always already present in time and in space. That is why our counter-playbook refuses the emptiness of linear time imposed by settler colonialism, disaster capitalism, and arsonist assault, which severs us from the fire dreams enchanting our present and hermetically seals them in a time called "past." The labor of speaking the names of southern Black women organizers past as present, of braiding their stories together with WWAV's own, and of carrying this Black feminist tradition across generations within the organization's own history—this labor is also the power of the erotic.[54] As theory on the ground, it calls us into "a new way to 'enter' into space (conceptually and materially)," one that uncovers a generations-honed geographic story to build worlds in which it is possible to live and thrive, and not just survive.[55] And it attunes us the to the fact that we already have the tools we need to free us. We live them every day.

This simultaneity of present, past, and future in WWAV's fire dreams is constitutive of the enduring, enchanted Black geography of New Orleans.[56] Indeed, remembering this truth is, as M. Jacqui Alexander taught us, "the antidote to alienation, separation, and the amnesia that domination produces."[57] It also calls to mind one of the elements of Alice Walker's definition of a "womanist" as: "Traditionally capable, as in: 'Mama, I'm walking to Canada and I'm taking you and a bunch of other slaves with me.' Reply: 'It wouldn't be the first time.'"[58] Speaking the fire dreams that fill our post-arson present has enabled WWAV to care for these transgenerational memories and stories in this land we call home. Care is life-giving; it is sustaining. This care holds the residues and forms of life that have been able to persist despite constant and lethal forms of surveillance. It also holds the always present possibility of abolishing racial capitalism and living into the radical transformation of worlds otherwise. There and then, here and now, our fire dreams are the creative and life-giving sparks from which new and more livable futures are rising. Centering our fire dreams does not just change the angle from which the story is written. It changes history itself.

Living the Future Now

Through *Fire Dreams*, we claim our thirty-five years of life-giving work at the intersections of Black feminist struggle and the "wellsprings of dreams" that have steadily been sheltered in these grounds for generations.[59] We track and refuse the histories of white supremacist dispossession, too often masked in the language of "progress," which erase the worlds otherwise that Black New Orleanians have held and nurtured in this place.[60] We render visible the tactics through which Black women and the worlds they make are systematically being isolated-blamed-criminalized-destabilized-erased-taken by the racial capitalism playbook.[61] We speak WWAV's future as an organization founded and led by Black women, by and for the people of New Orleans, into existence. And we call you, our readers, into doing the same. Telling this story is the first contribution of this book.

Part of telling this story is *showing* how we made the story together. And here we are also calling you, our readers, in. From its inception, this research has been framed by and accountable to the life and death questions that unfolded at WWAV in real time in the wake of the fire. We have known that our findings would need to be leveraged as interventions against the academic narratives and theories that have for too long been complicit in the systematic erasure of generations of southern Black women organizers' work—arson attacks of a different sort. However (or perhaps, *therefore*), the academy's questions have not been at the center of our work; our commitment to liberation has. Showing how we have made this story together means showing how we have come to understand that commitment through action. It means showing when and how we have leveraged, ignored, or flat-out refused the conventions of academic knowledge production. It also means showing the principles and practices we have crafted in order to approach this research as a project of liberation. This showing is the reason that the argument of *Fire Dreams* is not linear, but rather accumulates. Because this project refuses the white supremacist violence of "progress," it also refuses to yoke WWAV's liberatory work to its forms for marshaling arguments. This ethnography unfolds cyclically, iteratively, simultaneously. Events and stories are shared and repeated again, as new and different knowledge is produced, in the tradition of Black feminist storytelling. This showing is the second contribution of this book.

Typically, academic texts aim to make one of these two types of interventions: to change what story is told, or to change how it is told—that is, to change the tools we use to tell it. By doing both at the same time, *Fire Dreams* underlines the inseparability of these two dimensions of liberatory praxis and scholarship. Together, they push us out of a speculative mode of imagining beyond and enjoin us in the work of building together what must be. Tina Campt calls this the "grammar of black feminist futurity," which is defined by "a politics of prefiguration that involves living the future *now*—as imperative rather than subjunctive—as striving for the future we want to see, right now, in the present."[62] The principal question of our research as survival—*What is so threatening about Black women's leadership?*—underlines this imperative, as well as the contemporary and historical forces that have been leveraged to exterminate it. Throughout the years of our work together, we asked this question over and over again. It became a mantra of sorts, and provoked sustained, collective reflection. It mattered to us to be able to name that our existence is political, and to track how the world *must be* otherwise.[63] The labor of asking this question, however, was not the answer to it. But asking it over and over again did attune us to what was. As Alexis Pauline Gumbs writes in her essay "Are You Afraid of Black Feminists? Or Just Your Own Freedom?":

> I wonder if the freedom of Black women is a threat, not because it oppresses anyone else, but because it challenges all people to be free. Are you afraid of me and other Black feminists who consistently challenge oppression? Or are you afraid of the bravery it would take to live into your own freedom?[64]

As the WWAV crew repeated in unison on the front porch during one of our collective storytelling sessions, "They ain't ready." This is also the threat of *Fire Dreams*. Again, this is not simply a book to be read. It is also a counter-playbook for liberatory study and struggle. It calls you, our readers, into doing this work with us.

Using Our Counter-Playbook

For this collaborative undertaking with one another and with you, we have developed a layered methodology which we distill in activist form as a four-part toolbox: accomplice, refusal, otherwise, and speech.[65] We invite you, our readers, not only to use these tools from our counter-playbook to read this book, but also to practice them in the worlds that you make. That means that we are calling you in as *accomplices*, our first methodological principle.

The demand from within WWAV after the fire—to tell the story of Black women's organizing so that WWAV could not be erased or exceptionalized—is one that now reverberates globally. Hashtags like #TrustBlackWomen, #KnowYourHistory, #StopErasingUs, and #CiteBlackWomen have done immense work in the public sphere to push back on the mundane and exceptional forms of misogynoir through which Black women's work is attacked, invisibilized, and erased.[66] "Accomplice" is a methodological response to these calls. In using this term, we are invoking the contrast that Indigenous Action Media has drawn between accomplices and allies in their 2014 manifesto "Accomplices Not Allies: Abolishing the Ally Industrial Complex." Of academics and academia, they charge and demand:

> Although sometimes directly from communities in struggle, intellectuals and academics also fit neatly in all of these categories. Their role in struggle can be extremely patronizing. In many cases the academic maintains institutional power above the knowledge and skill base of the community/ies in struggle. Intellectuals are most often fixated on un-learning oppression. These lot generally don't have their feet on the ground, but are quick to be critical of those who do. Should we desire to merely "unlearn" oppression, or to smash it to fucking pieces, and have its very existence gone? An accomplice as academic would seek ways to leverage resources and material support and/or betray their institution to further liberation struggles. An intellectual accomplice would strategize with, not for and not be afraid to pick up a hammer.[67]

For Laura, as a white queer woman, an abolitionist, and an academic, to be an accomplice in this project is to be a partner at every level of the organizing, theorizing, and turning that theory into praxis. It is a commitment that Deon called her into, and one that she made to Deon, Shaquita, Catherine, and Danita before any part of our research as survival began. And it is why we have published *Fire Dreams* as a collectively authored book, with all royalties going to sustain WWAV's next thirty-five years of work. Being an accomplice is a skin-in-the-game approach of literally and figuratively driving the getaway car for the fugitive work already unfolding on the ground. Accompliceship is a stance that takes power away from the racial capitalism playbook and bolsters our liberatory work otherwise. To not simply call for a reconfiguration of local injustices, but to actually reconfigure; to not just make a case for reparations, but to actually repair. To, in our case, also not be afraid to pick up a match.

Accompliceship goes hand in hand with *refusal*, the second methodological principle in our counter-playbook. This project, in its very design, refuses the logics of violence that give shape to our world and that drove someone to set fire to WWAV; it also refuses the ways in which these same logics of violence prefigure the academy's own categories and modes of analysis. We understand this practice of refusal as it has been richly and deeply theorized in Black, Indigenous, and postcolonial studies, as well as on the ground in our struggles for freedom and liberation.[68] WWAV's goal is not to make slow, incremental reforms to systems, nor to be incorporated into them. WWAV is trying to build a world in which it is possible to live and thrive, and not just survive. In the early days, our foremothers turned neighborhood bars into underground needle exchanges, so they could quite literally keep abandoned and dying Black people who used drugs alive. In the wake of Hurricane Katrina, Deon similarly opened WWAV up to sex workers who were being criminalized into oblivion, so that they could make home, find respite, and organize into more livable futures. These barroom needle exchanges, like the NO Justice sex worker story circles, were embodied and relational practices of WWAV's refusal of the ways in which our community was consistently caught in the webs of the isolate-blame-criminalize-destabilize-erase-take racial capitalism playbook. Refusal as methodological practice in this project undergirds the framing of our questions and every level of our research as survival: the designing of our undisciplined study; the centering of WWAV's theory on the ground; the choice of which other theories to engage with and how; the form and manner in which our research is shared and presented through stories, photographs, and porch talks; and the ends toward which this living archive of WWAV's work is leveraged.

There is already a hint of the *otherwise*, our third methodological principle, in this description of how accompliceship and refusal are operationalized as methods in the writing of *Fire Dreams*. The otherwise is the accumulation and the ungrounding; it holds the liberatory epistemologies of WWAV's transformative knowledge production and world-building. The otherwise has been gaining traction among scholars from numerous disciplines who want to "glimpse" or gesture at the possibility for making the world differently, often drawing on phenomenological and continental theoretical lineages. We use the otherwise, however, in the tradition of global liberation movements and academic fields founded in these social movements, such as Black, Indigenous, Latinx, Asian American, postcolonial, queer, and gender studies.[69] These liberatory literatures not only attune us to the deeply enduring and resistant visions that could never fully be vanquished through colonialism, enslavement, and criminalization; they also emphasize how these often-hidden histories of struggle are growing, moving, and transforming our present into worlds otherwise. As Ashon Crawley wrote in the wake of the People's Uprising in Ferguson, Missouri, following the police murder of Black teenager Michael Brown:

To begin with the otherwise as word, as concept, is to presume that whatever we have is not all that is possible. Otherwise. It is a concept of internal difference, internal multiplicity. The otherwise is the disbelief in what is current and a movement towards, and an affirmation of, imagining other modes of social organization, other ways for us to be with each other. Otherwise as plentitude. Otherwise is the enunciation and concept of irreducible possibility, irreducible capacity, to create change, to be something else, to explore, to imagine, to live fully, freely, vibrantly. Otherwise Ferguson. Otherwise Gaza. Otherwise Detroit. Otherwise Worlds. Otherwise expresses an unrest and discontent, a seeking to conceive dreams that allow us to wake laughing, tears of joy in our eyes, dreams that have us saying, *I hope this comes true.*[70]

Otherwise as methodology, thus, means being with and caring for the deeply enduring and resistant visions that all of us at WWAV are carrying forward to build new and more livable futures. The materiality and urgency of this work is also the reason that space—and specifically the embodied, relational space of front porches—takes on such significance in this research. WWAV is not trying to speculate on the possibility of the world otherwise; we are trying to build it here and now, in relationship, and through the interstitial geographies of our present where our resistant visions have long been sheltered and stoked.[71]

This labor of being with and caring for brings us to the final methodological principle in our counter-playbook: *speech*. Speech has been a central ethic and tool of this work—to speak the stories of WWAV's pasts destroyed in the arson attack, to speak the analyses that WWAV has crafted, to speak also the histories of generations of Black women organizers in the South, to speak them alongside WWAV's own. This speech is creative: to speak into existence. It gives voice and care to the otherwise possibilities already around us. It disrupts the aural purification of our current order. It enchants our world with the sounds and stories of a new world a-coming.[72] This speech is also cautionary. Words have weight. They have power. As Toni Cade Bambara reminds us:

Words are to be taken seriously. I try to take seriously acts of language. Words set things in motion. I've seen them doing it. Words set up atmospheres, electrical fields, charges. I've felt them doing it. Words conjure. I try not to be careless about what I utter, write, sing. I'm careful about what I give voice to.[73]

In refusing to speak in the grammar of "progress," WWAV refuses to yoke our story to the eviscerating scripts of the racial capitalism playbook. Our refusal to speak some words also comes with the affirmation of WWAV's own world-building speech as prefigurative of the Black feminist futures we need.

Taken together, these four tools—accomplice, refusal, otherwise, and speech—have enabled us to expand the boundaries, forms, and methods of the knowledge we are sharing with you. Using them has also been an exercise in restraint. There is danger in shining too much light on the things that have been carefully concealed so that they might endure. There is also a reckless-ness in assuming that things must be visible to matter.[74] No one at WWAV is clamoring for "recognition" by the systems of racial capitalism that will our destruction.[75] Our demand from the front porch is simple and uncom-promising: to be able to live and thrive, not just survive. That demand is as much a refusal of what has been as it is a conjuring of what must be. "To be able to live and thrive" bespeaks a world in which fire dreams do not have to be sheltered from the glaring light of surveillance that wills their erasure, in which it is possible to simply be. This book is our counter-playbook for speaking that world into existence in real time, and we are grateful to share our stories and tools with you.

A Roadmap

Before we begin and take a seat on WWAV's front porch, we want to offer you a roadmap for the journey ahead. In each chapter, the body text holds our conversations *about* WWAV—about doing the work, about the social movements of which we are a part, about the theory on the ground we have built over the last three decades. The endnotes hold our conversations *with* WWAV's Black Feminist Library—conversations with what we have read, with the scholars, writers, poets, and artists who help us dream with our eyes wide open. As you progress through the pages of this book, we hope you will work with the theory on the ground that we share in the text—like the racial capitalism playbook and our counter-playbook—and reflect on it using the study and struggle practices of your own communities. That may look like drawing a diagram of the isolate-blame-criminalize-destabilize-erase-take playbook, or pulling out different steps and thinking them to-gether in different orders, or sharing stories about what each process looks like in your own lives and work. Our theory on the ground is meant to be used, and we hope that you visit the digital space we have created for *Fire*

Dreams in the online home for the Born in Flames Living Archive to share your own creations.[76] We also invite you to bring your own literatures, libraries, and book altars to those threaded through the endnotes of *Fire Dreams*. Ultimately, we have worked to keep this book grounded in the organizing and scholarly literatures read most at WWAV. We know there are texts that are beyond the bounds of our own conversations, even if they are very much in line with it. We honor the connections you make and hope that you will share them with us. We are so excited to learn from the work that *Fire Dreams* inspires, supports, and enlivens for you in your corners of the world and to bring it back to our own.

Our story begins in chapter 1 on the front porch of WWAV's first organizational home after the arson attack. It is late 2015; WWAV's rebirth is certain. From this interstitial expanse of southern storytelling, on the tenth anniversary of Hurricane Katrina, we take stock of the so-called resilient city of New Orleans and ask what is concealed in its official language of strength in recovery. This porch talk is the stage for setting up the contest between two very different systems for producing space: the enduring, rebellious logics of WWAV's "front porch strategy" and the white supremacist violence of "resilience space" that was being operationalized across New Orleans by government officials and developers alike (and which fueled the arsonists who set fire to WWAV). "Resilience space" is naturalized by disconnecting it from the historical circumstances of its production. This makes it seem as if "resilience space" extends indefinitely into the past and therefore also indefinitely into the future. "Front porch strategy," as a result, is denied the possibility of coevalness; it seems always secondary, reactive, and dependent, or somehow outside the time that "resilience space" has colonized.[77] We undertake a double move: first, provincializing "resilience space" by suturing the historical circumstance of its production back to it; and second, simultaneously rendering visible the physical, historical, and epistemological depth of the *fire dreams* that fuel WWAV's own "front porch strategy."[78]

To do this, chapter 2 dives into the intimate work of completing oral histories with the WWAV foremothers after the fire. Storytelling is essential theory and method at WWAV: we tell stories so that the work will continue. Through these oral histories, we enumerate the key principles for "doing the work"; we also build a sense of how these principles are bigger than WWAV in historical and geographic scale. WWAV makes worlds—worlds that connect deeply and radically, worlds that heal across generations. By listening to our foremothers' stories of what really happened, we learn what it meant for them to live and work in the incommensurability between the realities of anti-Black violence and the Black feminist possibilities they were nevertheless living as now.

Their focus on radical connectivity becomes our mode of analysis in chapter 3 for understanding the criminalization of WWAV's community in the wake of Hurricane Katrina through the CANS statute and its mandated sex offender registration. We lift up the key educational strategy from WWAV's NO Justice Project: asking people to think about how many times they have to show their IDs in the course of a day, and then asking them to think about the impact of having "sex offender" stamped on it in block red letters, as well as the matrix of everyday surveillance that it would capacitate. We then use this strategy as a hermeneutic for opening a window into the everyday and intimate texture of Black women's criminalization in the New Orleans pasts. Here, we underline how, throughout American history, technologies of surveillance had to continually be expanded and reasserted by official state actors precisely *because of* Black women's refusal of them. This fact brings historical momentousness to WWAV's founding vision, the challenge of the CANS statute, and our organizing work since.

Chapter 4 takes up this emphasis on Black feminism as a worldmaking politics and practice in order to trace the work of rebuilding WWAV after the fire. There are two levels to this tracing: first, Deon and Shaquita's constant work on the road to speak WWAV's fire dreams nationally and globally; and second, the steady reconfiguration by staff and partners of WWAV's New Orleans–based work in and for community. By tacking back and forth between these scales constantly, this chapter shows the dynamism of fire dreams, as the dreams that had long been sheltered at WWAV were stoked on the ground and on the international stage, in and through movements for liberation rising up worldwide. In so doing, we also illuminate how these multiple registers of doing the work steadily refined, reconfigured, and at times transformed the futures being imagined.

This local, national, and global work makes possible WWAV's homecoming in 2015. Chapter 5 opens on move-in day and flows with the WWAV foremothers and the organization's newer staff as they feel through the full archive of the organization's work that is being unpacked now that WWAV can again take place and have a space. It also zooms out temporally and spatially to reckon with how past, present, and future are held in the intimacy of this moment. In 2022, as we approached the tenth anniversary of the arson attack, our country was burning. It was hardly the first time. In the epilogue, we reflect on the stories and the practices—the what and the why, the dreams and the fire—that made possible WWAV's rising from the ashes. And we ask how we can be accomplices in bringing into being more livable futures by blowing on the creative and life-giving embers that are already smoldering around us.

FRONT PORCH STRATEGY

I have the stories of many women running through me and etched in my lifeline.
I know and am the hills and valleys of their lives. They speak to and through me.
This morning Sojourner Truth whispered to me: when they sold my last child my
baby boy a river broke inside me and I gave birth to myself. I was no longer Isa-
bella. I became Sojourner Truth.
—Ruby Sales, "From My Front Porch"

"We believe in the revolutionary things that happen on a southern front
porch."

It was mid-December, but Deon's affirmation hung in the air like humidity in July. It had been nearly four years since WWAV was made homeless by
the 2012 arson attack and only two months since we found our first home after
the fire. That Mid-City New Orleans space was in transition, just like the
neighborhood that surrounded it. It was nestled between a hipster bicycle
shop and an abandoned lot. And it was located at the four-way intersection
of North Broad Street and Esplanade Avenue where the neighborhood of
Tremé touched those of Bayou St. John, the Fairgrounds, and the Seventh
Ward. Before becoming WWAV's new home, the building had been the law

office of a Black elder, who had recently made his transition, and a family residence before that. Inside, the rooms flowed in a circle, with light pouring in through windows on all sides. Outside, a sprawling front porch emptied onto the North Broad Street foot traffic.

We christened that front porch with a conversation about the word *resilience*, the dubious slogan of the city's official "Katrina at 10" (or "K10," for short) anniversary commemorations four months prior. What exactly did *resilience* mean when 95,625 Black New Orleanians were still displaced and thousands more were living in prison cells as a result of intensified policing?[1] . . . when we knew that their permanent displacement was the penultimate step in the isolate-blame-criminalize-destabilize-erase-take racial capitalism playbook? . . . when we were bearing witness on that front porch right in that very moment to what was becoming of the buildings people were not allowed to return to?

As the rush hour traffic crawled by, we reflected on the vital work that WWAV was doing to hold the experiences of Black women—most especially Black women who were born and raised in New Orleans—as relevant and important. We imagined how telling their stories would help expose that there was an ongoing battle for space and for history actively underway in the new New Orleans. When we took this picture (fig. 1.1), Deon had just claimed WWAV's front porch as a site where that liberatory organizing could take place and have a space—where revolutionary things happen. The word *revolutionary* in WWAV's lexicon means "to have a plan."[2] Her affirmation prompted the recollection of another porch in WWAV's own history. In 1989, WWAV was just an idea thought up by a collective of Black women on a front porch in Central City. Our foremothers' plan was then, as ours still is today, to improve the lives of marginalized women and their communities by addressing the systems of oppression that hinder their health and well-being. That is where the word *resilience* came in.

In post-Katrina New Orleans, *resilience* had become the slogan to celebrate the rebuilding of the city after the storm. This usage of the word rested on a theoretical framework conceived in the wake of crisis to shift emphasis from pathology to strength. Specifically, what researchers and practitioners sought to do with it was to capture the strengths that people demonstrated that enabled them to rise above adversity. WWAV, however, was more concerned with what was obscured through this language of "strength in recovery." And we were not alone in our critique of how the focus on individual strength shifted focus away from the conditions that force people to have to be

1.1 Shaquita Borden, Mwende Katwiwa, Deon Haywood, Nakita Shavers, Laura McTighe, and Nia Weeks sitting on WWAV's front porch at 1226 N. Broad Street in New Orleans, Louisiana, December 16, 2015. Photo by Desiree Evans.

strong.[3] Interlocking systems of intimate, community, and state violence—not individual resilience—dictate who recovers, as well as how, where, and when. They always have. Beth Richie calls these interlocking systems the "violence matrix," and her scholarly and activist work is required reading for all WWAV staff members.[4] Richie's distillation of violence and Black women's worlds in our prison nation echoes WWAV's own foundational theory on the ground about our community's survival in the late 1980s and 1990s amid the escalation of the so-called war on drugs.[5] Against an unrelenting matrix of violence, the WWAV foremothers did what Black women have always done: they set their hands to building what their community needed to survive. Through this work, WWAV rendered visible and refused the ways in which American "progress" has always depended on long and practiced strategies for concealing violence and then claiming Black women are responsible for their own premature deaths—the racial capitalism playbook.[6] The city's official response after Hurricane Katrina, wrapped up in a celebratory narrative of resilience, also accelerated the lethal violence of this so-called progress.

In the intervening decade between the storm and that afternoon in late 2015, the biggest losers were Black New Orleanians and, most specifically, Black women. Together, we have been working to document how the fantasy of a new resilient New Orleans was built through the control and management of Black women's bodies and the destabilization of our communities. An important fact for all of us at WWAV and for any post-Katrina researchers worth their salt: the August 2005 disaster was created by *human* hands.[7] The tragedy that unfolded in the storm's wake was what Clyde Woods termed "a blues moment"; it brought long-standing structures of violence and domination into view.[8] Deon reiterated WWAV's position whenever she presented outside New Orleans: "We don't call it a *natural* disaster or a disaster made by *Mother Nature*. We call it the federal government failing a community, a city of people."[9] Decades of divestment predated the event of Hurricane Katrina, facilitated the immediate lack of response to the levee breaches, and prefigured the crisis in the storm's wake. In the intervening years, the result was the production of a new New Orleans that was decidedly whiter, both demographically and spatially. *Resilience.*

How have these violent logics of resilience been spatialized in the new New Orleans? And why is WWAV "respatializing" New Orleans?[10] In asking these questions, we work from the understanding that, as Katherine McKittrick has taught us, Black women's bodies are geographic.[11] To excavate the relationship between bodies and place in the new New Orleans, this chapter employs the four key principles of the methodological toolkit we outlined in the introduction—accomplice, refusal, otherwise, and speech. Our goal here is twofold: first, to track how the racial capitalism playbook has been operationalized across New Orleans at record speed to control and manage Black women's bodies as always already "out of place"; and second, to advance WWAV's own embodied spatial practices for creating liberatory futures in real time and "in place." The story itself unfolds nonlinearly; this is part of the point. We move iteratively in the simultaneous, layered traditions of storytelling that are practiced on front porches. But make no mistake. There is a single idea that animates this chapter and this book. "The front porch" is not a metaphor—as Eve Tuck and K. Wayne Yang remind us, decolonization is not either.[12] This chapter centers front porches as a particular kind of space: one where southern Black women have, for generations, sat and talked about the ideas that are important to them. That sitting and talking is how you build a shared understanding of the issues you are dealing with. It is also how you learn to dream that the world must be otherwise. Those understandings and dreams are also calls to action: to take place and have a space. That is why all of us at WWAV claim front porches as southern Black feminist geographies and honor the geographic knowledges of their making. Front porches are the grounds where revolutionary things happen.

To start this chapter, we gather on the front porch, and include a long-form transcription of the porch talk we had about resilience that mid-December afternoon. Allowing this porch talk to take up space in the text underlines each of the four methods of our counter-playbook. It *refuses* the official stories of the storm's afterlives and locates authority over post-Katrina displacement and gender-based violence with New Orleans Black feminist organizers as a practice of *accompliceship*. Doing so centers the *speech* through which the individual experiences of WWAV organizers are transformed into collective meaning and new worlds are then spoken into existence. It also emphasizes the importance of space to this engaged praxis for justice and liberation *otherwise*. The front porch is thus identified and theorized as the grounds of Black feminist liberatory knowledge production in New Orleans today.

The knowledge produced on front porches evidences very different logics of social organization from the new resilient New Orleans; it also works toward very different ends. The theory on the ground that was made during WWAV's mid-December porch talk exposed the acute violence and quotidian terror of the racial capitalism playbook—both in the wake of the storm and in the ongoing legacies of settler colonialism and chattel slavery that prefigure the post-Katrina landscape. It also summoned the pasts and potentialities that fill our present, through which generations of Black women have worked on southern front porches to build the world otherwise. WWAV's practiced refusal of the place-making systems of racial capitalism, as well as our steady stoking of the fire dreams of generations past on our own front porches, have all been sedimented in New Orleans through what we call "front porch strategy."[13] To excavate these histories of struggle, this chapter walks with the WWAV foremothers to extend the analysis of front porches back in the organization's past, and then further back to the front porches of enslaved Black women centuries prior. We then return to the Louisiana present through attention to state violence against people occupying the space of the front porch. This geographic story of confrontation and rebellion clarifies our belief in "the revolutionary things that happen on a southern front porch." It also brings into focus the contest for space and history that is actively underway in New Orleans today.

Front Porch Space

The seed for our December porch talk on resilience was planted during WWAV's move into our new home two months prior. In October 2015, while Deon was unpacking boxes that had been in a storage unit since the arson attack, she paused, observing that every single piece of paper in the box was dated 2012: "It's as if everything stopped." Her hands were covered in soot. Later that day, Deon was thinking out loud about how WWAV, as an organization interrupted, was going to have to explain itself. People had been patient after the fire. Now that WWAV again had a home, expectations were going to shift. "What was WWAV's story?" Resilience was a framework that people across the country were used to hearing whenever crisis and recovery in New Orleans were discussed, but *Lorde* was it a loaded word.[14] Deon wanted us to talk this out, tricycle effect style, "to give it the WWAV spin," before figuring out how she might broach the issue with funders and national movement partners.

We were ready to return to the topic a couple of months later, on one of those Friday afternoons when people would just start meandering onto the front porch. It was sometime between three and four o'clock, and we were just sitting and talking about stuff. That mid-December afternoon, our porch talk crew included nearly every member of the 2015 WWAV family: Deon, Shaquita, Desiree, Mwende, Nia, Nakita, and Laura. Desiree was WWAV's director of policy and communications. A writer, activist, and student of southern storytelling traditions, Desiree was born and raised in rural Louisiana, and joined the WWAV family the summer after the arson attack. Her programmatic and communications work was essential for sustaining WWAV through the years in exile, through to the organization's rebirth on the front porch where this conversation was taking place. Next to Desiree sat Mwende, a Kenyan, immigrant, shoga/queer storyteller, and the youngest of the crew. Mwende sought out WWAV for mentorship while they were completing their undergraduate degree at Tulane University and joined the WWAV team after graduating in 2014. Since, they had been growing work at the intersections of arts, education, and activism in New Orleans and globally. Within WWAV, that meant conceptualizing and launching the intergenerational Young Women With A Vision (YWWAV) program to promote the social, emotional, and cultural well-being and leadership of Black girls in New Orleans. Next to Mwende was Deon, then Laura, then Nia, then Nakita. Nia and Nakita had joined the WWAV staff only a few weeks prior as policy director and reproductive justice coordinator, respectively. Both were born and raised in New Orleans. Nia was a mother of four and had returned to New Orleans after several years living away to take a job as a public defender. Nakita was from the Lower Ninth Ward, the most flood-battered region of the city, and had founded her own organization after the storm to bring resources to her community.

Deon looked around at everyone gathered and asked if we were ready to talk about resilience, "to give it the WWAV spin." Desiree, Mwende, Nakita, and Nia all nodded. Laura asked, "Do we want to record this session?" Deon nodded, and Laura hopped up to grab the recorder we used for oral history interviews from inside. Still, there was no way to pull out a recorder and not change the space. Deon sensed that shift as Laura returned and put it out the in open.[15]

DEON So part of creating and doing this work with Laura, who's not only a friend, a colleague, part of the squad, and an ally[16]—a *white* ally—and I want to lay that out cuz all them ain't good [*laughing*]. It's true. Some people don't know what allyship is. The reason that she's here working on this project is that I do get how important it is to capture our voices. Right? And not sell it to the highest bidder, because "I got a story about some little Black women in the South." Like, this is a project that for all of us, even to y'all that ain't been here a month yet [*looking at Nia and Nakita*]. It's like the history of what we have the power to do, and how can we get away from—how can we use the word *resilience* in way that's better than what we do right now. Cuz I absolutely thought I was sick during Hurricane Katrina! Post-Katrina everybody use *resilience, resilience, resilience.* [*Mouths yuck!*] [*Desiree: Mmmhm.*] And I just feel, you know, Black people been resilient for a long goddamn time. Sometimes I don't want to be resilient. Sometimes I don't like that word to describe what we are doing. So the reason I personally feel like it fits is because it's true. Like there's so many organizations that didn't come back post-Katrina. There's so many—literally we got calls the morning after the arson attack from people in the DA's office, and different places like "Oh, so y'all are shut down?" "Oh, your doors are closed?" "Ohhhh! How does it feel after so many years to have to close your organization?" I was like, "Who said we were closing?"

MWENDE [*laughing*] I feel like resilience is one of those words where, like, I can say it, but you can't say it. Because of the way it's been used so much to paint that like "noble Negro" story of, "Oh yeah, you might be burdened but you're just so resilient!" [*Nia laughs.*] That, "it's okay." Like, "we'll just focus on your resiliency!" and not the actual cause of why someone *needs to be resilient*. People always focus on the resiliency of the person versus why they need to be resilient. [*Nia: Mmmhm.*] I know especially during K10 it was a word that just so much was being heard that it lost any and all meaning that it had. And it already had such little meaning, because of who it is that's usually using that term and what it is that they're erasing when they use that term. [*Deon: Mmmhm.*]

DESIREE I think it's so often coming from an academic context, right? It's used to describe populations, communities that have seen a lot of trauma, horror, war, violence, genocide. "Oh they're so *resilient*! They survive! They come back!" [*Deon shakes head.*] "What is it about this community? We gotta study this!" After Katrina it was just a word that kept being thrown around to describe New Orleans, to describe the Black population of New Orleans, to describe the Gulf Coast. And in a lot of ways it becomes, like "Oh they're *resilient*! They can take anything!" And so we really have to deconstruct this idea of resilience, to understand what does it really mean for us to survive in the face of so much oppression? And to create in this. "You know, I'm glad you love our Mardi Gras Indian tradition, I'm glad you love our music, but that doesn't mean that you get to keep oppressing us because we can create beautiful shit out of trauma and horror and damage." [*Deon: Right.*] You know, it's hard because we understand our communities are creative forces in the face of mass destruction [*Deon: Yeah.*] and displacement, and we are "magical be-ings." [*Mwende: Heyyyyy.*] We have made magical things happen in the context of our own survival, but at the same time we have to talk about system change.

DEON Riiiight. We can fix it, and we can be resilient, and [*Desiree: Mmmhm.*] we can work it, [*Mwende: Right.*] but can we run it? [*Nia: Right.*] And do we have the same support as our counterparts? It was grassroots organizations across the country that were in support of WWAV after the fire. In terms of city council? I don't think the mayor came to WWAV to see how we were doing. There wasn't this big out-cry to figure out who did it. And people were like, "Do you think it was based on who you are?" And I was like, "I don't know about anybody else, but as a Black woman who has a *clear* understanding of history [*Desiree laughs dryly.*] in *this* country and outside of this country [*Mwende: Mmmhm.*] with Black and Brown people and Indigenous people, *fire* means something. [*All: Mmmhm.*] Fire sends this really big message about *what* I want you to know and *how* I feel about you." Like, when you think about the stuff that we had then that we still haven't replaced. You know, breast models cost $700 and up. Birth control models, you know, those uteruses? Those kinds of things cost a lot of money. And they were all destroyed. And it wasn't like "I'm just gonna pour some accelerant and torch it." Like they took their tiiime to destroy certain things. So, historically, as a *Black woman*—who understands *history*—you were sending me a message. Right? [*All: Mmmhm.*]

DESIREE   So really thinking of these two horrors that happened to WWAV that we had to survive. Both of them are man-made. [*Deon laughs.*] Both of them [*Deon: Yes!*] were the result of white supremacy, patriarchy, and bigotry. So the system that failed us here in this city, that didn't care about poor people, that didn't care about poor *Black* people, that resulted in thousands of people dying, that resulted in thousands less Black people in the city of New Orleans than before Katrina, that didn't care about those people ever coming back, that is re-creating a city that is really about white professionals [*Nia: Yup.*], that is re-creating communities and environments to cater to people who are not about the people who are born and raised here. That *same* system is what fed this person who came and burned down WWAV [*dry chuckle, breathes in*] [*Mwende: Mmmhm.*] because of the work and the people WWAV was speaking for. And so we gotta understand that these twin traumas are basically children of the same system. And so how do we really think about our own survival in the context of that? Why should we have to keep having to survive? [*Nia: Absolutely.*] We should be able to live and thrive, and not just survive. [*Deon: That's true.*]

DEON   Just thinking about the word *resilience*—I do think that we are, but I hate the conditions that made us have to be. Right? [*Nia: Mmmhm.*] There is no class that coulda taught me how to do any of the stuff that I do at WWAV. Yeah, I may have to have certain kind of skills, but it's a hands-on kind of thing. Learn as you go. But it's just—it would be nice for people to put the same amount of effort as they do in white organizations in Black organizations, because in most situations we see the bulk of the people. [*All: Mmmhm.*] Right? I feel like we should videotape our day sometimes. Think about that. [*Mwende: They ain't ready.*] They ain't *ready*. People keep trying to make it something special, but we're not rewarded like we're special.

NAKITA You know, my goal in life someday, I want to have an organization, I want to make good in my community, I want to do great things. And to just come back to a city that has begun to thrive, and, you know, *Forbes* named it the "brainiest" city in America—but from *implants*, not necessarily the New Orleans citizens who have graduated, who have come back to make a better community for our people, you know. We don't get resources. We don't get praises. This city is no longer for young Black girls like me. [*Mwende: Hmph.*] [*Deon: Wow. Wow, that's deep.*] [*Desiree: That is deep.*] As much as I love New Orleans. [*Deon: You're about to make me cry.*] [*Desiree: Mmmhm.*] As much as New Orleans has taken from me, as much I've invested back in the city? It was no longer a place for young Black girls like me, who come from the 'hood, come from the Lower Ninth Ward–hood that has been taken away. Everything I love been taken away, you know. And everything that I am, I have given back. And, I'm not the one welcomed to the tables.

DEON Our struggle to get to the table? Is *always* hardest. [*Nia: Yes!*] As someone who fought to get to the tables we're at, I realize that I didn't even need to be at this table. I don't need to be here. These women aren't even ready for what I'm about to bring.

MWENDE See, we keep coming back to "they ain't ready!" [*All laugh.*] That should be like the tagline: "WWAV: they ain't ready."

NAKITA #TheyAintReady.

ALL [*laughter*]

DEON #TheyAintReady.

MWENDE I'm gonna put this down in my notes.

ALL [*laughter*]

Resilience Space

The conversation continued for at least another hour as the cars along North Broad Street slowed and then crawled and then stopped. We talked about the unreadiness of white feminists and funders, the violence of white tears, and the mediocrity of Abigail Fisher; about the since-Katrina abandoned bus routes in Black neighborhoods and the bike lanes that now snake through the neighborhoods occupied by transplants; and about the textbooks that tried to pass off the Middle Passage as a great American migration story.[17] *Resilience.* The term was refracted again and again through the intersectional pasts-presents-futures of all of us in porch conversation that day. Together, we coined the afternoon's second slogan: Black Resilience and White Fragility (#TheyAintReady). That turn of phrase spoke volumes about the violent logics that undergirded the new, shiny, "resilient" New Orleans.

Billions of dollars were poured into New Orleans after the storm in 2005. A decade later, the rich had gotten richer, and the city had gotten whiter. Black residents' permanent displacement was intentional. Naomi Klein dubbed it "the shock doctrine": the exploitation of shock in the wake of disaster to achieve massive societal transformations that the people would normally refuse and organize to fiercely protest.[18] Which also signals that the new New Orleans was not really all that *new.* As Deon said, "You know, Black people been resilient for a long goddamn time." With that single sentence, she connected the making of the new resilient New Orleans to the ongoing legacies of settler colonialism and chattel slavery. In so doing, she also exposed that two very different, centuries-old systems of place-making had long been in play in this battle for New Orleans—what Clyde Woods has called the Blues and Bourbon restorations.[19] Each had its own theory of time. In WWAV's front porch strategy, all of "racial capitalism's dramatically scaled cycles of place-making" past, present, and future were simultaneous and weighing: [20] "Sometimes I don't want to be *resilient.*" According to the resilience project, however, time, like modernity, was conceptualized and inhabited as moving linearly toward "progress." Black lifeworlds that did not fit that narrative of improvement were erased, and those that survived were often driven underground where they could be sheltered and protected. WWAV had "long memory"; that was also precisely what was under attack.[21]

Just after the storm, Richard H. Baker, a Republican representative from Baton Rouge, was overheard telling lobbyists: "We finally cleaned up public housing in New Orleans. We couldn't do it. But God did."[22] Joseph Canizaro, one of New Orleans's wealthiest developers, waxed slightly less theological as he expressed his designs on a new New Orleans: "I think we have a clean sheet to start again. And with that clean sheet we have some very big opportunities."[23] In the end, the only portion of federal disaster relief funds that many poor Black New Orleanians saw was the tiny fraction used to demolish the thousands of public housing apartments they once lived in.[24] Some of Katrina's displaced-made-homeless took up residence in the mixed-income units erected on top of their former homes. More were scattered—pushed out to neighborhoods where landlords would accept affordable housing vouchers and to far-flung cities nationwide.[25] This spatial process of containment and removal paved the way for the ultimate step in the isolate-blame-criminalize-destabilize-erase-take playbook: the influx of tens of thousands of white "transplants," who have *taken* the homes that Katrina's still displaced were forcibly prevented from returning to.[26] Meanwhile, the newly minted Downtown Development District Initiative has lined the arts and commercial districts with flags addressed directly to these transplants: "Welcome to your Blank Canvas."[27] *Resilience.*

Black (feminist) life in post-Katrina New Orleans took on a peculiar sort of presence—the sort of marveling that Mwende mocked when they said "You're just so *resilient!*" A debased construction of Blackness as criminal has been the flimsy justification for accelerating the total transformation of New Orleans in the storm's wake. Meanwhile, under the banner of resilience, a grotesquely caricatured portrait of Black culture has also been trotted out to authenticate and market this new resilient New Orleans on the world stage.[28] It is "the Disneyfication of New Orleans," as Desiree had described it to Laura many times.[29] Black people pop up like the colorful explosion of a jack-in-the-box, carrying brass instruments, laughing in the streets, praying in droves. And then they disappear again, as strangely and suddenly and magically as they arose. Within the new Big Easy modernity, this so-called authentic Blackness is thus presented as *timeless* (that is, out of step with the passage of time) and *placeless* (that is, unable to take up space beyond these scripted functions).[30] And that is how the whole racial capitalism resilience project is produced and reproduced. In a city that runs on tourism and maintains unemployment rates as high as 50 percent among Black men, identifying with this limited form of Blackness has become requisite affective labor that actual Black people have been strong-armed into performing in order to survive in the city that their ancestors built.[31] The alternative, as WWAV's participants know far too well, is to turn to the city's survival street economies to make ends meet and risk arrest and police violence daily.

However surreal the making of the new New Orleans might seem, it is important not to exceptionalize its genesis. Nationally, indeed globally, organized abandonment and expulsion have been wildly successful mechanisms for extracting the poor and people of color from territory and then grabbing the(ir) land. These are cold and exacting processes of bodily and spatial purification, which are developed and maintained through the place-making rituals, myths, and moral economies of racial capitalism.[32] The celebration of "a clean sheet to start again," the construction of a myth of Blackness as criminal to justify such cleansing, even the selection and parading of palatable elements of Black culture to authenticate the new New Orleans in the streets—the sole function of these anti-Black, racist imaginaries is to determine who and what is allowed to take place and have a space. They bespeak the deep and historically interlocking systems of "white supremacy, patriarchy, and bigotry" that Desiree named as producing the man-made post-Katrina crisis, and as fueling the arson attack that left WWAV homeless because of their work and the people WWAV was speaking for.[33] The result? Nakita named it, and Mwende, Deon, and Desiree underlined it: "This city is no longer for young Black girls like me."

The Grounds of Theory

If deeply and historically interlocking place-making systems of racial capitalism were producing the new resilient New Orleans, where did front porches figure into the mix? What could front porches teach us about the politics of space and the space of politics in the new New Orleans? What clues did front porches give us for understanding the production of space otherwise in New Orleans before the storm? What exactly was happening on WWAV's front porch?

The conversation on WWAV's front porch that December afternoon was physically, historically, and epistemologically about why the old New Orleans Black geography turned new New Orleans white resilience space was being inhabited, refused, and transformed by Black New Orleanians. Or, as Desiree put it, "I'm glad you love our Mardi Gras Indian tradition, I'm glad you love our music, but that doesn't mean that you get to keep oppressing us." Stepping onto the front porch transported one from the new New Orleans into a different sort of geography. The front porch was not just another "resilient New Orleans" space where scripted Black presence was made to pop up and perform. Nor was it simply a semipublic space where Black women were contained and tolerated. It also was not a space that could be found or discovered, as if placing it on a map of resilience space would thereby domesticate it. The front porch was at once immanently real and radically otherwise. WWAV's presence that December afternoon presented, as Katherine

McKittrick has put it, "a new way to 'enter' into space (conceptually and materially), one that uncovers a geographic story predicated on an ongoing struggle (to assert humanness and more humanely workable geographies)."[34] It was a living geographic story of Black women's bodies *in place*. That story challenged both its makers and onlookers to pause, to sit, and to become part of its slow sedimentation and ungrounding.

In the imaginative and material geography of the front porch that December afternoon, the everyday work of receiving stories and transforming them into collective knowledge—of producing theory on the ground—respatialized the past, present, and future of white supremacist domination and Black feminist revolutionary work. Our conversation flowed from one person to another to another, and then back to the first, to the third, and to another. Brake squeals threaded through sentences, and car horns provided the punctuation. Passersby bridged the aural and the visual with a simple nod or a "How you *doing*?" Each greeting returned to a person walking by then doubled back, as an interpretation of the exchange was shared in the front porch cypher.[35] Together, we were not only confirming what it meant for WWAV to take place; we were actively making this front porch space:

"We're well! How are you?" / "I knew it was important for us to be *here*."
"Good, good. How are you?" / "Yup, *this* is how we do outreach."
"All right. How are you?" / "Resilient, what? They ain't ready."

What was being said was inseparable from where it was being said, which was inseparable from why it was being said, which was inseparable from who was saying it. The conversation was reminiscent of a story circle, a community-building process that was developed by the Free Southern Theater and can be traced to the oral traditions that have long circulated through the Black Atlantic.[36] However, what unfolded was not simply a replication of (or even a riff on) this multigenerational oral tradition. This front porch conversation took *place*. And by taking up space, it provided an entry point for making the post-Katrina landscape otherwise.

To sketch the significance of this process of respatialization beyond those gathered in front porch conversation: each step in the conversation literally reversed the steps of the racial capitalism playbook (isolate-blame-criminalize-destabilize-erase-take). Those who could return after the storm assembled on the front porch and made visible the "absented presence" of Katrina's still displaced.[37] WWAV critiqued the continuous structures of Black suffering and Black death. We made our pasts present; we wrote our histories anew. We illuminated the futures that generations of Black women before us have long since been emplotting. In so doing, we resurrected the dead and gone on the land as we spoke; we spun into existence new relationships and potentialities; we exposed the wellsprings of dreams that have steadily been sheltered in these grounds. In these ways, we unraveled the racial capitalism playbook and made space for ourselves using the tools of our own counter-playbook. We literally made the world *otherwise*. This was no speculative project. Indeed, the WWAV family could hear the violence in any ungrounded, nonimperative formulation. The retort from the front porch underlined that deep and persistent truth: "They ain't ready!" Which also communicated another truth: "We right here? We've been doing that for ages."[38]

Working in the Interstices

In-betweenness is the territory of the front porch, indeed of Black feminist theory.[39] Front porches are thresholds: of language, of sociality, of embodiment, of possibility. Like their northern play cousins, the stoop and the public housing bench, front porches exist in the interstices between home and street, between private and public, between collective and intimate. They are Black geographies of communication, where news from the day can be passed on and incorporated or refuted and elaborated. They are also transitional spaces: of the pause, of passing time, of dragging your feet, of being not quite ready to be inside, but not quite ready to be out. What they are not is new New Orleans white resilience space.

Front porches on New Orleans's iconic shotgun houses are typically several-foot-deep stretches of wood flooring that adjoin to the front of a home (fig. 1.2). They are usually covered by that bit of attic space that juts out farther than the main floor. Between floor and ceiling, a line of pillars provides load-bearing support, leaving porches open on three sides. Architecturally speaking, however, front porches are crosses. Their expanse extends to the left and to the right, in a straight line that traces the perimeter between the home and the street. Their front steps cross forward and back, in a second straight line that reaches out to the street and back through the house's connected rooms to the back door. As geographical space, a front porch is a crossroads.[40] Southern front porches are spaces where Black women have long conjured the presence of generations past, just as they have opened pathways toward new futures for what must become.

1.2 Front porch of a home in the Mural House Program, Old South Baton Rouge, Louisiana. Art by Chemis. Photo courtesy of Museum of Public Art.

Crossroads, thus, is also an apt descriptor for the chance meeting that birthed WWAV more than three decades ago. After Catherine Haywood and Danita Muse met in that crowded health department conference room, they got to work—on the front porch. How and why they got to work will be the focus of chapter 2. Here, we want to emphasize *where* the work got done. Front porches are where Catherine and Danita gathered with family to make harm reduction and wellness packs for late-night outreach.[41] Front porches are where they sat talking with members of their communities who had at best been forgotten and at worst had been left to die. Front porches are where they brought their community members into networks of care and hope.[42] Front porches are where they pioneered models of harm reduction and community-driven outreach that continue to guide public health research today. Catherine explained the process to Laura like this:

> We didn't have an office. We would work from home, my porch. And my poor little mama (who's not here) would do condom packets and she'd say, "Ssshhhh! I'm not getting paid from Women With A Vision!"—because she *didn't*, I mean. But, you know, *everybody* did condom packets—the

children, my sister, my nieces, my mama. So, that's how we did. And we did that for a while.

But, how we did outreach, right? My thing is: you just can't go in somebody's house—in *their neighborhood*, in *their house*—and just start talking. So for weeks almost, I would go and sit in the St. Thomas. I would find a porch and just sit there. You need to get to know me before I start walking up and down your street, right? And you are still trying to figure out what I'm doing? So, I think that's part of what we did. Mmmhm. And then people ask you what you were there for and you're like, "I'm trying to build a relationship with you."

Gradually, Catherine and Danita's persistent presence in and with the community enabled them to build a network of community "gatekeepers" to disseminate vital health information and harm reduction supplies to those they did not touch directly through their street-based outreach. Front porches were, as Catherine explained, an in-between space—not home, but not the streets. They were places to sit, to pause, to stay for a while, and to build relationships. Front porches were also the grounds of theory production and revolutionary praxis. Front porches were where WWAV first came up with the idea to turn neighborhood bars into underground needle exchanges. Front porches were where our foremothers quite literally saved their communities.

Policing the Grounds

During a car ride retracing old outreach routes, Catherine explained to Laura, "WWAV can't do outreach like we used to anymore." They were driving upriver on Louisiana Avenue, just past the location of the former C. J. Peete (or Magnolia) Projects. After the storm, with tens of thousands of people still displaced, the housing projects where WWAV worked—front porches and all—were demolished.[43] The people who were able to return to the mixed-income units built in their place were rarely, if ever, surrounded by the familiar faces that populated their previous residences.[44] People were shaken up and strewn across redevelopment projects in a sort of intentional chaos reminiscent of the waves of forced removal under the Group Areas Act in apartheid South Africa and through urban renewal policies in US cities before that.[45] An array of new public housing restrictions, including ones limiting how many people could congregate on a front porch and what they could do on those porches, directly thwarted efforts to build community anew.[46]

Catherine was clear that the policing of front porches in the new New Orleans was about controlling and regulating the sights, sounds, and movements of Black livingness—indeed, the very possibility for Black life. But, as everyone at WWAV always says, such restrictions also had a history. That is why a key method of WWAV's own counter-playbook is to "provincialize" these racial capitalism place-making regimes by suturing back to them the historical circumstances of their own production.[47] In the case of new New Orleans front porch policing, such restrictions were quite plainly what Saidiya Hartman calls the "afterlife of slavery."[48] As early as 1680, colonial Virginia passed laws prohibiting enslaved Africans from congregating in large numbers, including for funerals, which were codified in Virginia's 1705 Slave Codes. The fear being stoked centered around what Black people would talk about without white surveillance. The lengths that enslavers went to police Black social life in order to try to prevent the formation of bonds through which insurrection could be planned exposed the everyday terror and extreme volatility of the chattel slavery system. Only under the watchful eye of the enslaver's chosen priest or catechist, in the time and space of the plantation mission, were Black people allowed to gather in any large numbers.[49]

Such fears were not for naught. Uprisings were organized no matter how much Black life was watched and policed. The 1811 German Coast Uprising along the eastern coast of the Mississippi River in Louisiana stands as the largest slave revolt in American history.[50] Insurrections such as these did not magically materialize. They were built through everyday forms of sabotage and subterfuge. They were built in intimate exchanges, in and through the domestically oriented survival work of enslaved Black women.[51] They were built on the slim thresholds that separated slave quarters from the rest of plantation life and beyond in the labyrinths of cypress swamps that concealed Louisiana's maroon colonies.[52]

When the line of sight is adjusted away from the transcendental horizons so often envisioned in modes of politics by overthrow, what comes into view are the immanent otherwise possibilities that are already unfolding around us, as well as the deep wellsprings of being, thinking, and doing otherwise on which they draw.[53] The policing of front porches in the new New Orleans is specifically and intentionally an attack on the sanctuaries of Black feminist organizing. Front porches are crossroads; they are the grounds of fire dreams. Black women have been making place, building community, sharing truths, and envisioning otherwise here for generations.

On Sunday, July 10, 2016, this power of front porches as a deeply persistent southern Black feminist geography, as well as the unrelenting violence of racial capitalism to will their erasure, were both shown to the world. Six days prior, Baton Rouge police had murdered thirty-seven-year-old Alton Sterling outside a convenience store where he was selling CDs. Protests had been unrelenting. Sunday was a huge day of mobilization by the Louisiana Movement for Black Lives. Hundreds of people statewide joined the local organizers in a march that first converged on the state capitol building and then headed toward the site of Sterling's murder. While en route, protesters were blocked and forced to retreat by a heavily armed police line. In the midst of the standoff, Lisa Batiste, a Black woman and longtime resident of Beauregard Town on the southern edge of downtown Baton Rouge, called out to protesters. She invited them to find safety on the front porch of her shotgun home. As she explained, she "just wanted them to have a safe place to voice their opinions."[54]

Within minutes, the police stormed Ms. Batiste's front porch to arrest protesters (fig. 1.3). None of the officers even acknowledged her when she told them that *they* did not have permission to be on her front porch. Instead, the police pushed protesters through the doorway of her home, in an attempt to arrest them. From the front lawn, the cries audible on protesters' own cell phone recordings repeated the refrain that they were on "private property."[55] And they were. They were also on hallowed grounds. The police were not simply stopping a protest; they were exacting violence against the past, present, and future of Black women's geographies of struggle.

In the evening hours later that day, Ms. Batiste reflected upon how "the police officers used this as an opportunity to extend their power and authority to the narrowest field of law."[56] When the media coverage from the Baton Rouge protests for Alton Sterling broke, Laura was in New York City. As soon as she saw one of the protesters' videos of Lisa Batiste's front porch, she called Deon and Shaquita. We talked in depth about the protests and the standoff, about the need now more than ever for WWAV to be holding space to understand these attacks on Black people and the Movement for Black Lives, as well as the histories of violence and struggle that give the attacks shape and meaning. The ferociousness of the Baton Rouge police officers' attack on Batiste's porch underlines the power of front porch strategy. By inviting protesters onto her porch, Batiste evidenced how southern Black feminist geographies can unravel the violences of racial capitalism and the production of white resilience space. Calling out to protesters was

1.3 Police barge onto Lisa Batiste's front porch on July 10, 2016, arresting people protesting the murder of Alton Sterling by two Baton Rouge police officers five days prior. Photo by Jonathan Bachman, Reuters.

a liberatory move; it revealed the absented presence of Black women and Black worlds in the southern landscape. In so doing, Batiste exposed the fire dreams that have long been sheltered and protected in these grounds. She also gave them power. For a moment, as protesters gathered in safety on her front porch, the otherwise not only ignited; it was able to flicker, to burn, to blaze. The police moved swiftly to put out this transformative fire rising.

After we finished talking, Laura shared an article about the standoff on social media,[57] with two sentences from our "tricycle effect" as comment:

> Southern front porches are revolutionary, sacred spaces. When the police stormed the protesters invited to gather in this Baton Rouge resident's front lawn and front porch, they exacted violence against the people and the places through which southerners have built community and shared truths for generations.[58]

Those lines were picked up by several friends and accomplices in New Orleans and moved through the national and international web of WWAV's own social media presence. The next day, Brentin Mock, a staff writer for *CityLab*, posted a story expounding on the Black front porch politics of the protests the day before, with the tag "Deon Haywood and Women With A Vision, Inc. been tryna tell y'all."[59]

Space Otherwise

"We believe in the revolutionary things that happen on a southern front porch."

In mid-December 2015, WWAV affirmed the power of southern Black women's geographies and geographic knowledges, as well as the stakes for continuing to produce WWAV's own theory on the ground here amid the materialization of a new New Orleans fantasy hell-bent on erasing all forms of Black livingness. Doing so unleashed the generations-honed geographic story of the front porch—a place where revolutionary things have long happened. We stoked the fire dreams sheltered in these grounds and claimed our power to ignite these visions to build and grow New Orleans otherwise. We also made plain the ways in which these rebellious geographies—even as they were being dismembered by politicians, restricted by property managers, and stormed by police—nevertheless were part of a full, complete, and liberatory *system* of place-making. And as a system, front porch strategy could, indeed *must*, halt the establishment of the new New Orleans resilient order and unravel the racial capitalism playbook. It already was. It was, because it had been doing so for generations.

Since that mid-December afternoon in 2015, we have been building a living archive of the front porch as a site for making knowledge to serve the liberation of our communities.[60] Through a steady series of porch talks, porch sits, and porch poses, we have been reassembling long-standing New Orleans networks and stitching in the occasional national and international visitor. May 2016 saw a series of "Black Feminist Porch Talks" on topics ranging from Black women's representation to state violence against Black women and girls (fig. 1.4).[61] In early July 2016, during the annual Essence Music Festival, director Ava DuVernay took a seat on WWAV's front porch to interview Marley Dias, the young visionary behind the #1000BlackGirlBooks project.[62] The months and years since have been filled with numerous impromptu conversations and photo shoots—including WWAV's staff and official visitors and people passing by on foot along the Broad Street corridor.

1.4 Event flyers and pictures from WWAV's inaugural Black Feminist Porch Talks, 2016. Flyers by Mwende Katwiwa; photos courtesy of WWAV Archives.

We have also organized porch talks on reproductive justice, HIV/AIDS, sexual health, community singing, healing justice, sex work decriminalization, harm reduction, and alternatives to calling the police.[63]

In relationship and in community, we are producing front porches as a deeply enduring geography for living Black feminist futures in New Orleans today. Together, we refuse the visual and aural purification of new New Orleans white resilience space and the ongoing legacies of settler colonialism and chattel slavery in this land; we also conjure the fire dreams of our foremothers and of the generations of southern Black women organizers who came before them. Our geographic story of the front porch extends these community and ancestral knowledges for healing the city, for imagining new futures, and for building a world that is more survivable than our present. In conversation, by taking up space, we are sedimenting the traces and genealogies of pre-Katrina New Orleans—and redefining the terrain (indeed, the possibility) of struggle in the process. Most importantly, we are exposing the immanent, revolutionary possibilities for a New Orleans otherwise that are already materializing around us.

As a system of place-making, our front porch strategy is nonlinear and nondeterministic; it is unpredictable and uncertain. Therein lies its power.

DOING THE WORK

The act of sharing stories *is* the theory and the methodology.
—Katherine McKittrick, *Dear Science*

WWAV's founding was an act of refusal and otherwise world-building. In 1989, the United States was rounding the corner on nearly two decades of the so-called war on drugs. From their own front porches, our foremothers bore witness to exactly how this latest reconfiguration of the isolate-blame-criminalize-destabilize-erase-take racial capitalism playbook was unfolding. Decades of divestment had gutted the social safety net and isolated their people from necessary supports and services. Meanwhile, racist stereotypes of "welfare queens" were being used to blame Black women for this violence, just as sensationalized stories about "crack babies" were being used to criminalize these women and destabilize their families.[1] The next step was *erase*. Rates of HIV infection were exploding, and the numbers of new infections among Black people were fast exceeding those among white people and have continued to ever since. By the early 1990s, HIV was the second leading cause of death for Black women between the ages of twenty-five and forty-four.[2] That lethal fact underlined for our foremothers that racism is, as Ruth Wilson

Gilmore has taught us, best understood as "the state-sanctioned and/or legal production and exploitation of group-differentiated vulnerabilities to premature death."[3] Place-making under mass criminalization, like place-making under all systems of racial capitalism, depended on regulating which bodies could take space, indeed, could *exist*.[4]

When our foremothers came together from their various health and human service positions citywide to take their community's health into their own hands, they were, in the words of Fannie Lou Hamer, "sick and tired of being sick and tired." They were also doing what Black women have always done. Black women's organizing in counterpurpose to the white supremacist misogynistic death logics of racial capitalism has been a durable force in American history. This is a necessary point to emphasize. Too often, even well-meaning critiques of our current order nevertheless extend its white supremacist logics by scripting Black people as mere recipients of aid or as victims of neglect, but never as health activists who create programs and change policy at every juncture. When our foremothers founded WWAV, they drew on the ideological and material tools of an unbroken line of Black women's health activism in the South.[5] They stood with the drug user and sex worker communities that no one else wanted to work with. In partnership with these communities, our foremothers demanded that the whole rotten system be transformed. And, most importantly, they showed that it *could be* transformed by being in community and making the world their people needed.

This chapter centers the knowledge that the WWAV foremothers made to serve the liberation of their communities by "doing the work." And it also cares for this knowledge by doing our work to *speak* this knowledge into the present so that it will continue. That is what theory on the ground looks like as a historical method. It is about recovering and reconstructing WWAV's own organizational history: what really happened. But it is also about why it matters so much to tell these stories—and what doing so demands of us all. The WWAV foremothers are telling stories so that the work they have done and the grounds they have established might be the foundation for new and more livable futures. What's past is prologue.[6]

Working in these two registers of theory on the ground as a historical method—(1) what really happened, and (2) why telling the stories matters—introduces a syncopated rhythm to this chapter. In the first half, excerpts from our Born in Flames life history interviews with Catherine, Danita, and Deon establish the grounds and theoretical texture of WWAV's liberatory knowledge production. Because WWAV history is movement history, telling the stories of what really happened in WWAV's three decades of work also means tracing WWAV's history across the intersections of Black feminist struggle in the movements of which we have always been a part. And there are a lot of them. As Audre Lorde taught us, "There is no such thing as a single-issue struggle, because we do not live single-issue lives."[7] Our foremothers grew their work on the ground in New Orleans at the intersections of social movements for harm reduction, sex workers' rights, women's health, ending gender-based violence, LGBTQ rights, ending the HIV epidemic, drug policy reform, overdose prevention, challenging criminalization, and realizing abolition feminism. WWAV's work has always been complex because our people's entire lives and beings were under threat. It was also dynamic, and it flowed with a swagger that was unwavering and unapologetic. As Danita put it, "For WWAV, practicing harm reduction in the South has demanded first and foremost the tenacity to believe in what we believed in. It's also helped us hone our ability to change with the times and continue to be open to new ways of doing things, which we are always developing in partnership with the drug user and sex worker communities with whom we stand."[8] In the first half of this chapter, we stay close to what our foremothers believed in and all that they developed to make their vision a reality.

In the second half of this chapter, these theories and methods are taught to new staff members through a collective storytelling session with the WWAV foremothers that was held shortly after the porch talk that grounds chapter 1. The mode of writing here is apprenticeship: to show how knowledge is passed at WWAV and why it matters so much to do so. We let this collective storytelling session take up space, on the ground and in the text. And we ask that you, our readers, settle into the pace of that front porch strategy with us—staying close to the stories that are shared in the order they are shared; listening with us to how our foremothers layer core WWAV slogans like "They Ain't Gotta Like You" to refuse the racial capitalism playbook; and also bearing witness with us to how the steps in this playbook have been weaponized against our foremothers through the theft of their work. That history of knowledge dispossession has shaped every bit of the undisciplined research that we have undertaken together in the wake of the fire, down to the collective authoring of this book. It has long been time to honor our foremothers' major contributions to harm reduction, mutual aid, and transformative justice—their fire dreams. Telling the stories of their work is creative and life-giving. Catherine, Danita, and Deon are not asking for

WWAV's history to be memorialized or set aside as an object of nostalgia. They make knowledge to serve the liberation of their communities and refuse the ongoing dispossession of Black women. Our foremothers want to teach the next generation—indeed, all of you reading this book now—how the work is done, so that it will continue.

The Relationship That Started It All

Both Catherine and Danita were raised in multigenerational Black New Orleanian families. Catherine is eight years Danita's senior, born in 1949 to Danita's 1957. She was the oldest child of three and is old enough to remember life in segregated New Orleans. She explained during her life history interview:

> I've lived through some segregation. I remember where I had to ride in the back of the bus. I also remember when my daddy couldn't take me in the store on Canal Street to use the bathroom, so I had to go behind a car, right? I remember the first time that we were allowed to ride in wherever on the bus and I sat in the front and a little white woman got up and I basically just looked at her. Because I thought as old as she was, if you were going to stand up because I'm sitting here, you go for it.[9]

Unwavering. That is the spirit that Catherine is known for. She got married right after high school, had her first child, Deon, shortly thereafter, and her second two children, Dawn and Charles, about a decade later. During that time, Catherine worked as a nursing assistant, as a barmaid, in a laundry, and at a bed-and-breakfast. Her entry into community work came when she got a job with the National Council of Negro Women (NCNW) as part of a new program for young women who had dropped out of high school, training them with the housekeeping skills they needed to be able to work in the hotels that were bursting with tourists each successive festival week or weekend. The program itself, as well as Catherine's participation in it, was the realization of NCNW's long-standing commitment to expand and protect the economic rights of Black women and girls by broadening their leadership in community services and advocacy.[10] And as such, this role provided Catherine with an unparalleled platform for witnessing the explosion of HIV in Black communities and taking action to provide the care that the government would not. From NCNW, she moved onto the Children's Pediatric AIDS Program, where she was hired as part of a project to find people who use intravenous drugs and connect them to HIV testing services. When her supervisor saw the skill and precision with which she moved in community, she told her, "I need you to meet this woman called Danita."

Danita was already making waves in the city's health and human services arena. When we did her life history interview, she talked about how she "always wanted to help people." Danita graduated from Southern University in New Orleans in 1978 with degrees in psychology and sociology, and she went on to get a master's in social work from Tulane soon after to make her passion legible and employable.

> I've always wanted to help people. I've always wanted to help people that most people didn't want. Because that's how I saw Black people. People really didn't want to help us. They just helped us because they felt sorry for us. And that was probably why I was interested in drug addiction treatment because those are the people who people *really* don't want to help. They don't want them to have nothing. They don't want them to be with nothing. They just don't want them with *nothing*. So I was drawn to them.[11]

Unapologetic. That is the spirit that Danita brought to all her work with WWAV. Naming how she was drawn to the people no one wanted to help, Danita laughed herself into an addendum to that story, which underlined how we all make choices to do what we have to do to survive: "Beside the fact that I got a job offer. Always helpful when you get a job offer. You're drawn to people where you can get a job."[12] That job was with the state of Louisiana—first in a ward for people with severe mental health issues and head traumas, then with child protective services, then with the Office of Substance Abuse, which is now called the Office of Behavioral Health. It was from that post that she started to work with community. From her "good government job," Danita ran groups with people struggling with addiction, which put her in a position to be the drug and alcohol representative to some of the earliest white-led HIV response efforts in the city.[13] These efforts, she learned, were willfully *not* reaching out to Black people in the city's ten housing projects; they were targeting the bars frequented by white gay men. That strategy was straight from the isolate-blame-criminalize-destabilize-erase-take racial capitalism playbook. Its implications were deadly for Black people. As Danita explained, "All of these people kept coming up HIV positive, and they *knew* that the intravenous drug users were not necessarily the gay people; they were just regular Joe's out of the housing projects. They *knew* that."[14]

Seeing this anti-Black racism in action was a catalyst. Danita knew that if she did not step up to make sure that HIV prevention and education resources got to her people, no one else would. And so she began to recruit other Black women who saw what was going on and were just as pissed off as she was. She met several in meetings at the Office of Public Health. Myra was a quick typist; Marion was a good bookkeeper. She invited both to dinner: "I started to tell them about this plan I had for this agency for women to be able to do stuff, to help HIV—to help *us*, to help poor people—to help."[15] What she was missing was a partner for community outreach. And then she met Catherine at yet another health department meeting. Danita's reputation preceded her.

The story of that meeting is one that we retell often at WWAV. Catherine and Danita locked eyes across a crowded conference table. The city had just gotten a big influx of funds to address a surging syphilis epidemic. This time, the outreach maps were following the epidemiology. When the city's zip codes were called out, Catherine and Danita claimed the ones to their Uptown neighborhoods, including all four of the Uptown housing projects: St. Thomas, Magnolia (officially "C. J. Peete"), Melpomene (officially "Gustavo"), and Calliope (officially "B. W. Cooper").[16] That was when their relationship started. Together, they drove the streets that fanned out through Central City and the Lower Garden District down to the Mississippi River—Calliope Street, Martin Luther King Jr. Boulevard, Washington Avenue, Louisiana Avenue. Danita was in her truck, Catherine in her car. The health department's orders were simply to take boxes of condoms and drop them at barrooms, grocery stores, beauty shops, and laundromats. It only took a few weeks before Danita and Catherine realized that the people who ran these businesses were taking their *free* condoms and then selling them for $1.50 apiece. And so Danita and Catherine quit bulk-dropping condoms, and started to try to figure out how to get them into their people's hands directly. That was when *the work* started.

The syphilis outreach funding dried up, and the HIV epidemic in their communities was steadily getting worse. Danita and Catherine decided to shift from work hours to after-work hours—from their vehicles to front porches. WWAV's first office was a closet in Danita's home. During these first years of work, Danita and Catherine built a network of what they called "gatekeepers." The term *gatekeeper* is typically used hierarchically to describe the people, usually low-level bureaucrats, who stand between community and the services they need. WWAV's foremothers deployed the term horizontally to talk about the different insider-outsider boundaries maintained by people in heavily criminalized and surveilled communities for their own protection. Gatekeepers for Danita and Catherine could be the person who ran a shooting gallery, or an old head who taught younger drug users how to inject safely, or a barkeep, or someone who kept a lookout for cops, or just someone everybody liked. Amid constant surveillance, survival depended on carefully and methodically concealing the intricacies and intimacies of everyday life. Working with gatekeepers maximized the impact of WWAV's outreach. Gatekeepers were able to get harm reduction tools into the hands of people Danita and Catherine would never see on the streets and people they might never know were using. Working with gatekeepers in this way also respected and strengthened the strategies that their communities had long used to care for and defend themselves.

In 1991, WWAV incorporated as a 501(c)(3), and opened our first office a couple of years later. Just like their unique outreach strategy, our foremothers' choice of location—and their choice of when and where to move—was always shaped by where people were already going and where people could feel comfortable. Between 1993 and 2005, WWAV maintained offices Uptown on Cleveland Street, LaSalle Street, Tulane Avenue, and Washington Avenue while continuing outreach on foot and by mobile van. One of our most prized outreach spots was Rose Tavern, located on the corner of Thalia and Dorgenois on the grounds of the Calliope Projects.[17] There, our foremothers worked with one of the bartenders to keep jars of condoms stocked on top of the bar and to establish an underground needle exchange behind it. Weekly, they would drop off a new case of clean needles and a new five-gallon sharps container, collecting the one that was filled. Needles started to disappear from the grounds of the Calliope, because the bartender did a one-for-one exchange with any needle used or found. Throughout these years, WWAV's squad also ballooned. Catherine and Danita were joined by Deon (fig. 2.1); by several other outreach workers, including Eisa, Angelita, and Sharon; by some part-time office staff, like Robert; by staff who supported outreach with the Latinx community as "Mujeres Con Vision," like Oscar; and even by Catherine's mama, who would help make condom packs on her porch. WWAV was family, and doing the work was a family affair. WWAV was also the Black southern anchor to the rapidly growing national harm reduction movement.

During Hurricane Katrina, WWAV's leadership was displaced, and most of our founding paperwork and supplies were lost in the floodwaters. It was

Danita Muse, and Catherine and Deon Haywood are women with a vision.

SAFE SEX ED

LOUISIANA GROUP WORKS TO REDUCE SPIRALING AIDS RATES AMONG URBAN BLACKS. **WORDS BY SHAWN E. RHEA**

2.1 Danita Muse, Catherine Haywood, and Deon Haywood photographed with red AIDS ribbons in their hands for a feature on WWAV in the *Source*, April 2001. A mounted copy of this article hung in the WWAV office and was one of the few things not destroyed in the arson attack.

our first bone-deep lesson in the ephemerality of Black archives, and how disaster would be continually exploited to dispossess our foremothers of the liberatory knowledge they made in concert. In the wake of the devastation caused by the government abandonment of Black New Orleanians, our foremothers made their ways back to New Orleans. In 2006, they came together to imagine how WWAV would continue. Catherine and Danita asked Deon to become WWAV's first executive director, because Deon was "the only one of the three of us who liked talking to people." There was deep trust in that ask. Catherine and Danita knew that everything that Deon did, she did "with the heart and soul of WWAV."[18] That meant relying on the same principles that had guided her mother and Danita since WWAV's founding; it also meant changing with the times, just like they had always done. Responsive to precisely how the new New Orleans was being built through the mass criminalization, destabilization, and erasure of Black communities, Deon led

WWAV in imagining and winning the policies that our communities needed to survive, much like Catherine and Danita had done with the harm reduction models they pioneered in the late 1980s and early 1990s. That was part of why Deon saw so clearly that the arson attack on our offices, which was a direct retaliation for our decriminalization work, was from the very same racial capitalism playbook that our foremothers had been refusing and resisting since WWAV's founding. By revolutionizing this knowledge into praxis, she transformed a fire that was intended to destroy WWAV into a portal for stretching our work to unprecedented reach and impact—locally, regionally, nationally, and internationally.

I Have This Feeling of *Belonging*

Our research as survival was a central part of that recovery and liberation work. Since the summer of 2013, we have been working together to document, reassemble, and grow the liberatory knowledge that our foremothers carried steadfastly in their relationships but were often too busy to write down: to assemble a living archive of WWAV's fire dreams.[19] True to their commitment to community and to the work, we began every life history interview we completed with the same question: "*Why* did you get into this work?" It was an open-ended question that allowed our foremothers, the early WWAV staff, and our current leadership alike to decide for themselves what "this work" is and why and when they "got into it." It also invited people to reflect on the central paradox that WWAV lived every day—the paradox of engaging with political institutions and public health officials that proved they did not care about Black drug users and sex workers.[20] Most staff explained the direct steps that led to them becoming connected with WWAV; Catherine (fig. 2.2) started with her childhood memory of being on a segregated trolley car in the 1950s and refusing to move.

For the next hour of Catherine's interview, she and Laura weaved through stories from her childhood, her connection to human services, and the early years of WWAV's work in community. It was slow going at first. Anyone who has ever sat with Catherine for any length of time has heard her say something to the effect of, "I don't like to talk. I like to *do the work*." The first minutes of their conversation ping-ponged between questions and short answers. "And what else do you want to know?" Catherine prodded, *what* being the operative word. When they shifted to talking about *why* she did it, Catherine's memories stretched out and filled minutes of conversation space at a time.

2.2 Catherine Haywood, cofounder of WWAV.

Why got us into the reality of living through the early HIV epidemic. From the beginning, the people most vulnerable to HIV were the very communities already treated as disposable in American society: queer people, Black people, people who used drugs, people who sold sex, people who were migrants fleeing violence. A landscape of willful government neglect, criminalization, racism, heterosexism, moralization, and media sensationalism was rapidly being erected to separate people living with HIV and those who fought at their sides from the rest of the so-called innocent population. AIDS activist Vito Russo spat that indictment from the steps of the Department of Health and Human Services at a 1988 ACT UP demonstration, "If I'm dying from anything—I'm dying from the fact that not enough rich, white, heterosexual men have gotten AIDS for anybody to give a shit."[21] The boundary between the disposable and the innocent was heavily policed— by the deafening silence of elected officials and all of the expected agents of the rapidly ballooning prison industrial complex, but also by public health officials and researchers who had been newly capacitated with the funds and mandates to "study" the epidemic that was unfolding. Catherine and Danita saw first-hand how this epidemiological surveillance was most often about managing and controlling Black bodies, and not about understanding the structures that made entire communities vulnerable to HIV.[22] In a vile sort of mathematics, their people were meticulously counted in the data that guided the paltry sum of resources that federal and state governments had allocated for HIV prevention at the local level, and then somehow their people all became invisible when it was time for local health departments and large, mostly white-led, HIV organizations to actually distribute those funds on the ground.[23] The consequences of that isolation from supports and resources were deadly. As Catherine explained, "My people didn't know a damn thing about it because the information wasn't geared to them. Right? And even though people were shooting up and doing whatever and becoming infected, they still weren't telling them enough about whatever."[24]

Catherine and Danita took action to stop this deadly order from materializing any further. They started collecting materials from their day jobs. Then, when they got off work at about five o'clock in the evening, they would walk "the housing developments and the neighborhoods that nobody else wanted to go into, because they were afraid of the people":

> We had no problem, you know? It got to where if something happened and they knew we were coming, they would let us know, "It's not a good day for y'all." Right? "Don't come to work." Or "Don't go out in the street working because this happened and that happened." So, they got to know us, and they trusted us, which is what—it's what you need when you work community. People have to trust you. And still this is, what, 2013? And all I have to say is my face, my name, and they trust me. And so I can't do anything that's going to jeopardize that—and make it where people will trust me whether I'm doing HIV or some—anything else, right? So I think, I think we had a great relationship with people within WWAV. Like family, I think we would fuss and whatever but that was okay, because it was what it was. Right?[25]

Being able to work with, build trust with, make knowledge with the very Black people that the city's white HIV providers and researchers were afraid of gave Catherine and Danita a righteous level of indignation. With these drug user and sex worker communities, they started working word of mouth to host home health parties that brought their prevention tools and education into a shared conversation space hosted by community gatekeepers. In so doing, they also explicitly and intentionally centered Black women's geographies and geographic knowledges. As Catherine saw it, "We're the ones who take care of the family. *Women* do that. They do it now, right? So, if she's well, then she's going to take care of all of you."[26]

The sheer impact of Catherine and Danita's early outreach work earned them a handful of public health contracts from the state and subcontracts with local researchers who were following the HIV and drug funding pipelines. That money enabled WWAV to open a storefront in Central City on LaSalle Street, where Catherine would cook supper and feed the community with lines around the corner. But she and Danita were also clear that the priorities of government agencies and academic researchers would not divert them from their very clear understanding of precisely how racial capitalism was killing their people. Funding could not change what they did, nor could it silence them; it only emboldened them. Grounded in the knowledge they were making with their community, Catherine and Danita continued to name at every meeting they attended how the war on drugs, AIDS moral panic, and the racism of white-led HIV responses were driving the epidemic in Black communities. The public health officials and researchers who had awarded them grants were enraged by the fact that they could not control what WWAV said or did. At one point during her life history interview, Catherine called out to Deon to ask if she remembered when one public health researcher, Tom Farley,[27] told her and Danita "not to say anything" at a statewide meeting for all the community agencies receiving HIV funding. The recollection washed over Deon's face, "I forgot all about that. I gotta tell Quita." Catherine continued, "And we looked at him like, mmm, 'I don't think that works.' Because you can't tell us that. We could say what we want to say. You don't have to agree with us, and you're not going to stop us from disagreeing with you. You are talking to the *wrong women*. Because we don't care. You know? We don't care."[28] Deon returned, "Quita's shaking her head." She brought a small glass of a new smoothie she had just made to share and stayed for a minute when Catherine asked her to help fill in a patchy memory about all of the places where WWAV had done outreach work.

That exchange with Deon carried us all into the next half hour of conversation about family, connections, and the work. It also framed "the feeling of belonging" that Catherine said she got from WWAV at the conclusion of her life history interview:

I have this feeling of *belonging*. And it's a different feeling. I BELONG. I'm clear. But this is a different feeling. And then the other side: I've done something. Right? I've done something that might help somebody else. Not so much a game. I'm not really a fun person. I really don't like to—work-wise I like to do the work. Half the time I don't give a damn whether my name is out there or not. Even though it is, I don't know that I *care* like that, right? But I think that the work is important and I think that it helps people, so I love it. I've gotten that from WWAV.

And I've grown. WWAV's grown. I've grown. That's a great thing. And I continue to grow. And it grows. And then watching the things that Dee do. It's *really*—Right? Like, okay, [*emotion catching in her voice*] *there's my child*. And so, she's growing and moving. And I'm the mama. And even though she'll say, "That's the co-founder" and I just look at her and say "Why you gotta keep saying that?" Right? But it's just a wonderful thing. So I get this great feeling because I can honestly say that I've been involved in THIS. If nothing else over here matter, I've been involved in THIS. And we were able to do THIS. And we've done THIS. Right? I love it.[29]

When she first spoke the word "belonging," Catherine caught herself, lest anyone think that she was describing some feel-good, multicultural, color-blind sort of racial acceptance. As a Black woman, she was *clear* that she BELONGED in American society and in the city of New Orleans. "I'm not going nowhere," she said, tracing back six generations of her family to the city and surrounding river parishes. She learned that lesson from generations of Black women organizers in the South; it was also the truth that spurred the founding of WWAV. In the early days, she and Danita turned neighborhood bars like the Rose Tavern into underground needle exchanges to literally stop the death toll of the war on drugs; in 2008, her daughter Deon similarly refused Black people's organized erasure after Hurricane Katrina and made home for hundreds of sex workers who were being criminalized. Catherine's clarification—"I BELONG. I'm clear."—rendered visible the weight of the deeply embodied, world-building ethics that she, Danita, and Deon all practiced through harm reduction and community outreach. For thirty-five years now, the course of action has been the same: stay put, take up space, build relationships, and do the work.[30]

An appreciation of that sense of belonging was important to understand the very different "feeling of *belonging*" that Catherine said she grew into at

WWAV. The barroom needle exchanges and the sex worker story circles were significant because of *why* each made a home for the people being erased under racial capitalism's violent place-making systems. Throughout WWAV's history, our foremothers cultivated relationships as sites for refusing dispossession and living into futures that are more survivable. Put differently, they fought back against the racial capitalism playbook by building Black women's relational geographies. In framing their relationships *as* geographic knowledge, we are bridging two dimensions of Clyde Woods's work: first, from *Development Arrested*, we take "blues epistemology," the plantation-birthed, Katrina-resurrected modes of "autonomy of thought and action in the midst of constant surveillance and violence"; and second, from his writing on New Orleans after Hurricane Katrina, we look to "the subterranean caverns that shelter the wellsprings of dreams during the seasons when hope can't be found."[31] At WWAV, relationships are both the means for maintaining independent thought and action amid constant surveillance *and* the caverns in which these thoughts, actions, and dreams are kept. They hold all that we have imagined for ourselves and the world.

When our foremothers founded WWAV, they did not turn to public health officials nor to church leaders nor to social workers nor to researchers nor to any other formal institution to authenticate their methods. They turned to each other. They turned to their communities. The proof was in the work and how they were able to help people. The proof was in the worlds they were able to create in the context of these relationships. Their presents were pregnant with possibilities. Emotion caught in Catherine's throat when she talked about watching the things that her daughter Deon did: "Like okay, *there's my child*." That pride of a mother, that power of across generations, brought Catherine deeper into describing "this great feeling" she got from doing the work and helping people, a feeling that was literally alive in relationships. She could feel it—as she grew and WWAV grew, and she continued to grow and WWAV continued to grow. And she could honestly say that she had been involved in THIS, and she had done THIS.

You Can Do This and Be a Black Woman

If *why* WWAV did the work was critical to understanding Catherine's "feeling of *belonging*," *what* WWAV did shaped the appreciation Danita (fig. 2.3) had of the importance of WWAV's work in a country swept up in panic over rising HIV rates. Every single bit of what she and Catherine were able to do was

2.3 Danita Muse, cofounder of WWAV.

brand *new*. The work they pioneered—work that would be stolen out from under them and used to underwrite researchers' careers—all started with their shared commitment to actually talking to and learning from the sex worker and drug user communities that no one else wanted to work with.

A few years in, Danita and Catherine started surveying the country to find networks where they could learn from and with other people working in community like they were. That search landed them at the first National Harm Reduction Conference in Oakland, California, in September 1996. Harm reduction had its roots in the health and self-determination work of multiple liberation movements in the United States—the Black Panther Party's creation of community survival programs like Free Breakfast for Children and Free Health Clinics; the Young Lords' launch of an acupuncture program for heroin users in the Bronx; the women's health movement's work to bring reproductive care and education under women's own control; the Black feminist organizing to address violence against women without involving the police; and the grassroots responses to the growing HIV crisis.[32] From these threads, those gathered in 1996 wove a vision and practice of harm reduction that birthed the movement we know today. That conference, in Danita's words, "made a whole lot of sense to us." Whatever pushback she and Catherine had been getting back home in Louisiana, person after person in Oakland confirmed for them:

> We were actually doing the right thing. The fact that we were actually in the community. That we didn't wait for the community to come to us. The fact that we went to places where they went. And most of all is that we were from the community. We weren't outsiders. We would walk the streets and people would say, "You are so-and-so's daughter." They would get me mixed up with my sisters, because my sisters ran the street; I didn't run the street. So they would call me one of their names. I'd say, "No, those are just my sisters." You know, so um, so that made sense to us.[33]

Being a southern anchor to the growing harm reduction movement propelled WWAV into myriad just-forming harm reduction networks. Our foremothers were often the *only* people in attendance from the South and some of the only Black women. Gradually, people across the country started to recognize WWAV and depend on Danita and Catherine for their expertise in *doing* community outreach—expertise "around packaging, around what to put it in, what's the logic behind it and everything." They turned that expertise into a slogan for some of their first outreach T-shirts: "Risk Reduction in the Dirty South."[34]

Moving as the southern experts in harm reduction spaces was one thing. However, Danita and Catherine were also intent on making inroads into the mainstream HIV prevention efforts in the South so that they could change how work was being done region-wide. During her life history interview, Danita talked at length about a presentation that she and Catherine did at a "little hole in the wall in Texas," which put a point on their theory on the ground about the importance of community outreach in making Black women's geographies. That story unfolded with the same embodied "We don't care what people think of us" ethic that Catherine had shared earlier:

> DANITA We went to some little hole in the wall in Texas, Catherine and I did, in our African garbs. We sure did, because we were *pissed off.* So she and I went to Union Station, right out of Texas A&M. Right there, she and I went and we presented. She did something on something; I

did something on something else. And we did these workshops. And people were so enthused by the fact that we were Black women, and that we could talk with sense, and that we just kind of told them stuff that they thought was wrong but that was working for us.

LAURA Like what?

DANITA Actually *going to the community*. They really thought that they didn't have to do that. Now, this is in the mid-1990s, so they really didn't think that they needed to go, or they had issues with people coming in. And we just kinda laid it out for them: "What you expect? Why would they come see you? What you got? I mean WHY? They don't know you. Their mama and them don't know you. Their neighbor on the street don't know you. The person that might know you, they don't like! So why would they come see you? You ain't nobody. Say, 'We got this thing!!!' So?? The store got something for them, too, but they gotta pay for that shit, too. So what."

And it was like, we would tell them things that—it kinda made sense to them. That they needed to change the manner in which they tried to get people in for the services. Because at this time, there was a lot of money for minorities to receive treatment. And the minorities were not going in. So the funding sources started to blame the monitories for not going in. When it wasn't them. It was the people that were providing the services. Because they didn't know how to get the minorities in. Because they probably didn't have no Black people working for them—Black people, or people of color *period*, working for them. So that was one of the things that we showed them was that *you can do this and be a Black woman*.[35]

"You can do this and be a Black woman." This was Danita and Catherine's watchword. The two were lifelong outreach partners. Their trust in each other and the unwavering, unapologetic swagger with which they moved were pivotal to the harm reduction models they pioneered. Each of them brought a unique focus to the work (and, by extension, to one another). Catherine traced the "infrastructure of feeling" that flowed in and through relationships at WWAV;[36] Danita zeroed in on the tangible stuff that enabled WWAV's work to take place and have a space. Both were clear about the other's strengths. Their differences were complementary and generative, opening them both into the liberatory possibilities they were making together in community. Where their focuses met was in the meticulous way

each analyzed the political sense of the communities they lived and worked in: "Why would they come see you?"

The community the WWAV foremothers worked in solidarity with was the very class of so-called undeserving poor who have long been presumed incapable of autonomy, much less of collective action. That was what Danita was naming when she said, "Those are the people who people *really* don't want to help. They don't want them to have nothing. They don't want them to be with nothing. They just don't want them with *nothing*." That perception has not been without challenge. Much ink has been spilled by scholars and community workers alike to understand and *underline* poor Black people's capacity for action. Against the "culture of poverty" thesis and the "underclass" debate, Black feminist ethnographers have descended into the bowels of neoliberal governmentality and its intersections with other political-cultural formations like welfare offices, battered women's shelters, and mixed-income developments to explore the political agency of poor Black women in the midst of their dispossession.[37] Likewise, Black feminist historians have traced poor Black women's transformative organizing as a steady, unbroken tradition in the South—one with deep material gains for Black people in the areas of food security, housing access, welfare reform, prison abolition, and the long struggle for reparations.[38] Together, these scholarly works shed light on how inequality is lived by poor Black people as a consequence of state policy, as well as on the forms of collective action and "choreography" that Black women and girls have used to disrupt the hierarchies and narratives that marginalize them—to make life in the face of the structures that produced premature death.[39]

Nonetheless, Danita's story was a reminder about precisely how long these racist myths have been greasing the wheels of the isolate-blame-criminalize-destabilize-erase-take racial capitalism playbook. When the question of poor Black people's everyday lives was raised by providers or funders or researchers, Danita and Catherine watched how often the gaze shifted subtly to view their people as objects of regulation or of moral indignation.[40] It was, in Danita's words, the methodical way that white-led agencies and public health researchers were "getting all the money" and "just fucking over our people." Seeing that again and again solidified Danita and Catherine's own practiced refusal of the racial capitalism playbook:

> We do have a history—back in the day we had a history of not playing well with others. And I think some of that was because we knew we were

good. We knew that people could not measure up. And we had a high standard of what people needed to do to help the community. Whereas some folks were just kind of stabbing at it, we were actually *doing it*. So we didn't take shit from people. We really didn't. And we didn't care that they didn't like us. We didn't care that they talked about us. But they respected us. That was enough. Sometimes today that's still enough.[41]

The story about the conference in that "little hole in the wall in Texas" mattered, because it exemplified how Danita and Catherine handled the gaze on themselves and their communities through their own counter-playbook. They did so through practices of solidarity: through their dress, through their conversation, and through their work. Every facet of the knowledge Danita and Catherine made, lived, and embodied in service of the liberation of their communities was immanently real and radically otherwise.[42] They had no interest in playing nice with people who could not see them, nor the communities with whom they stood. They showed up in their African garbs because they were *pissed off*. They told a burgeoning network of HIV educators and funders that they were *wrong*. And they demonstrated how, by respecting the long-standing patterns of community caretaking that were essential to Black women's own geographies and geographic knowledges, it was possible to have a massive impact on entire communities' health and well-being. "*You can do this and be a Black woman.*"

We're Home

The WWAV foremothers made history. They made history in both senses of the word: as actors who created the conditions of their own liberation, and as narrators who shaped the analysis of what their work was and how it should be understood. These are, again, the two registers of theory on the ground as a historical method—what really happened, and why telling the stories matters. As actors, Catherine and Danita labored to stop the latest reconfiguration of the racial capitalism playbook in the late 1980s and the premature death it was wreaking for Black people. They did so by going to drug users and sex workers, by making knowledge with them, by building innovative health programs that grew directly from their lived realities, and then by working with them to imagine and create the world otherwise. As narrators, they also expressed the promise of their fire dreams in every space they occupied, funders and politicians be damned. In so doing, they created space for visualizing and actualizing the ways in which the health work, spirit work, and justice work of Black women could open very different worlds—ones built through solidarity, respect, and care.

That was the work that Deon (fig. 2.4) was raised in and the legacy she was entrusted to carry forward when she became WWAV's first executive director after Hurricane Katrina in 2006. But the New Orleans in which she was continuing to live WWAV's mission was also being rapidly transformed in yet another reconfiguration of the racial capitalism playbook. Rose Tavern, which had been the anchor of WWAV's pre-storm work, had shuttered its doors, never to reopen. Meanwhile, developers and legislators exploited the disaster to accelerate the racist violence that the WWAV foremothers had come together to fight in the context of the early HIV epidemic—along with its attendant practices of hoarding resources, stealing Black women's knowledge, blacklisting them from funding, denying their people services, and criminalizing them into oblivion. A decade later, we would critique this targeted destabilization of Black worlds, whitewashed under the slogan of "resilience," from WWAV's post-arson front porch.

Becoming the organization that had that porch talk and held that space was no small feat. Deon saw it immediately when she and Shaquita, and her mama Catherine, and her children Cynthia and Brandon, and her first grandchild Little Brandon, and Danita, and all of Danita's family were able to make their ways back home after the storm. There was a battle for land and for history actively underway. Continuing WWAV's work meant staying true to the foundational theory on the ground that Catherine and Danita had built; it also meant changing with the times, just like they had always done, to grow into all the horizons of what WWAV could and needed to become. Deon systematized that continuity and change in a 2019 interview:

> We are a collective of Black women who do amazing community organizing, policy, community engagement. *We're home.*
>
> I became executive director of WWAV after Hurricane Katrina. It was a very tough time. It was extremely hard to rebuild, to come back. Being a small nonprofit, I don't know if we knew we would be *able* to come back. After Hurricane Katrina, I knew that if we were gonna survive, somebody was gonna have to be in charge and take charge.
>
> When we started out, WWAV just did harm reduction and street outreach and HIV prevention. It wasn't until after Hurricane Katrina that we realized that the work needed to shift, that we needed to start looking at

2.4 Deon Haywood, executive director of WWAV.

policy and services for people in our community. And so it's become a part of our organizing that we provide case management services, as well as organizing, as well as integrated voter engagement.[43]

Even as the work continued to grow, the vision remained the same. WWAV is, was, and will always be a collective of Black women making knowledge to serve the liberation of Black drug user and sex worker communities.

As Deon led WWAV in this new focus on policy change, she did so by staying true to the methods that have defined WWAV since our founding in 1989. Whenever Deon showed up at any national or international policy table, she always talked about the people who were being left out, just like her mother and Danita had always done, funders and politicians be damned. In movements to end mass criminalization that too often naturalized the experiences of cisgender men as normative, she emphasized the difference it made to build analysis and strategy from the knowledges of women, gender-nonconforming, and transgender people. She put Black women's comprehensive reproductive justice demands front and center in white women–led movements for reproductive rights and abortion access. In the work to build a national HIV strategy, which too often tried (and still tries) to sanitize the lives of people living with HIV as respectable victims rather than indict the systems that willed their premature deaths, she also called out racism and lifted up sex workers. And she centered active drug users in projects for women's health that operated with the same normalized shame and stigma. Most importantly, she championed the South in all of them—not as a region to be pitied, but as a part of the country that has *been* rising up in and through Black women's organizing and leadership. These connections sound almost commonsense now as we are writing this in 2022. In 2006, however, they were not. That is why our comrade and NO Justice Project attorney Andrea Ritchie calls Deon "the embodiment of Black feminism."[44] Deon helped frame a whole generation's understanding of how criminalization is the tactic our current system uses to come for Black women's bodies. Deon is also why this conversation is rooted in the South and in the history of Black women's organizing here, most especially WWAV's.

The knowledge that Deon leveraged to move national and international policy has always been made in the geography of the South in partnership with the people of this region. That is why, back home in New Orleans, the fight to ensure that WWAV would continue was just as methodical. With Catherine and Danita, Shaquita, and a whole new squad of staff members, Deon led WWAV in making space for Black drug user and sex worker communities in a city hell-bent on erasing them. It was a radical act of refusal and otherwise world-building, as unwavering and unapologetic as the decades of history on which it rested. And it was just as life-giving. WWAV is, as so many in our community have affirmed, "a place I knew was sacred."[45] When you walked through WWAV's doors or sat on the front porch, you were stitched into a Black feminist family that had been living the future as now for generations. Doing THAT, protecting THAT, growing THAT, was tiring, as Deon readily acknowledged. But her commitment to making WWAV's vision a reality as unwavering as her mother's and Danita's:

> Someone once asked me, "Oh you, you don't get tired?" Yes. Yes, I get tired. But that doesn't mean I *stop*. And I also think, suppose we would've stopped after Hurricane Katrina? Then I wouldn't be celebrating this

thirty years, and I wouldn't be celebrating the amazing work and history of what it means for Black women to live in the vision of the possibilities of who we are.[46]

What really happened matters. In order "to live in the vision of the possibilities of who are," our foremothers knew that Black women needed to have some*where* to rest, to be together in community, to talk about the forces impacting their lives, and to feel the fire dreams that are always already sheltered in these grounds. Catherine, Danita, and Deon have lived that truth in community for more than thirty years. That is what it has meant for WWAV to be *home*. On these hallowed grounds, as Arundhati Roy reminds us, "Another world is not only possible, she is on her way. On a quiet day, I can hear her breathing."[47]

The Work Will Continue

Sharing stories is how we make that world present. In the years since the fire, we have recorded hours of stories about WWAV's first decades of work—stories about the home health parties that gatekeepers hosted to share sexual health information, about the education events that targeted the wives of the men that WWAV's people were selling sex to, about the expansion of WWAV to the Latinx community as "Mujeres Con Vision," about the quick and dirty demonstrations on how to "cheek" a condom, about the staff member losses to relapse and overdose.[48] These stories have weight. The theory on the ground accumulates. Speaking WWAV's history, sharing the liberatory knowledge that our foremothers made in partnership with drug user and sex worker communities pushes back against the racial capitalism playbook that has willed their erasure for too long. That speech is creative: to speak into existence. It gives voice to the otherwise possibilities already around us by disrupting the aural purification of our current order and filling our world with the sounds of a new world a-coming.[49] It also enjoins all of us to the work of continuing to make WWAV's vision a reality.

Speaking these possibilities is also *for* WWAV. There is no way to survive the constant and lethal surveillance of our current order without being impacted by it. *All* of our imaginations have been harmed. (In this *all*, we include you, our readers, too.) Sharing stories *again and again* makes them real *again and again*. Catherine's feeling of belonging, thus, is also a discipline of hope: "I've been involved in THIS. And we were able to do THIS. And we've done THIS."[50] It is a practice that sediments the traces of WWAV's own pre-Katrina past and the liberatory knowledge WWAV is steadily making—that the work can and will continue to be the grounds for building new and more livable futures. And *that* is what is so threatening about Black women's leadership. As Danita put it, "We knew we were good."[51] Knowing that meant teaching it to every new person who joined the WWAV family. Catherine, Danita, and Deon tell stories about what they were able to do together, so each person who walks through WWAV's doors or sits on the front porch knows where they come from.

In the years since the storm, there have been a lot of new people to stitch into the WWAV family. That apprenticeship work has been constant, iterative, and involving. About ten years into Deon's tenure as executive director, in 2016, she formalized that apprenticeship under the banner of a strategic planning retreat. WWAV's work had expanded in ways that the foremothers never would have dreamed possible. We had just hired three new dedicated staff members, one to move statewide legislative policy (Nia), one to coordinate reproductive justice work locally (Nakita), and one to launch an integrated voter engagement program (Raven). This trio joined the cohort of staff who supported WWAV's rebirth in the wake of the arson attack, holding down communications and programming (Desiree), anticriminalization work (Christine), youth organizing (Mwende), and case management (Michelle). As joyous as that expansion was, there was also a disconnect. This was the first time in WWAV's history when we had staff members who only worked in one program area. Our founding method, however, required that all staff moved in formation and in accordance with the embodied, world-building ethics of southern Black women's organizing that they were trusted to carry forward every day. And so Deon asked Catherine and Danita to help her make WWAV make sense to some of the newest members of the WWAV squad by doing what they had always done: telling stories, so the work would continue.

They Ain't Gotta Like You

The storytelling circle that day in 2016 was more than twelve-round. Deon opened the space by asking Catherine and Danita, "What made you want to get out on the streets and start doing this work?"[52] The rest of us who were gathered were sitting at the feet of our elders. Mwende and Laura both pulled out their cell phones to make sure that the audio from this session was recorded, like all of our porch talks. We knew the pace would be slower this afternoon. This was not a conversation that would flow from one person to another to another, and then back to the first, to the third, and to another. We were all apprentices. We were also bearing witness. There were lethal realities we needed to hold with Catherine, Danita, and Deon about the violence that was materializing nationally in the late 1980s and early 1990s, as well as the acute harm done locally by researchers, public health officials, and legislators—to WWAV and our people—that had never been acknowledged, much less transformed. We also needed to learn how our foremothers became ungovernable, and what harm reduction methods and principles they pioneered by being in community and working in partnership with drug users and sex workers, locally and nationally, to refuse premature death and save their own lives.[53] There was an incommensurability here—between the realities of anti-Black violence and the Black feminist possibilities WWAV has always lived as now.[54] That is what we, those who continue the work (including those of you joining us now as readers), were being entrusted to hold.

Deon's question hung in the air, as Catherine and Danita looked at each other and back at her. After an eye-contact-only *"Please, Mommy!"* from Deon, Catherine sighed and began:[55]

CATHERINE Our people—Black people—were not getting the same information that gay white men were getting about HIV and AIDS. At all. It wasn't going in the communities. So Danita and I—and her "good government job"[56] [*laughter*], you know, and my job at Pediatric AIDS Program—would go out in the evening when we got off from work and pass out information and give out condoms. We would start at five, maybe five-thirty, and possibly work 'til nine o'clock.

But you do know when you're doing that kind of work, you have to build a relationship with community. You just can't walk in people's areas and start talking. And so, we had to do that. We didn't really worry about crime, because people got to know us. And they would say "Don't come in here today. This is what's happening," which we thought was a great thing, right?

We worked in the three housing developments, and we worked in Hollygrove and Gert Town—in areas that other people did not want to go into because they were afraid, you know? We weren't paid for it, not in the beginning. And then we did get, it wasn't a whole lot of money. You know, it could get about a few things and some beer, but—[*laughter*] I mean, let's be honest. It *could* do that. But we were able to get, like, the whole family involved. Down to my mama who made condom packets for us. [*Wowwwww*] So you know, we cussed a lot, but we like what we do—or we did then—and we liked being able to educate our people around things that they needed to know more about.

> So that was—I mean Danita could jump in *AT ANY TIME HERE*.

DANITA Well you're doing good!

CATHERINE You know, my only thing: we all had each other's back. And we really didn't have that many problems in the community with people. And we still have people who know us. And so I think that's a really good thing.[57]

That was a cue to newer staff. Of the two foremothers, Catherine was not the talker; she liked to do the work. And so Danita could jump in *AT ANY TIME HERE*. Those words were really superfluous. Danita knew that Catherine would outline the principles they would keep coming back to throughout the storytelling session: the misinformation and everyday violence their communities were enduring; their refusal of this world and their will to build otherwise; the centrality of relationships to their theory on the ground; the strategies they used to protect each other; the involvement of their entire families; and the durability of their work to this day.

The newer staff nodded. Raven vocalized what they were all learning quickly: "We *still* have clients who come in and remember you and Danita." And for good reason. By being on the ground in the ways that they were—day after day, week after week—Catherine and Danita actually worked with their communities to change the entire culture around how condoms and drugs were used and how sex was sold.

DANITA I think one of the best things we ever did was that we made condoms normal for people. People didn't used to use condoms—Black people didn't used to use condoms, poor people didn't use condoms—when we started. If you went to the Walgreens to get a condom, you had graduated from college. [*Mmm-hmmm*] So we made condoms normal. And I think that was the biggest thing we did.

> And we also normalized people shooting dope. [*Yessss*] Cuz before us, there is a hierarchy of drug use in America. You shoot dope, you are the lowest of the lowest of the lowest. Your mama don't even

trust you with her beer money. So, we normalized that relationship in the community with that population.

They began to *love us*. They stole our shit, and we had to hem 'em up a few times [*laughter*], and then they brought our stuff back. But we made that normal. We made syringe exchange normal. They *looked* for syringes from us.[58]

That culture change was life-giving. In a country that was denying Black people the tools and information they needed to protect their health, Danita and Catherine made drug use normal and excised decades' worth of stigma in the process. Their work helped communities accept that drug use is part of our world and choose to work to minimize its harmful effects, rather than simply ignore or condemn them. That was the foundational principle of harm reduction.

Everything Danita and Catherine were doing at that time was illegal. Activists in cities like San Francisco, New York, and Philadelphia organized to get their mayors to sign executive orders declaring health emergencies due to HIV, which enabled local groups to skirt state laws prohibiting the distribution of syringes without a prescription; New Orleans would not see such an ordinance passed until 2017, when the opioid epidemic hit white suburban homes. That reality forced Catherine and Danita to get creative.

DANITA We had a bar in central city, the Rose Tavern (fig. 2.5). Thank *JESUS* for Rose Tavern. [*a'ight*] Yeah. They did syringe exchange for us. In that bar, you could buy heroin. Across the street you could buy weed and cocaine. Down the street you could buy pussy and dick. In that order if you wanted it. In the Calliope Projects. They did syringe exchange for us.

In those housing projects, you could buy a syringe for a dollar. We cut into their business. Cuz that was somebody's hustle. We cut into their business. So they had to quit swapping out syringes, because they had threatened to do stuff to her bar. So we said "OK." So we cut that loose. Stopped that. Cuz it was gonna hurt her business, it was gonna hurt her bar.

We talk about partners? We had the Drop-in Clinic. The Drop-in Clinic would actually take the syringes, cuz you have to dispose of those things a certain kind of way. We would drop 'em—I'm talking about five-gallon containers of syringes—we would drop 'em at the

Women With A Vision's message is clear

By Cassandra Lane
Contributing Writer

As the sultry beats of a love ballad pumped from the jukebox at Rose's Tavern, Danita Muse stood pouring condoms into a large plastic jar. When she was finished, she placed the overstuffed jar back on the counter and turned her attention to some women clustered in a corner of this tiny bar, which sits under a streetlight across from the B.W. Cooper housing development.

The women clowned around a bit, using laughter to talk openly and easily about sex. They crowded around Muse, stretching their palms out for free packages of male and female condoms, and anything else she carried to help make their lives safer.

"Thank you for saving my life," yelled one woman with dark, satiny skin and a sincere smile.

Muse and her fellow "street outreach workers" wore T-shirts with the message, "Risk Reduction in the Dirty South," emblazoned

Continued on Pg. 8

Women With a Vision assemble before their most recent 'Night Out.' (Photos by Nijme Rinaldi Nun)

2.5 *"Women With A Vision's* Message Is Clear," *Louisiana Weekly* 75, no. 26, week of March 19–25, 2001. In the image at left, Deon Haywood, Catherine Haywood, and Danita Muse are distributing harm reduction supplies in front of Rose Tavern. At right, the WWAV crew is assembling for street outreach. Photos by Nijme Rinaldi Nun.

> Drop-in Clinic and they would take 'em away for us. *No questions asked.*
>
> **DEON** No questions asked.[59]

Each piece led to the next. By going to Rose Tavern after outreach, Danita and Catherine built a relationship with the woman who ran the bar. That relationship is why she started doing syringe exchange with them; it is also why Danita and Catherine pulled back when doing exchange was no longer safe for her and leaned instead on other partners and gatekeepers.

The team at the Drop-in Clinic helped them, *"No questions asked."* Danita said it and Deon repeated it for a reason. That was how the WWAV foremothers demanded to be treated. And they wanted the newer staff to get it.

> **DANITA** I mean, they didn't tell anyone that they were helping us, cuz it wasn't a cool thing to help WWAV. We wasn't always polite. [*chuckle*] But then people didn't fuck with us either. And we figured—I don't know about Lady—but I figured that if you gonna step to me, you

gonna have to step right, because I'm always gonna be right. I'm not gonna be wrong. If you gonna step, you gonna have to step right. And I want you to be afraid of me. [*laughter*] I want you to be. I really do. Cuz otherwise you not gonna question what I do. Cuz if you afraid of me, that means you respect me.

That's all you gotta do. *They ain't gotta like you.* We ain't never cared if people liked us. Y'all might think that, but we ain't never cared if people like us.

CATHERINE I don't think we still do.

DANITA No. [*laughter, hands clap*][60]

"*They ain't gotta like you.*" Another lesson passed. This one was the perfect rejoinder to the porch talk mantra: #TheyAintReady. The newer staff already understood that most people could not last a day at WWAV. What Catherine and Danita explained was that the work was not about changing them. It was to change the whole rotten system that gave them power and resources.

We Just Did It, Somebody Else Took Credit

Being in community in the ways that Catherine and Danita were was a constant practice of experimentation.[61] WWAV was literally creating groundbreaking methods of harm reduction with drug users every single day and was also starting to apply those methods to work with other communities. Next, Deon prodded Danita and Catherine to share some about "the sessions we used to do with sex workers on Oretha Castle Haley till two and three in the morning."

DANITA Oh! Jeez! When we first started doing work with sex workers— this was around 1993, 1995, all the way into 2000, 2004, maybe. Before the Hurricane came, we was *still* doing stuff with sex workers.

In the African American community there was always certain kind of "niches." We were from Uptown. Uptown means Martin Luther King, Claiborne, Broad Street, over towards Louisiana Avenue. So we were all from around there. And we knew everybody, and everybody knew us. We started working with the sex workers, and they were in little pockets around Martin Luther King and Rampart Street. There was a bar named Sam's and there was another bar on the front called Pete's. Then there was The Detour, which was down that street.

I don't know, all y'all little young children might not know about this—

CATHERINE They don't know cuz it's *gone*.

DANITA Yeah, it's gone.

DEON They don't know nothing about it. You had to be *grown* just to walk through the goddamn door.

DANITA Yeah. So Sam's was literally a bar and restaurant. You could go in there from three o'clock in the afternoon to five o'clock in the morning. They had the best ham sandwiches. They had Chisesi ham that they cut right there for you. You talking about *goooood* ham sandwiches. And their Yaka meat was delicious. They had a five-foot bar where you could walk up and get a cocktail in those little bitty round cocktail glasses that they don't make no more. They had a juke box, and they had a pool hall—a couple of pool tables in the back. That's where all of the *business* took place. *Business.* [*Business*] Cuz again, you could buy heroin, crack, weed, pussy, and dick all in Sam's.

There were three sex worker houses within a half a block of Sam's. One place was right next door in the back. They had this set of twins. Remember them twins? [*Mmm-hmmm*] The twins lived there. And they would talk to us from the balcony. Me, Lady, and Dee, and— Dee had an outreach worker???

DEON Was it *Eisa*?

DANITA *Was it* Eisa?

DEON Or was it *Angelita*?

DANITA *Angelita*! Angelita. So then we started talking about doing *safe* work [fig. 2.6]. We *never* told them to stop. That has never been our philosophy. We always tell people, "We can't feed you, and Lady ain't cooking." [*laughter*] "She ain't cooking and bringing this food around here cuz it's too much trouble." And they would just laugh at us. So we never told people to stop doing your work cuz that's your job. I go to work to do something. They go to work to do this. "Just be safe."

They told us about what condoms to buy. Flavored condoms cuz certain ones liked certain ones. Some of 'em didn't like the chocolate and the strawberry. Some of 'em did. Some of 'em liked grape and strawberry. So we would buy what they liked.

And I want you to know: throughout this whole time, there was no documentation, there was no research, there was nothing. *We just*

2.6 Catherine Haywood, Danita Muse, Angelita Bolden, and Deon Haywood leaning over the back of Danita's pickup truck filled with harm reduction outreach supplies, ca. 1998. Photo courtesy of WWAV Archives.

> *did it*. Somebody else took the credit for it. But we just did it. There's no proof that we did this—*we* don't have our own proof that we did this. Somebody else has our proof. Office of Public Health, Dr. Tom Farley—*he* got our proof. But we don't have proof that we did all of this work. It's just in our memories.[62]

That last point underlined for newer staff why we were now, after the fire, taking such pains to document what WWAV did and to claim everything that was new. It also drove home the pain of dispossession that undergirded our foremothers' stories about what really happened.

Through their relationship with the twins, Danita, Catherine, and Deon translated the core principles of harm reduction to sex worker organizing. That relationship opened up space for experimenting on a whole range of strategies to make sex work safer.

> DANITA People would actually come to us and talk to us. So we would do sessions with them about doing what they do safer. Like telling 'em how to not be so high when you're giving a blow job, or how you can start drinking after you get your work done. You know, work for a certain time, *then*—. And you could see that their brains were like, "Oh, yeah, I don't have to be high all the time when I'm working. I'll

get more money. I'll work more efficiently. I'll get more people to me if I'm *not* high." So they started doing stuff like that. So to us that was the first phase of harm reduction, cuz we never said *stop*.

We taught them how to cheek a condom. That's why they always had certain flavors, cuz you're gonna hold it in your mouth. I mean, men don't usually look. I don't know if y'all know this, but men don't look where they put they stuff. They just kind of stick it. [*laughter*] So these women just kind of knew how to cheek a condom, so that they could have a condom on, and give em a blow job, and tell them that it was without a condom. So they made more money that way also.[63] So then they really started *looking for us*.[64]

"Looking for us" was the definition of trust. It was also the power of relationships. Danita and Catherine and Deon wanted newer staff to understand that. Through harm reduction, WWAV was building new oppositional geographies that unraveled each step in the racial capitalism playbook. Our foremothers *took* back their city; they went to communities that were being *erased*; they worked relationship by relationships to counter the *destabilization* of these communities; they refused *criminalization* as the response to drug use or sex work; they also refused to *blame* their people for what they were doing to survive; and they brought them the tools and information they were being *isolated* from, so they could save their own lives. This was what it looked like in practice to be ungovernable. That understanding washed over the faces of all gathered in the storytelling cypher.

WWAV's relationships with sex workers did not go unnoticed by local public health officials, nor by HIV prevention specialists nationally. These outreach stories were all happening around the same time that Danita and Catherine had gone to that "little hole in the wall in Texas" and told a whole roomful of service providers and funders that they were doing outreach wrong. Back in New Orleans, public health officials and researchers were clamoring for data from the very sex worker communities that WWAV was building liberatory knowledge with. And they started to offer WWAV some funds—like Catherine said, enough to "get about a few things and some beer"—to bring people together for surveys, focus groups, and other interventions. These bridges between researchers and community were actively being encouraged and funded by the Centers for Disease Control and Prevention (CDC) throughout the 1990s through the Diffusion of Effective Behavioral Interventions (DEBI) program that was officially rolled out in

2002. The goal was to bring the academic researchers working on empirically based models for HIV prevention rooted in theories of psychology and behavior change together with the community-based organizations who had long honed homegrown strategies for addressing their communities' health, so that they could together produce evidence-based interventions to disseminate nationally. The program was critiqued rigorously by a growing movement of HIV prevention justice activists, WWAV included. Not only did the DEBIs turn community-driven work into abstractions; they reified huge power imbalances in knowledge production. Too often, the community-based organizations who partnered with researchers were treated as gatherers of data rather than architects of the work and erased from the peer-reviewed papers that rested on *their* theory on the ground. This was the reprise to Danita's earlier story about how "We just did it. Somebody else took the credit for it." Their dispossession was not a onetime thing. It happened again and again. Danita took the newer staff members there, with Catherine and Deon's help.

DANITA We would just have all of these group sessions. We knew the sex workers who were renting out beds to other sex workers cuz that's how she made her money. One sex worker, she was like the mama to all them: Pat. And the Office of Public Health needed to have a focus group. They contacted us. So we contacted Pat. We told OPH that you have to pay this lady, cuz they wanted them to do it for free! [*hmph!*] And we's like, "NOOOOO. These people working for a living. They can't just be here cuz you want em to." [*Mmm-hmmm*]. "They don't like you like that. And they don't like white people like that." [*laughter*] So we made them—we *suggested* to them [*laughter*]—that they pay Pat $35 an hour for the use of her room and everybody who came got $15.

CATHERINE And a beer

DANITA And a beer.

DEON And food.

DANITA Yeah. And food. "If you want 'em here to participate, you have to buy food and give 'em what they drink. And you gotta give 'em all $15. Cash. We ain't talking 'bout no check."[65] [*chuckle*] "Cuz they ain't got that." So everybody who went got that. Catherine and I held the money, cuz they wasn't gonna fuck with us. So we paid the people when they left the room. And we paid Pat.

And all that data that they collected? We have *yet* to see. We *never* saw it. But they *collected* that data.

DEON That was the DEBIs. Just so y'all know. CDC doesn't really use DEBIs anymore. But *this* is where the DEBIs was designed. Out of the work that WWAV did.[66]

That story drove home the magnitude of dispossessions that the WWAV foremothers have survived. The knowledge that *they* made to serve the liberation of their communities was literally captured by researchers, whose so-called objective methods extended each step in the racial capitalism playbook, like we outlined in the introduction: *isolate* yourself from the people you "study," *blame* them for the violence they survive by turning them into data, *criminalize* them by attaching their lives and choices to academic theories that were only ever meant to oppress them (which are often also used to make laws that criminalize them), *destabilize* the knowledge they produce about their own lives and liberation, *erase* the communities in which this knowledge is grown and made actionable, and then *take* their theorizing and pass it off as your own. Looks of outrage registered around the storytelling circle. Outrage, but not shock. Even the newest staff members knew better.

People See Us the Same as They See Them

Deon scanned the faces of everyone gathered in a circle that afternoon. "Outreach skills," she would often say with a smile. She could read any group of people in the blink of an eye—on the streets, on the porch, or in a collective storytelling session like this one. Deon could see clearly that the history of what WWAV did was beginning to register and accumulate, but many of the newer staff were still struggling to understand how the WWAV foremothers did what they did. And so Deon shifted focus subtly to center the intimacy of the relationships that she and Danita and Catherine had with one another, and how that intimacy was what enabled them to establish relationships of solidarity built in care with their communities.

DEON So, can I share one thing?

DANITA Sure!

DEON I know you've heard me say that I would never send y'all out by yourself, that we never did outreach by ourselves, and why it's important. We talk about the changing New Orleans, but it wasn't safe *then*—but I don't think we cared. Like, crime in New Orleans has always been crime in New Orleans. And Danita and I actually got up at one in the morning! I'll never forget that. We went to Pat's—

DANITA Oh, Pat's! Yeah. We got UP!

DEON We got up out the bed and went to Pat's. And we're *tired*.

And it's always this thing I make the joke that I only do outreach with certain people, because it means something to me to know somebody got me. So I'm doing my presentation, and I know that Danita is watching what I can't see, because I'm talking to people. And so one woman brought her boyfriend with her and kept saying, "Well I think I might have something." And he said, "I done told her she ain't have anything."

Now that may sound silly, but this is serious because it was all wrong from the get go. There was no way we could back out of this presentation. In situations like that, I don't like being far away from a door or a window [fig. 2.7], cuz if I gotta fall, bitch, I'm falling out the window. I don't have no problems jumping. But this time, our back was to the wall. And he was like "I should just stop fucking with her, and I should fuck you." That's what he said to me. I was like, "Well you ain't fucking *me*." And he was like, "I'll do it if I want." And Danita said, "Nah, bro. We not. We ain't doin' none of that." And then he jumped up.

I want to be clear why I'm telling you this story now. Because there are times when people have been willing to come for us. The same way people perceive the women we work with—they come for us that *same* way. That's why I tell y'all that you don't save *nobody*. That women are not victims. That we need to see the women we work with as powerful. Cuz when *we* out there? People see *us* as the same as they see *them*! So *WEEEEEE* (motions around circle at each person) are one. It's why that piece is so important when y'all are doing this work.[67]

That point was huge. "People see *us* as the same as they see *them*!" Deon was not just talking about one man at one home health party at Pat's. She was talking about the researchers who erased the WWAV foremothers from the public health literature that rested on their work. She was talking about everyone who challenged WWAV's ability to stand with drug user and sex worker communities and demand that the whole rotten, racist system be changed. She was talking about the violence matrix that Black women survive daily.[68] WWAV's answer to that dispossession was solidarity: "*WEEEEEE* are one," Deon emphasized, calling in every person around

2.7 Deon Haywood midpresentation at a WWAV home health party in the Magnolia Projects, standing in front of Sexually Transmitted Disease posters, with the door immediately to her left, ca. 1998. Photo courtesy of WWAV Archives.

that circle. "There are no victims at WWAV. We claim the power we were born with."[69] Deon had been drilling that message into staff for weeks. This story was why.

Always treating community as powerful had palpable material effects in the world. Newer staff had already seen that in action. People *know* when you are looking at them as an object of regulation or of moral indignation. That was why Deon had been telling the newer staff, "You don't save *nobody*." WWAV's community could feel that solidarity. And they returned it, too. That is how Danita and Deon made it out of Pat's house safely that night.

DEON If that other guy wasn't there and wouldn't have jumped in, me and Danita would've been in a *hard* fight. Cuz he wasn't gonna fuck me, that was *clear*.

DANITA That other guy, that was Pat's husband.

DEON Yeah, that was Pat's husband.

DANITA He knew better.

DEON Yeah. He punched this guy and put him out. And the next day, we went to work, and everybody knew about it. Everybody want to check to see if we were okay. And he can't come to nothing else. But it was the protection of the community that was so important. If you stole something from WWAV, I'm pretty sure the next day it was gonna be at the door. Cuz somebody was gonna get it back.[70]

There were more times than Deon, Danita, and Catherine could count when their people had their backs just like that. That was what solidarity looked like in action.

Deon had another story to share about how WWAV moved in formation on street outreach, and this one was a WWAV classic. She also told it the day of Danita's first life history interview.

DEON There have been other times when a can of roach spray and an empty coffee pot saved our lives. Now that sounds silly, but Catherine and Danita had "Don't fuck with me" attitudes. So they walking through the project together was kinda different from me and Angelita who was kind like "oh, you know" [*flips her locks over her shoulder*]—not that we were like that in the street, cuz we weren't. And Eisa: born and raised in the Magnolia Project. She was our administrative assistant, and she was a baaaaad ass administrative assistant. Got her training from the Magnolia Community Center. *Awesome* [fig. 2.8].

But that day, this man walked up to our RV. And he was like, "You bitches got to get the fuck from around here." So Eisa was like, "Say, bruh, wassup?" And he was like, "This property don't belong to y'all. Y'all always coming around here. HIV is brought to us by these white people.[71] And y'all fucking bitches falling for it." You name it, he must've told it to us. Without talking—and *this* is the beauty of when Black women organize and work together—

DANITA And Eisa is a big woman. Eisa's about six foot two—

2.8 Deon Haywood, Angelita Bolden, Danita Muse, Catherine Haywood, and Eisa Scott sitting together in a barroom booth, ca. 2000. Photo courtesy of WWAV Archives.

DEON Eisa's six-two, about two-hundred something pounds, all booty, all titty—

DANITA Yeah.

DEON And without talking to each other, without ever saying a word— You see, Eisa was behind him, cuz she was outside the RV. Angelita and I was inside the RV, and he was moving to come up the RV. So I picked up the roach spray, and Angelita picked up the coffee pot [*chuckle*] and we went at him. By the time Danita and Catherine came back around, everybody was there. And the people took care of him. But it was like: I never even looked at Angelita. It was like we just knew.[72]

Sometimes it was said with words, other times with nothing but eye contact, and still other times "we just knew." That was the power of being in deep, committed relationship with one another. That power kept them safe. It also gave them the energy to always go back and keep working to make genuine change in the world.

The Legacy Is in Place

Danita and Catherine each went another round of sharing stories. Danita talked about Whaler, a "bigtime ex–drug dealer" who owned a custom T-shirt shop in Hollygrove. Behind the counter, he kept a sawed-off shotgun and a nine-millimeter. In the back where he printed the shirts, the walls of the shop were lined with automatic rifles. He provided WWAV cover to do HIV testing in the neighborhood. In exchange, WWAV got all of our T-shirts printed by him. Catherine talked about their work cleaning up used syringes in schoolyards, so children would not come across them on their way to and from school, or during recess. That story jogged Danita's memory about how much the grounds of the Calliope changed while they were able to keep the needle exchange up and running at Rose Tavern. The stories could have kept on coming.

Remembering those stories—*speaking* them—was creative work. It rendered perceptible the otherwise possibilities already smoldering around us and enjoined newer staff as accomplices to blowing on these embers and igniting these fire dreams. But some of the newer staff members were also struggling with how to turn those stories into action. The cypher opened as several of those newer staff started to reflect back the weight of WWAV's accumulated history, but also to express some skepticism about the viability of WWAV's methods in the new New Orleans. Catherine and Danita were quick to shut those doubts down, helping newer staff understand that the core WWAV principles were unchanging, even if the practice of them changed with the times.

DEON We weren't thinking about writing them down back then.

DESIREE This is just Black women doing what we do.

CATHERINE [*shaking her head*] We weren't thinking about documentation. But we should have been.

SHAQUITA Naw. Y'all were doing what you were supposed to do. Taking *care* of the community.

RAVEN [*sighing*] But the times have changed.

DEON [*looking at her confused*] What does that mean? "But the times have changed"??

RAVEN Like how they say that they can walk through the community and get that respect. Now, you can't do that. I mean you *can*, but we definitely won't get that respect. Or people may avoid us.

CHRISTINE Well, and lots of communities have been destroyed, too.

RAVEN And then the communities that they were in are no longer there. The people are no longer there.

CATHERINE You're killing me. I'm sorry, I love you, but you're killing me. The thing says that you have to build a relationship regardless. Once you build that relationship ... [fig 2.9]

It took me—St. Thomas Project, I'd just go out and sit on people's porch, and they say "What you doing here?" And I'd say, "I'm sitting here, but my name is *Catherine* and I'm doing *this*." But, I didn't even try to give them anything or try to educate them. I told 'em what I was doing. And then after a couple of weeks or so, it was good. And then I could go in and do what I do. And I think this same thing holds for now.

The thing is, you have to build a relationship with the community, so that you can do what you do. It's not impossible. And I don't care what color they are. If you build that relationship, then you're good to go. No, some of them may not like you, but if they don't like you then don't deal with them no more!

DANITA But you also have to figure out where you fit. And what community means to you. Cuz community to you ain't the same thing it means to me.

Yeah, it's gonna look different. It's gonna be different, for a long time to come. But that don't mean those people ain't just as crazy as those other negroes who used to live there. [*chuckle*] They *still* need the services. They might not think they do, but they still need the services. They might think they better than most folks who used to live there, but they ain't got no services either. They ain't living there because they *want* to. They living there because they got to, you know?

So it's just different. Your community might just be women. And that's fine. Wherever you find them is wherever you find them. But don't ever sell yourself short talking about "It's different." It ain't that different.

CATHERINE And you can't be afraid.

DANITA Well, you can be afraid. You just can't—

CATHERINE Can't show it! We don't want you to go out on the street and be stupid.

RAVEN Oh, yeah, yeah, yeah.

CATHERINE But we want you to go out, and do what you need to do.[73]

2.9 People lined up at the WWAV RV during outreach in the Melpomene Projects, ca. 2000. Photo courtesy of WWAV Archives.

That last exchange drove home the point that the new New Orleans was not really all that new. It was just the latest reconfiguration of the racial capitalism playbook. People were *still* being isolated from services, even if the means for doing that looked different, which meant the reality materializing was just as lethal as it always had been.

After the storm, Catherine and Danita trusted Deon to carry the WWAV vision forward and stop the new New Orleans from materializing any further. Danita named that explicitly as our session concluded, and Deon explained what it felt like to carry that obligation forward:

> DEON The legacy is in place. And I never want to have to call Danita and Catherine and say "It's failed. It's broke. I can't fix it. We closing the door."

DANITA She better call us *before* she get to that point. [*Mmm-hmmm*] You not supposed to really wait till the end, and be like, "I'm done." [*laughter around the circle*]

Can I say something? [*pausing for laughter and talking to die down*]

And—what I wanted to say is—it's emotional. [*tears welling in her eyes*] It's emotional, because I trust Deon. I don't trust the rest of you muthafuckers. But I trust Deon. And whatever she does, she does with the heart and soul of WWAV. [*voice shaking as she cries*]

It took me a minute to trust Des, because that muthafucker there, whoa, she rock! Y'all ain't *never* got to like Des. She ain't care. And that puts her in the mind with me and Lady, because we don't really care if you like us or not, we really don't. But we trust Deon. Quita comes with her as a package. And Laura has built her way to be in this. One of the few white women who wants to be in this.

SHAQUITA [*nodding*] For real.

DANITA And that's a lot. It's a lot. But I trust Deon. [*voice shaking again with tears*] And if I got to go back to work, I will. I don't want to, but I will. [*laughing, wiping her eyes*] And if she can pay me, she'll pay me, and if she can't, she won't. But the work continues. The work will continue to get done, no matter what.[74]

Suppose We Would Have Stopped?

"No matter what." Danita's words hung in the air, reminding all of us of the history we walked in daily at WWAV, of the work we had been called into. Only Catherine could break that silence, "Well shit, y'all made Danita cry. [*laughter*] I ain't never seen her break down like that about WWAV. Y'all made my friend cry." Catherine's laughter summoned Danita's own, inviting us all in, too.

WWAV is both a vision and a practice.[75] It is the vision of "what it means for Black women to live in ... the possibilities of who we are," and it is the practice of building that world together.[76] Catherine and Danita refused a world caught up in HIV panic by being ungovernable. Through a practice of solidarity built in care, they reassembled the very Black feminist worlds that the isolate-blame-criminalize-destabilize-erase-take racial capitalism playbook was trying to destroy. They were relentless. They had to be. "People see *us* as the same as they see *them*!" because we know that "*WEEEEEE* are one."

The WWAV vision was clear, and all of us gathered were entrusted to carry it forward. Each step led to the next. When something failed, we had to try a different way, applying the lessons we had learned to the next experiment. It was, as Ruth Wilson Gilmore has put it, "life in rehearsal."[77] This was not the recitation of rules; it was the practice of our own liberation.

Catherine, Danita, Deon—each told the stories so that the work would continue. And that was what was so threatening about their leadership. They *knew* they were good. And they consistently told people what they were doing wrong and taught them how to do it better. That meant that they approached every single person as someone who could be moved in service of liberation. In so doing, they invited all people to live in the possibilities of who *they* were and who *they* could become. That truth recalls Alexis Pauline Gumbs's questions about the threat of Black women's freedom: "Are you afraid of me and other Black feminists who consistently challenge oppression? Or are you afraid of the bravery it would take to live into your own freedom?"[78] Catherine and Danita would probably say both. One of WWAV's first principles was, of course, "They ain't gotta like you." Catherine and Danita refused to be complicit in anything that was killing their people. But make no mistake: their unwavering, unapologetic swagger was also an invitation to doing the work—your work, our work. It still is.

3

WE SPOKE OUR TRUTHS

Nobody in the world, nobody in history, has ever gotten their freedom by appealing to the moral sense of the people who were oppressing them.
—Assata Shakur, *Assata: An Autobiography*

On March 30, 2012, the energy at WWAV was electric. A "small but mighty" community of staff, participants, and volunteers piled into the front meeting room of our Mid-City office.[1] Some were standing. Others gathered on couches and chairs by the front window or around the donut-shaped conference table in the center. On the slender overhanging porch out front, a few people lingered to wave others up the steps to the second story of the house that sat off North Norman C. Francis Parkway. Deon[2] beckoned people to start coming through the archway and down the central hallway, which extended past staff offices and into the meditation alcove and then the kitchen. There, several folding tables for street outreach had been lined up end-to-end to form a long banquet table. The whole expanse was draped in purple cloth and decorated with bright yellow flowers and small baskets of sweets. At the center, a sheet cake proclaimed: "We Won!!!!"

That victory had been more than five years in the making. In the wake of Hurricane Katrina, Deon, Catherine, and Danita had taken to the streets to find the people for whom they had been the primary safety net for decades: Black cisgender and transgender women living and working in the city's street-based economies. With the housing projects set for demolition, the schools dismantled, and the return rates still waning, their city was a shadow of its pre-Katrina self. Still, little could have prepared them for the first time they saw one of their people with her new photo identification card. In the bottom right corner, immediately below her picture, the words "SEX OFFENDER" were stamped in block red letters. All she knew was that she had been charged with a "crime against nature."

What was a "crime against nature"? Where did the statute come from? What was happening to women in their city? As one story became ten, and ten became twenty, Deon, Catherine, and Danita did what WWAV has always done: reached out with immediate aid and support, held space for people to come together, and rallied behind their community's own visions for liberation. WWAV's conversations with some of the first people to be placed on the sex offender registry after Hurricane Katrina helped uncover the criminalization crisis underway. For the simple act of trading sex for money to survive, hundreds of Louisiana cisgender and transgender women, 80 percent of them Black, had been convicted of a felony-level Crime Against Nature by Solicitation (CANS) and forced to register as sex offenders for a period of fifteen years following a first conviction and for life after the second.[3] CANS convictions were often piled on top of prostitution convictions, and so were the debilitating penalties.

As people convicted under the statute saw it, "There is NO justice in Louisiana."[4] Their words became the organizing call. Together, WWAV staff and participants assembled a chorus of local, national, and international allies to mount a constitutional challenge to the CANS statute within a comprehensive grassroots organizing project to transform this latest reconfiguration of the racial capitalism playbook in post-Katrina New Orleans. Now, after years of fighting, the WWAV coalition, led by people directly impacted by the statute, and the NO Justice Project legal team had secured a federal judicial ruling. On March 29, 2012, US district judge Martin Feldman found that nine plaintiffs, all WWAV participants, had "been deprived of equal protection of the laws in violation of the Fourteenth Amendment to the U.S. Constitution."[5]

The next day, as slices of cake were passed around the table, Deon affirmed for all gathered the truth of the NO Justice Project. "Today, we celebrate with the [people] who courageously stood up to combat the criminalization of their lives—and *won*. Today, we celebrate a victory for *all* people who have told their truths that justice might be done. WWAV has always just been a catalyst for [people] affected by this."[6] Zina Mitchell, a longtime participant turned staff member, articulated what so many of the people WWAV had long provided safe haven for were feeling: "I've never been to court and had a judge side with me. We did it. *We* won. *We* made history."[7]

In this chapter, we trace WWAV's process of organizing against the CANS statute in post-Katrina New Orleans. Our goal is twofold: first, to show how WWAV built an analysis of this criminalization crisis as an afterlife of settler colonialism and chattel slavery; and second, to clarify the historical depth and momentousness of the victory Deon claimed in March 2012 "for all people who had ever been criminalized."[8] This story rests on the legacy that Danita and Catherine built in the first decade and a half of WWAV's groundbreaking harm reduction work with drug user and sex worker communities. This is also the story of WWAV's ability to continue to change with the times as the racial capitalism playbook was being reconfigured at record speed in the wake of Hurricane Katrina, and WWAV had to incorporate new tactics to fight the white supremacist dispossession of our people—our counterplaybook. WWAV's history of being in community put Catherine, Danita, and Deon on the front lines, bearing witness to the making of this criminalization crisis as people were being forcibly placed on the sex offender registry list and their communities destabilized.[9] Catherine and Danita had just asked Deon to become executive director, and they were clear: "You gonna let it stand???? You gonna do something, *right*?" For Deon that meant "We better *do* something."[10]

Over the next decade, Deon would oversee the expansion of WWAV—from the organization Danita and Catherine had founded, through to its present as one of the leading national voices on Black women and criminalization in the South. That growth was built using the same theory on the ground that had always guided WWAV's work. Immediately, Deon could see clearly that CANS criminalization rested on historically interlocking systems for invisibilizing Black cisgender and transgender women. No one was talking about the impact of structural violence in their lives, and no one was making the connections between things like CANS and the policies of criminalization and rescue that were circulating globally. At the "Know Her Truths" southern Black feminist conference at the Anna Julia Cooper Center at Wake Forest University a decade later, Deon explained all that was held in this moment:

> We understood what it means for Black women, for trans women to be invisible. *How* we're invisibilized. This law was created for white gay men—to keep gay men from having sex in the French Quarter—and then they coming for *you*, too. And it wasn't just that you are charged [with CANS], and it went on your ID. It was an *automatic felony conviction*. And we *know* what criminal laws and the criminal justice system can do to the lives of people.
>
> And so post-Katrina, we realized that we could continue [to do the work that we used to do], but we also needed to think about "what does this look like?" because it seems like *nobody* is talking about it. We're not having the conversation about what it means for structural violence to happen in the lives of Black women and trans women. It actually puts them at risk for HIV; it puts them at risk for further criminalization. And mainly the reason they're involved in sex work is, "I need to eat." "I need to survive." "This minimum wage is not enough." "It's not enough for me." . . .
>
> [We have] taken our mission and taken our work and connected it to global issues, as well as national issues. All still being predominantly served and run by a queer Black woman. And taking that work where people are making the connection about what is happening in the South, what is happening in India, what is happening in Africa, because we are connected to the global sex worker network. So it is now where we have taken the work and our main focus is still all the things we used to do around public health, but we are also asking people to look at what *policies* are being pushed in your area. And what are on the back end of these policies that you think are going to save women but actually put them at risk for criminalization.[11]

That is how, even with this significant growth in scale, Deon ensured that the organization remained rooted in WWAV's foundational methods of relationship-building and community care. Staff were fully in and of the same communities as WWAV participants; they worked together to provide mutual aid and support so that people with CANS convictions could be at the helm of the organizing; and the work unfolded step by step as one victory led to the next and to the next. In so doing, WWAV successfully disrupted the use of CANS as a strategy of predatory policing and targeted criminalization. By refusing their erasure from the city of their birth, WWAV not only rendered visible the violence against Black cisgender and transgender women in the wake of the storm; we also opened new horizons for struggle and for liberation.

This chapter unfolds, like all WWAV's work, in the intimacy of these relationships. It also brings together a range of sources: the testimonies, policy briefs, educational materials, and legal analyses amassed throughout the NO Justice Project; the personal notes and reflections transcribed during the conversations where Deon would talk and Laura would type, much of which lives on the WWAV website; the Born in Flames life history interviews and ethnographic fieldwork we conducted with WWAV staff and participants after the fire; and further work in state archives and secondary literature to contextualize the CANS statute and WWAV's NO Justice Project. What we do not have is WWAV's own organizational archive of the NO Justice Project: the interviews that staff conducted and the testimonials gathered with people convicted of CANS, as well as the meeting notes, outreach materials, and flyers made during different phases of the organizing work. Our archive was destroyed in the 2012 arson attack.[12] The quotes that are included in this chapter are drawn from the electronic records and public presentations that survived the attack, as well as the files kept by the NO Justice Project legal team members. We also rely on the skeletal structure of WWAV's collaborative, relational methods of building knowledge to serve the liberation of our communities, which we have already charted in chapters 1 and 2. What we do *not* do is attempt to re-create the flows of conversation through which the NO Justice Project community organizing strategy was being collectively built among WWAV members, as one person spoke and passed to the next, and that person passed to another, and then to the next... These silences were produced by the arson attack. We let them stand, loudly.

By listening across these sources and sitting with these silences, we work to describe and connect a series of responses—from institutions and from individuals—through which Black cisgender and transgender women were identified as a social and political problem in post-Katrina New Orleans. This chapter moves chronologically, in step with the process of organizing the NO Justice Project, in order to underline a core principle of organizing:

wins like this do not magically happen. They are grown in the subterranean caverns where fire dreams can be sheltered and protected and where Black study happens.[13] And they are unfurled on the streets where the contests for history and space, for bodies and movement, are actively underway. Wins like this, thus, are as much about the tactics that people use to render themselves visible as they are about the meticulous forms of study and self-education that make those renderings strategic. This chapter begins with study: a historical exposition of the research into Louisiana's Crime Against Nature statute that was done by the members of the NO Justice legal team and WWAV, showing how, in Deon's words, "this law was created for white gay men—to keep gay men from having sex in the French Quarter—and then they coming for *you*, too." We then complicate the legal history with WWAV's ongoing street outreach and grassroots organizing to map the everyday implications of CANS sex offender registration in community. This quotidian violence of CANS, we argue, pressed WWAV to reframe CANS criminalization through a Black feminist analysis of carceral control, in which staff and participants connected their struggles to the policing of Black women in the Jim Crow South and Great Migration North. We then show how this historically informed Black feminist analysis of racial capitalism shaped WWAV's narration of the post-Katrina CANS crisis and the organizing of the NO Justice Project.

Throughout our fight against CANS, all of us at WWAV and the partners who stood with us documented how the fantasy of a new New Orleans was being built through the evisceration of Black cisgender and transgender women—and we worked together to render our communities visible against the historic violence of invisibilization, and also against their hypervisibilization through policing and surveillance.[14] We show how WWAV's staff, participants, and accomplices artfully exposed and evaded the interpretive and self-referential framework of this post-Katrina criminalization crisis. Grounded in the knowledge of our communities, we worked to map the reinforcing nature of the systems of oppression that gave the law meaning in the wake of Hurricane Katrina. Then, all the people with whom we stand threw the whole of their lives up as the precondition for social change; they countered social death with a defiance of living.[15] This was the theory on the ground of the NO Justice Project: intimate, historical, unwavering, unapologetic, and ungovernable. That theory not only disrupted the logics of the systems of oppression that sought the erasure of our communities; it also spun into life new possibilities—our New Orleans otherwise.

Creating a Crime against Nature

Crime Against Nature by Solicitation. The statute had an unmistakably Christian ring to it. The subject of "nature," as well the crimes against it, has prompted centuries of theological argumentation around sex and sexuality and also around race.[16] King Henry VIII is to be credited with helping the concept jump the tracks from ecclesiastical legalities into civil law when he made sodomy a formal crime in England in 1533. But it was eighteenth-century legal scholar Sir William Blackstone who first coined the definition of a "Crime Against Nature" in the fourth and final book of his *Commentaries on the Laws of England*, the criminal code "Of Public Wrongs." Published in England in 1769 and three years later in the American colonies, Blackstone's commentaries were required reading for all colonial lawyers. In the fifteenth chapter of the final book, Blackstone describes the "infamous *crime against nature*, committed either with man or beast" as a "crime not fit to be named; '*peccatum illud horribile, inter christianos non nominandum* [that horrible crime not to be named among Christians]." [17] The punishment for this crime, Blackstone specified, was derived from the biblical edict in Sodom: "to be burnt to death." In the context of eighteenth-century England and its colonies, Blackstone surmised that the customary punishment for all felonies would suffice: hanging. As the American colonies became states, settlers and enslavers refashioned Blackstone's language as an essential tool of racial capitalism in the new nation.[18] In 1803, Blackstone's commentaries were hand delivered to Louisiana by the Virginia lawyer William C. C. Claiborne, who became the first governor of the newly acquired "Territory of Orleans." [19]

Our research into the solicitation of "that horrible crime not to be named among Christians" picked up in the nineteenth century in Louisiana. As we developed a strategy to win, the members of the NO Justice legal team worked tirelessly to trace the evolution of the Crime Against Nature statute in Louisiana law, paying close attention to the role the New Orleans Police Department (NOPD) played in making its solicitation a felony.[20] In 1805, Louisiana enacted its first criminal code, which included explicit prohibition of the "abominable and detestable Crime Against Nature, committed with mankind or beast." [21] The Louisiana Supreme Court and legislature refused to specify what conduct constituted a Crime Against Nature until the turn of the century, when the state's Black Codes were being made law after the violent disassemblage of Radical Reconstruction and these questions of "crime," "nature," and "sex" were further inflected with a white supremacist Christian genealogy.[22] In 1896—the same year that the US Supreme Court enshrined the "separate but equal" doctrine into law through *Plessy v. Ferguson*—Louisiana revised its state constitution and amended the Crime Against Nature statute to read:

> Whoever shall be convicted of the detestable and abominable Crime Against Nature committed with mankind or with beast with the sexual organs, or with the mouth, shall suffer imprisonment at hard labor for not less than two years and not more than ten years.[23]

The Louisiana courts further clarified in 1913 that the statute prohibited anal and oral sex, irrespective of consent, the sex of participants, and their marital status.[24]

In 1942, the Louisiana legislature undertook a comprehensive revision of the state's criminal code, with specific attention to the raced and gendered boundaries of sex. All previous miscegenation acts and rulings were consolidated into a single statute in the state's "criminal neglect of family" articles.[25] Prior statutes around "sexual immorality" were also consolidated to include a series of articles prohibiting prostitution and related offenses, as well as an additional series of articles aimed at "stamping out" prostitution around army camps in Louisiana. The Crime Against Nature statute was amended to read:

> Crime Against Nature is the unnatural carnal copulation by a human being with another of the same or opposite sex or with an animal. Emission is not necessary, and, when committed by a human being with another, the use of the genital organ of one of the offenders of whatever sex is sufficient to constitute the crime.[26]

The maximum sentence was reduced from ten years to five, with a fine of up to $2,000. The solicitation of such acts was *also* explicitly discussed in 1942. The legislature claimed that "the sexual pervert who frequents parks and other public places and *solicits* abnormal sexual practices" exhibited "a very reprehensible conduct." They also affirmed that this conduct "had given the police department in New Orleans and other large cities considerable trouble."[27] However, the legislature deemed that this conduct did *not* constitute a Crime Against Nature. Instead, it was added as a subarticle of the state's misdemeanor obscenity statute, which included "the sale or display of any indecent material."

Forty years later, in 1982, the NOPD advocated again for a felony-level addendum to the state's Crime Against Nature statute, claiming that they needed a tool to clamp down on a "growing problem in male prostitution."[28] Nationally, sex workers and gay men were being scapegoated and criminalized in a mounting AIDS panic. There were calls for quarantines, for mandatory testing, for contact tracing, and for public registration of all "prostitutes" and licensed brothels.[29] Conservative religious leaders such as Donald Wildmon of the Mississippi-based American Family Association famously bolstered his lobbying efforts through direct-mail appeals that warned, "These disease-carrying deviants wander the streets unconcerned, possibly making you their next victim."[30] A fifteen-part series called *Cruisin' the Streets* brought that rhetoric home to Louisiana. Airing statewide over a three-week period on the late news on WVUE-TV, this so-called exposé alleged to have uncovered an underground male prostitution ring in New Orleans's French Quarter, and claimed that the police were powerless to do anything about it because of the wording of Louisiana's existing antiprostitution laws, further stoking the AIDS panic.[31] In this climate, the NOPD could argue that the solicitation of oral and anal sex had become more than just an obnoxious *practice* (an "obscenity" in the state's own language); it was now a *deviance* that threatened the moral social order.

On June 17, 1982, Jim Donelon, a young Republican legislator, addressed his fellow members of the Louisiana House of Representatives Administration of Criminal Justice Committee on the topic of expanding the "Crime Against Nature" statute to include solicitation, with penalties significantly harsher than were currently on the books for prostitution. He presented this proposal (formally introduced as HB 853) as a concrete step that the legislature could take to protect the health and well-being of its citizens.[32] Warning that "a serious problem" was exploding in the streets of New Orleans, he spun fantastical tales of young "male hustlers" lurking in the shadows of the French Quarter, selling sex and artfully evading police surveillance. He played clips from *Cruisin' the Streets* to bolster his case.[33] The bill was passed out of committee without objection and was signed into law by Governor Dave Treen six weeks later. Under the new felony-level Crime Against Nature by Solicitation statute, soliciting anal or oral sex was now punishable by a term of imprisonment of up to five years, with or without hard labor, and/ or a fine of not more than $2,000. Additionally, once Louisiana launched its sex offender registration scheme in 1992, a single CANS conviction mandated fifteen years on the sex offender registry; two CANS convictions required life-time registration as a sex offender. Nationwide, CANS was exceptional among registerable offenses, as it was, as all of us clearly saw, "just a talking crime."[34]

Mapping the Violence of Criminalization

The role of the police in advocating for the adoption of the Solicitation clause in 1942 and again in 1982 is critical for understanding how the CANS statute was quickly extended beyond the "male problem" it was designed to address. Police had sole discretion over whether to charge someone with CANS or prostitution. Through their patrolling and booking practices, they mapped the CANS statute onto the gendered and racialized bodies of Black cisgender and transgender women working in street-based economies. As NO Justice Project attorney and our comrade Andrea Ritchie explained, "It should also come as no surprise that a law rooted in condemnation of sexual acts deemed 'deviant,' and enforced in a context in which Black women's sexualities are 'queered' by the historic and present day legacy of gendered racial discrimi-nation which frames women of color as inherently sexually deviant, was also discriminatorily applied to African American women."[35] This was, as Deon said, "*how* we're invisibilized." By 2011, when the NO Justice Project was in full force, 97 percent of women registered as sex offenders in Orleans Parish were mandated to do so because of a CANS conviction.[36] Consistent with the United States Department of Justice's 2011 finding that "NOPD engages in a pattern or practice of discriminatory policing" that is "so severe and so divergent from nationally reported data" that it constitutes "a violation of constitutional and statutory law," 80 percent of people registered because of CANS were Black.[37]

That analysis took time to come into focus. In 2008, Deon and the WWAV foremothers were bearing witness to the sheer number of people in the WWAV network who had suddenly been placed on the sex offender reg-istry list. That truth raised a lot of questions for WWAV. What was happen-ing in our city? Were these new charges? If not, why had people not had to register before? What had changed? How were these people found? Who was next? *What was happening in our city?* Even while the contours and genesis of this crisis remained uncertain, the need for WWAV to do some-thing was not. WWAV has always stood in solidarity with drug user and sex worker communities, because, in Danita's words, "those are the people who people *really* don't want to help. They don't want them to have nothing.

They don't want them to be with nothing. They just don't want them with *nothing*." CANS was no different.

As more people in WWAV's communities were able to return to New Orleans after the storm, the implications of the CANS licenses became clear. WWAV drop-in hours had become a vital time for crafting what would become the strategy to end criminalization under CANS. Sometimes WWAV participants would meet one-on-one with staff. Other times weekly regulars would be joined by as many as ten to fifteen more. Those conversations flowed like the porch talk that grounds chapter 1 and the collective storytelling session that concludes chapter 2. Together, people shared stories of the everyday violence of living with a CANS conviction: completely losing any sense of privacy, not being able to walk their kids to school or go to their children's graduations, having people use the sex offender registry to track them down and harass them at home. "It was like my life just stopped," one woman explained. People shared stories of being called "rapist" whenever they got carded while buying cigarettes. Some had stories of being denied access to drug treatment programs because "We don't serve your kind." Others started carrying around envelopes stuffed with all their court paperwork when applying for jobs, so that they could prove that they had histories of drug addiction and sex work, not of child molestation. Then there were the photos printed in the local paper, and the court-mandated postcards they had to buy and mail to neighbors alerting them that "this violent predator lives in your community."[38] One WWAV participant explained that when her probation officer told her she had to pay $500 for these postcards, she laughed in his face in disbelief: "Where am I supposed to get that kind of money when I just got out of jail? What are you telling me, I gotta go turn tricks?"[39] The debilitating impacts of CANS sex offender registration hardly stopped with the financial burden. Another WWAV participant explained, "It's like the Scarlet Letter. I am trying to put that in my past—but it's not gonna be in my past because it's in my present, and it's going to be my future for the next thirteen years." That truth reverberated through the WWAV space as participants assembled a careful framing of how this kind of labeling worked: "Once you been labeled as a convict, or a prostitute, or a drug addict, or some type of criminal. The minute they find out, they ostracize you. You know what I mean?"[40]

While the everyday terror of being on the sex offender registry was debilitating, WWAV staff and participants alike were also clear that it was *not* especially shocking.[41] And WWAV refused to pitch our messaging in that register. For the vast majority of people with CANS convictions, this modern-day "Scarlet Letter" was just the latest in a long line of small and great injustices to be weathered. Deon and all of us at WWAV were clear about "what it means for structural violence to happen in the lives of Black women and trans women. It actually puts them at risk for HIV; it puts them at risk for further criminalization." Most people in WWAV's network had been raised in multigenerational households that managed the reality of systemic economic oppression through decades-honed practices of mutual aid. Starting in the mid-1980s, however, their family units were being scattered across state and federal prison systems; already scarce family funds were diverted behind prison walls to support those serving decades-plus drug sentences. The passage of the 1996 Welfare Reform Act shook what semblance of a social safety net remained. In this climate of persistent economic hardship, many had turned to street-based economies to survive: "I need to eat." "I need to survive." "This minimum wage is not enough." "It's not enough for me." The SEX OFFENDER label on their photo identification cards all but ensured that those streets would remain their only viable source of income. CANS, thus, was an essential tool in expanding and consolidating the racial capitalism playbook in post-Katrina New Orleans—a tool for forcibly removing hundreds of Black cisgender and transgender women from Louisiana society and concealing this structural violence under the banner of "resilience." That is why people with CANS convictions proclaimed, "There is NO justice in Louisiana." Their words called all of us to action.

Policing Black Womanhood

To frame these complexities of CANS enforcement in the NO Justice Project, WWAV relied on a long-standing Black feminist hermeneutic fashioned at the intersections of art, protest, and scholarship: the excavation of Black women's simultaneous *invisibility* and *hypervisibility* in systems of white supremacist dispossession.[42] What the NO Justice Project emphasized was how race and gender intersected in Black cisgender and transgender women's lives through historically changing systems of power to, at times, render state and interpersonal violence against them wholly invisible, and, at other times, mark their movement as a hypervisible threat to be disciplined. Doing so brought into focus a different historical genealogy than that of the Crime Against Nature statute's own religious and colonial genesis and AIDS-era expansion.[43] WWAV staff and participants each had their own way of explaining the effects of being both "out of the frame" and "in the spotlight." Invisibilization was a means for accelerating each of the isolate-blame-criminalize-destabilize-erase-take steps of the racial capitalism playbook. When you are not seen, it is easier for you to be devalued, to be isolated from the support you need, to never get credit for work you do. But when the lights of surveillance turn on, when you become hypervisible, those very same things that went unseen become reasons to blame you for the strategies you use to make ends meet, to criminalize you for your survival, to destabilize your communities. WWAV staff and participants saw it every day: "Do you know how many times women call the cops because they're being beaten by their partners and there are no services, no nothing in their communities, and then *they're* the ones who end up in the back of the cop car?"[44]

This was the theory on the ground that WWAV used to strategically render visible the intimate, communal, and structural violence of CANS criminalization—and the whole racial capitalism playbook that gave it power and meaning. Intimate and interlocking systems of oppression invisibilized Black cisgender and transgender women's criminalization under a statute intended to target gay men, and also made their very existence in post-Katrina New Orleans hypervisible and hypersubject to predatory policing. This truth gave shape and language to WWAV's everyday political work; it also placed the fight against CANS in the post-Katrina moment in conversation with a whole body of literature on the history of Black women's criminalization before imprisonment became "mass incarceration." At WWAV, we use "mass incarceration" in quotes not only to signal its specificity as a term intended to name the dramatic expansion of the carceral state since the 1970s, but also to underline how this term has produced a sense that the problem with incarceration is simply the "mass," not the incarceration. Here, we are thinking with our comrades and scholars, Black feminist abolitionists like Beth Richie and Andrea Ritchie, who have long been two of our touchstones, and with Mariame Kaba, Dorothy Roberts, Hazel V. Carby, Saidiya Hartman, Cathy Cohen, Sarah Haley, Ruth Wilson Gilmore, and Angela Davis.[45] For them, and for the millions like us who have influenced and been influenced by their work, invisibility and hypervisibility are essential analytical tools for naming and tracking how anti-Black violence under chattel slavery and amid the assemblage of Jim Crow modernity was at once racialized *and* gendered.[46]

We are well acquainted with the story of how the southern prison system became a principal vehicle for exacting and reproducing modern state racism under Jim Crow. What has received less attention are the ways in which "gender structures the prison system," as Angela Davis taught us—and, thus, how this entire system also reproduced white normative gender.[47] Through the making of the Jim Crow carceral sphere, white women became a protected class, while Black women filled the courts.[48] All of us at WWAV knew the afterlives of this reconfiguration of modern state racism all too well. The few white women who did stand trial during Jim Crow were most often charged with miscegenation. Black women, however, were assembled in droves, booked mostly for petty crimes such as larceny and selling whiskey. At sentencing, they were steadily funneled into the convict lease system (and then later into chain gangs and the domestic carceral sphere after the convict lease system was outlawed state by state),[49] often as the sole woman among a band of a hundred male convicts, forced to live with the mining boss or prison manager and subjected to all forms of sexual, physical, and emotional violence.[50]

Sarah Haley's work has been especially helpful for us in understanding how invisibilization at the start of the twentieth century worked much as it did in the start of the twenty-first in post-Katrina New Orleans. In her research on Jim Crow Georgia, Haley uncovered how even when state law explicitly prohibited sending *women* to work on chain gangs, white women were the only ones diverted; Black women were still sent by the thousands. As she opened her groundbreaking *Signs* article, "Georgia's Jim Crow carceral regime produced women every day, and all of the women were white."[51] The point for Haley, and for all of us at WWAV, is not a call for parity (i.e., to be treated "*like* white women"); rather, the point is that when we strategically render the invisibilization of Black women visible, we can clearly see the violence of normative gender that is always already racialized as white (i.e., that "women" by default refers to *white* women), and also how Black women's fugitivity and flight within this carceral order literally unravels it. Again: this is what is so threatening about Black women's leadership.

Beyond this ever-expanding latticework of Jim Crow carceral invisibility, the street-based economies of survival sex work were, as WWAV knew well, the sites in which Black women's movement and lives always became hypervisible.[52] In the postbellum South, Black women were depicted as naturally licentious and prone to prostitution, and irredeemably criminal should they be convicted of any number of gendered crimes. This was, again, the violence of normative (white) gender—and the impossibility of Black women's fire dreams and survival strategies to be captured by it. That impossibility was the threat. That was what made Black women hypervisible in different historically interlocking systems of racial capitalism. To quote historian Mary Ellen Curtin, "The image of the fallen woman in the South had everything to do with race. Black women prisoners were seen as inherently immoral, while white women prisoners convicted of sex crimes lost their racial privilege."[53]

As WWAV has continued to write our own long history of sex work and Black cisgender and transgender women's criminalization in the context of the NO Justice Project and beyond, *movement* has emerged as a critical analytical tool. We are inspired by the work of Hazel V. Carby, who, in her field-defining essay "Policing the Black Woman's Body in an Urban Context," argues that it was precisely Black women's movement during the first decades of the twentieth century—between rural and urban areas and between southern and northern cities—that made Black womanhood a hypervisible threat, capable of generating "a series of moral panics."[54] To build this argument, Carby looks not only to the police in these cities, but also to the many softer agents of everyday surveillance who had a vested interest in reasserting a racial capitalism order they see devolving. In these communities, Carby finds people who were alarmed by the changes afoot in their cities, and who identified Black women migrants' definitions of and searches for freedom as innately criminal and sexually deviant. She poses the following questions to clarify this point, each of which map onto those asked by people with CANS convictions in the wake of Katrina:

> If a black woman can claim her freedom and migrate to an urban environment, what is to keep her from negotiating her own path through its streets? What are the consequences of the female self-determination evident in such a journey for the establishment of a socially acceptable moral order that denies the boundaries of respectable sexual relations? What, indeed, is to be the framework of discipline and strategies of policing that can contain and limit black female sexuality? These are the grounds of contestation in which black women became the primary targets for the moral panic about urban immorality.[55]

From their posts at various institutions and agencies, a whole range of elites and churched folks manufactured reams of reports and retraining programs for southern Black women and girls. This corpus of work, backed by the structural power of the police and the courts, produced a self-referential, interpretive framework about Black women's so-called vulnerability to vice and failing moral character throughout the Great Migration. It also dramatically expanded the surveillance and criminalization of Black women and girls, as well as the matrix of intimate, communal, and structural violence to which they were subjected.[56]

Decades and miles separated these southern migrants from their post-Katrina kin. Nonetheless, this enduring Black feminist common sense about how movement triggered the policing of Black women's bodies also undergirded the NO Justice Project's theory on the ground about the CANS crisis in post-Katrina New Orleans. People were displaced, homes were lost, businesses had not reopened, and services were gone. All this made the people that WWAV had long worked with even more vulnerable to violence and poverty, and pushed them to make ends meet however they could. Needing to do what they had to do to survive put the people WWAV stands with in the streets; it also put them in the crosshairs of local and federal surveillance—formal kinds like the New Orleans Police Department and the US Marshals Service, as well as informal kinds like rescue missions and pastors' associations. There was, for example, the judge who ran a diversion program out of her court for young women and girls, in which she court-mandated them to things like etiquette classes and beauty pageants. There were the hundreds of pastors citywide who banded together when the local jail was on the verge of going into federal receivership due to deplorable conditions, and held a pray-in outside the Orleans Parish Prison—not for the people held captive inside, but rather to ask God to give Sheriff Marlin Gusman $8 million in Federal Emergency Management Agency (FEMA) money so he could build another new jail. And there were all the good white ladies with their big house for "victims of human trafficking," who were being emboldened and resourced through a growing global moral panic that erroneously conflated sex work with sex trafficking and in so doing expanded a classic carceral feminist tactic: to use intensified policing, surveillance, and criminalization to address violence against (white) women, and in so doing wreak terror in the lives of Black cisgender and transgender women and girls.[57]

These were some of the many players who were producing and reproducing the racial capitalism playbook that destabilized the communities WWAV stood with. Criminalization was the constant background noise. More jail beds were being built, which meant these beds would be filled. Meanwhile, the options for staying out of jail required Black cisgender and transgender women to perform narratives of their own moral failing in order to be worthy of something other than imprisonment. If they were young enough, they could choose the finishing-school-and-manners route. If they were not, they would have to spin a fantastical tale of violation that hit the notes of the antitrafficking script. In these ways, WWAV knew that CANS was but one of many tools (in a long history of tools) being used to control nearly every aspect of Black cisgender and transgender women's freedom and living. The work of the NO Justice Project, thus, was to continually render visible not only the violence that WWAV's communities were enduring, but also the whole racial capitalism playbook that made CANS make sense.

Making a Post-Katrina Crisis

Rendering this violence visible helped put the specificities of CANS policing and enforcement after Hurricane Katrina into place. As WWAV's theory on the ground underlined, the pre-Katrina enforcement of the CANS statute emerged within a social and political climate in which Black women had long been subject to interpersonal, communal, and structural violence, and then blamed for the strategies they used to survive through sensationalized narratives about criminality and sexual deviance. The everyday policing of Black cisgender and transgender women working in street-based economies, thus, was unremarkable. So, too, were the coercive strategies that police officers used to arrest them. As one of the Black women who would become a leader in WWAV's challenge of the CANS statute explained:

> I have been selling sex since I was 13 years and the police are always stopping me. I have done had the police tell me: "If you give me head I'll let you go." So I do it and they still bring me to jail.[58]

After being entrapped into agreeing to sell oral sex at the behest of their arresting officers, Black cisgender and transgender women were sometimes charged with *both* prostitution *and* CANS, an overbooking practice that police use nationally to strong-arm the people they arrest into entering guilty pleas in exchange for sentencing leniency.[59] This was how Black women were invisibilized through a stringent project of gendered and racialized criminalization once CANS was enshrined into law in 1982.[60]

However, there was an ironic loophole in this system of punishment by expulsion. In the absence of an integrated electronic database to facilitate cross-reporting among the various branches of the New Orleans criminal justice system in the 1980s, 1990s, and early 2000s, the CANS sex offender registration requirement had often been, in practice, too tedious to enforce. In fact, many people in the WWAV network did not even know that they had to register. For them, CANS had become just another charge accumulated in the course of everyday survival. And then suddenly survival itself became uncertain. It was late August 2005. Tropical Storm Katrina had strengthened to a Category 5 hurricane. Black people were on the move—gathering their families, finding shelter, making ends meet by whatever means they could.

In the wake of Hurricane Katrina, with tens of thousands of people still displaced, WWAV observed how local officials and developers created the sensationalized media that positioned Black cisgender and transgender women as a hypervisible threat to moral order in the Crescent City. Immediately after the storm, the Department of Justice made more than $20 million available to New Orleans to rebuild the city's criminal justice system, which included a mandate for targeting and apprehending "violent felony fugitives" such as registered sex offenders.[61] In the state of Louisiana at this time, those charged with CANS comprised nearly half of the people required to register as sex offenders and nearly all the people who had failed to do so. And so, in the wake of the storm, with the assistance of the US Marshals Service, CANS "fugitives" were tracked down, often saddled with increased penalties for having failed to register previously.

The timing of Hurricane Katrina and post-storm US Marshals Service intervention also coincided with the passage of the Adam Walsh Child Protection and Safety Act (AWA) in June 2006, a federal statute that established different tiers of sex offender registration, mandated lifetime registration for those deemed most serious, and made failure to register a felony offense.[62] On January 1, 2008, the same year WWAV saw a surge in participants showing up with "SEX OFFENDER" licenses because the registration requirement was increasingly being enforced, the Louisiana legislature amended the state's existing sex offender registration laws to bring them into conformity with the provisions of the AWA. The amendments mandated that a central registry of sex offenders be maintained by the Bureau of Criminal Identification and Information; the bureau was also mandated to participate in the National Sex Offender Registry. Again, by 2011, 97 percent of the women in the Orleans Parish sex offender registry had a CANS conviction; 80 percent of people in the registry were Black.[63]

Thus, as WWAV's own Black feminist study meticulously traced, it was the post-Katrina enforcement of CANS—made possible with federal dollars and a federal mandate—that gave this draconian AIDS-era relic new life and new moral urgency. Black cisgender and transgender women had long been the invisible targets of New Orleans policing since the CANS statute was made law in 1982. After the storm, the presence of Black cisgender and transgender women became a hypervisible threat to developer Joseph Canizaro's vision for "a clean sheet to start again."[64] Criminalization was the tool that made the whole racial capitalism playbook run.

Organizing to Win

For WWAV, challenging criminalization, therefore, did not simply mean challenging the NOPD and the new New Orleans developers. It meant unraveling the playbook that gave these particular actors license to orchestrate the erasure of our people. It also meant uprooting the histories of systemic domination, which overlapped sexuality, race, gender, and class, to make CANS make sense. For that reason, WWAV affirmed that any challenge to CANS needed to unfold within a transformational project that refused the structural violence that Black cisgender and transgender women moved through daily in New Orleans and be built otherwise. We use the word *transformational* here as Cathy Cohen does in her pathbreaking article "Punks, Bulldaggers, and Welfare Queens" to underline "a politics that does not search for opportunities to integrate into dominant institutions and normative social relationships, but instead pursues a political agenda that seeks to change values, definitions, and laws which make these institutions and relationships oppressive."[65] Striking down the law would not matter if WWAV could not also change the climate that made Black cisgender and transgender women's criminalization thinkable. The police would just find another tool, another tactic, and the complicity of parole officers, job interviewers, and store clerks would remain unchecked. However, if WWAV could disrupt the totalizing surveillance of Black cisgender and transgender women, even in small ways, then we could begin to frame and actualize a vision for our community's survival.

Affirming this truth of transformational organizing changed the horizon of struggle for the NO Justice Project. This was no campaign in which the repeal of the CANS statute was lingering as a lofty goal on the horizon. Rather, the liberatory work of NO Justice was stitched in the everyday fabric and relationships of social life, just like it always had been at WWAV. People with CANS convictions needed immediate relief. So Deon and the WWAV foremothers called on (and dropped in on) local service providers and advocates in health, housing, and legal aid fields to help them build an emergency response and referral network for people on the sex offender registry. The list of "Organizational Outreach Targets" for this emergency response and referral network included domestic violence programs, emergency shelters, rent and utility assistance programs, health outreach programs, HIV/AIDS education programs, mental health programs, job training programs, job placement programs, food banks, substance use treatment facilities, youth shelters, transitional housing programs, and an array of faith-based missions and houses. This list was regularly maintained and updated to allow for organizations that did not survive after the storm as well as the new ones that were formed.

The referral network gave people with CANS convictions a bit of breathing room. What becomes possible when you can catch your breath? And when you can catch it again and again? What happens the first time you can safely let out a long and deep sigh? In the context of the NO Justice Project, the people that WWAV stood with began to dream about—and in so doing to strategize toward—more lasting transformation beyond their immediate survival. They talked about strategies for combating the drug testing of welfare recipients; about microfinance projects for expanding their employment possibilities; about health education courses for addressing disease disparities in their communities; about trauma healing circles for sustaining their community with one another; about going to their children's graduations and being present in all the vibrancy of their lives.[66] In so doing, they began to articulate and live into the contours of justice as the liberation of our communities, even while so much conspired to make this justice feel impossible in the present.[67]

From this visioning space, WWAV began the hard work of building community consensus around CANS. Throughout this time, Deon and Laura continued to deepen their relationship by phone: Deon would talk, Laura would type. First, they worked together to transcribe the story of how WWAV uncovered the CANS criminalization crisis. Then, they made a draft brochure layout. They talked about colors, fonts, and the aesthetics of WWAV's self-representation. They revised the brochure; they talked some more; they revised it again. As outreach began in earnest, Deon talked through the running list of questions in her mind: "What would the goal be? How would we move forward? Who needed to be contacted first? Who needed to be approached with deep grace and care?" These were the subtle and relational ways that she was assembling a working coalition just like her mother and Danita had always done. It was important to have WWAV's "ride-or-dies" in from the beginning—most especially the longtime Black harm reduction and HIV prevention workers in New Orleans. But the work could not move forward without bringing in new faces, like the legal fellow working at the public defender's office who had defended women with CANS convictions, or the local reporter who had written a story drawing attention to the massive increase in the number of women on the state's sex offender registry list. And then there were the trusted national allies who could be called on to sound the alarm when directed, but would not push so hard as to shame the southern lawmakers and shut down the whole organizing project before it got up and running.

WWAV continued to reach out to grassroots organizers, health care advocates, public defenders, reporters, community-based researchers, and community people. On July 22, 2009, we hosted the first daylong strategy meeting to launch a citywide NO Justice coalition, with Deon and Laura facilitating (fig. 3.1). The agenda we made grew out of WWAV's foundational method of building relationships. After group introductions, we worked together to craft a story of doing the work: *Why was CANS a problem? How did it affect people who were criminalized? What did everyone gathered believe needed to happen? What could they commit to doing?* When we got to the third question, the floor erupted with ideas. Deon and the WWAV foremothers kept that conversation focused on the stories of our people and the visions they were already crafting for their own liberation. We left that day with three guiding principles for the NO Justice Project: (1) engage, support, empower people most at risk; (2) influence key players in the criminal justice system to immediately reduce and/or halt further prosecutions; and (3) secure systematic challenge to the statute through the courts. These were relatively straightforward priorities, as organizing projects went. But they also told a story. The truths and solutions of our people were at the center of everything. Their truths guided short-term work to try to interrupt CANS criminalization; their solutions also dictated the vision of the NO Justice Project and our practice of liberation.

These priorities demanded that WWAV formalize and expand the storytelling work that was already happening during drop-in hours. Deon started a "Women's Empowerment Meeting" for Black cisgender and transgender women to come together and document their stories of CANS-related violence[68]—the formal kinds like legal and police abuse, and the more insidious ones like the everyday surveillance they encountered at stores, schools, and benefits offices—and to document their visions for liberation. Their stories of CANS violence were interwoven with WWAV's own study on criminalization in the South; their visions for liberation were, likewise, held within the long

3.1 Deon Haywood and Laura McTighe facilitating the July 22, 2009, daylong strategy session to launch the New Orleans NO Justice coalition. Photo courtesy of WWAV Archives.

and unbroken history of southern Black women organizing. WWAV then worked to disseminate this theory on the ground through independent media and national movement circles, and among community leaders closer to home.

As a central component of this storytelling strategy, Deon wanted to maintain a living archive of the NO Justice Project on the WWAV website, and asked Laura for support to make it happen.[69] This virtual dissemination of the work, however, was no substitute for sitting face-to-face with people. And so another pillar of the NO Justice Project strategy was physically going to and talking with community—service providers, church ladies, activists in other movements—to build relationships and solidarity, just like Catherine and Danita had always done. Whenever she sat down with people, Deon knew that WWAV needed to address plainly and simply the paths that led people with CANS convictions into sex work, because these questions would be at the front of people's minds. The point of this opening work was to meet people where they were at and then invite them into WWAV's own methods for doing the work differently. Every community outreach presentation centered WWAV's theory on the ground about Black women's invisibility and hypervisibility. The flow was designed to make people *feel* the mundane terror of CANS criminalization and sex offender registration. First, we

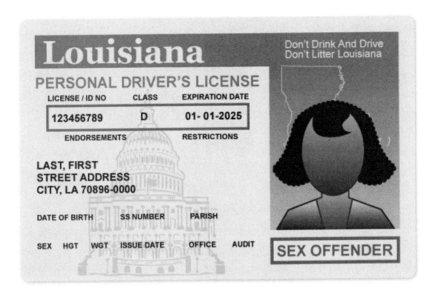

3.2 This mock-up of a Louisiana driver's license with the words "SEX OFFENDER" below the silhouette of a Black femme figure was created by the Center for Constitutional Rights. As the NO Justice Project progressed, WWAV and the NO Justice legal team used this graphic, rather than renderings of people's actual licenses, to protect confidentiality. Graphic courtesy of Center for Constitutional Rights.

would ask community members to pull out their own photo identification cards. Then, we would ask people to think about how many times they have to show their IDs in the course of a day. Sometimes people would call out the places they had gotten carded already that day. Then, we would show a mock-up of CANS licenses with the SEX OFFENDER label (fig. 3.2). We would recount the stories we were entrusted to tell—of our people being denied jobs, of being excluded from drug treatment, of being kicked out of emergency housing. We would explain what it felt like for them to have to carry stacks of paperwork at all times in order to clarify the real circumstances of their arrests to store clerks and housing officials alike. It was rare that a meeting did not end in a collective expression of shock and outrage. And that mattered to Deon. In the state that was then the incarceration capital of the world, WWAV was actively crafting a messaging strategy that could mobilize broad-based community support for striking down the CANS statute and for realizing the liberation of their communities.[70]

Using Legislative and Legal Tactics

Next, WWAV began to explore the viability of bringing a constitutional challenge of the CANS statute. The attorneys who had come to the first local NO Justice coalition meeting in July 2009 were skeptical that the law could be challenged. WWAV needed to find someone who was not. That is how our comrade, Black feminist abolitionist attorney Andrea J. Ritchie, became the anchor for building a NO Justice legal team. Andrea served on the national collective of INCITE!, had cochaired the Color of Violence III Conference held in New Orleans, and was a longtime organizer around the policing of Black women and queer and trans people. She first learned about what was happening in New Orleans in 2009 from Laura when the two met at a sex worker organizing meeting in New York City. At the time, Andrea was the director of the Sex Worker Project and Laura was the director of Project UNSHACKLE.[71] Andrea was already connected with other organizers in New Orleans—most especially her INCITE! comrade Shana M. griffin, who was the cofounder of the Women's Health & Justice Initiative (WHJI) and a longtime WWAV board member—and was aware of WWAV's work before the storm. When Andrea journeyed to New Orleans to meet with Deon and others in the WWAV family, she did so as a Black feminist abolitionist committed to using legislative and legal tactics in service of Black cisgender and transgender women's own visions for liberation, not as ends in and of themselves.

That connection with Andrea also provided WWAV with a litmus test for any attorney who would join the NO Justice legal team. Attorneys needed to have a commitment to what the legendary lawyer and Loyola University New Orleans College of Law professor Bill Quigley described as "social change lawyering": lawyers take their direction from activists because they "start with the idea that history shows us that systemic social change comes not from the courts or heroic lawyers or law reform or impact litigation, but from social movements."[72] Bill had just joined the Center for Constitutional Rights (CCR) as their new legal director. With Deon, Andrea reached out to him about the possibility of forming a partnership with WWAV to develop a legal strategy for the NO Justice Project. From their conversations, the core partnerships grounding the legal team were formed. Alexis Agathocleous and Sunita Patel also joined from CCR, as did Professor Davida Finger from the Stuart H. Smith Law Clinic and Center for Social Justice at Loyola University New Orleans.

All of us at WWAV knew that sustained grassroots organizing would be essential for grounding a legal challenge of the CANS statute within the transformational vision of the NO Justice Project. We started by bringing our longtime local organizing partners into tighter formation. In the spring of 2010, Shana M. griffin of WHJI and Rosana Cruz of Voice of the Experienced (VOTE), who were both WWAV board members, and Wes Ware of the LGBT Youth Project at Juvenile Justice Project of Louisiana (which would become the LGBTQ youth collective BreakOUT!) joined us in further developing the NO Justice Project community organizing strategy. We began with the three founding project objectives established the summer before: (1) engage, support, empower people most at risk; (2) influence key players in the criminal justice system to immediately reduce and/or halt further prosecutions; and (3) secure systematic challenge to the statute through the courts. As part of our strategy development, the NO Justice legal team members—Andrea, Alexis, Bill, Davida, and Sunita[73]—also worked closely with us and presented a range of possible legal, legislative, and policy strategies that were in line with these objectives. Each of these had to be vetted by WWAV and agreed to by the communities with whom we stand before any work could move forward, a central step in all movement lawyering. Together, we broke down each of these proposals into tangible, actionable steps and goals. We also named that public advocacy, community education, and media advocacy needed to be central in any actions we took moving forward. To reduce CANS prosecutions, we decided to partner with the Vera Institute to try to get NOPD to stop charging people with CANS and the DA's office to stop prosecuting. The pathways forward for a constitutional challenge of the statute were less clear, since every person we spoke with (beyond our legal team) continued to claim that this was an unwinnable fight. The legal team proposed filing multiple legal claims that they believed were viable, so that we could see what argument would hold water in the courts, and we agreed with this all-hands-on-deck option.[74] Based on our success in building community outrage around the everyday impacts of having to register as sex offenders, one equal protection claim seemed to be especially compelling: had arrests been prosecuted under the state's prostitution statute, those convicted would not have been required to register as sex offenders.

The care that the legal team took in building legislative, legal, and policy strategy in partnership with us confirmed for all of us that using the tactics we agreed to would bolster, not detract from, the transformational work we were already doing to expose the violence of CANS criminalization and to

3.3 Members of the NO Justice legal team gathered with WWAV staff, board members, and accomplices on the courthouse steps for a press conference after the *Doe v. Jindal* case was filed in the Eastern District of Louisiana, February 15, 2011, on behalf of nine plaintiffs who had been forced to register as sex offenders as a result of a Crime Against Nature by Solicitation conviction. Photo courtesy of WWAV Archives.

posit the possibility of the world otherwise. Our community-building work also needed to be intensified and supported, even and especially while the NO Justice Project shifted into a more public, legalistic mode. And so WWAV doubled down on the four-part model that had gotten the NO Justice Project this far: (1) building power with people directly affected, (2) reaching out to accomplices citywide for relief and support, (3) carefully circulating stories through local and national organizing networks, and (4) maintaining WWAV's own online living archive of the project.

On February 15, 2011, with WWAV's support, the NO Justice legal team filed a case in the Eastern District of Louisiana Court on behalf of nine of the more than eight hundred people who had been forcibly placed on the sex offender registry because of a CANS conviction (fig. 3.3).[75]

Immediately after, we held a press conference on the courthouse steps. The first to speak was a young Black transgender woman, who addressed those gathered anonymously. She described the conditions of racist, gendered profiling that led to her being arrested and charged with CANS in her midteens:

> Hi, my name is Tatiana. I'm nineteen. I was charged with Crime Against Nature at the age of sixteen. I was walking down the street while I was asked by a male individual if I needed a ride. I considered his offer and shortly after I got into the car I was swarmed by NOPD officers who accused me of being a prostitute. And later on I found out after I came into the juvenile detention center, that I was being charged with Crime Against Nature. I spent a week in the juvenile center and was released to the custody of my parents, and shortly after that I started trial. I spent a year in trial going back to court where eventually the judge did dismiss my case. But it did affect me because I missed a lot of schooling and it was just not called for and I'm very disturbed.[76]

While her charges were ultimately dismissed, this was not true for the vast majority of Black cisgender and transgender women with whom WWAV stood. Deon offered the following words on their behalf:

> The women we serve are grandmothers, mothers and daughters. All of them have struggled with poverty and many have struggled with addiction. They did what they had to do to survive, put food on the table, but because they are poor, because they are Black, because they are street-based, because they struggled with addiction, they were singled out for this charge. Mothers who picked up this charge twenty years ago now can't get their children into daycare because they have sex offender on their ID. Women who have struggled with addiction, violence, trauma, and poverty all of their lives and haven't been able to get the services they need are now even more shut out. No DV shelters, drug treatment programs, or homeless shelters will take them.[77]

Shana M. griffin followed Deon, speaking to the impacts of this structural violence on Black women's lives and worlds:

> The public demonization and the complete disregard of the health and safety of women of color impacted by this statute entraps them in a dangerous cycle of violence, poverty, and criminalization. The sex registry mandate condemns them to a vicious cycle of excessive fees and restricted access to jobs due to discrimination, which leads to the possible need to engage in high-risk choices, thereby exposing themselves to daily violence

just to comply with the law. The challenges faced by women of color, who are maliciously marked as "sex offenders" by the state because of their sexual behavior, profoundly affect their health and safety and severely limit their access to resources, thus relegating them to a lifetime of shame and fear.[78]

Andrea Ritchie stitched together the intimate, communal, and structural layers of violence in Black cisgender and transgender women's lives, ending on a quote from one of the WWAV participants who was a plaintiff in the lawsuit:

> In New Orleans and across the country, women of color and transgender women are routinely profiled as being involved in prostitution, and often report that they can't walk down the street without being picked up for loitering for the purposes of prostitution. That's bad enough when it's a misdemeanor. In Louisiana, on a second offense it's a felony, and requires registration as a sex offender for fifteen years to life. Not only are the individuals we are talking about today survivors of rape and domestic violence, they are also survivors of police violence, including sexual harassment, physical abuse, improper strip searches, and rape by law enforcement officers. As one of our clients told us: "I was raped and used many times myself, and I never hurt anyone—why am *I* on the registry as a *sex offender*?"[79]

Finally, Rosana Cruz spoke to the debilitating and often lifelong impacts of criminalization in the incarceration capital of the world:

> Every day dozens of New Orleanians come home from extended periods of time in jail or prison. They face obstacles that make it nearly impossible to find jobs, rent apartments or to access sorely needed resources like educational loans or housing subsidies. We know that many of them also face discrimination because of their records. But the brave women and men who have stepped forward today face an even more insidious roadblock. In addition to having the social stigma of having been in the criminal justice system, they also have to contend with a modern day scarlet letter, a sex offender charge emblazoned across their ID cards. For years after their release, those red letters continue to close doors in their faces. Instead we should help them to clear a path for their success, as they struggle to make a new and better life for themselves and their children.[80]

Rosana's closing words drove home the core tenets of the WWAV outreach script and the Black feminist theory on the ground that it rested on. And just like WWAV always did, they put this forth as an invitation and also a challenge: "*We* should help them to clear a path for their success, as they struggle to make a new and better life for themselves and their children."

The next day, WWAV was back on outreach and strategy-crafting. Deon knew that if WWAV was to have any hope of winning the case, we would have to continue to build a climate in which the judge could safely rule *against* the state of Louisiana. And so the state itself became the next target of the NO Justice Project advocacy efforts. Barely a month later, the NO Justice team persuaded Representative Charmaine Marchand-Stiaes—who represented the most flood-battered district in Louisiana, the New Orleans Ninth Ward and Lower Ninth Ward—to introduce HB 141, which would make CANS penalties equal to those for prostitution. On May 24, 2011, the Louisiana House Committee on the Administration of Criminal Justice heard testimony on the bill. When Bill Quigley and Deon spoke, they were asked to explain the sexual practices criminalized under the CANS statute in graphic detail. Following their testimony, the House committee unanimously approved the bill. After the session ended, Deon turned to Bill and asked, "What do we do next?" He replied, "I don't know. We don't usually win."[81] One month later, the bill had passed the Louisiana House, Senate, and governor's desk. No one convicted of CANS would ever have to register as a sex offender again. However, the bill was not retroactive.

In the wake of what had only been a partial victory at the state level, WWAV and the NO Justice legal team doubled down on the federal lawsuit.[82] The legislative change made a favorable ruling in the lawsuit seem obvious: If people would not have to register as sex offenders for new CANS convictions, why should those previously convicted remain on the registry? However, as the legal team advised, that was not an argument that could be made in court under the equal protection claim. WWAV knew that we needed to, once again, build community awareness and outrage about the Black cisgender and transgender women still on the sex offender registry. We had to organize a groundswell of community support demanding that the CANS statute itself be declared unconstitutional and every person on the registry be removed. The methods for doing so were the same ones that had guided the NO Justice Project since 2007: (1) keep building power with the Black cisgender and transgender people being directly criminalized, (2) continue to lean on

3.4 The Krewe du Vieux 2012 "Crimes Against Nature" cartoon, featuring Queen Deon Haywood in a police lineup with a chicken and a goat to her left and a sheep and a pig to her right. Illustration courtesy Krewe du Vieux.

accomplices citywide for relief and support, (3) circulate carefully crafted stories through local and national organizing networks, and (4) maintain WWAV's own online living archive of the project. WWAV continued. And the community responded. For the 2012 Mardi Gras season, Krewe du Vieux even chose Deon as their queen and made "Crimes Against Nature" their theme (fig. 3.4).[83]

"Our Win"

Five weeks after Mardi Gras Day, on March 28, 2012—before a courtroom filled with WWAV staff and participants, local community activists, New Orleans religious leaders, and legal allies from across the Deep South—US district judge Martin Feldman heard oral arguments on Louisiana's reasoning for requiring people convicted of CANS to register as sex offenders when people convicted of prostitution were not—and whether that reasoning violates equal protection principles. The next day he concluded that Governor Bobby Jindal and his codefendants "fail[ed] to credibly serve up even one unique legitimating governmental interest that can rationally explain the registration requirement imposed on those convicted of Crime Against Nature by Solicitation. The court is left with no other conclusion but that the relationship between the classification is so shallow as to render the distinction wholly arbitrary."[84]

The next morning, on March 30, 2012, a letter entitled "OUR WIN" began to make its way through social media networks before the Friday morning East Coast commute was underway. In it, Deon centered the stories of the Black cisgender and transgender women who led the fight against CANS, and the southern Black feminist organizing tradition of which WWAV is a part.

Dear friends and allies,

There are few times in our work when we are truly brought to the point of being speechless. For all of us at Women With A Vision, today is one of those days. Today, we celebrate with the women and men who courageously stood up to combat the criminalization of their lives—and *won*. Today, we celebrate a victory for *all* people who have told their truths that justice might be done. WWAV has always just been a catalyst for women affected by this.

So many times, people tried to tell us not to do it. They didn't believe that poor, uneducated women could win a victory on this scale. They didn't think that our women were important enough, or that they had the ability to change their own lives. Let this be an example of people standing together through grassroots organizing to change their lives. We didn't back down even when we lacked the funding to do this. We did not back down when person after person said that they were unsure about standing by us. We knew what we were doing was right. We did not waver. We did not compromise what needed to happen. We just stayed the course and fought the fight.

At a time in this country right now when we feel like justice is not on the side of the people, the people most affected spoke their truths—not some abstract "speak truth to power," but *their* truths from *their* hearts— and that is what made the difference.

This was not a legal fight or a legislative fight. This was a fight for women's lives and wellbeing. This was a fight, simply put, about everything. This was about the freedom of people to make choices for themselves. This was about public health. This was about sex worker rights. This was about human rights. This was and is about everything. Which is why we cannot pick apart injustice. We can't decide that something is wrong for one group and right for another. We can't decide we don't like this law for women, but it's okay for gay people or trans people.

Especially in the South, most people feel like we come in last. But this is where the civil rights movement started. And today it continues in the South.

We have seen too often that the way problems are solved in Louisiana is through incarceration. But over-incarceration is not going to solve things. It's not going to make our communities safer. It's not going to make our communities better. The issue here is poverty. Over-incarceration is not going to solve that.

For once, women and men won. And we believe that this is not just a win for us. This is a win for every group that has ever been criminalized. Our win today proves that when we stand with folks who have been wrongly charged, we *can* make a difference.

With this win, the women of NO Justice can begin to heal. With this win, we can begin to renew and rebuild our lives.

And the struggle continues,
The women we stand with, Deon Haywood, the staff of WWAV, and our Board of Directors. [85]

Later that day, everyone gathered around the banquet table and the "We Won!!!!" sheet cake. The WWAV office was a mess of open eyes, tear-streaked eyes, and eyes that could not look up.[86] Most people had not believed that they would see their sex offender registration periods end so abruptly. Indeed, many had never been to court and had a judge side with *them*.[87] Ms. Michelle expressed what so many people with CANS convictions experienced: "I can taste my FREEDOM!"[88] All at WWAV were also clear that this victory was but one step in realizing the transformative healing envisioned through the NO Justice Project. And so, Deon concluded, "Today we celebrate. And still we rise."[89]

Over the coming days and weeks, everyone at WWAV was consumed in almost constant conversation about *how* we had been able to win. Some insisted that we won because the people most affected spoke *their* truths from *their* hearts. For others, what mattered most was that *no one* had been left out: WWAV organized from the experiences of the people most marginalized under CANS so no one could be left out or picked off. Still others waxed prophetic about the continuation of the long Black freedom struggle. Amid all these interpretations, Deon insisted that WWAV needed to do more than just claim "OUR WIN." WWAV needed to work with every person who had been part of the NO Justice Project to document the steps in the organizing process.

As all of us at WWAV talked more about the *how* of "OUR WIN," it became clear just how important it was to specify *what* victory was being claimed. The federal ruling in the CANS case was far from an unfettered pronouncement of liberation. In the name of equal protection under the Fourteenth Amendment, Judge Feldman *limited* the state's ability to further criminalize some people convicted of prostitution. It was significant, then, that in her letter about the win, Deon asserted that the NO Justice Project "was not a legal fight or a legislative fight"—it "was a fight for women's lives and wellbeing."[90] The decision to counter social death with a defiance of living had grown out of a wholesale rejection of both the violent dispossession exacted through CANS and the strategies that advocates typically used to effect piecemeal policy change. Grounded in knowledge that was made to serve the liberation of our communities, WWAV arrived at a novel strategy for challenging this criminalization crisis and for unraveling the whole racial capitalist playbook that gave it shape and meaning. Our approach, with its own historically rich Black feminist analysis, exposed and disrupted the interlocking systems of oppression that produced the post-Katrina crisis and conspired to erase Black people from the city of their birth. Moreover, it enabled Deon to distinguish *WWAV's* victory from the limits of the CANS litigation.

While the federal ruling on CANS was a moment to be celebrated, it was also a moment that only made sense in community—in a process of becoming—through which people began to heal, to rebuild, and to renew with one another using the tools of our own counter-playbook: accomplice, refusal, otherwise, speech. Deon had begun her letter by saying: "They didn't believe that poor, uneducated women could win a victory on this scale. They didn't think that our women were important enough, or that they had the ability to change their own lives." She then refused the white supremacist violence of abstraction, and lifted up WWAV's own otherwise analysis, grounded in the intimacies and radical connectivity of human life and the transformative power of speech: "The people most affected spoke their truths—not some abstract 'speak truth to power,' but *their* truths from *their* hearts—and that is what made the difference." She further refused the modern detachment and fragmentation of our world into separate spheres and categories of being, repeating twice: "This was and is about everything." Constructively, she affirmed WWAV's role as an accomplice to the people most impacted, who were the actors and narrators of their own histories, but she also went deeper than that. She spoke about the geography of the South as "where the civil rights movement started" and used a historically inclusive "we" throughout her text. This was more than a rhetorical device. By claiming the

NO Justice victory as the continuation of the civil rights movement, she told a history of the long Black freedom struggle that put Black cisgender and transgender women at the center; she also stitched WWAV into this history. How did that victory become possible? As Deon explained, "We just stayed the course and fought the fight."[91]

Like a Phoenix

WWAV was never supposed to win a victory on this scale. We knew it. Governor Jindal knew it. Even the federal government knew it. Those afforded first-class citizenship within the United States' own borders were supposed to emerge as saviors after the storm. Black cisgender and transgender women were supposed to fade into the background, invisibilized and criminalized further as state capacity expanded. That, of course, is not what happened. However, that is how some members of the local media chose to tell the story.[92] And so, as part of this victory and also well after it, WWAV and the NO Justice Project legal team wrote and published *our own* press releases, op-eds, and articles, just as we had been doing throughout the years of the NO Justice Project organizing.[93] Deon, Shaquita, and Laura also began to dream of launching an oral history project that summer to document the theories, methods, and new forms of knowledge that we produced during this so-called unwinnable fight, so that we could offer these tools and lessons to support other movement comrades in making the impossible possible. We tentatively titled it, "We Spoke Our Truths."[94]

Two months later, before we could begin that love offering, the very violence that we had refused and organized to transform was turned intimately against us. On May 24, 2012, as the clock approached midnight, our offices were firebombed and destroyed by still unknown arsonists.[95] First, the arsonists whittled the dead bolt off the back door by the kitchen. Then they moved through the space, up the hallway where the NO Justice celebration table had been set up. They set small fires in the meditation alcove, singed the faces off Black cisgender and transgender women in posters that hung on the walls, and tossed WWAV's awards into the alleyway. Inside the outreach office, they stacked WWAV's educational breast models three-high, covered them in accelerant, and ignited a blaze strong enough to melt the blades off the ceiling fan fifteen feet overhead. Decades of client files, harm reduction supplies, and outreach materials—and all the NO Justice Project materials—were reduced to ashes. It was a vile act of hate intended to exterminate WWAV's

3.5 Deon Haywood standing at the center of WWAV's firebombed outreach office on May 25, 2012, the day after the arson attack. Photo by Eliot Kamenitz/ *Times-Picayune*/Landov.

efforts once and for all. The pain of walking through the charred rubble was gut-wrenching (fig. 3.5). In a single breath, Deon explained the intimacy of this violence, as well as how WWAV was being invisibilized in the aftermath of this terror: "There are moments like this that remind us how you're criminalized in more ways than the media will ever show you."

Days later, at a local fundraiser, Deon addressed WWAV's community for the first time. She affirmed that all of us were deeply shaken but recovering. Most of all, she and the WWAV foremothers were worried about how we were going to provide for our community during the rebuilding. WWAV was only beginning to realize the transformational change that had been envisioned in the context of the NO Justice Project. To make matters worse, people with CANS convictions had recently been dealt yet another blow. The state decided to interpret Judge Feldman's ruling as conservatively as possible: only the nine people directly named in the lawsuit were removed from the sex offender registry. For several weeks, people who were still on the registry had been gathering at WWAV to teach each other how to file petitions to be removed from the sex offender registry list, with the support of staff member Zina Mitchell and local movement lawyer Nikki Thanos.

They were continuing the work of freeing themselves in the place where that work began. With the arson attack, our community lost more than a space to meet; they lost their *home*, a home filled with memories of the slow conversations and pained exchanges and joyful celebrations they shared as people who had come together through grassroots organizing to change the conditions of their lives. Losing the people, places, and things that make up one's emotional ecosystem is a deep and intimate shock.[96] And that loss had happened over and over and over again for everyone in the WWAV network. The coming weeks would bring much uncertainty. And WWAV's work *would* continue. "Fire has long been used as a tool of terror in the South," Deon explained, "but it can also be a powerful force for rebirth."

That night Deon spoke WWAV's rebirth into existence. That is the power of fire dreams. We worked to support Andrea, Alexis, Bill, Davida, Sunita, and Nikki as they expanded the legal team to include Philadelphia civil rights attorneys David Rudovsky, Jonathan Feinberg, and Seth Kreimer, and brought a new lawsuit to extend the ruling in *Doe v. Jindal* beyond the nine original plaintiffs. On June 27, 2012, just a month after the arson attack on our offices, this new federal class action was filed.[97] A year later, on June 10, 2013, that lawsuit was settled and the state of Louisiana agreed to remove all of the more than eight hundred people still on the sex offender registry due to a CANS conviction.[98] Methodically, Deon then led WWAV in turning this victory into a systematic challenge of the criminalization of poor Black women and girls in New Orleans. With city council support and judicial partnerships, WWAV worked to establish a diversion program founded on Black feminist and abolition feminist principles to redirect people arrested for street-based prostitution out of the criminal justice system and into the WWAV organizing community. Inside the Orleans Parish Prison, WWAV staff further organized to support the release of hundreds of women who were locked up because they were too poor to make bail. In so doing, we amassed rare and intimate testimonies, observations, and glimpses of a system in crisis. On the tenth anniversary of Hurricane Katrina, August 29, 2015, we began unveiling this analysis of how the new New Orleans has been built through the evisceration of Black women.

Two months later, WWAV walked into the home that was the grounds for the porch talk in chapter 1. The site was still temporary, but it was a *home* nonetheless. It was near impossible to overstate the significance of reopening this Black feminist home and the labor that made it possible. The new

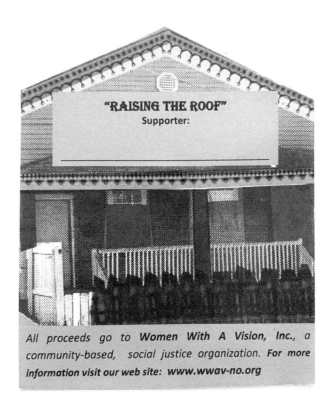

"RAISING THE ROOF"
Supporter:

All proceeds go to **Women With A Vision, Inc.,** a community-based, social justice organization. **For more information visit our web site: www.wwav-no.org**

3.6 In the months following the arson attack, people locally, nationally, and globally hosted fundraisers to ensure that WWAV's work would continue. These "Raising the Roof" cards were part of a New Orleans–led effort to ensure that we would continue to have a home in our city.

New Orleans was actively being built through the organized abandonment and expulsion of Black New Orleanians. But the end had not been written yet. After an arson attack that could have been fatal, at a time when 95,652 Black New Orleanians had not been able to return, the WWAV community rose with the unwavering support of our community (fig. 3.6) to take place and have a space. On this contested land, these fire dreams were just beginning to rise from the ashes.

WORKING WITH FIRE

You have to act as if it were possible to radically transform the world.
And you have to do it all the time.
—Angela Davis, Lecture at Southern Illinois University Carbondale

There was no manual for WWAV's rising from the ashes. We had to move forward day after day, just like our foremothers had always done, creating what our people needed to survive. These acts were not somehow separate from the futures we sought; they are how we built them. Working with fire in these ways—and *choosing* to do so—required attentiveness and discernment. Like Deon said immediately after the arson attack, "Fire has long been a tool of terror in the South, but it can also be a powerful force for rebirth." This paradoxical character of fire was always present. One had to, in the words of M. Jacqui Alexander, "become intimate with this danger zone in order to re-create anew; to enter the fire not figuratively, or metaphorically, but actually, that is, in flesh and blood."[1] That is what it meant to work with fire. And in the wake of the terror of the arson attack, amid the horror of the resilient new New Orleans materializing around us, this destructive quality of fire *loomed*.

Deon challenged all of us to not lose sight of fire's creative potential. With her, we learned to see just how important but malleable this distinction between destruction and sustenance could be. Doing so attuned us in new ways to the revolutionary power of WWAV's theory on the ground for analyzing and transforming our world. It also helped us to commit to the core methods we would need to use for working with fire: first, being in deep *relationship* with one another; second, claiming *space* in New Orleans and working across scales with movements nationally and globally; and third, exploding the fiction of linear *time*.

"You have to build a relationship." Catherine's words are the foundation that makes everything we do possible at WWAV. They are our guide for nurturing the connections that give life and severing those that kill. "Love is contraband in hell," Assata Shakur has taught us, "cause love is an acid that eats away bars."[2] But what is this affective force, built through love, that is capable of entering fire and destroying the racial capitalism playbook? Most simply put, life is complicated, and it gets to be at WWAV. *WEEEEEE* move as one, but our "thick solidarity" is also a shield to protect the complex forms of livingness that the arsonists' fire attempted to destroy—violence that official narratives after the attack tried to blame us for in order to finish the job.[3] All of us knew well that for the racial capitalism playbook to work, our people had to be cut off from relationships and treated as objects of regulation or moral indignation that could be isolated, blamed, and criminalized.[4] We also saw how the softer agents of racial capitalism (providers, funders, public health officials, and faith leaders) trafficked in a quasi-Christian idea of empathy that was no less harmful—what Savannah Shange and Roseann Liu call the "slender *if* of empathy—as *if* I were you."[5] In the wake of the arson attack, WWAV was not interested in platitudes from people who claimed to feel our pain but did nothing to stop it from happening again, still less in being forced to care about people who had tried to destroy our life's work. The antidote to racial capitalism is not to deny difference, nor to repress dissent; it is to change the conditions under which violence has prevailed.[6] *To enter fire.* That is why being in relationship at WWAV *honors* difference—the differences between each member of the WWAV family, the complexities within the communities with whom we stand, the contradictions internal to each one of us.[7] Holding difference is the foundation of harm reduction: to check your own beliefs about what someone should do and meet them where they are at. It is also how we get to the grounds of theory: literally the space between us and within us that could become the grounds through which we stand together in solidarity. That is why throughout WWAV's history we have put so much emphasis on building relationships that allow our people to be with difference, to stand in their truths, to claim the power they were born with, and to grow these relationships in and through the movements for liberation rising all around us. These relationships prefigure the world otherwise. Being in relationship was our central method for working with fire.

Space was the second. WWAV proudly and firmly claims the geographies of New Orleans and the Gulf Coast as home. Our foremothers also share an irreverence for the manufactured cordoning off of the South from the American nation and the world. Their rootedness here has always held within it a global, diasporic consciousness of liberation, which made the connections between seemingly disparate struggles happening here and there, and over there, and over here. Like our foremothers, indeed *because of* them, we knew that the firebombing was no isolated attack on a singular organization at a single moment in time. The violence wielded against WWAV was part of the unbounded destruction that the racial capitalism playbook has long wrought, through space and time for centuries. This playbook was first fashioned in the Atlantic world by the settlers and planters who set out to make the Crescent City by layering interlocking systems of imperialism, colonialism, and chattel slavery that extended up and down the Americas. It was also steadily refined and reconfigured, always in crisis, in response to the constant rebellion and fugitivity of Native Americans, Africans, Afro-Creoles, and African Americans, who also understood their struggles to be just as hemispherically and globally significant as the violence they were fighting. WWAV is an afterlife of these histories of struggle. And in Deon's hands after the fire, these global, diasporic histories were intimately and spatially connected to WWAV's own; they were also anything but past.

This brings us to the third method for working with fire: time. The arson attack on WWAV underlined the long, racist history of fire being used in the South to destroy Black geographies and the traditions they keep. We knew why. The deep and enduring histories of struggle sheltered in these hallowed grounds conjured futures that were always already present with us. Our appreciation of this fact grew from our refusal of the emptiness of linear time and the simultaneity of past, present, and future in WWAV's fire dreams: our "infrastructure of feeling." We used this term in chapter 2 in reference to "feeling of belonging" that Catherine gained through WWAV, as well as the stories that she and Danita shared so that the work would continue. After the arson attack, we also learned to hold the term more expansively, in the fullness of Ruth Wilson Gilmore's naming. To set our dreams afire, we had to expand our horizons beyond what had been, and steadily organize in the present toward the freedom that must be. "Such change," Gilmore explains, "is not just a shift in ideas or vocabulary or frameworks, but rather in the entire structure of meanings and feelings (the lived ideology, or 'taking to heart') through which we actively understand the world and place our actions in it."[8] The Black Radical Tradition of which WWAV is a part is the accumulation of these "structures of feeling." What holds it together? This is what Gilmore calls the "infrastructure of feeling":

> The Black Radical Tradition is a constantly evolving accumulation of structures of feeling whose individual and collective narrative arcs persistently tend towards freedom. . . . What underlies such accumulation? What is the productive capacity of visionary or crisis-driven or even exhaustion-provoked reselection? The best I can offer, until something better comes along, is what I've called for many years the "infrastructure of feeling." In the material world, infrastructure underlies productivity—it speeds some processes and slows down others, setting agendas, producing isolation, enabling cooperation. The infrastructure of feeling is material, too, in the sense that ideology becomes material as do the actions that feelings enable or constrain. The infrastructure of feeling is then consciousness-foundation, sturdy but not static, that underlies our capacity to select, to recognize possibility as we select and reselect liberatory lineages.[9]

This consciousness-foundation was what enabled all of us at WWAV to work with fire. It far exceeded the "structure of feeling" of WWAV's own specific temporal and spatial location in post-Katrina New Orleans; it connected us with all the accumulated "ancestral and community knowledges and practices" in the Black Radical Tradition, past, present, and future.[10] As Deon led the WWAV community in rising again, she did so by caring for and carrying forward the fire dreams of hundreds of thousands of Black southern women organizers past who knew that what they had was not all that was possible. Together, we blew on these otherwise embers that filled our present, so that they could catch, ignite, and set new and more livable futures afire.

In the sections of this chapter that follow, we show how WWAV worked with fire in relationship, in space, and in time to rise from the ashes of the arson attack. We begin with the literal loss of WWAV's home and trace how we made space over the coming year by being in relationship. From there, we move across geographic scales, following Deon and Shaquita's constant work on the road to conferences and international gatherings of AIDS activists, human rights defenders, drug policy makers, and more, as they spoke WWAV's fire dreams nationally and globally. We also hold their creative speech alongside the steady growth of WWAV's liberation work back home in New Orleans through the launch of a new sex worker organizing program to "divert diversion" and the struggles and histories that this program carried forward. In doing this work, WWAV was not only contending with our own placelessness but also with the steady reconfigurations of the racial capitalism playbook through global wars that purport to "save" women in order to conceal the expansions of the military and the police. The mantras of Black reproductive justice are braided together with WWAV's longtime harm reduction and anticriminalization work: #TrustBlackWomen #WeAlwaysResist. By moving in relationship across these local, national, and international scales constantly—and by living past, present, and future simultaneously—this chapter shows the dynamism of WWAV's fire dreams, as the knowledges long sheltered in our infrastructure of feeling were stoked on the ground and on the international stage, in and through movements for Black liberation rising up worldwide. Through these multiple registers of entering and working with fire, WWAV rose from the ashes. We also steadily refined, reconfigured, and at times transformed the futures being imagined.

Holding Space

Immediately after the fire, WWAV set up temporary shop in an annex room at First Grace United Methodist Church a few doors away from the firebombed office. The gift of space was impossible to refuse in the months following the arson attack, but the everyday juxtaposition of packing condoms and syringes into outreach packets in a small conference room while congregation members held meetings for adult and youth ministries on the other side of the door had quickly become difficult to navigate. Tellingly, WWAV's longtime harm reduction participants were reluctant to "drop-in" at the new space. That hesitation may have come as much from assumptions about what kind of God was called into a church as it did from the very real tensions that were present inside. First Grace was a hybrid: born out of the post-Katrina union of two United Methodist congregations, one all-white, the other all-Black, that had decided to join forces to keep their respective churches from dying out with post-storm return rates still waning.[11] The two congregations, now become one, were now actively working through the layered and embodied histories of that marriage in order to build engaged theological responses to racism both internally and citywide.

To be sure, it was intensive and urgent work, but it was also of a different nature than WWAV's. First Grace was embroiled in a difficult process of reparation in a city that was rapidly being whitewashed. The people WWAV worked with, however, were not suddenly made out of place by the storm; Hurricane Katrina was rather a vehicle for accelerating processes of displacement and abandonment that had long been underway. Moreover, while WWAV maintained a decades-long history of working in community, we were most certainly not a religious organization. The majority of WWAV's staff were not "churchgoing women." Our participants historically were the very people who were believed to be too far gone to be heaven-bound—people who sold sex, used drugs, cycled in and out of jail, and who stood unapologetically in these dimensions of their own experience. WWAV valued and affirmed their lives through risk-reduction (rather than saving-people) methodologies. For WWAV to be able to stay at First Grace for any length of time, staff would have to work with First Grace congregation members to build a capacity for walking alongside people who were unchurched and in active addiction—and for seeing these people as *powerful*. It could have been a meaningful undertaking in the long-term. First Grace was, by Deon's estimation, one of those "churches that we work well with, because they get it."[12] Immediately, however, WWAV's participants needed clean needles, cookers, cotton, tourniquets, and condoms.[13] And so, as winter approached, we packed the next month's outreach supplies into staff members' trunks and stored the overflow in the front rooms of our founders' homes.

After six months of "getting back to our roots" as a street-based outreach organization without walls, WWAV moved daily operations into yet another temporary space in the summer of 2013: a small office room on the upper floor of a converted produce warehouse.[14] The building was a shabbier version of the new New Orleans Central Business District blank canvas projects. ArtEgg Studios boasted artist lofts and nonprofit meeting space at prices well below the steadily ballooning rents that were consuming the Crescent City. Perhaps that was partially due to location. ArtEgg Studios was near impossible to find if you did not know the city. The repurposed warehouse was located on the bit of Broad Street that had been laid fallow when Interstate 10 was erected on top of the city's Black thoroughfares in the 1960s urban renewal projects. By car, you could only access the space through a few small streets that were lined with industrial buildings and riddled with industrial-tire-sized potholes. By foot, you could take a metal staircase (that was only slightly more stable than an extension ladder) down from the overpass that buttressed the Orleans Parish Municipal and State Court Houses. That pedestrian access made ArtEgg ideal for the communities that WWAV had been working with for decades—the very sex worker and drug user communities who were most reluctant to come into the First Grace church annex room. ArtEgg was the perfect pre- and post-court stop-off location, especially for people who had been out all night on the street-based hustle and needed to catch their breath (and a change of clothes) before standing in front of a judge and going out again.

Stopping off, however, was about all that anyone could do in the summer heat. ArtEgg Studios kept their rents reasonable, in part, by skimping on amenities like insulation, heat, and air conditioning. On cold days, the inside office temperature could plummet to near-zero. Hot days bade the opposite problem. Even with the curtains pulled and the window air conditioning units pumping, the east-facing windows on WWAV's office funneled in enough sunlight to bake the space to a ninety-degree swelter by midday. We had tried to hold many meetings in that heat, only to have the conversation devolve into a heat-induced dribble when it was too hot to even take notes. It was the sort of stubbornness one might expect from an organization that had been made homeless a year prior and was damn well going to inhabit the little bit of space we had been able to secure for ourselves and our participants as if it were the *perfect* meeting room. However, it was ultimately a stubbornness that was too taxing on all our bodies.

And so for the rest of the summer of 2013, we shifted to Deon and Shaquita's dining room table. Laura was staying at Mary Frances Berry and Mindy Chateauvert's apartment on the edge of the French Quarter. She would head up Esplanade Avenue to pick up Desiree, who had just joined the WWAV staff, from her home in Mid-City right around the corner from the old, fire-bombed office. Then Laura and Desiree would cut over Canal Street to City Park Avenue to the Gato Negro on Harrison Avenue to pick up homemade guacamole and chips before continuing on to Deon and Shaquita's home in Lakeview. We spent hours around their table that summer, eating and drinking, and speaking the vision for WWAV's work going forward.

Before the fire, WWAV had started making plans for expanding the NO Justice Project and its story-driven organizing model into a statewide effort for Black women's health and well-being. Deon had insisted that plan was still on: "This is no new beginning; we are going to continue to do our work the way we always have. We will come through this, bigger and better than ever." All of us knew that "the way we always have" meant starting with the voices of our communities and building relationships with the people we had not met yet. That summer, WWAV launched the "Community Voices Project" through four storytelling and listening sessions: one for formerly incarcerated women, one for Black women survivors of violence, one for LGBTQ survivors of violence, and one for anyone impacted by drug overdose. These intersections of race, gender, and sexuality—of intimate violence, state violence, and medical neglect—were well-plotted at WWAV and in community. Desiree suggested potential event locations that could hold each conversation; Laura offered to make a flyer using the WWAV logo with four women's profiles (fig. 4.1); Deon outlined which of WWAV's longtime outreach spots should be targeted for each event; and Shaquita proposed designing a baseline questionnaire to supplement the qualitative storytelling process.

From the stories and visions shared in those four conversations, we worked to design a service-linkage program for Black women survivors of violence, an intergenerational Black LGBTQ mentoring project, a whole host of programming against criminalization, a similarly expansive focus on reproductive justice, intensive street-based harm reduction outreach, and in-house trainings on vein care and overdose prevention. The work was intimately local and community based. But it was also conceptualized in concert with organizers working across the US South and Global South to be regionally, nationally, and globally impactful.

On the Move

Catherine and Danita had been working at the intersections of community health, harm reduction, Black liberation, economic justice, and more since they cofounded WWAV. Their work was a living testament to Audre Lorde's enduring wisdom: "There is no such thing as a single-issue struggle, because we do not live single-issue lives."[15] That truth was precisely what pressed Deon to stitch together WWAV's anticriminalization work with our reproductive justice work, antiviolence work, and harm reduction work after the fire: *to work across movements*. Her history in the All-African People's Revolutionary Party, as well as her ongoing presence in global movements for harm reduction, HIV prevention justice, and sex workers' rights, had also trained

4.1 The outreach flyer for the four community conversations that launched WWAV's "Community Voices Project" in the summer of 2013. Flyer by Laura McTighe.

her to make connections between the struggles happening in the US South and those happening globally: *to work across scales.*

Weeks after the arson attack, Deon and Shaquita had traveled to Washington, DC, for the 2012 International AIDS Conference. It was the first international meeting to be held on US soil in more than twenty years. The same HIV panic that facilitated CANS becoming law in Louisiana had also paved the way at the federal level for a law restricting the movement of people living with HIV into the United States. When President Barack Obama formally lifted what was colloquially referred to as the "travel ban," the International AIDS Society brought the biannual conference to the nation's capital to celebrate this change in US foreign policy. WWAV attended to shine a spotlight on how US domestic policy was failing Black women in the South and putting our entire communities at greater risk for HIV. In a press briefing called "What's Up Down South?," which we organized with our partners at the Atlanta-based SisterLove, we charged:

> While it is indeed a historic occasion for the International AIDS Conference to be held on US soil, WWAV, SisterLove, and our allies attest to how the US's lack of investment in public health–informed domestic policy has created an HIV epidemic among women in the Deep South that is on par with those in countries in the Global South like Botswana, Ethiopia, and Rwanda. Without attention to the conditions of systemic poverty, poor access to health care (including mental health), gender violence, over-incarceration (through immigration detention and the criminal justice system), and the targeted discrimination suffered by transgender women, a world without AIDS will continue to be beyond our grasp.[16]

This analysis was not new for WWAV, nor for SisterLove. Both of our organizations had been working for decades with the knowledge that HIV vulnerability was produced by the structures and policies that made people have to choose between their daily survival and their long-term health, and that real HIV prevention needed to be just as structurally focused. Centering Black women in the South rendered visible the systems of oppression that WWAV had worked to unravel through the NO Justice Project: poverty, homelessness, gender-based violence, and the criminalization of drug use and sex work. "In the South," Deon always said, "we come first in everything bad and last in everything good." And the epidemiology numbers proved it. As SisterLove's director Dázon Dixon Diallo explained, "The Deep South is ground zero for the domestic AIDS epidemic."[17] And just like the architects of the 1977 Combahee River Collective statement, WWAV and Sister-Love used this position at the bottom (and their clear understanding of the structures producing it) to extend the foundational Black feminist call to action: "If Black women were free, it would mean that everyone else would have to be free since our freedom would necessitate the destruction of all the systems of oppression."[18]

Throughout AIDS 2012, Deon worked to scale up that analysis through the policies that circulated globally to produce the HIV crisis in the US South. In sex workers' statements from around the world, similar concerns were echoed, including funding restrictions that impede prevention for sex workers; the criminalization of sex work and the dangerous public health situations it creates, such as reduced use of condoms and increased violence; the use of other discriminatory laws to repress and punish sex workers; the exclusion of migrant sex workers; and the increased targeting of the clients of sex workers. With members from the global sex worker network, Deon explored how laws that criminalize sex work, sexuality, drug use, and the transmission of HIV all contribute to a global climate of intimate, communal, and state violence for people living with HIV and those most vulnerable to HIV infection. She offered WWAV's organizing through the NO Justice Project as an example of what it looks like to take a structural approach to HIV prevention by ending the criminalization of Black cisgender and transgender women. And she also showed people around the world what happened when Black women dared to change these structures. It was two months to the day after the aggravated arson attack on WWAV when she cochaired a session on "Criminalizing Sex Work."

Working across these movements and scales, like Deon did, helped expose the fiction that violence like the arson attack only happened elsewhere. The US South had an HIV epidemic on par with countries in the Global South because the same systems of oppression were driving it, even if the details looked different as the racial capitalism playbook was materialized in different local contexts. That fact—and Deon's persistent speaking of WWAV's analysis of the arson attack in global context—earned her an invitation to the Seventh Dublin Platform for Human Rights Defenders in October 2013 alongside 145 activists from ninety-five different countries. Hosted by Front Line Defenders, this was an international forum designed to build a community for organizers who have faced violent retaliation in their home countries to share experiences and learn from each other, and for them to come up with new and more effective strategies for their protection and liberation. Deon was the only person in attendance from the United States who was invited as a survivor of targeted, structural violence.

Deon made that journey to Dublin in community: with Shaquita, her mother Catherine, her daughter Cynthia, and Laura. At the conclusion of each day, she debriefed with us, asking us to listen to the stories that she had been entrusted to hold as the mic passed from person to person. She also spoke to the complexities of holding that space as a person from the United States, a country that purported to be a global defender of human rights abuses in order to conceal the structural violence exacted daily against its own people. When addressing the global community of organizers, Deon spoke of "making a choice":

> To be a human rights defender is to make a choice between standing up for what is right and defending the rights of others, or passively accepting that there is no other way. Being here with 145 other human rights defenders from every corner of the globe, all of whom face very similar risks, reminds me of the rightness of our cause. When you see the energy and the commitment of the people in this room, then there is a real cause for optimism for the future.[19]

That energy propelled Deon in the weeks and months and years to come, as she kept making connections and talking about the people who were being left out, just like her mother and Danita had always done. And she championed the South in everything she did—the radical history we carry forward every day, the power of the drug user and sex worker communities with whom WWAV has always stood, and the Black feminist abolitionist vision that holds us steady through it all.

Carceral Feminism and the Racial Capitalism Playbook

Being in those rooms and speaking WWAV's truths also brought into sharper focus the global pathways through which the policies of sex work criminalization that WWAV was fighting at home were being repackaged and recapacitated through a growing antitrafficking movement, which humanitarians, politicians, and pundits alike were calling "modern-day slavery."[20] This language has been rigorously critiqued by WWAV and our accomplices globally as being "haunted by the specter of racial slavery even while it feeds off it parasitically."[21] WWAV has worked for decades to end all forms of intimate, communal, and state violence against Black women: the afterlives of slavery. This includes any and all ways in which Black women are forced into sexual labor through violence, fraud, or coercion (e.g., sex trafficking).[22] Our long memory and meticulous study of Black women's simultaneous *invisibility* and *hypervisibility* in systems of white supremacist dispossession has enabled us to distinguish sex trafficking from the moral panic that has been built up around it. We know that Black women have been terrorized for centuries through sexual, emotional, and physical violence at the hands of the very white people who make the laws and enforce them.[23] The panic against "modern-day slavery" gained power using these very same tactics.

By rhetorically conflating sex work and sex trafficking, the antitrafficking movement has been able to rally broad-based public support for resourcing the very criminalization apparatus of racial capitalism already well practiced at exacting violence against Black women and at concealing this terror in the process.[24]

The start of the antitrafficking panic in New Orleans can be tied to the 2013 Super Bowl, which, like major sporting events before and after, was mythologized as "the largest sex trafficking event in the US" with little to no evidence to support this incendiary claim.[25] In New Orleans, indeed, nationwide and globally, the antitrafficking panic long outlived the event that triggered it, thereby becoming a vehicle for expanding policing, surveillance, and imprisonment domestically in the name of "saving" women—a tactic that is now widely recognized in the academy and on the ground as the hallmark of "carceral feminism."[26] It did so by moving globally hand in hand with the whole apparatus of "colonial feminism," which similarly mobilized the language of rescue to conceal the violence of militarism and conquest.[27] Key to this panic, as WWAV was bearing witness to, was the repurposing of war on drugs criminalization strategies in this new "war on" sex trafficking.[28] Naming how carceral and colonial feminisms were essential to the operation of the racial capitalism playbook across time and space helped bring WWAV's anticriminalization work after the fire into sharper and sharper focus.

As 2013 drew to a close, Deon and Shaquita were again on the move, this time to the biannual international meeting of the Drug Policy Alliance in Denver, Colorado, with Laura and Desiree. Shaquita and Laura had both been invited to speak as part of the new research track: Shaquita, on the politics of drug policy research; Laura, on opening a space of ethics and religious imagination for our movements. Deon was holding down four different sessions in the organizing, education, and policy tracks. When she took the stage for a panel on "Organizing While Criminal: Can We Build Power in the Face of Stigma and Criminalization?" she did so walking strongly in the lessons learned through the NO Justice Project and the connections WWAV had long made to movements for HIV prevention justice. But she was also determined to engage these drug policy experts in strategizing with her about the repurposing of war on drugs technologies in the new "war on" sex trafficking—and to center the experiences of women, especially Black women in the South, while doing so. She carried that analysis into her next panel, "When the War on Drugs Becomes a War on Women: Sisterhood,

Strength and the Struggle for Justice." At the session's end, organizer Andrea James approached the stage wearing a shirt that said "FREE HER." Andrea was just beginning to lay the foundation on the outside for the expansive, locally rooted network of the National Council for Currently and Formerly Incarcerated Women and Girls that she and several other founding members had codreamed while on the inside, incarcerated in the federal prison in Danbury, Connecticut. Deon's unapologetic centering of currently and formerly incarcerated women was what had caught Andrea's attention and earned her lifelong respect. As they spoke, Deon began to share in more depth about precisely how WWAV was challenging these intersections of carceral feminism and racial capitalism in New Orleans.

The last year and a half had been a time of constant motion for Deon and Shaquita, as they moved across scales, refusing the violence of an arson attack intended to erase WWAV's work once and for all. Rooted firmly in the decades of knowledge that WWAV had been making to serve the liberation of our communities, they connected with others nationally and globally who were fighting these same systems of oppression in their own local contexts. Visions for reproductive justice, for HIV prevention justice, for harm reduction, for sex workers' rights, for abolition feminism, and for ending violence rippled through these geographies. Revolutionizing these visions into praxis also exposed the particular ways in which the racial capitalism playbook materialized on the ground through distinct if interrelated histories of dispossession. Back home in New Orleans, WWAV was steadily working to divert the very drug war courts that were being repurposed to brand sex workers as "sex trafficking victims" and force them into rescue programs (fig. 4.2). To rise from the ashes, WWAV had to continue to fight. And in the shadows, beyond the surveillance that willed the destruction of our communities, we were building something truly life-giving.

Diverting Diversion

"I came through the very first class of Emerge, and now I'm working giving tours!" Diamond paused and scanned the faces around the table in WWAV's ArtEgg office.[29] Three out of the four people who were court-mandated to be there had just broken eye contact with her. She knew that subtle shift well—the "Oh, this bitch found ____ (insert: sobriety, God, a job, etc.) and now she thinks she's better than us" shift. The thing was, Diamond did not.

4.2 Zina Mitchell and Desiree Evans carrying WWAV's "NO MORE WAR ON DRUGS!!! The Drug War Is A War On Women" banner at the Southern Harm Reduction Conference action at City Hall, December 13, 2013. Photo courtesy of WWAV Archives.

She just had to perform that for her "good day job." She was still wearing her uniform. Slowly, Diamond breathed in and out, and released her respectable daytime cover.

"I'm not saying there's anything wrong with doing sex work. Hell, I still have to do it when bill money is short or when my son needs something. But for me, I was just having a hard time taking care of my son and working the streets at night. So I wanted a job I could work while he was in school. WWAV helped me figure out how to do that. I put it as a short-term goal on the vision board I made during our first Emerge class. You all made vision boards, right?" Diamond paused, scanning the faces again and then scanning the ArtEgg walls.

WWAV introduces the practice of vision boards on the first day of every Emerge class. Participants and staff each take sheets of poster board and cut out pictures and headlines and slogans from magazines. On the poster board, we create stories of ourselves—right now, in six months, in a year, and well into the future. Then we explain these vision boards to one another, speak the change we desire in our lives into being, and hang them on the walls.

Our work in Emerge is to begin to materialize the visions we have scripted in word and image on paper. Thus, as a storytelling exercise, vision boards are one vital way that WWAV supports people in claiming their power and in claiming one another. It is also how we underscore Deon's principle: "*WEEEEEE* are one."

Each of the three skeptics nodded their heads slowly and let out a distinctive New Orleans "Mmm-hmmm." Anyone who has spent any length of time in the city knows how those flat tones of the "Mmm" and the "hmmm" signify a whole mouthful of words, like "Did you hear what she said?" and "Yeah, I know that's right." Here, "Mmm-hmmm" was a reply to Diamond's question. But it was also an affirmation of the hustle she had chosen to balance her family and her finances. Diamond had the group's attention again.

"I designed this workshop to teach you what WWAV taught me."

Diamond passed out the manila folders that WWAV staff and volunteers had assembled for her. Inside there were guides on résumé-making, dressing for job interviews, and preparing for questions, as well as pictures showing dos and don'ts and fill-in forms for getting started. The materials were what one might expect at a run-of-the-mill job training program for formerly incarcerated women. Emphasis in Diamond's packets was placed on documenting nontraditional forms of work (like babysitting), navigating gaps in work history (because of having children), and building a professional wardrobe (on a limited budget). *People started shifting in their seats again . . .*

Emerge had grown out of WWAV's victory in the NO Justice Project. Following this win, in the immediate aftermath of the fire, Deon was invited to join a citywide Racial Justice Improvement Project. Through this project, WWAV built a partnership with municipal court judge Desiree Charbonnet, who was ready to use the leeway she had within the city judiciary to design a program for diverting people arrested for prostitution to WWAV.[30] People who completed the program (called "Crossroads" in court, "Emerge" at WWAV) would have the prostitution charge wiped from their record. The model had been adapted from drug courts and was usually only available to people with simple nonviolent charges. That separation of the nonviolent (read: innocent, deserving) crimes from the violent (read: guilty, undeserving) crimes raised the ire of prison abolitionists, because it was often a Trojan horse for seeming to advance criminal justice reform while actually smuggling in harsher sentences for others and thereby expanding the carceral state.[31] Within sex worker organizing circles, the heavy, community-based surveillance drew further concern. Nationally, service organizations that agreed to partner with diversion programs often had to screen people for drugs, remand people to custody for positive tests, and teach antiprostitution curricula that required people to disavow sex work and perform a normatively gendered script of "sex trafficking victim" to be eligible for graduation and a reprieve from criminal charges.

On each of these fronts, how WWAV had been able to "divert diversion" through Emerge was remarkable. With Judge Charbonnet, Deon advocated for the most expansive inclusion criteria possible; no enhanced charges for people who were not eligible; and public defender help to comb arrest records for people who were eligible but had not been offered the option of participating because of booking time, location, or some other issue. Moreover, the work that WWAV would carry out through Emerge was not someone else's antiprostitution curriculum; it was a space of WWAV's own production. Deon agreed to move forward on these terms, because, in what was then still the incarceration capital of the world, the frequency of arrests and the number of prostitution convictions people accumulated were debilitating. As we had meticulously tracked through the NO Justice Project, these forms of targeted gendered and racialized criminalization set our communities up for longer and longer prison sentences in ways that organizers in other states were used to seeing only with repeated violent convictions.

This process of negotiating the inclusion criteria with Judge Charbonnet also illuminated some very different expectations on the internal workings of Emerge.[32] In meeting after meeting with Judge Charbonnet, the public defenders, and representatives from the district attorney's office, Deon explained why WWAV used a harm reduction approach to work with people who were engaged in street-based sex work. An assistant district attorney was reprimanded and suspended from the project after accusing WWAV of further victimizing women by not trying to "rescue" them from prostitution.[33] Deon flatly asked, "What do you do when you have a friend in a bad relationship? You love her, you support her, and you trust that she knows much more about her life than you do." That consistent and straight-from-the-hip approach honed through decades of doing the work in community was how Deon had been able to carve out the space to construct the Emerge curriculum however WWAV saw fit—and also how she kept staff from having to report on participants if they were using drugs or selling sex while in the program. There was no expectation that participants would stop doing sex work. The goal was to do what WWAV had always done. The goal was to *Emerge*.

The Emerge program, thus, exemplified WWAV's methods for working with fire—in relationship, in space, and in time. Emerge made space for sex workers to come together. Caring for these relationships also meant making time. Other programs often insisted on scheduling meetings in the middle of the afternoon when parents needed to be available for their children. We opened our doors when we knew our people would be able to walk through them and stay for a while, talk about what was happening in their lives, and build an analysis about the structural forces that produced those experiences together. WWAV staff leaned on our own Black feminist histories, and our ancestral and community knowledges, to further refine that analysis and support our people in realizing whatever visions were articulated in these life-giving conversations. In *Freedom is a Constant Struggle*, Angela Davis talks about how we need to expand the concept of intersectionality spatially and temporally, to make connections with freedom struggles globally and throughout time; it is imperative for us to figure out "how to create windows and doors for people who believe in justice to enter and join in."[34] Her book was required reading at WWAV when it was released. Deon knew that the brutal violence of racism was made tangible in the ways it decimated our ability to imagine otherwise. She also knew that WWAV could be a catalyst for supporting entire communities in becoming "the people whom we have to thank for imagining a different universe and making it possible for us to inhabit the future."[35] This *power*—and how unapologetically WWAV stood in it—was what the arsonists had tried to stamp out. Making Emerge, thus, was life-giving, *including* for the whole WWAV family. In the wake of the fire, Emerge was one of the ways that we all learned to create new windows and doors: moments when "social realities that may have appeared inalterable, impenetrable, came to be viewed as malleable and transformable."[36] Emerge was a fire dream for us all.

Diamond's return to the Emerge class sessions was part of *her* vision supported by WWAV staff. After graduating from Emerge, she, like many other participants, did not want to leave. She kept coming back to the office, and she kept seeing people from her Emerge class doing the same. After a few weeks, they decided to start a program called Groundworks to honor their groundbreaking and foundation-building work together: "To provide a safe space for sex workers and former sex workers to exchange ideas on building a professional brand and explore avenues of self-growth. This is a no-judgement space, geared toward comradery and community outreach."[37] Diamond had been invited to share some of the tools she had been developing in

Groundworks with soon-to-graduate Emerge participants by Leslie Davis, the current Emerge facilitator. Leslie was a baby in the organization at twenty-three, but she had an old soul and a way with WWAV's participants that came from being raised by a Black mother who was an active heroin user for nearly all her childhood in Virginia. Leslie was part of a small team of social work and public health interns who had worked together to craft the Emerge curriculum and launch the program through a combination of listening to the stories that WWAV elders shared about the old days of street outreach and to the more recent ones of organizing the NO Justice Project; studying the digitized resources and training materials that had survived the arson attack; and working to fill in the gaps in these stories and resources through the sex worker–led curricula, health education programming, Black feminist thought, and abolition feminism praxis that were produced by WWAV's accomplices, both nationally and globally.

Diamond eyed the people shifting in their seats and continued, "Okay, so that's what you can find online. I know you're thinking what I did: 'How the hell is this going to help *ME* make a résumé out of all the things that I've done?'" Rolls of laughter fell like dominoes around the table. Diamond stood up and flipped over the first page of the flip chart to expose a sheet titled "Informal Work Experience in Professional Terms. What Skills Are Transferable?" (fig. 4.3). She passed the marker to Laura and asked her to take notes. Then Diamond took a seat alongside the Emerge participants at the table.

> DIAMOND Okay, so what types of work have you done before?
> LADONNA I worked at a bar.
> ANGELIQUE Yeah, I worked as a waitress.
> DIAMOND Yup, everyone in New Orleans has done some kind of food service. Hospitality city. And what sorts of skills did you need to do that job well?"
> LADONNA It was all about multitasking—
> ANGELIQUE —and being able to talk with folks.
> DIAMOND Totally. So customer service, right?
> LADONNA AND ANGELIQUE [*in unison*] Yes!!!
> DIAMOND Okay, so what other jobs? [*looking around the table*] [*Everyone was silent.*]
> DIAMOND Okay, well, why are we all here?

TANISHA Um, sex work?

DIAMOND Thank *YOU*! [*tapping her hand on the table for emphasis*]

TANISHA But how am I going to put that on a résumé and expect anyone to hire me?

DIAMOND Well, you don't put *SEX WORK*. You call it something else. What skills do we need to be sex workers?

JEANETTE People skills for real, for real. [*arching an eyebrow*]

LADONNA And negotiating skills. I mean, I *am* my own business.

DIAMOND Right. Which means being really good at managing money, right?

TANISHA I am an *un*-certified accountant! [*smiling*]

ANGELIQUE Yeah, but negotiating also means communication—with johns and with other girls on the streets.

DIAMOND Right! And not just on the streets. What about backpage?

LADONNA Seriously. Between placing and managing ads online and by phone, I've got a background in telemarketing.

DIAMOND That's what I'm talking about!

TANISHA Yeah, but I can't just make things up. I mean, someone is going to want to check references for my "good accountant job," aren't they?

DIAMOND Well, yeah, but that's where you have to get creative.

[*Ladonna, Angelique, Tanisha, and Jeanette all looked at her, heads cocked and eyes wide.*]

JEANETTE Creative?!?!

DIAMOND Yes, *creative*. Let me tell you what I mean.

[*Diamond nodded at Laura, who flipped to a new sheet of flip chart paper (fig. 4.4).*]

DIAMOND So one option: apply to places that have really high turnover rates. They won't look at your résumé that closely, because they're always looking for somebody. They'll just be glad to have someone who has any experience.

JEANETTE Right, right!

DIAMOND Another option: if you are going to make something up—like passing off sex work as an accounting business—make sure you pick a place that really existed but has closed down, okay? That way, the person checking your references will know that the place is legit, but won't be able to verify whether you worked there or not.

TANISHA Dayum, Diamond, okay. I see you!

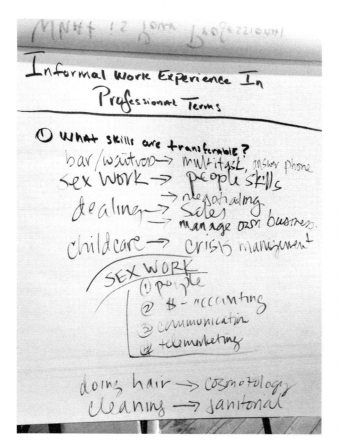

4.3 Flip chart from the Emerge/Groundworks Training on Reframing Informal Work Experience in Professional Terms, March 27, 2015. "What skills are transferable?" Photo by Laura McTighe.

DIAMOND   And last thing: anyone can be a reference for anyone. You just don't want to pick someone with your last name. So Angelique, you could be a reference for Ladonna, and Jeanette, you could be a reference for Tanisha, and vice versa. [*The pairs looked at each other and nodded.*] You can also ask the WWAV folks here to speak for you, if it's a position where being part of an educational program would look good. Right, Leslie?[38]

Leslie nodded, as Ladonna, Angelique, Tanisha, and Jeanette all dove back into résumé-building. By the end of the session, they had reframed drug dealing, childcare, doing hair, and cleaning. "That's how we do at WWAV!" Diamond smiled, extending her arms to signal that time was up. "I hope you'll think about joining Groundworks after graduation." Applause led into thank-yous passed over the shuffle of papers, as Ladonna, Angelique, Tanisha, and Jeanette each stood up to collect their things. And with that

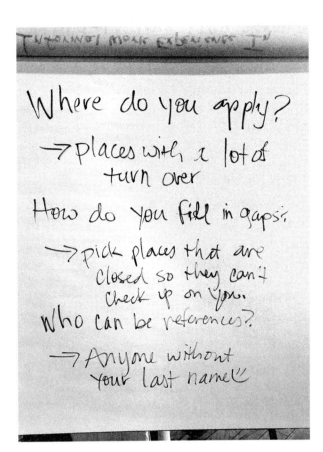

4.4 Flip chart from the Emerge/ Groundworks Training on Reframing Informal Work Experience in Professional Terms, March 27, 2015. "Where do you apply?" Photo by Laura McTighe.

they were each off for what the day held for them next. Diamond was grinning from ear to ear. She lingered only briefly, soaking up all that they had dreamed together and spoken into existence.

Later that night, Laura shared pictures from the Groundworks session with Deon, as had become their regular practice on days whenever Deon was on the road or on conference calls or otherwise not able to be physically present in the office. Tired from the day, Laura started somewhat stream of consciousness, going through the details of where Diamond had taken Ladonna, Angelique, Tanisha, and Jeanette, and how unapologetically the whole workshop stood in the audacity of WWAV's abolition feminism praxis—just like the stories that Catherine and Danita had shared about the early WWAV days and the Our Space events Deon organized after Hurricane Katrina and the NO Justice Project meetings after that . . . Laura paused and turned to look at Deon. Deon's eyes had not moved from the pictures.

"I absolutely love this," she beamed. "There are no victims at WWAV. We claim the power we were born with." Diamond was teaching the current crew of Emerge participants how to turn that liberatory vision into practice. Deon continued, still looking at the pictures, "It's about that moment of just owning all of you. It's something about owning all of who you are, without taking it apart."

Interrupting Carceral Feminism

That afternoon around the Emerge table showed how the vision and practice of WWAV's rising had been passed from Deon to staff to participants and among one another in the wake of the fire—how we were all creating new windows and doors to liberation. By doubling down on our relationships in space and in time, we were all experiencing new ways of being in the world—and catching glimmers of new worlds in formation. The conversation that Diamond led around the Emerge table that day was one of these glimmers. It was so faint at several points during the conversation that Diamond had to recenter and dig deeper so that she did not lose Ladonna, Angelique, Tanisha, and Jeanette. And she taught them how to be ungovernable. To do so, she modeled a praxis that she had learned at WWAV to honor how she had done what she had to do to survive and had also been able to find alternate ways to make money other than selling sex. In order to hold both of these truths—that is, to not *dismember* herself—she had to find a way to honor the reasons she wanted to change her life course that did not require her to demean sex work.[39] She had to tell her life story in such a way that this story did not hinge on divorcing herself from her own self. This was no "once I was lost and now I am found" tale. Hers was an unapologetic tale of care and humor and steadfast determination. That is how Diamond claimed the power she was born with. She turned even the most banal job training materials into tools for writing her own story. In so doing, she came into a different relationship with the survival skills she learned and honed on the streets. All the parts of herself arrived in the present. She spoke the complexity of herself in community. There are no victims at WWAV.

The focus that WWAV placed on belonging in relationship, in space, and in time was what helped render visible the violence in the "victim narrative" that WWAV refused as well as the history that made it make sense. WWAV was no place to tell stories about the Fall and about sin, about women polluted and deplored—about how sometimes these same women could be saved and redeemed. Nor was it a place that tolerated the rationalizing and capacitating of any part of that white supremacist Christian script through the project of carceral feminism and the wheels of the racial capitalism playbook that it greased. The victim narrative left a person first dismembered, then displaced, and then disassembled from their community. You belonged nowhere and to no one until you shed those facets of yourself that did not fit in the constructed order (perhaps even your entire self).[40] WWAV's theory on the ground, on the other hand, played with multiplicity and difference, with present, past, and future all held simultaneously. There was nothing wrong with anyone who walked through WWAV's doors. What each of them had lost (been robbed of) by the systems of dismemberment were the life-giving connections through which a person can begin to know and also exceed themself. At WWAV, they could stand in the fullness and complexity of who they were and who they wanted to become. There are no victims at WWAV.

The problem with all this "no victims" talk was that it could fall harshly on the ears of people not accustomed to the spatially and temporally expansive definition of intersectionality that WWAV was leveraging, much less to the liberatory worlds we were making after the fire. Within the confines of normative gender, to be a victim was to be worthy of support. Victims survived crimes; victims survived violence; victims survived abuse. The state's recognition of "victimhood" was something that white women had fought long and hard for: intimate harm was real and recovery took work. "Victim" was a group-differentiated category that, with the support of the police and the courts, could open up a whole matrix of services, programs, and supports. No one at WWAV was unaware of that context. Which was precisely why Deon used such jarring language. What she was drawing attention to was the long history of white feminists—*carceral* feminists— claiming that they were "saving" women from victimization while they were actually leveraging the entire apparatus of state criminalization to rescue *white* women and do more harm to *Black* women and other people outside the boundaries of normative (white) gender.[41] That was how Black cisgender and transgender sex workers were getting caught up in the whole "modern-day slavery" antitrafficking panic, just like they had in the post-Katrina CANS panic before that. Our staff and participants saw it every day: "Do you know how many times Black women call the cops because they're being beaten by their partners and there are no services, no nothing in their communities, and then *they're* the ones who end up in the back of the cop car?"[42] It was also why WWAV got *blamed* for our own offices being firebombed and destroyed.

In the wake of this attack, all of us at WWAV became practiced at tracing the interlocking histories of white supremacist Christianity and carceral feminism. Since the dawn of the penitentiary era, women (and people classified as "women" by the state) have been going to prison for having sex and getting high. When the first separate women's prisons opened in Massachusetts, New York, and Indiana in the late nineteenth century, as many as half of those confined had been arrested for being drunk, and a third for prostitution.[43] Within the emerging latticework of the separate women's carceral sphere, white middle-class and elite Christian women appointed themselves the "mothers" of these so-called fallen women and contrived elaborate programs to "re-parent" women held captive, whom they often referred to as "children."[44] To nurture purity, piety, domesticity, and submissiveness, their carceral programming was often modeled on household chores and household duties, infused with a heavy dose of prayer, music, and Bible study.[45] However, the liberties many of these early carceral feminists took were not limited to ritualizing white middle-class and elite women's socialization under racial capitalism. By the turn of the twentieth century, these state-appointed female keepers started merging religious discipline and eugenics inside women's prisons. Building on their existing program of protracted religious punishment, in which release was determined not by a judge but by the prison matron herself, they further demanded unbridled access to incarcerated Black, Indigenous, and immigrant women indefinitely held captive "until we have probed her mental processes . . . and studied her physical capacities as thoroughly as the knowledge of medicine will permit."[46] All of us at WWAV knew exactly how those experiments played out. Since the late 1970s, women's incarceration has exploded nationwide, increasing more than eightfold and at twice the rate of men's.[47]

"There are no victims at WWAV" was at once a refusal of how white supremacist Christian and carceral feminist logics structured the victim script *and* also a meticulous observation of precisely how these logics invisibilized and eviscerated Black women. By standing in our own power, WWAV refused to order the stories we told about our lives and the lives of our communities using the plotlines and stock characters of the victim narrative: "*We* are not victims." We also exposed the ways our communities were systematically denied the *ability* to be victims: "We are not *victims*." This second meaning of "no victims" rendered visible the racialized and gendered logics that undergirded this group-differentiated category, logics that were threaded through the whole racial capitalism playbook. By saying "We are not *victims*," we refused the logics that treated us as powerless; we also refused the logics that blamed us for the strategies we used to protect our own selves. Throughout the NO Justice Project, we had to continually name how these white supremacist Christian and carceral feminist logics made the criminalization of Black cisgender and transgender women under CANS thinkable and *actionable*. Likewise, during the porch talk that grounds chapter 1, Desiree also had to name how the "two horrors" that WWAV had to survive—first, the post-Katrina government abandonment of Black people and, second, the arson attack on our offices—had been produced by the *same* system:

> So really thinking of these two horrors that happened to WWAV that we had to survive.[48] Both of them are man-made. [*Deon laughs.*] Both of them [*Deon: Yes!*] were the result of white supremacy, patriarchy, and bigotry. So the system that failed us here in this city, that didn't care about poor people, that didn't care about poor *Black* people, that resulted in thousands of people dying, that resulted in thousands less Black people in the city of New Orleans than before Katrina, that didn't care about those people ever coming back, that is recreating a city that is really about white professionals, that is recreating communities and environments to cater to people who are not about the people who are born and raised here. That *same* system is what fed this person who came and burned down WWAV [*Mwende: Mmmmmm*] because of the work and the people WWAV was speaking for. And so, we gotta understand that these twin traumas are basically children of the same system. And so how do we really think about our own survival in the context of that? Why should we have to keep having to survive?[49]

The urgency in Desiree's question "Why should we have to keep having to survive?" came after three years in exile, hearing story after story shared in the ArtEgg office, during street outreach, at public events, and over meals. All bore witness to a single uncomfortable and persistent truth: *There are no victims at WWAV*.

Rising in the Streets

That is why at WWAV: *We claim the power we were born with.*

Deon's words held the diagnosis and also the cure. Throughout the years of our rebuilding after the fire, she consistently spoke about WWAV and the Black feminist histories we carried forward. This was far from an auto-biographical process of self-contextualization. The practice of speaking the resistance histories that filled WWAV's post-arson present enabled Deon and everyone else in the WWAV fold to care for and carry forward these histories of struggle, so that we could build new and more livable futures. That is why, at WWAV, names are everything. Together, we speak the names of Harriet Tubman, Sojourner Truth, Callie House, Ida B. Wells, Anna Julia Cooper, Pauli Murray, Shirley Chisholm, Ella Baker, Rosa Parks, Fannie Lou Hamer, Oretha Castle Haley, Audre Lorde, Toni Morrison, and many other Black feminist ancestors who have left this earth.[50]

WWAV's three decades of labor to care for the ancestral and community knowledges that give our work shape and meaning dovetail seamlessly with work inside the academy and beyond to build a body of scholarship on Black women's political lives and vision. Some of the field's first social historians took us into slave quarters, postemancipation church pews, and Great Migration rail lines to explore the sacred and secular texture of Black women's everyday lives amid systems of seemingly totalizing social death.[51] With the 1993 publication of Tera Hunter's *To 'Joy My Freedom*, a new era of scholarship on poor and working-class Black women's history was born. Since then, scholars have recovered numerous narratives of poor and working-class Black women as they founded mutual aid societies, negotiated public housing, joined labor movements, and challenged the carceral state.[52] These histories, biographies, memoirs, and novels fill Deon and Shaquita's home. Slowly after the fire, month by month, copies also began to make their way to ArtEgg as WWAV's first Black Feminist Library was created by Deon, Desiree, and Mwende. The Born in Flames Living Archive we were steadily in the midst of building was also part of this library.

All of us at WWAV read these collected works methodologically and theoretically as windows and doors that can and do open our collective imagination. These are precisely the windows and doors that so-called American progress has tried to seal shut. In naming the new resilient New Orleans as an afterlife of settler colonialism and chattel slavery, we emphasize that the endgame of the racial capitalism playbook has always been the literal destruction of the physical, material, and aural *presence* of Black people, Indigenous people, and other people of color in space and on land. We also refuse the white supremacist stories of "empty lands" and "clean sheets" that attempt to conceal the strategies through which these lands have been emptied and these sheets have been cleaned. These strategies of erasure may have "evolved" from policies of outright genocide to more palatable forms of legalized containment and slow death.[53] They may have "evolved" to the proliferation of carceral feminist narratives of "victimization" that enlisted enslaved and colonized peoples and their descendants in performing the emotional and physical labor of evacuating their own presence. But these were all nevertheless tactics from the racial capitalism playbook.

Every day before and after the fire, WWAV refused racial capitalism's place-making systems, which tried to erase Black women's lives and work, and sutured back to these systems the centuries of violence that prefigured them. Deon's work to correct the historical erasure of WWAV's NO Justice Project by claiming "OUR WIN" embodied the steps and process of this Black feminist analysis. In her hands, the NO Justice victory exploded the fiction of "progress" in post-Katrina New Orleans in much the same way that Danita and Catherine had done in that "little hole in the wall in Texas." The point was not simply that Black southern women *could* enter history as the architects of movements to build the world otherwise. The point was that Black women had been doing so for generations. The presence of Black women's geographies and geographic knowledges could never be contained, extinguished, or evacuated. Deon and Shaquita showed this as they moved nationally and internationally, speaking WWAV's rebirth into being, and they trusted staff and interns to do the same locally.

The summer of 2013 made the stakes of WWAV's methods for working with fire painfully clear. On July 13, George Zimmerman was acquitted for murdering seventeen-year-old Trayvon Martin in Sanford, Florida. Shortly after the news broke, organizer and strategist Alicia Garza posted on Facebook, "We don't deserve to be killed with impunity. We need to love ourselves and fight for a world where *Black lives matter*. Black people, I love you. I love us. We matter. Our lives matter."[54] Together with Patrisse Cullors and Opal Tometi, she would turn that "Love Letter to Black Folks" into a movement for Black liberation nationally and globally: #BlackLivesMatter.

In New Orleans the next day, hundreds of people gathered for a Solidarity Rally for Trayvon Martin. Deon was asked to speak, and she took the mic as a Black queer woman, an activist warrior, a mother, and a grandmother

4.5 Deon Haywood speaking at the Solidarity Rally for Trayvon Martin at Washington Square in New Orleans on July 14, 2013, which was organized in the wake of George Zimmerman's acquittal. Photo by Melinda Chateauvert.

(fig. 4.5). This day, she put WWAV's vision and practice for liberation out into the universe, calling each person into this revolutionary work:

> Am I crying because yet again the criminal justice system, or the US system of so-called justice, disappointed me again? I felt like a jilted lover because yet again, I looked for you to do something different, and you didn't. And you hurt me again.
>
> This morning when I thought about it, I just had this overwhelming feeling of, please please please, let people feel and move—and be reactionary, because that's the first urge we get—but please can we move to *revolution*.
>
> When I was in my early twenties, I used to go to meetings for the All-African People's Revolutionary Party. And I didn't think it fit me as a Black queer woman, but it fit me in terms of what I felt needed to

be done for my community. Remember I'm one of those people, always trying to decide what side I need to take.

I want a revolution. I want and I'm calling for a revolution, not in a very violent way. And I want to make sure people understand that. Sometimes when you say revolution, in this country, we fear that in some way that means violence. What it means is to have a plan.

You don't have to join Women With A Vision. We get it all the time: "Y'all don't talk enough about men." But sometimes you don't want to stand with me, because we do talk about queer people and women and their issues and criminalization.

What I'm asking for is join somebody! I am almost pleading, and holding back the level of emotion I'm feeling. *Do something*!

I've been talking to people all day. I don't want to hear one more person, in front of me—y'all can do it with each other, whoever you are, but not with me—tell me, "Well, young Black men kill each other all the time, so George Zimmerman couldn't respect Trayvon." Two separate issues!

I have no desire to change the minds of people like George Zimmerman. I will NOT waste my energy on that. Because I'll be dead and gone and my grandchildren will be still trying. But what we all can do is lend our energy to [fighting] those systems and the ideology that makes us think a certain way.

That we work within our communities so young Black men value themselves. How can you value what other people do not?! So if you hear somebody say that to you, challenge them. You tell them that what they are dealing with is oppression, and poverty, and lack of education, and lack of love for self, and internalized racism. You tell them that.

I am not a begging woman, but I am almost pleading—pleading for every one person who is not here. I do not want this moment to go away, like every historical moment goes away, until another one happens, and we're talking about "The last time—" and "Remember—" because it always happens!

I really want this time to be different. I want to figure out who we meet with this week, next week, once a week, once a month, and what community are we going in, what group are we going to work with, what conversations are we going to have within our community, with our families, about making things different?

I want to know next time OPPRC [Orleans Parish Prison Reform Coalition] is out there challenging the criminal justice system, or anybody in this city who is fighting for someone's LIFE—we talk about rights, but sometimes there's a thin line between rights and your LIFE—I want you to stand up. And I want you to be angry and frustrated enough that you can no longer sit down. That you get up in the morning, you say, "What am I gonna do today?"

And for those of you who feel like you can't. If you feel like you cannot do it, then donate to those who will. Figure out how to support them. For somebody who runs a grassroots organization, I can tell you, the reason we exist, after an act of violence, was because of so many people out here. Whether it was a small party of $100, $500, it means another day for us to fight oppression and injustice in this city. So I ask you. Don't let this moment end and feel like, "I went to the park! And I supported that event in the park!"

Tell me six months from now that you're still supporting this event. Tell me a year from now you are still supporting this moment. That you wake up! I like putting things out in the universe: That *you* speak. That *we* speak.

This day, we use our energy for revolution.[55]

To "use our energy for revolution" meant embodying WWAV's methods for working with fire. When Deon spoke about revolution, she spoke to *these people* in *this place*. She asked them to figure out what community means to them and to build a relationship with someone. She emphasized the momentousness of the present, past, and future held in our relationships. She also called out the lethal violence of prisons, policing, and surveillance—of resilience space, of victim narratives, of crimes against nature, of arsonist assault. And she beckoned, she asked, she pleaded, she begged. She spoke the historical depth of the Black Radical Tradition to people for whom this rally might just be a singular moment of action. This day, Deon put out into the universe that all those gathered in the park would see clearly how the racial capitalism playbook was actively being reconfigured in our midst, and that we already held the building blocks of a new world a-coming in our hands—the possibility that the world could be otherwise. This day, she spoke the presence of all gathered into movements for doing the work.

In the coming months, Deon led WWAV in adding another tool to our decades of work at the intersections of Black feminist struggle: reproductive justice. This framework had been created in 1994 by a group of Black women who gathered in Chicago immediately after the International Conference on Population and Development in Cairo to critique the women's rights movement's persistent leadership by and representation of middle-class and wealthy white women. And just like the WWAV foremothers had done, the Women of African Descent for Reproductive Justice refused to flatten Black women's lives into single issues, positing instead their wholesale opposition to the racial capitalism playbook. Together, they affirmed their work to defend the needs of Black women and other women of color by combining reproductive rights and social justice toward three imperatives:

We believe that every woman has the human right to:

1. Decide if and when she will have a baby and the conditions under which she will give birth;
2. Decide if she will not have a baby and her options for preventing or ending a pregnancy; and
3. Parent the children she already has with the necessary social supports in safe environments and healthy communities, and without fear of violence from individuals or the government.[56]

The last point put into words the pain that so many Black women and birthing people experienced in the wake of Trayvon Martin's murder. A few months later, Mwende reflected on making their sign for the Solidarity Rally on July 14, 2013 (fig. 4.6): "I was (without even realizing it) connecting the struggle for Reproductive Justice."[57]

In 2014, the movement for reproductive justice, often called "RJ" by organizers, celebrated its twentieth birthday, and WWAV was part of the chorus uplifting this milestone in Black women's history and the Black women organizers who had made it possible. And then, in late July, Planned Parenthood, the flagship organization of the white-led reproductive rights movement against which the entire RJ framework had been created, publicly announced that they were shifting from working reproductive *rights* to reproductive *justice*, without even mentioning the Women of African Descent for Reproductive Justice who created the RJ framework, or a single woman of color organization that had built the movement since. The *New York Times* and *Huffington Post* both ran stories about Planned Parenthood's mission change, reproducing this erasure of Black RJ.[58] The response from Black women organizers was swift. Monica Simpson, the director of Sister-Song, which was founded by Women of African Descent for Reproductive Justice foremother Loretta Ross, wrote a public letter condemning the violence of this dispossession of Black women's thought and work.[59] Mwende ran

4.6 Mwende Katwiwa at the Solidarity Rally for Trayvon Martin in New Orleans on July 14, 2013, seated with a sign on their lap that reads "I FEAR HAVING A SON." Photo courtesy of NOLA.com.

social media for the #KnowYourHistory #StopErasing Twitterstorm. That action helped open intergenerational conversations on the history of Black women's organizing and the long-standing linkages between movements for reproductive justice and ending police violence. WWAV held space for that conversation locally by hosting a screening of "We Always Resist: Trust Black Women," a film made in the early 2010s as part of the Black women–led RJ movement to combat the vile billboards erected in Georgia, Missouri, Florida, Texas, California, and Tennessee that claimed, "Black Children are an Endangered Species" and accused Black women who accessed reproductive health care of genocide.[60] Following the film, Deon and Paris Hatcher, a cofounder and former director of SPARK Reproductive Justice NOW and founder and current director of Black Feminist Future, opened a conversation with all gathered about the past, present, and future of Black RJ, underlining why it was so important for Black women to continue to be *leaders* in defining what RJ means and looks like in their lives and their movements for liberation.[61]

Days later, the people rose up in Ferguson, Missouri. Black teenager Michael Brown had been shot and killed by white police officer Darren Wilson on August 9 with a brazen callousness that shook the nation. His was the fifth high profile murder in less than a year, following those of Jonathan Ferrell (September 14, 2013), Renisha McBride (November 2, 2013), Eric Garner (July 17, 2014), and John Crawford (August 5, 2014). When Michael Brown's body was left baking in the August sun, Black people in Ferguson took to the streets. Their steps were matched nationwide, as walkouts, vigils, marches, and moments of silence cascaded from New York to Washington, DC, to Atlanta, from Chicago to Detroit to New Orleans, from Los Angeles to Oakland to Seattle, just as when George Zimmerman was acquitted for murdering Trayvon Martin. A sign held by France François, a Haitian-born, US-raised writer and activist, became one of the most iconic protest images: "I CANNOT BELIEVE I STILL HAVE TO PROTEST THIS SHIT!!" (fig. 4.7). The hashtag beneath her words refused the now familiar murder roll call: #TooManyToName.

On August 14, 2014, in New Orleans, hundreds of people gathered in Lafayette Park as part of a national moment of silence. Reporter Darian Trotter ran a simple image-free story online for WGNO, the local ABC affiliate, covering only the scripted portion of the vigil in which Chanelle Batiste read aloud the names of Black people who had recently been killed by the police and called on everyone present to raise their hands in the now iconic "Don't Shoot" pose.[62] What the WGNO coverage omitted was that there were several Black feminist leaders in the front row of that protest crowd, including WWAV's Mwende and Desiree, and several of the people they worked with through Wildseeds: The New Orleans Octavia Butler Emergent Strategy Collective.[63]

When the August 14 vigil crowd began to disperse, Mwende turned to the people sitting next to them and asked, "*Really? Is that it?*" Then they pushed to the front and addressed the crowd: "*EXCUSE ME! Is that all?* I know too many busy people here who could be somewhere else but chose to be here. For Mike and others. There is too much collective energy here to waste. If we took to the streets, would you join us?" They did. And the people joined. More and more continued to join as the vigil-turned-march crossed Poydras Street, continued through the Central Business District, turned onto Canal Street and took the neutral ground, before crossing over onto Royal Street and into the French Quarter (fig. 4.8). The march had grown to four hundred people strong before occupying the French Quarter police station on Royal. There, a community that was already well-organized against the everyday surveillance and terror of its local police force hurled demands and grievances.

4.7 France François at the National Moment of Silence/Day of Rage protest in Washington, DC, August 14, 2014, holding a sign that reads "I CANNOT BELIEVE I STILL HAVE TO PROTEST THIS SHIT!!" Photo courtesy of @callmedollar.

After the march, Desiree emailed everyone in the core WWAV collective with an update:

I'm going to make y'all smile!

Just so you know, Mwende, my friend Mshi, and I might have been the ones to start the march through the streets of New Orleans today.

Whoops.

Everyone's okay though! It just hit me though that it was a decision made by three Black women, two of them from WWAV, that ended up seeing a crowd of 250+ people march through the streets of New Orleans for a couple of hours.

Mwende did a great job speaking at the rally when it landed at Jackson Square, introducing the cousin of Mike Brown, who gave an incred-

4.8 The view down Canal Street in New Orleans from the front of the spontaneous vigil-turned-march organized by Mwende Katwiwa, Desiree Evans, and others following the National Moment of Silence/Day of Rage vigil, August 14, 2014. Pictured left to right are Anita Dee, Samai Lalani, and Mwende Katwiwa. Photo courtesy of @Small_Affair.

ible speech. And then Mwende was a part of marching into taking over a police station.

I'M JUST SAYING, YA'LL.

It was a beautiful sight and I wanted to give mad props to Mwende because this day wouldn't have been as amazing as it was without your leadership out there.[64]

It took local news outlets more than a month to upload a small photo gallery of the action, a complicity with white supremacist dispossession that the Movement for Black Lives had been fighting since the #BlackLivesMatter hashtag was started.[65] WWAV was also well practiced with this. Just like had been true throughout the NO Justice Project, the coverage of this vigil-turned-march had to be penned by the WWAV organizers making the history themselves. Mwende ultimately published "On White People, Solidarity, and

(Not) Marching for Mike Brown" on their own blog.[66] In a post on social media immediately after the vigil-turned-march, they underscored what they saw as the point of this vital documentary work:

> So thankful for the support and leadership of Black women yesterday and every day. The moment of silence was nationally started by a Black woman, the NOLA moment of silence was led by a Black woman and the march that followed in downtown NOLA was started and led by 5 Black women, three of which are pictured here. Even though our battles against police brutality and the impact it has on us at the intersection of Blackness and womanhood are largely untold, we know them. We live them. We may be forgotten but we must not forget ourselves. #TrustBlackWomen #WeAlwaysResist #BlackLivesMatter.[67]

Their words would be an anchor for all of us at WWAV, as nationally the campaign to #SayHerName was founded at the year's end to render visible the names and stories of the Black cisgender and transgender women and girls who had been victimized by racist police violence.[68] We honor Mwende's posts just like we honor Deon's "This Day, We Use Our Energy for Revolution" speech and "OUR WIN" letter and all the Black feminist histories, written and not, that have been created by WWAV: as a living archive that testifies to the complex ways in which southern Black women organizers have long navigated the chasm between the "group-differentiated vulnerability to premature death" to which they have been subjected through the racial capitalism playbook, on the one hand, and the embodied, relational practices of their own life-giving, liberatory work, on the other.

WWAV's history-making flies in the face of a whole series of interpretive strategies in the racial capitalism playbook through which Black women's organizing is exceptionalized, isolated, and erased, or constructed as reactionary and not as the continuation of generations-honed *movements* for liberation in time and space. In the months following these actions, the nation was embroiled in a debate over whether Ferguson would "be a moment" or "become a movement."[69] Pundits, organizers, and scholars alike charged that the "be a moment" camp was trafficking in respectability politics, since it tended to depict protesters in Ferguson as disorganized, reckless, even dangerous.[70] They pointed out that a sanitized version of the civil rights movement—stripped of its poor, young, and female leadership, stripped of its vibrantly radical and rebellious Dr. Martin Luther King Jr.—undergirded such critiques.[71] Through these civil rights fables, we were made to believe that Ferguson, like the WWAV-led vigil-turned-march in New Orleans, must "be a moment," because real movements did not look like this. The language "*become* a movement" hardly offered an alternative to this sanitizing gaze. It was based in another series of assumptions about how change happens—what we call the "jack-in-the-box approach" to movement history. "Real movements" pop up, like the old-fashioned toy, when people make a demand, and they go down when that demand is met. Movements are thereby exceptionalized and so, too, are the conditions they seek to address. By this logic, we could only ask if the groundswell of #BlackLivesMatter organizing in 2013 and 2014, of which WWAV was a part, would "become a movement," because we were already telling a story of United States history in which there was no continuity of Black struggle, much less a need for it.[72]

When the country "exploded" after George Zimmerman's acquittal and stayed "sprung" after Michael Brown's murder, Black women were on the front lines. Black women cofounded the Movement for Black Lives. Black women also forced the nation to #SayHerName and worked intersectionally to make #AllBlackLivesMatter. Many asked where these organizers came from, who they were, how they were so organized, how they immediately commanded attention and respect. The same was asked of the vigil-turned-march in New Orleans and of the leadership Mwende, Desiree, and others brought that day. Slogans like "not your grandfather's civil rights movement," though pithy, seemed to confirm that there was a break—not that the story had been being told wrong all along (and in ways that reproduced and further naturalized the logics of our current order). The Black Lives Matter "explosion" of the 2010s did not come from nowhere, and neither did WWAV.[73]

Resurrecting Ourselves

This claim is as historiographical as it is theoretical.

At WWAV, we work from the truth that being in America involves being with Black women's organizing. This is what it means to work with fire: to discern, embrace, and live that important, yet malleable, relationship between destruction and creation. Throughout history, southern Black women have organized in counterpurpose to the possibilities and limitations that the racial capitalism playbook imposed on them; they have had to. But that does not mean that their resistance was ever *predicated* on this violence or reducible to its logics. That is why our counter-playbook follows Cedric Robinson in prescribing a necessary limit on the degree to which the excessive, violent systems of place-making under racial capitalism can penetrate and re-form social life, thereby creating entirely new categories of human experience.[74] We can see this in Alicia Garza, Patrisse Cullors, and Opal Tometi's call for Black Lives Matter; in Monica Simpson's protest of the erasure of Black RJ; in Mwende and Desiree turning a vigil around police murder into a march on an NOPD station; in Diamond teaching a whole crew of Emerge participants how to translate off the books work into résumé-ready terms; in Deon and Shaquita traveling the country and the globe to see WWAV rise after the fire. These are but glimpses into much longer traditions of struggle and liberation: the windows and doors that open our imaginations, the infrastructure of feeling of the Black Radical Tradition. To appreciate the *breadth* of spatial and temporal experience that informs this tradition, all of us at WWAV learned that we had to commit ourselves to *resurrecting* the events that have systematically been made to vanish from our intellectual consciousness. We also had to work accountably—in relationship, in space, and in time—to learn how these events, like the histories that WWAV was steadily in the process of producing, pressed on our present, demanding justice. Or, like Cedric Robinson so artfully put it, "For the realization of new theory we require new history."[75]

The histories made by all of us at WWAV refuse to script our work as reactionary, episodic, localized, or somehow secondarily reactive to the oppressions we are resisting. This is how WWAV rose from the ashes. The exiled pasts and ancestral knowledges that we carried forward each day of each month of each year after the fire had transformative effects when they were spoken into our presents. They rendered differently visible, and therefore differently actionable, the contours of our current order, much like Mwende did by pushing to the front of the National Moment of Silence vigil and asking the crowd: "EXCUSE ME! Is that all?" And they also enabled otherwise possibilities to emerge, grow, thrive, and transform our present, just as Mwende's observation ("There is too much collective energy here to waste") and question ("If we took to the streets, would you join us?") were the catalysts to move four hundred people to join a march that snaked through New Orleans streets and occupied a police station. To be certain, this world-transforming theory was rarely comfortable for the people that WWAV met in the process of our rebuilding. It *did* render visible the logics of the racial capitalism playbook and expose even the most subtle complicity with them. But when people could hear this challenge and unite with its critique, WWAV's theory on the ground could also become a catalyst. It could turn allies into accomplices. It taught people how to move in community with us, across space and through time. It opened new ways to live, think, be, and do otherwise—in the intimacies of our relationships and our being in the world; in the pages of our ethnographies and the texts we wrote in the streets.

That change was bigger than "a shift in ideas or vocabulary or frameworks," to recall Ruth Wilson Gilmore's words; it was a shift "in the entire structure of meanings and feelings . . . through which we understand the world and place our actions in it."[76] It was the change that unraveled, rather than widened, the racial capitalism playbook. It did so because it leveraged the whole infrastructure of feeling of the Black Radical Tradition to open the windows and doors of our imaginations, letting in all the accumulated stories and lessons and struggles that kept us tending toward freedom. And that put a point on the truth that Danita and Catherine and Deon would speak to staff once WWAV had set foot into our new home on Broad Street, a truth that included and also far exceeded WWAV's location in that precise moment in New Orleans: "The work will continue to get done, no matter what." *That* is how WWAV rose from the ashes. It is also why we could.

THE GROUNDS

Freedom is a place.

—Ruth Wilson Gilmore, "Abolition Geography and the Problem of Innocence"

On October 19, 2015, WWAV rose to take place and have a space again in the heart of Mid-City New Orleans. It was ten o'clock in the morning, and we all arrived ready to get to work. The sun was shining overhead and streaming across the front porch of 1226 North Broad Street. The side door was standing open. Cars lined the slim driveway that extended to the building's right side. It was rare to see so many people in the office this early in the day. Between the fleas, the mold, the sweltering heat, and the frigid cold, ArtEgg had been hard on the system. The space itself also held energy in a way that was hard to move with smudging.[1] If someone showed up nodding from heroin and needing a safe space to ride out her high, or in crisis after her old man had beat her within an inch of her life, or terrified that she was going to lose her kids because her landlord found out she was a sex worker and he now wanted her rent "paid in pussy"—you could feel it for days, even weeks. Which was strange, because the ArtEgg office had a whole wall of windows and ceilings that were warehouse high. Somehow though the sunlight could never quite penetrate, much less permeate, the space.

Walking through the open door at 1226 was breathtaking. Every wall, every floorboard, every face was drenched in sun. Christine rushed past with a box in her arms, and Michelle was wedging a blanket under a file cabinet to drag it into Deon's office. The long hallway ahead was lined with artwork propped up against the baseboards. It was like déjà vu. The last time Deon, Shaquita, and Laura had been in a long hallway lined with WWAV artwork was days after the fire, and we were crouched on the floor wrapping sheets of brown paper around the few that had not been burned by the arsonists or thrown out the window and shattered. Now, those pieces of art were propped along the wall at floor-level, right below where they would be hung. It had been four years.

Just to the left of the front door was the room that had been designated the reception area. It opened into what would become Desiree and Christine's office. Desiree was explaining the layout. She had pictured it since finding the space and convincing Deon and Shaquita that the move was necessary, even if it was not a move into a permanent home, *yet*. To the left of her office was where Deon and Shaquita would sit. Desiree demonstrated how the big pocket doors could be pulled closed for privacy whenever they were on calls. "Or whenever y'all get to be *too much*!" Deon fired back jokingly, her fingers flipping quickly through stacks of files that had been dumped into boxes during the fire cleanup. A faint smell of smoke wafted from them. To the right, Desiree gestured, would be the office for the three new staff members to be hired: the policy person, the reproductive justice person, and the outreach person. That office opened into a slim hallway that ran the entire back of the building. "Storage," Desiree pointed, "Wendi's desk, volunteer desk, and the kitchen." A kitchen had long been a requirement at WWAV for storing and serving hot food whenever Catherine cooked.

The kitchen opened into Michelle's office, which shared a wall with the office for the staff to be hired. Michelle was the only person with her own space. "Finally, you'll have privacy for Emerge sessions and one-on-ones," Desiree smiled. Michelle Wiley had joined the WWAV team a few months prior to take over facilitating Emerge when Leslie returned to her family in Virginia. Michelle was, on paper, an unlikely pick for the position—a Mississippi native and part-time New Orleans resident who, at fifty-three, had most recently been working in customer service. Deon had a gut feeling that

Michelle would be a good fit for WWAV, a feeling that was confirmed when Michelle described her years of work in youth detention and social services. She had left the field when her mother died, but the work that was supposed to be less emotionally intense while she was grieving was not really her passion.[2] The people who came through Emerge took to Michelle in a way that most of us had only ever heard tell of through stories about Danita's skills as a social worker. Michelle was the only person who could move the stuck and lingering energy in the old ArtEgg office. "Yes, that's right, Des, my own office. Whatchu think about these pictures in here?" Michelle asked with a smile and wink, her voice smooth like molasses. Then we were back in the reception area, and the conference room was just beyond that. There, running nearly wall to wall, was the four-piece oval conference table from the front room at the old North Norman C. Francis Parkway office. It had survived the fire mostly unharmed, because it was on the other side of the blaze that the arsonists set in the outreach office. More artwork had been unwrapped and laid out on that table.

We had just walked in a circle. Each room had a door in and a door out, but not all the rooms were easily accessible. "The flow matters," Desiree explained. "We all have really distinct personalities. The space needs to move the ways that we move, the way that WWAV's work moves. Mwende is the first person you see," Desiree continued. "They have their finger on the pulse of everything. Next you run into me and Christine. We are like the gatekeepers." Christine Breland had joined the WWAV family the summer after Desiree, in 2014. Born and raised in New Orleans, Christine had lost one of her best friends to overdose and had worked in his memory ever since as a dedicated harm reductionist and prison abolitionist.[3] She was also one of the only other white women besides Laura to be invited into the WWAV circle. Christine built her position as the coordinator of WWAV's anticriminalization work through a whole lot of pavement-pounding volunteer hours. After helping build the Emerge curriculum during a summer internship for her master's degree in public health (MPH) program, she carved out a space for herself as the informal case manager for Emerge participants. That brought her into much more intimate contact with the everyday violence that the program's participants were living through, and it enabled her to start mapping structural and policy interventions around policing, charging, and reentry services. In the late fall of 2014, she accompanied Deon on a tour of the Orleans Parish Prison (OPP) women's pods for people awaiting trial who could not afford bail.[4] During that tour, Sheriff Marlin Gusman introduced WWAV as "your new reentry program," much to Deon and Christine's surprise. Christine made creating that program her final project for her MPH program. Based on input from people she interviewed at OPP, Christine recruited several agencies from across the city to offer intensive courses for people preparing for release. And she took on the bulk of individual tracking, following people through medical care, grievances, court, release, and (sometimes) rearrest. WWAV's was the first program to reach people on the women's pods in OPP since Hurricane Katrina. And it was wildly successful. Nearly everyone Christine met in OPP called or showed up at the office after release. Slowly, she was not only amassing a damning report on conditions in OPP, she was also building a base who wanted to advocate for changing the conditions in which they were kept, as well as the policies that landed them there. That was why Christine needed to be seated across from Desiree, just past the reception desk and visible to anyone coming in, especially those newly released from OPP.

"You can't get to Deon and Quita, or to the new folks, without passing by us." We could hear a "That's right!" from the other side of the conference room. "And that's why I love you, Desiree Evans," Deon added. Over the last three years, we had all grown to deeply appreciate Desiree's watchful introverted self and masterful organizational skills. If you wanted a color-coded spreadsheet for tracking a year's worth of activities across twenty different programs, Desiree was your person. Still, this office selection and organization was a very particular feat. Desiree had never set foot in the WWAV office that was firebombed; she had only known the organization in exile. How could the space be so perfect? Were we just stunned by what it felt like to be in an open space again? Had Desiree gained an intuitive sense during her last three years of managing policy and communications of the way that WWAV *felt* in the years before the fire? Or was it something deeper, something not unique to WWAV at all, something about the history of how Black women have long gathered and occupied space in the South—around a kitchen table and on a front porch?[5]

From the next room, we could hear Deon exclaim, "Oh my god—" We poked our heads through the doorway. She was sifting through a box marked "Deon's office." She continued when she felt us approach, not breaking eye contact with the box contents: "—it's just file after file, all marked 2012. It's as if everything stopped." Her hands were covered in soot. As she brushed

5.1 A collection of photos that survived the fire laid on top of a laminated copy of the continuation of the *Louisiana Weekly* story "*Women With A Vision*'s Message Is Clear" (fig. 2.5). Clockwise, starting top left: WWAV member at the kitchen table with a foil tray full of Catherine Haywood's famous crawfish pies; Danita Muse standing in the back of her pickup truck filled with harm reduction outreach supplies; Deon Haywood and Danita Muse tabling; a coffee table covered in safer sex supplies during a WWAV home health party; the original WWAV RV; and Oscar Salinas tabling for Mujeres Con Vision. Photos courtesy of WWAV Archives.

off her hands, she picked up a stack of photos and placed them with the clippings that used to fill her bulletin board (fig. 5.1). "Danita's truck! Lady's crawfish pies! The old WWAV RV! Mujeres Con Vision!"

"Wait, is that Oscar?!"[6] Laura asked.

"Oscar?" Christine and Desiree inquired.

"Oscar," Deon confirmed. "Back in the day we had support to do home health parties with Latinx women. I guess there are a lot of stories we haven't shared since the fire..."

That moment helped clarify the *feeling* we had since entering 1226 that day. It goes without saying that places are not simply bricks and mortar, nor do they merely serve their expressed functions (shelter, office, grocery store). They are emotional ecosystems. Space is made through stories spun into existence in the everyday interchanges of social life. What had made WWAV's old office space on North Norman C. Francis Parkway a home had been the stories passed from person to person, the dreams etched into the carpet as someone tapped their foot to the music playing in the background, the bowls filled whenever Catherine made her famous gumbo, the sighs that could finally be exhaled when a judge said, "Your rights were violated." What happens when a space is destroyed, but the things that used to fill it remain? What happens when a lineup of framed posters and art triggers a memory of a space that can never be visited again? What happens when the process of opening a box of papers dated "2012" finally allows someone to say, "It's as if everything had stopped"? What happens when just seeing an image of Danita in the bed of her pickup truck triggers joyful laughter and a story about "back then"? What happens when a picture with a WWAV sign in Spanish leaves newer staff dumbfounded?

Archives are often thought of in material terms. Letters, photographs, documents, ephemera. That was certainly part of what was being unpacked during WWAV's move-in day. But those boxes contained more than mementos, pictures, and soot. Even the staff members who had not known WWAV before the fire could feel that. Artwork, posters, photographs: all were laid out for Deon to go through and place. Each was a portal—to a story, or a memory, or a feeling that had been retracted after the arson attack and put away for safekeeping. What Deon was unpacking, and in so doing, regrounding, was WWAV's *living archive*.[7]

Our understanding of this living archive was something that came into focus slowly in the wake of the arson attack, when decades of our work literally went up in flames. Reckoning with the full extent of the erasure being willed against WWAV attuned us to the ways in which the violence of racial capitalism is made manifest through the absences and silences in our archives, through the obliteration of lives, through all the things that we cannot know. And yet, Black cultural and feminist historians have always challenged us to go deeper, to be "undisciplined," in the theories and methods we use to produce knowledge about what does remain.[8] From Mary Frances Berry, we learned how to scour government archives and respectable sources to reconstruct the *threat* that southern Black women organizers have always posed.[9] Following Marisa Fuentes, we read these records "along the bias grain" in order to study our own absented presence in the new New Orleans landscape and "see" what was hidden in plain sight.[10] With Saidiya Hartman, we practiced "critical fabulation," like our Louisiana Black elders did "storying," both strategies that helped us awaken the historical depths of the erasure wielded against us—that is, to use storytelling to imagine not only what was, but also what could and must be.[11]

Being with these theories and methods changed our understanding of what was destroyed in the arson attack, what we always sustained through our practices of working with fire, and what we were "rebuilding" through our research as survival. The roots of our own relational praxis extended back, as Jessica Marie Johnson has taught so many, to the very intimate and kinship practices through which Black women have been shaping what living freedom means in the Gulf Coast since the eighteenth century, thereby laying the groundwork for centuries of resistance to come.[12] We are an afterlife of their fire dreams. *Our relationships are a living archive.* Relationships are the means through which we have maintained and passed down our independent thought and action amid constant surveillance, and they are also the caverns in which these thoughts, actions, and dreams have been kept for generations. Our relationships hold all that we have imagined for ourselves and the world. At 1226, this *feeling* materialized, spread out, and began to take root. Rebuilding WWAV's living archive, thus, was not simply a matter of reconstructing the paper record that had been destroyed; it meant ensuring WWAV had a place that could never be erased—neither from the geography of New Orleans, nor from history.

Desiree had intuited enough to choose and craft this space for WWAV's living archive. However, from the first boxes unpacked, it was also clear that a lot from the old days had not been shared since the fire. Hell, a lot of the details of the arson attack had not been shared. On one of the harder days in the ArtEgg office, Mwende had remarked, "It feels like WWAV is building the car while driving it." Deon insisted then, "We already *had* all of this stuff. We have been around since 1989, incorporated since 1991." There, in Deon's boxes, were the surviving policy and procedure manuals, dating back to the first binder that Danita had made not long after WWAV's founding. Most were too charred or smoke-stained to be salvageable.

What is breathed into a space when the stories of a photo are told? What is unleashed when memories have a geography to occupy? What is made tangible that was long thought dead? Deon opened another box and pulled out a small wooden sign that read "Life Is a Journey."

"Wow, Lady got this for me years ago in acknowledgement of the spiritual journey I was on," Deon smiled with her eyes. "See how *supportive* my mother is?"

Shaquita nodded in agreement, "That's Lady."

Deon placed the sign on the mantel behind her desk, just beneath the copper goddess silhouette, next to a small bottle of rum. "I want to get Sula to do a house blessing for us . . ."[13] She trailed off, looking through the box.

"Wow, what time is it?" Deon asked Shaquita.

"Six o'clo—" Shaquita began.

"Six O'CLOCK?!?! And y'all are still here?!?!" Deon looked at Desiree and Michelle, who were sitting at a small table where Desiree's desk would soon be. "I couldn't *get* y'all to come to the old office!" Both laughed. As Deon came to sit at the table, her granddaughter Bailey, or "Bunny" as she was more often called, got out of the chair she was sitting in. Deon stretched out her arm for Bunny to stand by her as soon as she was seated (fig. 5.2).

"Wow, y'all. This really reminds me of the old outreach days at WWAV," she smiled. "We would work all day, then do outreach all night, then head to Rose Tavern. I want to bring that back. I want to be in community like that again."

We all nodded, and began to gather our things, slowly making our way to the door.

While Shaquita locked the door and activated the alarm, we lingered on the front porch steps, looking out over the North Broad Street late rush hour traffic, as the cars crawled along and people passed them by on foot.

"All right. How are you?" Deon waved back at a person who greeted us from the sidewalk.

She then turned back to all of us on the porch and repeated with emphasis, "To be in community like *this*. This is our homecoming."

5.2 Shaquita Borden, Deon Haywood, Bailey "Bunny" Haywood, Desiree Evans, and Michelle Wiley seated around a table on WWAV's move-in day at 1226 N. Broad Street, October 19, 2015. Photo by Laura McTighe.

My Existence Is Political

That day, we were able to make sure that WWAV's decades of liberatory work could again take place and have a space. We did so by firmly placing our truths within the histories and the geographies that gave them shape and meaning. These histories were carried with us through the Black Feminist Library of books and movement posters and framed artwork that would come to line every wall in the new office. The grounds for living this archive would quickly become that sprawling front porch that emptied onto North Broad Street. As days turned into weeks, and weeks into months, we bore witness to the revolutionary things that could happen on that southern front porch. This threshold between WWAV's office and North Broad Street was not only where we connected with the people who lived and moved through Mid-City. It is also where we shared stories from our days; where we talked about the histories we were steadily making across local, national, and global scales; where we learned from the knowledges of the ancestors who taught us why we fight; and where, in so doing, we began to articulate the politics for how we could unravel the whole racial capitalism playbook. On these grounds, WWAV was continuing the generations-passed rituals of imagining that the world must be otherwise. Doing so was sacred work. It resurrected the fire dreams that have long been sheltered in these interstices. It also taught us what it felt like to make spaces where Black women and girls born and raised in New Orleans could stand fully in their power and reclaim their city. *Why* did we believe in the revolutionary things that happen on a southern front porch? And *how* exactly did those revolutionary things happen? To appreciate the place of the front porch in WWAV's southern Black feminist politics, *why* questions matter just as much as *how* questions.

Here, we recall Robin D. G. Kelley's vital distinction between *why* and *how* questions, which has guided our social movement ethnography thus far. For Kelley, *how* questions tend to reify traditional expectations of what counts as political, whereas *why* questions expose the paradox of engaging with political institutions and processes that traditionally have not proven to be very attentive to the concerns of poor and working-class Black people.[14] Our call to action for this book, indeed throughout the history of WWAV, has been the refusal of the often-subtle ways in which the racial capitalism playbook structures our understanding of what legitimate politics are and where we should go to find them—Kelley's critique of *how* questions. *Why* questions, however, have helped us expose the violence of the arson attack and the histories of erasure that preceded it; they also underlined the liberatory hermeneutic of WWAV's rebuilding.

Q *Why did the arson attack happen?*
A Fire has long been a tool of terror in the South, but it can also be a powerful force for rebirth.
Q *Why did WWAV rise from the ashes?*
A There are no victims at WWAV. We claim the power we were born with.

By refusing erasure and claiming our power—that is, by occupying the grounds of *why*—we also arrived at a different inflection of *how: How* did we unravel, rather than widen, the racial capitalism playbook? *How* did WWAV do the work?

Outreach is and always will be the lifeblood of WWAV's organizing practice. For thirty-five years now, everything we have done or made to serve the liberation of our communities has begun with Catherine's first step: you have to build a relationship. The WWAV foremothers knew that their people had razor-sharp analyses of the systems of structural oppression they moved through daily, and that they could name the precise things that needed to change in order for the pressures of suffering to relent. Our foremothers also knew that their people often did not have the time to show up to more traditional forms of organizing. They were too busy making ends meet day-by-day, minute-by-minute. Their people needed relief here and now if they were going to lead the work to change the structures that made that relief necessary. Through outreach, by sitting with their people on front porches at the end of the day, the WWAV foremothers were able to build relationships and figure out what immediate support looked like. *That's how WWAV did the work.*

Then, while passing out harm reduction supplies or serving up a home-cooked meal, our foremothers talked with their people about the issues they were dealing with and what it would take to bring some deeper, lasting change. In time and in concert, these porch talks grew into new political possibilities. Putting the communities that WWAV stood with at the center of everything we did exposed the violence of normative politics—politics that erected and reified a boundary between organizations that provided services and those that worked for social change. It also attuned the WWAV foremothers to the geographies where otherwise possibilities could and did materialize. Black women organizers in the South have *always* approached mutual aid and reparations work as inseparable and interconnected goals.[15] *That's how WWAV unraveled, rather than widened, the racial capitalism playbook.*

It is also how we made our foundational theory on the ground. Our foremothers connected their work to the infrastructure of feeling that undergirds the Black Radical Tradition by building relationships. Politics at WWAV, thus, have never been separate from lived experience. Politics are the everyday struggle to create liberatory spaces and otherwise worlds beyond the structures and agents of racial capitalism that destabilize our communities. Politics are matters of life and death. And because the whole racial capitalism playbook is about exaggerated and lethal systems of *place-making*, we also know that the grounds of our own liberatory systems are just as essential for doing the work that is life-giving. This is the place of the front porch in WWAV's southern Black feminist politics. It is from the front porch that we can see the new world we are building taking shape all around us. These grounds connect us with the past, present, and future of the Black Radical Tradition, across geographies and generations. They also bring us into deeper touch with the power of the stories that have been shared here, so that the work will continue to get done, no matter what.

Honoring these fire dreams does not simply mean saying the names of those who came before us, though this is important. It also means engaging with their practices, learning from their failures, and speaking their truths, so that we can grow futures more livable than our present. It is an intimately and complexly human process. As Lila Abu-Lughod has put it, "We respect everyday resistance not just by arguing for the dignity or heroism of the resistors but ... by letting their practices teach us ... about the complex interworkings of historically changing systems of power."[16] WWAV gathers on porches, we make knowledge there, and we engage in politics to speak into being a world in which we can live and thrive, and not just survive. And we do that through our living archive by being in relationship—not only with one another in the present, but also with the generations of southern Black women organizers past who have imagined otherwise on these grounds, as well as with the generations who are still to come. WWAV's mantra? "My Existence is Political" (fig. 5.3).

As the sections of this chapter unfold, we occupy the grounds of WWAV's front porch. And from that front porch, we breathe together, we break bread, we laugh, we share stories, we make the superheroes we need, we imagine what safety feels like, we love this city and its people, and we teach our accomplices nationwide and globally why it matters so much to do so. In other words, we live "My Existence Is Political" as both a vision and a practice, and we root our living archive firmly in this land. That is how we ensure that WWAV has a place that can never be erased—neither from the geography of New Orleans, nor from history.

Black Feminist Santa

"We believe in the revolutionary things that happen on a southern front porch." It had been two months since WWAV rose to take place and have a space at 1226 North Broad Street, and Deon's words had become the refrain of WWAV's regrounding. One afternoon in December, we were again kicked back in conversation on the front porch, watching the falling sun paint the New Orleans sky pink, orange, purple, and yellow. After Desiree snapped a picture of us in full porch pose, Mwende jumped up and bounded inside. They returned moments later with a bright red Santa hat, eyeing Deon:

5.3 Catherine Haywood and Deon Haywood wearing matching "My Existence Is Political" T-shirts, standing on WWAV's front porch at 1226 N. Broad Street, December 9, 2016. Photo courtesy of WWAV Archives.

"We're not leaving for the day without doing a photo shoot." Deon replied in kind, gesturing at her gold peplum shirt: "Don't you see I dressed for the occasion?" She then shook her head in mock frustration, as she slowly stood up from her porch recline and followed Mwende inside.

A few days prior, WWAV staff had been gathered around Deon's desk. It had a solid wood top that stretched at least six feet wide and four feet deep. The monstrosity was a remnant from the law office that had occupied 1226 previously. The room Desiree had picked for Deon and Shaquita's office was in the very front of the building, likely a parlor or sitting room in some not-too-long-ago household configuration. Behind Deon's head there was fireplace with an inset mirror above the mantel. She began building an altar on that thin stretch of wood on move-in day, starting with the small wooden "Life Is a Journey" plaque from Catherine, which was still placed beneath the copper goddess silhouette and next to the small bottle of rum. Since, Deon had incorporated pictures of her grandchildren along the opposite side of the mantel. The newest addition was a bouquet of fresh flowers in the middle. "We will always have fresh flowers in this office," she affirmed.

Deon's desk was the unofficial meeting space for both formal and informal WWAV business. It was a fitting turn of events after Deon had (by choice) been without a desk for all three of the years that WWAV was holding temporary space in ArtEgg. She insisted that limited desk space go to the staff who were running programs and doing direct work with participants. Now, with more space than WWAV had had in years and with three new staff members just having come on board (Raven, Nia, and Nakita), everyone chose to gather around her desk when we were not out on the front porch. Deon was able to leverage that physical closeness to do some critical staff training on WWAV's history and methods for doing the work. Conversations flowed from drug policy to criminalization to reproductive justice to women's health to LGBTQ rights to sex and to dating to friendships to family. Older staff members were called to share stories about participants or about their trials in the courts, on the streets, or with gatekeepers. Deon connected the dots as these stories ricocheted from person to person; the emphasis was placed on showing why and how WWAV moved as one. Whenever a staff member suggested a strategy that she knew would widen rather than destroy the racial capitalism playbook, she broke it down and dismissed it. "WWAV doesn't grovel, and we certainly don't play with systems like that," Deon explained. "The WWAV foremothers had *swagger*." As if on cue, Mwende or Michelle or one of the other the more senior staff members would walk across the room to the opposite wall, turn around, and fold their arms across their chest. "Ha! Exactly! Just like that. Straight into a room, and to the back, eyes *watching*. No one fucked with them. It's going to take a minute before you new people realize what it means to walk like *that*, to walk in *that* power, to walk in *that* history."[17]

This December afternoon, the topic had been of a more playful variety. Desiree insisted the office be decorated for Christmas. Earlier that year, while we were still in ArtEgg, she had us laughing with her stories about growing up Baptist in Catholic Louisiana and wanting with all her little self to be Catholic during Lent so she could get ashes on her forehead and eat fish like all her friends. "Now I just eat fish on Fridays," Desiree laughed. For

Christmas, she proposed a tree, garlands, and stockings. The real clincher, however, was the Secret Santa gift exchange.

"Secret *who*???" asked Raven.

"Yeah . . . how does that even work?" Shaquita followed.

As Desiree described the process of pulling names from a hat and bringing a present for the person whose name you pulled to the staff holiday party, Mwende was the first to volunteer that they had not been raised believing in Santa Claus. Nearly everyone around Deon's desk let out a "*Me neither*!"

Deon offered a story to bolster that consensus. When she was a teenage mother, she had worked two or three jobs and put items on layaway in order to make a Christmas for her children. "After all that work, I wasn't about to let some rosy-cheeked white man take credit for providing for my children. I was young and poor and didn't want my kids to be left out, so I worked hard to make sure they weren't. We kept the holiday spirit, but we didn't lie about where it came from." That point opened into conversation about how the making of Christmas as a commercial, family-oriented holiday had a history.[18] And, like with so many of the rituals of American capitalism, the presence of Black families and poor families in these stories was either highly caricatured or entirely erased.[19] We then all began musing about a holiday figure who would spread joy, love, and revolution. As the words passed from Mwende to Desiree to Raven to Shaquita, #BlackFeministSanta was born. Deon was cajoled into embodying her on camera.

"What I let y'all *do* to me!" we heard Deon playfully chiding Mwende as she walked toward the door to the front porch. Pictures inside by Desiree's tree were finished. Now it was time for a few outside. Those of us still seated on the porch walked to the bottom of the steps to provide feedback. "They ain't ready!" Mwende repeated the porch talk slogan once more, as they put away their camera and called it a day.

The next day at the office, Mwende was turning Christmas songs into #BlackFeministSanta holiday wishes, callouts, demands, and visions. The memes broke the internet when Mwende unveiled them on social media.[20] #BlackFeministSanta was "Making a list, checking it twice, gonna find out who is still in OPP because they can't pay their fines and why the public defender's office is so underfunded." She said "Ho ho" to remind everyone, "Hoes deserve not to be slut shamed for exercising bodily autonomy." She sang Christmas classics like "Baby, It's Cold Outside" for "Black families in Louisiana facing housing discrimination." She called Bobby Jindal a Grinch for "cutting benefits to Louisiana families." She reminded everyone "to buy

Black this holiday season, but also that capitalism is inherently flawed and anti-Black." And she was "Dreaming of a White Christmas where #BlackLivesMatter." Hordes of friends, comrades, and accomplices nationwide called, emailed, messaged, and tweeted about how to order copies of the full set (figs. 5.4–5.11).

All of us at WWAV were calling "bullshit" on the Christmas fiction of white Santa, with his elves making toys up in the North Pole, and his reindeer delivering them by sleigh. We decried the violence of Black mothers being expected to hand over power to "some rosy-cheeked white man"—the violence of having to participate in the invisibilization of their own labor. And then, using our counter-playbook, we dreamed up an icon and a rallying cry for rendering visible the violence of the new New Orleans and for celebrating Black feminist visions for change. In a city that was actively policing the sights and the sounds of Blackness, #BlackFeministSanta sat on the front porch and theorized from these grounds. Her speech was creative. She refused the isolation of Black families from necessary supports and services and the housing discrimination that blamed them for the abuses they survived. She calculated the number of Black people who were languishing in jail cells, criminalized because they were too poor to make bail. In so doing, she named and reversed these steps in the racial capitalism playbook. By envisioning an end to this white supremacist terror, she showed us all that the world could be otherwise. #BlackFeministSanta dreamed out loud of a day when all Black lives would matter; she also made space for those dreams to exist on the front porch here and now. Her presence was at once imaginative and material. As a political practice, #BlackFeministSanta showed how the whole WWAV family was refusing the scripts we had been given, claiming our own power, claiming each other, and working—in relationships, in space, in time—to make more livable futures together. In this way, #BlackFeministSanta was a revolutionary practice. This was how we started to make a plan.

Safety and Love

The Christmas season gave way to Twelfth Night on January 6, the official start of Carnival season, which would end at the stroke of midnight on Mardi Gras Day. In 2016, Mardi Gras Day fell on Tuesday, February 9, nearly four months to the day since WWAV had taken place at 1226. As we settled into Lent, and with it, the weekly practice of Friday fish fries, we were also taking stock of the state of WWAV's anticriminalization work.

ALL I WANT FOR CHRISTMAS

GET YOUR JINGLE ON

IS AN END TO WHITE CIS HETERO PATRIARCHY
#BLACKFEMINISTSANTA #WWAV

MAKING A LIST, CHECKING IT TWICE

GONNA FIND OUT WHO IS STILL IN OPP BECAUSE THEY CAN'T PAY THEIR
FINES AND WHY THE PUBLIC DEFENDERS OFFICE IS SO UNDERFUNDED
#BLACKFEMINISTSANTA #WWAV

HO HO

HOES DESERVE NOT TO BE SLUT SHAMED FOR EXERCISING
BODILY AUTONOMY #BLACKFEMINISTSANTA #WWAV

I'M DREAMING OF A WHITE CHRISTMAS

WHERE WHITE COLLEGE STUDENTS GET ASKED IF THEY WERE
ADMITTED DUE TO RACE #BLACKFEMINISTSANTA #WWAV

**BLACK FEMINIST SANTA REMINDING YOU TO
BUY BLACK THIS HOLIDAY SEASON**

GET YOUR JINGLE ON

BUT ALSO THAT CAPITALISM IS INHERENTLY FLAWED
AND ANTIBLACK #BLACKFEMINISTSANTA #WWAV

BABY IT'S COLD OUTSIDE

FOR BLACK FAMILIES IN NEW ORLEANS BECAUSE OF HOUSING
DISCRIMINATION #BLACKFEMINISTSANTA #WWAV

5.4–5.11 All eight of the #BlackFeministSanta cards that Mwende Katwiwa made, featuring Deon Haywood, December 17, 2015. Photos and memes by Mwende Katwiwa.

Shortly before the move to North Broad Street, WWAV's access inside OPP had suddenly dried up without warning. The prison staff who managed volunteers decided to keep on all the agencies that Christine had recruited to provide the classes and trainings requested by women inside—and ditched WWAV. At first, it still seemed like there might be a chance of renegotiating access. As the year drew to a close, even that hope was lost. We all agreed that it was time to move on the stories of abuse that women were enduring at the hands of police, prosecutors, and prisons. Deon, Christine, and Desiree caught WWAV's new policy director, Nia, up to speed and began to imagine releasing these stories as a white paper on gendered criminalization. By the end of Carnival season, that white paper was blossoming into a plan for a criminalization-focused grassroots campaign modeled on the NO Justice Project. The stories of women from inside OPP would drive the analysis of the complex interworkings of these systems of power. In partnership with women who had been released, we would work together to name the life and death fights, who (or what) we could put pressure on to bring relief for our communities, and *how* we could do so. WWAV had the people, the stories, and the analysis. However, where we were struggling was on identifying the "nonreformist reforms" to demand—that is, the policy changes that would take power away from the prison industrial complex and help us grow abolitionist futures in real time.[21] As we knew all too well, the problem was not a single policy issue; it was the whole rotten system. "It's like a hamster wheel to hell!" Christine spat.

Deon invited a dear national Black harm reduction colleague, Allen Kwabena Frimpong, to facilitate a two-day meeting with the WWAV team to narrow focus and craft an organizing strategy. Allen was coming off a major win in his home state of New Jersey around building safer neighborhoods by getting local governments to divest from hiring cops and invest in the supports that communities need—the very things that the racial capitalism playbook isolates people from as a precondition for blaming them for their abuse and then criminalizing them. He had also just left his "good foundation job" to cofound his dream organization: a movement-building, skills-sharing laboratory to build better analyses of how change happens in order to effect deeper, more transformational wins. By working outside of traditional funding and foundation circles, Allen was able to more easily root his work in the spatially and temporally expansive practices of study and struggle that had been honed in global freedom struggles, past and present—practices that defied the tactics most funders would commit grant dollars toward.[22]

What Allen brought to WWAV for that two-day meeting was a theory on the ground that he built in community through his own organizing in New Jersey: "The Movement Cycle." This framework named, and in so doing, reimagined, the usual rollercoaster of normative policy campaign work, in which bursts of targeted organizing were unleashed in reaction to crises and then receded when the crisis was over. Allen explained to us all how such reactive "reformist reforms" rarely attacked the underlying structures of white supremacist dispossession that made particular policies thinkable and actionable; more often, "reformist reforms" relied on these structures and expanded them. They also failed to realize two essential goals of any "nonreformist reforms": first, effecting personal and collective transformation among those doing the work, and second, (what Allen called) "creating the new." Put simply, for "nonreformist reforms" to be viable, the policies of the racial capitalism playbook needed to go—*and* something constructive needed to fill their place, *and* that something constructive had to be created by people who were nourished through the process of organizing for their own liberation and would be freer still as "the new" took shape.[23]

We all agreed that Allen's framework around "creating the new" aligned strongly with WWAV's now more than three decades of organizing at the intersections of Black feminist struggle. His framework also underlined the traditions of revolutionary theory and practice that undergirded our work. As Deon had shared at the Solidarity Rally for Trayvon Martin after George Zimmerman's acquittal, what revolution means is "to have a plan."[24] It is not "about destroying, destroying," as freedom fighter Kwame Ture taught us, "it's *creating*."[25] Or in Allen's words, it is "creating the new." What WWAV also knew was that "the new" was never entirely *new*; it built on and extended those glimmers of the world a-coming that we had been creating in community for generations. In post-Katrina New Orleans, "the new" for WWAV was the first time our communities caught their breath in the context of the NO Justice Project; it was the feeling of "I can taste my FREEDOM!" after our win; it was continuing to organize for sex work decriminalization; it was launching the Emerge program to divert diversion; it was turning an opening at OPP into an inside-outside organizing project. "The new," thus, was *precisely* what was being attacked by the myriad people, places, and things that were building the whole "hamster wheel to hell" that was the new resilient New Orleans. That lesson was intimately and catastrophically felt by all of us at WWAV after the arson attack that tried to destroy our work and the histories we carried forward. And we also saw it growing daily as we bore witness to the destabilization of New Orleans's Black communities from our front porch.

In late March, we gathered around the WWAV conference table to turn that knowledge into a plan. Allen guided us in making a list of the threats before us with a simple question: *What are you seeing?* That focus on sight was intentional. It reminded us all of Deon's "outreach skills" and conjured the image of WWAV's foremothers standing at the back of the room, arms folded, *watching*: all the forms of "dark sousveillance" that WWAV was well practiced at doing to survive amid constant and lethal surveillance.[26] It also lifted up another register of sight in WWAV's lexicon: the constructive, world-building vision that was our founding call to action and undergirded all our practices for supporting our people in claiming their power and standing in their visions for their lives. What Allen was, in essence, facilitating us through was an all-WWAV vision board–making session. He had opened the space that morning by asking everyone to close our eyes and imagine a time when we felt completely safe. That exercise underscored the power of sight in WWAV's storytelling, both for assessing a situation clearly and for imagining it otherwise. By speaking together a vision for our communities' safety and contrasting that with the violent erasure we were observing as the new New Orleans took shape, all of us at WWAV could clearly see and name just how deadly the nexus of predatory policing, overcharging, eroding services, and failing public defense was. The next step was to imagine the transformation that our communities needed—to dream with our eyes wide open—and then to map the tactics we would use to make those dreams reality, just like our foremothers had always done.

ALLEN I want to give you a structure for moving from what you see to what you're going to do. What is your goal? What is your tactic? Put these together, and you'll have your community change. [*He wrote* GOAL + TACTIC = COMMUNITY CHANGE *on a sheet of flip chart paper.*] In Jersey, we explained it like this: DIVEST HIRING OF COPS plus INVEST IN COMMUNITY ALTERNATIVES equals SAFER NEIGHBORHOODS.

DEON How do we narrow down to a *single* goal? [*She shook her head.*] There are so many moving parts here.

[*Christine, Desiree, Nia, and Laura nodded in agreement.*]

ALLEN Well, that's the point. This is what we are going to work on tomorrow. Once you have this GOAL plus TACTIC equals COMMUNITY CHANGE equation figured out, we can start mapping out the story of your work, the strategy, and the structure. So don't cross any items off your big list. Just figure out what the overarching goal is, what the tactic is, and what change you want to see. After that, we'll see which items fit into the organizing process as short-term strategies or strategic escalation techniques. I'm going to give you all about thirty minutes to identify your goal, tactic, and community change.

[*Allen tore off a sheet of flip chart paper for us and put markers on the table.*]

DEON Tiggy, will you take notes? [*She slid the markers to Laura.*]

LAURA Of course. [*She wrote "Goal," "Tactic," and "Community Change" on our paper.*]

DEON Where should we start, y'all?

[*We all looked around the room at each other and then up at the paper.*]

LAURA What if we just go one by one? I'll keep a running list and then we can try to narrow down at the end?

[*Everyone nodded in agreement.*]

NIA Okay, so goals . . . How about: increasing political engagement among native New Orleanians? I mean, it's kind of what I was hired to do. But we talk so often about this city is being taken away from those of us who were born and raised here . . .

DESIREE Mmm-hmmm. Which means that we need to arm the public with the tools they need to advocate for themselves in this city. We need to demystify the whole political process. Secrecy and entitlement are how bad policies are getting through.

CHRISTINE I totally agree, and I think that things being so bad for so long has also taken a real toll on a lot of the people we see. People don't believe things can change; they have only been seeing them get worse. The toll of that is something we cannot underestimate. We're going to have to create a desire to fight with some of the people we work with—especially the people who have been most impacted and most need to be at the front of this.

DEON Exactly. Our people have been told for so long that they ain't shit, they're not entitled to shit. We have to cultivate a *feeling* of entitlement.

LAURA Okay, so how do we do that? What are the tactics? [*She drew a line to close the "Goals" stack for the time being.*]

DEON We do what we always do. We get back into community. We listen to people's stories. It's how we make change at WWAV. Community drives everything.

CHRISTINE Okay, so I get this is a lot, but I really want to see that asshole Canizaro OUT of office.

SHAQUITA ME, TOO. He's got to GO. And we need to replace him and all the rest of his crew with people who actually understand and follow best practices.

DEON BOOM! [*She knocked her fist on the table for emphasis.*] So does that mean we want to be the ones vetting people?

CHRISTINE Mmmmmm—[*She tilted her head to the side, as if asking a question.*] Maybe we should get some more people on board to help us with that?

NIA Well, I still have all of my contacts in the public defenders' office— [*Everyone started to shift in their seats.*]

Nia had left a job working as a city attorney to take the policy job at WWAV in late 2015. Those first months had been rocky, because Nia was trained as a lawyer and analyzed everything in terms of tactics that would work within the criminal legal system. WWAV, however, "specialize[d] in the wholly impossible," to quote that famous motto of Nannie Helen Burroughs.[27] Our work was the radical embodiment of Angela Davis's injunction,

"You have to act as if it were possible to radically transform the world. And you have to do it all the time."[28] WWAV's commitment to movement-first, lawyers-second had created some tensions as Nia settled into the position, but Deon kept repeating that the space to think and dream as expansively as possible was going to be one of the biggest gifts WWAV gave to her. Nia glanced around the table seeing the reaction when she had again brought up the lawyers, and clarified:

NIA   I just wonder if there's a way that we can use the fact that the public defenders' office is in crisis to help shift the narrative.

DEON   Like how?

NIA   I don't know, maybe to bring the focus back onto our participants? To keep Black women from New Orleans at the center? First, they've got to deal with a crazy district attorney, then there are no public defenders.

DESIREE   I like that. Which brings us back to Deon's point about creating a *want* to fight. We have a real opportunity here to train a whole new generation of activists—

CHRISTINE   If Mwende were still here today, you know they'd tell us to expand the focus to girls.[29]

DEON   Yes, Mwende would. Black women AND girls.

NIA   My girls will be the first ones! My eldest daughter blossomed as a writer and performer in Mwende's poetry classes.

LAURA   [*Drawing another line on the flip chart paper.*] So what's the Community Change we want? I mean, we've got this morning's conversation about what *real* safety looks like . . .

CHRISTINE   Right. NOT incarceration.

DEON   When all of us who are from here told our stories about feeling safe, we talked about memories from before Katrina. Which means we're not *just* talking about criminal justice system. We're talking about everything. We're talking about the whole new New Orleans. We're talking about what this whole narrative of resilience is doing to our city. We have to believe that *that* can change—that New Orleans can change. I love this city. I want this to again be a city for New Orleans Black women.

DESIREE   [*nodding*] What we're talking about is *freedom*—

DEON   Yes!

DESIREE   What we're talking about is taking back this city, taking back the *power* of this city.

DEON   Standing in the power we were born with!

LAURA So, I think we're really close, don't y'all? Do you want me to try to say back what I've been writing up here?

DEON Go ahead, Tiggy.

LAURA Okay, so for a Goal, we've been saying we want to build the power of Black women AND girls to take back political power in New Orleans.

DEON Damn. That's good. That *is* what we've been saying. Except I think we need to be really explicit that we're talking about *poor* Black women and girls. We're talking about low- or *no*-income Black women and girls. We're talking about the women no one else talks about.

NIA Yes, definitely. [*Christine echoed her.*]

[*Laura scribbled out and rewrote "poor Black women and girls."*]

LAURA Okay, the Tactics are what WWAV does. Train the people. Tip the system. Hold elected officials accountable.

DEON Yup, yup.

[*Desiree, Christine, Nia, and Shaquita all nodded.*]

LAURA And if we combine that goal with those tactics, the Community Change we're going to see is: Build a *new* new New Orleans.

[*Laughter roared around the table.*]

DEON A *new* new New Orleans! What are the lines that you have beneath that? I can't read them.

LAURA Oh, I was just trying out slogans. Like "Down with Criminalization!" though you already said what we're fighting is bigger than just the criminal justice system. So then in the affirmative, "Up with Safety and Love!" because of what everyone has said about what real safety looks like and how it grows out of a love for the place of New Orleans and a love for the people of New Orleans (fig. 5.12).

DEON I like that. Safety and Love. [*She spoke the words slowly, feeling their frequency, their power.*] The Safety and Love Project.

ALLEN [*Poking his head around the corner*] It sounds like you have a name!

DEON You know, I think we do. What do y'all think?

DESIREE Safety and Love. We're trying to make New Orleans into a place of safety and love.

NIA We *work* from a place of safety and love.

CHRISTINE Yup, I think we have a name and a vision.

The next day was Good Friday. Deon, Shaquita, and Allen arrived at the office together. "Hey everybody," Deon called. "So we did a lot of work

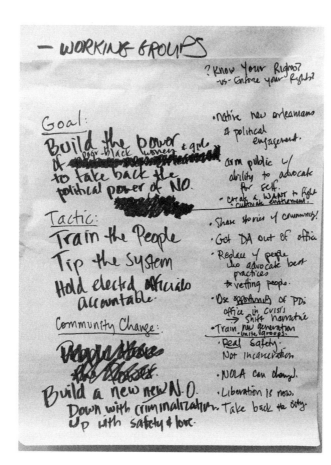

5.12 Our completed Goal + Tactic = Community Change flip chart for the Safety and Love Project, March 24, 2016. Photo by Laura McTighe.

yesterday. I've asked Allen to leave materials with us for the next steps in our planning, but I'd like to give him and all of us the rest of the day off so that we can just sit and relax. There's a fish fry happening in the back. Mama Kat made tons of food.[30] Let's spend the afternoon basking in what we just dreamed up."

Everybody knew she was right. To make liberation, you had to practice it in community. How else would you know how to realize something as transformational as: "*Safety and Love?*" Desiree called; "*Safety and Love!*" Christine responded.

The first pan of fish had just come out of the fryer. "Come on and make plates while it's hot!" No one had to be asked twice for that one. With bellies full, we all piled onto the front porch. The sun was blinding and beautiful. It was springtime in New Orleans.

5.13 Christine Breland, Jonathan (Christine's husband), Nia Weeks, Allen Kwabena Frimpong, Laura McTighe, Desiree Evans, Michelle Wiley, and Shaquita Borden spread out on the steps of WWAV's front porch at 1226 N. Broad Street in the spring sun, March 25, 2016. Photo by Deon Haywood.

"Don't move y'all!" Deon called from the front walk a few feet beyond the porch steps. "I want you to see yourselves just the way you are right now" (fig. 5.13).

Front Porch Strategy

A month later, we were like salmon swimming upstream in the Louis Armstrong International Airport. It was the second weekend of the 2016 New Orleans Jazz and Heritage Festival. Hordes of people were coming into town. Deon, Shaquita, Mwende, and Laura were about to board a plane to North Carolina for the Anna Julia Cooper Center's Know Her Truths: Advancing Justice for Women and Girls of Color Conference at Wake Forest University. Together, we formed the WWAV contingent tasked with unveiling our vision for "front porch strategy" on the national stage—and the new institute called Front Porch Research Strategy we were launching to support our ongoing work at the intersections of service, activism, and research.[31] WWAV had been invited by Melissa Harris-Perry to talk about what now more than three decades of Black women's organizing in the South looked like—and why it mattered so much for this work to take place and have a space as the fantasy of a new resilient New Orleans was being materialized across the Crescent City at an alarming rate.

By terming our work *front porch strategy*, we claimed the everyday community-building work that we had been doing on the front porch at 1226 as meaningful and significant. We stitched together our #BlackFeministSanta cards, the Safety and Love visioning session, and every porch talk and meal shared in between. We claimed them all as the building blocks of revolutionary transformation, as the glimmers of this new world a-coming that we were making with our own hands. We also refused a whole slew of assumptions about normative politics and where change was supposed to happen in the South. Front porch strategy, in WWAV's theorization, demonstrated the deeply enduring spatial latticework of southern Black women's geographies for sharing stories, developing political analysis, realizing community care, and building the world anew: "We believe in the revolutionary things that happen on a southern front porch." *Strategy* (like revolution) means to have a plan. *Front porch* tells you where to find it. In these ways, front porch strategy opened up a whole range of possibilities for talking about WWAV's decades of organizing for reparations and mutual aid alongside southern Black women and girls. It also rooted our *research* in the long traditions of Black study and the practices for making knowledge to serve the liberation of our communities, which WWAV carried forward in everything we did. That focus had earned us a spot in the conference's first-day plenaries showcasing model projects and justice organizations.

Melissa Harris-Perry was getting ready to call the room to order. Mwende, Deon, Shaquita, and Laura were seated to her left, behind two rectangular tables draped in black cloth. Circular banquet tables fanned out toward the room's corners and doors, providing seating for the sold-out room of Black women scholars, organizers, and reporters, peppered with four male accomplices and three white women. At each table, a few of the eight chairs were still waiting on their people. Initially, WWAV had been scheduled to present immediately before lunch, but the morning's conversations had run over. After taking a read on the room and quickly rearranging the program, Harris-Perry asked if we would come back as the post-lunch conversation restarters, because she knew that it would be better to be talking to a room full of people with full bellies rather than standing between people and their lunch. With a nod to us, she took the mic and offered a story to refocus everyone's attention. The night before, Deon had been part of a dinnertime meeting with the steering committee for the Anna Julia Cooper Center's new Intersectional Research Agenda. During that dinner, Harris-Perry's best friend, Blair Kelley—a public historian of Black social movements who "was not easily impressed by the living"—was sitting at the other end of the table from Deon. At one point, Kelley leaned in and said, "Ohhhh. You're Ida B. Wells." Harris-Perry described how she replied, "Ohhhh, shiiiiit, Deon got Blair," to roars of laughter from our panelist table and the audience beyond, "It is going down." With that, she asked the room to join her in welcoming us. Mwende was ready, mic in hand.

So how y'all doing? My name is Mwende, and I am a program assistant, executive assistant, slash just-hanging-out-at-Women-With-A-Vision cuz I like to be in their space. And I'm really excited to be here to present with these people, because each of these people up here, and Deon especially, has been a mentor to me. Full disclosure to start: I am not a researcher. I'm a poet, I'm an organizer, and I'm an activist. And I really believe in blending social justice and arts. I came to WWAV in 2014, and there were four staff members and me in this tiny room in this large warehouse. We were just doing what we could with the resources that we had.

Those are the roots of WWAV. WWAV was started in 1989 by eight Black social workers from New Orleans. They just looked in their community and realized that HIV/AIDS was actually impacting Black women more than anyone in New Orleans, but it was still wearing the face of gay white males. Right? So these eight women said, "You know what? We're gonna do what Black women have always done and look out for ourselves." So they went into their communities. They did some underground needle exchanges—really focusing on harm reduction among Black women based on the spread of HIV/AIDS.

And then 2005 came, Hurricane Katrina happened, and some of our priorities had to shift and expand specifically because the landscape in New Orleans was so bad for Black women and no one was talking about it, right? The women who kept coming into our office—poor Black women, cis and trans—all had this "SEX OFFENDER" label on their licenses. Huge red label. And we were wondering, "How is it that women are coming in here, don't identify as pedophiles, and are all labeled as sex offenders?"

And we started listening to their stories.

That's one of the things that is foundational about WWAV: storytelling. And knowing that women hold their *truths* in their stories, and they also hold their *solutions* in their stories.

So listening to these women, we figured out that they were all being systematically targeted by the police cuz they were transgender women or because they were sex workers or because they were at the intersection of Black womanhood and all of those things. And not only that. Not only were they being criminalized; they were specifically being given higher sentences because of their identity. So there were two ways it could go down. You could get a prostitution charge which is a misdemeanor, or you could get a "Crime Against Nature" charge which is a felony, and then you would also get put on the sex offender registry list for fifteen years. The police had the authority over what they charged you with when they got you on the street. And when they were arresting Black cis and trans women and gay men as well, if they were Black, they were giving them this Crime Against Nature statute.

So WWAV got together with people from around the city and lawyers from around the country, who brought this lawsuit all the way up to the Louisiana Supreme Court and got over eight hundred women removed from the sex offender registry list in Louisiana, right? Which was a *major* victory. And also at a very small level. Something as simple as being able to go to your kid's graduation, right? You weren't able to do that if you were a sex offender, because you couldn't be within a certain vicinity of a school.

And this was the time when I started to understand just how important research really was. We talk a lot about that gap that exists between policy and person, right? That gap is really what we try to work in at WWAV. And one of the things we've been talking about is how research informs policy, right? And so if you're doing research that's centered in and rooted in the community's stories, it follows then that your policy, if it's based on that research, will also do the same thing. So I'll let them take that on because they're actually going to talk about the research.[32]

Mwende turned to Deon and smiled, "That is where we're coming from as WWAV." Deon nodded in agreement.

Mwende had provided the skeletal structure of WWAV's decades of work in New Orleans. Each of us had become practiced at that narrative, and we each put our own spin on it. Mwende's made plain the intersections that were in play at each turn in the story. They drilled down into how the criminalization of Black cisgender and transgender women in post-Katrina New Orleans destabilized their most intimate relationships. What did WWAV win through the NO Justice Project? A mother was now able to go to her child's graduation. Storytelling was the theory and the method for all of us: "Knowing that women hold their *truths* in their stories, and they also hold their *solutions* in their stories." Deon built on the foundation that Mwende had laid by sharing stories about the history of WWAV as a Black women–led organization in a Black city—and also about "the new" that WWAV was steadily creating in New Orleans and in partnership with national and global movements for liberation.

Hi y'all. You heard that? *Y'all.* So one of the things that I wanted to share, to pick up where Mwende left off, is what it looks like to have to "change your strategy" after—Now, we don't call it a *natural* disaster or a disaster made by *Mother Nature.* We call it the federal government failing a community, a city of people. New Orleans has its issues, but I absolutely LOVE my city. I love the people. I love the culture and the richness of Blackness. That when people from the Continent come over they say, "This feels like home." When people from the Caribbean come, they say, "This feels like home." It says something about the rich history and about the people who *really* built this city, and why it's important that we sustain ourselves and make a place to know our truths, right?

And so post-Katrina New Orleans, when we got back—everything that Mwende said was true. But what was unique about it was that the Feds gave the state of Louisiana millions to target "harmful and violent offenders."[33] And that was *these* women. That was the people who are most policed. It was the communities that are under surveillance, which are normally Black and Brown communities, right? And so when we got back, we didn't know what we were going to do about this. We had no clue. I just knew—I talked to a couple of WWAV's founders, and they were like, "Well shit. You gonna let it stand???? You gonna do something, *right?*" And that for me meant, "We better do something," if you know our foremothers. We also understood what it means for Black women, for trans women, to be invisible. How we're invisiblized. This law was created for white gay men—to keep gay men from having sex in the French Quarter—and then they coming for *you*, too. And it wasn't just that you are charged and it went on your ID. You could get fifteen years. It was an automatic felony conviction. So we know what criminal laws and the criminal justice system can do to the lives of people.

And so post-Katrina, we realized that we can no longer do the work that we used to do. We can *continue* that, but we also needed to think about what *this* looks like because it seems like nobody is talking about it. We're not having the conversation about what it means for structural violence to happen in the lives of Black women and trans women. It actually puts them at risk for HIV. It puts them at risk for further criminalization.[34] And mainly the reason they're involved in sex work is, "I need to eat." "I need to survive." "This minimum wage is not enough." "It's not enough for me." And so we decided that the changes were gonna have to be: *How do we grow ourselves?*

This year Women With A Vision has been around for twenty-six years. I don't know about y'all but that makes me very happy. Mainly because Black women started this organization, and it was at a time when many people didn't think that Black queer women and Black cisgender women could be in the same room and organize together. They *did*.[35] They were all born and raised in New Orleans. Some of them went to the same high schools. And to have an organization that has taken our mission and taken our work and connected it to global issues as well as national issues. All still being predominantly served and run by a queer Black woman. And taking that work where people are making the connection about what is happening in the South, what is happening in India, what is happening in Africa, because we are connected to the global sex worker network. So it is now where we have taken the work and our main focus is still all the things we used to do around public health, but more at asking people to look at what policies are being pushed in your area. What are on the back end of these policies that you think are going to save women but actually put them at risk for criminalization?[36]

Deon turned, "And so this is where the work is and I will pass it off to Shaquita—"

The emphasis Deon placed on public health was part of the segue to Shaquita's work as a researcher and practitioner. We had all heard her pass that baton many a time, always carefully carving out space for the analysis

Shaquita was about to drop. This time, there was a particular sweetness to that pass. At a deeper, more intimate level, the timeline of WWAV having to "change [our] strategy" was also the timeline of Shaquita's presence in the organization. She and Deon had become partners not long before Hurricane Katrina. After the storm, Shaquita had decided to change her career.

So how's everyone doing? Awesome. So for my part, I've probably been with WWAV for ten years? Being around the work that was happening and meeting the founders led me to change my career, which is how I really got started.

And so it occurred to me as I was doing an MPH and getting more involved in public health that WWAV had *literally* done *everything* that I was reading about—amazing programming, to work with sex workers, to work with low-income women around HIV. But WWAV's work was not documented.[37] It was something that didn't matter to them given the grassroots way that they came about. But now being on this other end in academia, I could see how documentation becomes something that is really important and legitimizes your efforts. So working with WWAV and also meeting other organizations, it just seemed like the capacity wasn't necessarily there to do this kind of work. So I started thinking about "How does WWAV begin to move our own research agenda forward?" Which is extremely important because the women that we work with are considered "unique populations" by public health. But they also have these really unique experiences that we need to begin sharing broadly and disseminating broadly.

You know, I feel like one of the problems that we have in New Orleans is that it's very hard to get any kind of data from the state, from the police.[38] So having access to our own data becomes extremely important when we're trying to make the case to funders, when we're trying to make the case to politicians. "Yes, we want data," but there's also this attention paid to "What's the moral decision?" around certain issues. So right now we're trying to look at some old arrest data for women who were charged with "crime against nature" and for women who were charged with "prostitution." And we literally are having to sit down and go over *printed* copies of the seven hundred different records that we're trying to look at. It's absolutely completely nuts.[39]

In any case, we think it's extremely important to start doing our own thing. That's how "front porch strategy" came about. I actually went to a public health gathering where different folks were talking about outcomes that folks wanted to see in their communities. We were talking about the front porch as this very uniquely southern cultural idea for folks, and as a place where people literally sit and talk about ideas that are important to them. So, for us, that drives what we feel like is a strategy that will hopefully build the capacity of not only WWAV, but also other small grassroots organizations. And build folks' social capacity and their shared understanding for the issues that they're dealing with.[40]

With that, Shaquita underscored the importance of WWAV moving our own research agenda, and concluded, "So I guess I'll turn it over to Laura—"

Shaquita and Laura had shared many an afternoon talking about research. They began their graduate school journeys at the same time, and both had strong and aligned feelings about what worked and what did not when it came to community-driven research practices. Their different academic trainings, however, often enabled them to come at these questions in complementary ways: Shaquita's theoretical grounding is in public health and Laura's is in religious studies; Shaquita has training in mixed quantitative-qualitative methods, and Laura in collaborative ethnography and oral history. "Having access to our own data" meant being able to ask and answer our own questions about the systems of violence that WWAV's communities were surviving. Those systems profited from white supremacist Christian ideas and practices that had long worked to accelerate and widen the racial capitalism playbook—all the layers of saviorism and carceral feminism that Deon had trained staff to be able to hear in the uttering of a word as seemingly simple as "victim."[41] The precision of WWAV's theory on the ground also underlined for us that the knowledge produced by southern Black women organizers should be taking up space in the academy and beyond.

How are y'all doing today? My name is Laura McTighe. I've been working with WWAV for almost a decade now. I also am a PhD candidate at Columbia University in the Department of Religion. And I think it's especially important for me to locate myself in this space today as a white woman. I've been doing community-based organizing at the intersection of HIV and criminalization since 1997—at the side of people who are moving through police lockups, jails, and prisons across our country— to amplify the strategies that they already know work to decarcerate our communities. It was in the context of that work that I first met Deon in 2008. And the first time I came to New Orleans, I was invited. I was invited by Deon to be the facilitator for the launch meeting of the coalition that took on the "Crime Against Nature" statute. Then over the next four years, I was back and forth to New Orleans every couple of months. In between, Deon and I would spend hours talking by phone. She would talk, and I would type. And now reflecting on this, I understand that what was happening in that moment was that I was being apprenticed in the twenty-six-year history of WWAV's work.

So as Quita and I both entered into graduate programs in 2011, we were asking: "What does it look like to have the type of work that we've both been privileged to be part of on the ground be what's driving academic research?" And that's a particularly dicey question to be asking as people who don't even have PhDs yet. And then we really started having to figure it out together because of another story—a story that was the follow-up to WWAV's huge constitutional victory in March of 2012. Two months later, the very violence that WWAV had organized to transform was turned against us. On May 24, 2012, WWAV's offices were firebombed and destroyed by still unknown and uninvestigated arsonists.

In the wake of that fire, we started asking three questions. First, what is so threatening about Black women's leadership? Then, what would it look like to tell a history of Black women's organizing in the Deep South where WWAV's work had a place? And, last, how would doing that change the way that we tell American history proper? We've spent the last several years trying to figure out how to answer those questions, and how to do it in a deeply collaborative way. From turning those questions into ones that could be put to an Institutional Review Board, to designing together research methodologies for how to answer those questions, to pushing back against methodologies that would say, "These stories should be anonymized, they should be stolen out of people's mouths."

And so we built this beautiful oral history project to recreate the archive that literally went up in flames. And we have been going back through every person who has touched WWAV, with a focus on their life histories. The choice of life history interviews was really important to us, because at any given moment, WWAV is the sum of all of the life experiences that gather in the rooms. Another thing that we've been doing are these collective storytelling sessions. We did the first one pretty soon after the tenth anniversary of Katrina, while the word "resilience" was being thrown around and really thrown in the face of Black residents in the city. And so we were like "What does it look like for WWAV to really engage with this word—to theorize, to retheorize, to cast off, and to talk about this with the predominantly New-Orleans-born-and-raised staff of WWAV?"[42]

Laura paused and looked down the table for Mwende to jump in next.

The story Laura was telling was the story of *Fire Dreams'* conceptualization, framing, implementation, analysis, and collective authorship. Meaning at WWAV was so often made—as we were showing at this conference—in conversation. With front porch strategy, we transformed "research" into study; we also emphasized the importance of *where* those stories were being shared. This framework had a huge impact on all of us at WWAV, like giving something a name so often does. By claiming that when we were informally gathering on the front porch, we were in fact having *strategy* sessions, we opened a new horizon of programming at WWAV. In the months following our porch talk on resilience and the #BlackFeministSanta photo shoot, Mwende grew our late afternoon porch rituals into a full Black Feminist Porch Talk series.[43] Two were coming up: first, a porch talk on Black women, representation, and Beyoncé's *Lemonade*; and second, a #SayHerName porch talk on state violence against Black women and girls. Mwende took the mic again to invite all gathered into that story:

> When I started working at WWAV, it was four people. We didn't have an office, we didn't have a front porch. And this was something that started happening really organically after we moved into the new office. Every Friday people would just start meandering onto the porch. And sometime between three and four o'clock everyone would be on the porch just sitting and talking about stuff. And we started to realize—I think Laura was the person who said: "Why aren't we recording what's being said here?" So much of what was actually informing the work that we were doing inside of our office was happening on the front porch, so we decided to actually make this into something.
>
> And in addition to the research thing, we actually started doing these Black Feminist Porch Talks. We'd literally just invite Black feminists to come sit on our porch and talk to us about Black women's issues. It's just been such an amazing experience, because I think people really identify with the simplicity and the complexity of having to come and sit on the porch and speak southern Black women's truths in a place that was really one of the few places that's ever been able to hold it.[44]

The front porch was not only a gathering point for conversation. It was also the launch point for doing the work, the foundation for building more livable futures, the place where we grew those otherwise possibilities in community. It had been so for generations. Deon, Shaquita, and Laura all nodded in agreement as Mwende sat back from the mic.

To demonstrate that power, Deon brought our front porch strategy presentation to a close with a story about a new sex worker outreach project that some of WWAV's longtime participants were taking on, in much the same spirit that Diamond had cofounded Groundworks after graduating from Emerge. That, for Deon, was the threat of Black women's leadership. The women WWAV works with are not victims; they are powerful. And "*WEEEEEE* are one."[45]

> One of the last things I'll say: Our clients never leave y'all. They come back. They put on a WWAV T-shirt. They go out into the community—women who are involved in sex work, they're like, "We're gonna talk to our own people. We're gonna talk about what it means to be a sex worker, what it means to be hungry, what it means to be a mother, what it means to be a student. We're gonna go talk to those people." And it's just amazing to see Black women stand in their leadership, because we never take it from them. We never ever say, "Poor you! Oh, it's horrible you had to sell yourself." *Nahhh*. We say, "It's nice that you were able to feed yourself. Sorry for the way it had to happen."
>
> And many people may not agree with the ways we see it, but what we do know is that we acknowledge the power that exists in women who are oppressed every day. It is amazing to see women blossom out of that. And what we've seen is women who want to give back, women who want to work at WWAV. And many of them have gone on to other careers and doing things that they never thought they would do. But just the beauty of what we've been able to create.[46]
>
> It's really what this conference is about today: "What are our truths? And how are we going to make people know them?"

With those words, she claimed the conference vision as WWAV's own, and spoke the visions of the people WWAV stands with to all who were gathered. There was a challenge in her words, but there was also an invitation. There always was. The stories that we had shared were not simply stories to be heard; they were the theory and the methodology: "To see Black women stand in their leadership, because we never take it from them."

This Is Sacred Work

Deon's words invited reflection from us all, as we gathered with the "Know Her Truths" conference attendees on a university porch that evening, and then began the journey back to New Orleans the following day. Our presentation had traced WWAV's nearly three decades of work at the intersections of Black feminist struggle in the South. We knew those stories, we worked to archive them, we lived them every day, we honored the generations who made them possible. And we shared those stories so that the work would continue to get done, no matter what. But thinking about WWAV's participants pushing off from the front porch to do sex worker outreach, thinking about Black women standing in their leadership because we never take it from them, also raised another question: How much further along will we be in thirty more years?

It is difficult to imagine, but it is also important. This is sacred work. "The fight to save your life is," as #BlackLivesMatter cofounder Patrisse Cullors has named it, "a spiritual fight."[47] How else could we term the work to refuse the reformist reform question "What do we have now and how can we make it better?" and instead to ask, in the words of Mariame Kaba, "What can we imagine for ourselves and the world?"[48] In saying this, we are *still* not giving any time or space to the white supremacist Christian ideas and practices that have greased the wheels of the racial capitalism playbook for centuries. Rather, we are lifting up the deep and enduring world-building knowledges through which our Black, Indigenous, queer, trans, womanist, feminist, and disabled kin have survived centuries of colonial, capitalist, and carceral warfare. *This* is sacred work.[49] Black women organizers have been using these liberatory practices to cross worlds, open portals, and conjure revolution for generations.[50]

When we walk in their legacies, we are able to see the new world a-coming that we are steadily building all around us. We are able to do so because the futures that we seek are already here with us. They have been for ages. This is the truth of enchantment at WWAV. That is why it matters so much to all of us to honor the community and ancestral knowledges and practices through which people have long dreamed with their eyes wide open, beyond the violence of racial capitalism—and the geographies in which they could do so. When we open the windows and doors to all these fire dreams past, when we stand in the power of the infrastructure of feeling of the Black Radical Tradition, we are also able to touch the futures we are creating in real time.

5.14 Desiree Evans, Michelle Wiley, Raven Frederick, Mwende Katwiwa, Deon Haywood, Nia Weeks, and Dianne Jones on WWAV's front porch at 1226 N. Broad Street, August 9, 2016. Photo by Laura McTighe.

This book was never simply a text to be read. It has always been a toolkit for making knowledge to serve the liberation of our communities and a call to revolutionize that knowledge into praxis in order to build the world otherwise. When we began this journey, we called you, our readers, into the process of learning with us how to unravel the racial capitalism playbook that prefigures WWAV's present. We asked that you hear—indeed, speak with us—WWAV's history in and through the stories of generations of southern Black feminist organizers. In so doing, we called you into the work of ensuring that these deeply enduring resistant visions for living and thriving otherwise—these *fire dreams*—could take place and have a space; that they could root and stay rooted.

And so we now invite you to take a seat on the front porch, to imagine with us, to share your truths, to speak the histories you honor (fig. 5.14).

How much further along will *WEEEEEE* be in thirty more years? So Be It! See to It![51]

EPILOGUE
FORWARD EVER

You cannot, you cannot use someone else's fire. You can only use your own.
And in order to do that, you must first be willing to believe that you have it.
—Audre Lorde, *I Am Your Sister*

On the evening of Friday, December 6, 2019, the WWAV family gathered with our community at Latrobe's on Royale for our Thirtieth Anniversary Gala. Staff were all dressed in gowns and tuxes that sparkled in shades of the WWAV deep purple, with gold, turquoise, and lime accents to match. Community from across the country—longtime leaders in Black reproductive justice, HIV liberation, harm reduction, drug decriminalization, and sex worker organizing—poured in to join all our local partners at these intersections. There were signature drinks, photo stations, areas to share stories. The New Orleans Baby Dolls were even in attendance, with custom-made second line umbrellas bearing the WWAV logo and signature colors, and the Pinettes, New Orleans's only all-woman brass band, were due to make an appearance before the night was over. The awards ceremony lifted up the work of three of our local "sheroes": the "Hustle Hard Award" went to Ashley Hill Hamilton, founder of The Uptown Doula; Ashley Shelton, director of the

Power Coalition for Equity and Justice, was given the "Visionary Award"; and the "Freedom Fighter Award" went to Ursula Price, director of the New Orleans Workers' Center for Racial Justice. Before the dance floor opened again, Deon took the mic to address us all:

> This celebration was intentional. We deserved to get dressed up. We deserved to feel pretty. We deserved to come together in celebration of liberation and justice. All of the work we do comes from being in community. To you, our community, our supporters, our friends, our family: WE LOVE YOU!

As a gift to WWAV, Andrea Ritchie and Laura produced a full-color report and a video for the occasion, with support from our staff and foremothers, Carol McDonald, and Angélique Roché. *Our Existence Is Political* traced WWAV's thirty years of Black feminist struggle: the interlocking gears of the analysis, the methods for doing the work, the people who set the vision into motion, and the people who carried it forward today.[1] The cover featured an illustration of that 2001 photograph of Danita, Catherine, and Deon with red AIDS ribbons in their hands, which had accompanied the article on their groundbreaking harm reduction outreach methods, by and for Black southerners, in the *Source* (fig. E.1).[2]

To write the *Our Existence Is Political* anniversary report, Andrea and Laura drew on the oral history interviews, porch talks, speeches, and writings we had gathered and produced through our research as survival in the first four years following the arson attack, from 2012 to 2016. But the anniversary report also exceeded these sources; it had to. In the three years since, WWAV's work had grown exponentially. Reproductive justice was now a dedicated program, and the sex worker and drug user communities with whom we stand showed us how RJ needed to intersect with all our anticriminalization work. As 2016 drew to a close, we were on the front lines of a massive statewide organizing project to dethrone Louisiana from its dubious title as the "incarceration capital of the world" and bring thousands of our loved ones home. Deon and Christine held the WWAV position in this coalition fight, ensuring that the policy reforms signed into law in mid-2017 took meaningful steps toward ending the criminalization of Black cisgender and transgender women and femmes. Furthering this decarceration work at the county jail level, WWAV was the New Orleans partner to the national 2017 and 2018 Mama's Day Bail Outs organized by Southerners on New Ground and the National Bail Out collective. Through this labor of love, WWAV was

Women With A Vision
Our Existence is Political:
30 Years of Black Feminist Struggle

E.1 The cover of the WWAV 30th-anniversary report, coauthored by Laura McTighe and Andrea Ritchie, with Women With A Vision, 2019. Illustrations by Whitney Rivers; design by Iván Arenas.

able to pay bail for several Black mothers and caregivers awaiting trial so they could be home with their families. Michelle Wiley and Dianne Jones also relaunched our harm reduction outreach work, serving as our eyes and ears to street-based policing and surveillance. Behind the scenes, we were crafting policy to further unravel the power of the police and courts through a dedicated focus on sex work decriminalization, which we were growing in partnership with national and international movements for sex workers' rights. This work was buttressed by the groundswell of grassroots community organizing that WWAV had been sustaining in New Orleans and statewide through our Integrated Voter Engagement program, headed by the core program team of Raven Frederick and Elyse Degree and supported by dozens of outreach workers. This network was precisely what we leveraged when WWAV was asked to spearhead efforts to build an HIV strategy for the state of Louisiana in 2019 for bringing new infections to zero by naming and transforming the lethal operations of racial capitalism in our daily lives and communities. It almost seemed absurd that we had sat on WWAV's Broad Street front porch in 2016, asking, *How much further along will we be in thirty more years?* Could we have even imagined where we would be in three?

There was a rightful and righteous sense of awe here. Awe, simply put, at how much WWAV had been able to do. But that awe was not an arms-length, hero-worship sort of awe. It was the awe that comes from honoring what the work is and how it has always been done. For more than thirty years, WWAV has just kept acting, in Angela Davis's words, "as if it were possible to radically transform the world."[3] We have done so by working with fire, by claiming our power and claiming one another. And we have kept doing it day after day after day after day. There was no roadmap for this work. What our foremothers shared was a vision for liberation and a commitment to making that vision a reality. From a front porch in Central City New Orleans in 1989, they set out to build a world that was more survivable than the present. It was intimate work. Their relationships carried the movement. To do the work, they did not need to have the answers. How could they? The answers had not been written yet, because they had not been on *these* grounds before, making *this* knowledge to serve the liberation of their communities. Our foremothers' commitment to one another and to the work was simply and profoundly to continue to walk together to figure those answers out. That is how our foremothers grew futures with all the beauty that life should hold. Staying true to their vision is precisely how we made it to thirty years of WWAV (fig. E.2).

WWAV is alive in us—through the belief that the world must be otherwise and the precision of building relationships; through the fire of doing revolutionary work and the spirit of experimentation that infuses it all; through the invitation that is always open and the knowledge that we, too, will be transformed in the work. That is what Deon passed to staff, participants, and accomplices, nationally and globally, during those years in exile after the fire. She helped us all learn how to adjust our eyes so we could see the possibilities already flickering around us, to join the people in our own corners of the world who were already creating liberatory futures in real time, and to make more and more still. In this way, there is nothing surprising about how much further along WWAV was after three more years. Our awe is a respect for WWAV's methods. The theory on the ground that the WWAV family has steadily been making—about sex work decriminalization, reproductive justice, HIV liberation, and building the political power of poor Black women and girls—has exploded the sense of what even we

E.2 Michelle Wiley keeping the traditions of our foremothers alive by teaching Deon Haywood's grandson Brandon Haywood Jr. how to make harm reduction packets. Photo courtesy of WWAV Archives.

thought was possible. And nevertheless, we could see the through lines. We could see how every new facet of the work being done in these years built on decades—indeed, generations—of organizing, even while each also forged a new and uncharted path to freedom.

Sex worker organizing was at the core. Our unapologetic, unwavering commitment to harm reduction and sex workers' health had begun in the early days of the AIDS epidemic, and had expanded to include a policy focus after Hurricane Katrina through the NO Justice Project. That win made possible our work to divert diversion after the fire through the Emerge program, as we continued to support sex workers in standing in their own leadership, refusing the perniciousness of carceral feminism, and creating visions for their own liberation. We worked to spatialize those visions in New Orleans in 2017 and again in 2018 when we hosted our second annual Black and Brown Sex Worker Second Line on December 15 (fig. E.3), the annual International

E.3 Raven Frederick and Elyse Degree in their "Sex Work Is Political" T-shirts, holding red umbrellas before the second annual Black and Brown Sex Worker Second Line begins on the International Day to End Violence Against Sex Workers, December 15, 2018. Photo courtesy of WWAV Archives.

Day to End Violence Against Sex Workers, culminating under the Claiborne "bridge" (of the Interstate 10 overpass) with tables full of the resources our communities needed. Behind the scenes, we were also steadily growing our sex worker liberation work toward new horizons.

In the spring of 2021, WWAV unveiled our Deep South Decrim Project. This project was made possible by working from the core principles that had grounded our work for decades: centering sex workers' leadership, challenging the conflation of sex work with sex trafficking, refusing criminalization in all forms, moving nonreformist reforms through the legislature to unravel the policies of white supremacist dispossession, and living into a vision for

Black women's liberation. The release of the toolkit *Deep South Decrim: Towards Sex Work Decriminalization and Justice in Louisiana* coincided with the founding of our Sex Worker Advisory Committee during the height of the COVID-19 pandemic and the reintroduction of a model bill in the 2021 Louisiana legislative session to fully decriminalize sex work.[4] We brought hundreds of sex workers to the state capitol to testify about the violences of criminalization in their lives. Meanwhile, billboards erected statewide proclaimed the abolitionist vision of this work: "No Jail for Any Job: Decriminalize Sex Work" (fig. E.4).

The movement to defund the police and abolish prisons had exploded nationwide in the wake of George Floyd's murder by Minneapolis Police in May 2020. For all of us at WWAV, the commitment to abolition as both a vision and a practice was always already rooted in our relationships and our deep livingness with one another. As the *Deep South Decrim* toolkit made clear, "Our abolitionist perspective demands that we dismantle interlocking systems of oppression in their entirety while investing in the ongoing safety and success of those most marginalized. Decriminalization of sex work is one of the many ways we are advocating for freedom, justice, and liberation for all."[5] This vision to "dismantle . . . while investing" grew quite literally from the "Safety and Love" seed that we planted on the WWAV front porch, back in the spring of 2016.[6] That vision was blooming because it was rooted in the unapologetic and unwavering trust we place in Black women's leadership, knowledges, and power to build the intersectional, liberatory systems we need. And it was watered daily, like everything WWAV did, by continuing to work together to free ourselves.

WWAV staff across program areas took on myriad support roles during the years of moving this decriminalization work forward. That was out of necessity. As of the writing of this epilogue in 2022, on the tenth anniversary of the arson attack, Deon is now a two-time breast cancer survivor. She was first diagnosed in July 2016 and then again in August 2019. Deon undertook these fights, in the words of the late Audre Lorde, as "an act of political warfare."[7] And she asked us all to be there with her—learning, growing, sharing, and fighting at her side (fig. E.5). True to WWAV's vision and practice, she began recording short videos to share her journey to healing—first from the porch, then from her couch. By choosing to make her own journey public, she also "collectivized" her experience.[8] She rendered visible the intimate and everyday violence of the health care system. She did so by contextualizing the particular forms of intimate, community, and state violence she experi-

E.4 The Deep South Decrim billboard in New Orleans, 2021, which reads, "No Jail for Any Job: Decriminalize Sex Work." Photo courtesy of WWAV Archives.

E.5 Deon Haywood seated at center, surrounded by WWAV's cofounders and staff, all wearing "Fuck Cancer" shirts, middle fingers up, August 21, 2016. Photo courtesy of WWAV Archives.

enced while accessing breast cancer treatment within the histories of medical abuse, neglect, and criminalization that Black women have long faced in America. She also refused the invisibilization of Black people, thicc people, and lesbians in the white supremacist, heteronormative educational materials that were available. As she unapologetically chose her own living and thriving, she also taught us all how to do so: by resting, by claiming joy, by putting herself and her family first, by allowing herself to just be, whatever that meant on a given day.

Deon reflected at many points about how much she had learned from women living with HIV about how to navigate health care systems that were never made for you by taking your education into your own hands. And her fight sharpened WWAV's commitment to again put HIV liberation at the center of our work. Another through line. In 2018, WWAV was asked to lead the state of Louisiana in building a strategic plan for Ending the HIV Epidemic (EtE).[9] We launched the project in January 2019 with the newest additions to our WWAV staff team: Jenny Holl, who came to us with a background in public health, and Charles Haywood, Deon's younger brother, who had been raised in WWAV's outreach model and was himself a person living with HIV. Charles and Jenny took charge of the program before a packed auditorium in Lafayette in early 2019. After a daylong meeting that identified key barriers, opportunities, and threats to this work, they were tasked with drafting a racially just EtE strategic plan that was grounded in human rights principles. To do so, they built relationships with health care providers, with public health officials, with staff from community organizations, and most especially with people living with HIV. Where did Charles and Jenny gather? On the front porch, of course (fig. E.6). As with all our post-homecoming work, building an EtE plan for Louisiana rested on and extended Black women's leadership in movements for liberation well beyond our state. Most obviously, we were guided by and accountable to the "Declaration of Liberation" developed by the United States HIV Racial Justice Now network, of which WWAV is a founding steering committee member.[10] But we also undertook our EtE work amid some of the biggest attacks on reproductive justice that our country had witnessed in decades. Our HIV work, RJ work, and anticriminalization work were all interconnected. They always had been.

In May 2019, we delivered a ten-point platform for abortion justice to the Louisiana State Legislature, in partnership with the New Orleans Abortion Fund, the New Orleans Workers' Center for Racial Justice, the New Orleans

E.6 The flyer to join WWAV's Ending the Epidemic (EtE) program, featuring Charles Haywood and Jenny Holl on the front porch at 1226 N. Broad Street, March 27, 2019. Subsequent program flyers announced the start of the traveling EtE statewide porch talks. Flyer by Jenny Holl.

People's Assembly, Black Youth Project 100, and the New Orleans Hospitality Alliance. That kicked off a week of solidarity actions to oppose abortion bans and stop the attacks on reproductive justice. Getting signs ready was a family affair (figs. E.7–E.8).

It would be more than a year until the US Supreme Court would finally declare that Louisiana's "admitting privileges" bill, which would have reduced the number of abortion clinics in the state from three to one, was unconstitutional. It was a judicial ruling, just like the NO Justice win, that only made sense in community. That analysis needed to be shared, and Deon needed the WWAV team's support to do so. By March 2020, our country was on COVID lockdown and Deon was again fighting for her life. And so she spoke her vision aloud to staff, so that they could craft an email blast claiming this victory with her words:

E.7 Bailey "Bunny" Haywood, Deon Haywood's granddaughter, works on a sign that reads, "HANDS OFF MY BODY." Photo courtesy of WWAV Archives.

Who said Black queer women don't lead? This is what it means for Black queer women to lead. To be steadfast and unwavering in our beliefs and to continue to fight for them and never give up. To work to make change in our communities and then to take it one step further, to the state level, the national level, and even the international level. We must continue to fight and never give up. Our fight is for Black queer women AND our fight is for everyone. *Forward Ever.*[11]

Deon's words were ablaze with a fire that was much bigger than this victory. It was the fire that she knew in herself, the fire of Black queer women's leadership, the fire of more than thirty years of doing the work, the fire of all the dreams long sheltered in these hallowed grounds, the fire of what we could make in thirty more if we kept coming together and doing the work.

E.8 Jaliyah Davis, Deon Haywood's niece, works on a sign that reads, "You're NOT stopping abortions. You're just stopping them from being SAFE." Photo courtesy of WWAV Archives.

Two years later, as we approached the tenth anniversary of the arson attack in 2022, documented COVID-related deaths in the United States surpassed one million. In March, we gathered two of our steadiest touchstones, mentors, and friends—mother of the reproductive justice movement Loretta Ross, and historian and activist Mary Frances Berry—for a conversation on "Where Do We Go from Here?" (fig. E.9). Our table talk that evening was livestreamed to gather close our people, both far and near, to reflect together on the attacks on reproductive justice we knew were coming, the stakes of the midterm elections, and the truth that again and always, *history teaches us to resist*.[12]

On the evening of May 11, our country was sent into a spin when a leaked draft opinion revealed that the US Supreme Court could be on the cusp of eliminating the constitutional right to abortion, and states across the South made haste to expand the systems of criminalization already in place by in-

E.9 Mary Frances Berry, Deon Haywood, and Loretta Ross seated around the table in Deon's office following the "Where Do We Go from Here?" conversation, March 5, 2022. Photo courtesy of WWAV Archives.

troducing bills that would classify abortion as homicide. Three days later, while our New Orleans community was gathered in tandem with millions nationwide for a day of local actions against abortion bans, a white supremacist terrorist murdered ten Black people in a Buffalo grocery store. Then on May 24, the ten-year anniversary of the arson attack, a gunman murdered nineteen Latinx children and two Latinx teachers in a Texas school.

We know this place.[13] Like the arson attack on our offices, none of these acts of violence was an isolated event at an isolated moment in time. The forces that drove the arsonists who set fire to WWAV are the very same ones driving these attacks on bodily autonomy and on life itself. We know that these are precisely the times when hope can seem a near impossible discipline to practice. And we also know that the work will continue to get done no matter what. As people living through these times, we must grieve and rage and do whatever we need to do to refuse this terror being wielded against us. And as organizers, we also must talk to our people. We need to be one with our community, to know who each other are, to learn from those who have already been fighting back. The racial capitalism playbook works by dismembering and disappearing our communities. That is why we have to get closer, and closer still. It is the only way we can protect one another and provide sanctuary, just like our foremothers have always done; it is also the only way we will be strong enough to work with fire and continue to build together the world that must be.

Deon often reminds people that "at WWAV, we understood a long time ago that we are the outlier, the radical, the come-to, the gonna-bring-all-the-weapons-to-fight organization here in Louisiana and throughout the South."[14] The vision is clear. The invitation is open.

Forward Ever.

NOTES

Introduction: Born in Flames

1   At the time of the arson attack, Norman C. Francis Parkway was still named Jefferson Davis Parkway. In August 2020, following sustained protests in the wake of George Floyd's murder by the Minneapolis Police Department, the New Orleans City Council unanimously voted to rename this street in honor of Dr. Francis, a Black educator and institution builder whose vision transformed Xavier University of Louisiana during his tenure as president from 1968 to 2015.

2   Throughout this book, we mirror the intentional (non)capitalization of names that activists themselves use.

3   Deon Haywood recounted this story during her presentation at the Know Her Truths: Advancing Justice for Women and Girls of Color Conference organized by the Anna Julia Cooper Center at Wake Forest University on April 29, 2016. See Haywood et al., "Front Porch Strategy: Organizing for Black Women's Lives at the Intersection of Service, Activism, and Research"; Speeches, Presentations, and Writings in the Born in Flames Living Archive.

4   Haywood et al., "Front Porch Strategy."

5   The first three layers of this playbook map onto Beth Richie's discussion in *Arrested Justice* of the intersections among intimate, community, and state violence against Black women, or what she calls the "violence matrix" (133).

6   In describing this as a "racial capitalism playbook," we are building on and contributing to generations of collective work rooted in a commitment to Black liberation. Since the first usage of "racial capitalism" by anti-apartheid activists in South Africa to its elaboration by political theorist Cedric J. Robinson (*Black Marxism*, 1983), the concept has underlined the interlocking relationships between race and class in global capitalism. We specifically draw

on Ruth Wilson Gilmore's "Abolition Geography and the Problem of Innocence," which helps us understand the connections among what she calls "racial capitalism's dramatically scaled cycles of place-making" (266), as well as how criminalization functions in each cycle by naturalizing certain people, bodies, ways of being, and forms of life as always already out of place.

7 In emphasizing the continuities among these historically changing and nevertheless interconnected systems of racial capitalism, and also emphasizing the precarity of these systems in the face of the constant rebellion by Native Americans, Africans, Afro-Creoles, and African Americans, we are building on the work of Clyde Woods, especially his contribution to Woods, Camp, and Pulido, *Development Drowned and Reborn*, and carrying forward the stories that have long circulated among Black and Indigenous peoples in the Louisiana Gulf Coast. We will return to these systems in chapter 1. We also take inspiration from Rashauna Johnson's meticulous reconstruction of enslaved people's social and cultural worlds in antebellum New Orleans in *Slavery's Metropolis*, and Jessica Marie Johnson's history of how Black women in the Atlantic world, and in New Orleans specifically, used their intimate and kinship ties to develop a practice of freedom that laid the groundwork for nineteenth-century emancipation struggles in *Wicked Flesh*.

8 As Saidiya Hartman writes in *Lose Your Mother*, "I, too, am the afterlife of slavery" (6).

9 Joseph Canizaro, one of New Orleans's wealthiest developers, quoted in Rivlin, "Mogul Who Would Rebuild New Orleans." See also Saulny, "Clamoring to Come Home to New Orleans Projects."

10 We revisit "otherwise" in greater theoretical depth at the end of this introduction. What is important to underline now is that the "otherwise" is not something to speculate or abstractly imagine. It is already *here* with us.

11 Women With A Vision, "Rebuilding Our Archive"; Speeches, Presentations, and Writings in the Born in Flames Living Archive.

12 Sharpe, *In the Wake*, 13. We discuss the theories and methods we made together in the second half of the introduction. At this point, we want to note that we have chosen to use real names throughout this book (except when stated otherwise) as a practice of our research as survival and a refusal of the erasure willed against us.

13 We trace this history of violence against Black women back through Jim Crow terror with the support of Danielle L. McGuire's *At the Dark End of the Street*, and back through chattel slavery with Angela Davis's "Reflections on the Black Woman's Role in the Community of Slaves." Our Black Feminist Library includes many more histories and biographies of Black women's organizing in the South and across the nation, with focuses on reparations, mutual aid, anticriminalization work, housing advocacy, and other interlocking struggles. We explore this library in depth in chapter 4.

14 Rodney, *Grounding with My Brothers*, xi; see especially the introduction to the 2019 edition by Carole Boyce-Davies.

15 See, e.g., Berry, *My Face Is Black Is True*; Ritchie, *Invisible No More*; Kaba, *We Do This 'til We Free Us*; Kaba and Ritchie, *No More Police*; Ransby, *Ella Baker and the Black Freedom Movement*; Cohen, *Democracy Remixed*; Cohen, "Punks, Bulldaggers, and Welfare Queens"; Haley, *No Mercy Here*; Gore, *Radicalism at the Crossroads*; Thuma, *All Our Trials*.

16 Kelley, "We Are Not What We Seem," in *Race Rebels*, 78.

17 See especially McKittrick and Woods, "No One Knows the Mysteries at the Bottom of the Ocean"; and Katz, "Bad Elements."

18 The phrase "interlocking systems of oppression" was introduced by the Black feminist Combahee River Collective in their 1977 "Combahee River Collective Statement" and further developed as "intersectionality" by Kimberlé Crenshaw in "Demarginalizing the Intersection of Race and Sex" and "Mapping the Margins." The triad of "white supremacy, patriarchy, and bigotry" is one that Desiree Evans advanced as part of the porch talk that grounds chapter 1. See "Resilience"; Collective Storytelling Sessions in the Born in Flames Living Archive.

19 Kelley, *Freedom Dreams*, 2.

20 Kelley, *Freedom Dreams*; A. Davis, *Freedom Is a Constant Struggle*; Imarisha and brown, *Octavia's Brood*.

21 We call this "a meeting at the crossroads" to underline its power for our foremothers and the boundary they crossed together. In many Black religious traditions, the crossroads symbolizes a mystical barrier that separates the material world from that of the ancestors and the divine. A meeting at the crossroads thus conjures the presence of generations past, just as it opens pathways toward new futures for what must become.

22 Centers for Disease Control and Prevention, "Mortality Attributable to HIV Infection among Persons Aged 25–44 Years."

23 We will return to this point in chapter 2, using Ruth Wilson Gilmore's definition of racism from *Golden Gulag*: "the state-sanctioned and/or legal production and exploitation of group-differentiated vulnerabilities to premature death, in distinct yet densely interconnected political geographies" (28).

24 Center for Constitutional Rights, "Just a Talking Crime." We discuss these statistics, as well as the tremendous research that the NO Justice legal team undertook to produce them, in chapter 3.

25 See, for example, Haywood, "OUR WIN"; Speeches, Letters, and Writings in the Born in Flames Living Archive. For the decision, see Center for Constitutional Rights, "Judge Rules That Sex-Offender Registration for 'Crime Against Nature by Solicitation' Convictions Is Unconstitutional." See also Alexis Agathocleous's "When Power Yields to Justice" and "Building a

Movement for Justice"; and Andrea Ritchie's "Crimes Against Nature" and *Invisible No More.*

26 See Kaba and Ritchie, *No More Police*; A. Davis et al., *Abolition. Feminism. Now.*; Bierria, Caruthers, and Lober, *Abolition Feminisms Vol. 1* and *Abolition Feminisms Vol. 2*; and Bernstein, "Sexual Politics of the 'New Abolitionism.'" We intentionally specify the Black feminist and abolition feminist lineages we work in due to the co-optation of "abolitionism" by anti–sex work activists. See, e.g., Bernstein, "The Sexual Politics of the 'New Abolitionism.'"

27 These words were spoken by Desiree Evans during the porch talk that grounds chapter 1. See "Resilience"; Collective Storytelling Sessions in the Born in Flames Living Archive.

28 Their work around HIV criminalization in Philadelphia in the early 2000s is the focus of McTighe, "Our Relationships Carry the Movement." See also McTighe, Shabazz-El, and Miller, "Refusing to Vanish."

29 This structural approach brings into focus the immediate and long-term health impacts of incarceration's sustained destruction of familial bonds, social support systems, economic relations, and more. Rucker Johnson and Steven Raphael ("Effects of Male Incarceration," 2009) were among the first to show that the structural link among race, imprisonment, and HIV is so strong that it almost completely explains the disproportionate impact of HIV in the Black community. See also Fullilove, "African Americans, Health Disparities and HIV/AIDS."

30 McTighe, "Project UNSHACKLE."

31 In his keywords essay "Affect," Joshua Javier Guzmán explores the power of relational bonds through a beautiful reading of Lizzie Borden's film *Born in Flames* (1983), emphasizing the "textured ways we come to know about each other's suffering—the *sensing* of commonality—while transmitting a willful desire to feel the world differently" (16, emphasis in original). See Guzmán, "Affect" in *Keywords for Gender and Sexuality Studies*. As Audre Lorde taught us, this is the power of the erotic, of love between women.

32 We titled the oral history project "Born in Flames" because this was a core slogan of our rebuilding after the arson attack; it was also a shout-out to Lizzie Borden's film of the same name. We discuss in the next section of the introduction how this oral history project grew into the Born in Flames Living Archive, which fills this book.

33 Lorde, "Uses of the Erotic" in *Sister Outsider.*

34 Ewing, "Mariame Kaba."

35 Anzaldúa, "New Speakers" in *The Gloria Anzaldúa Reader*, 24–25.

36 In chapter 2, we discuss this principle of solidarity at WWAV through a lesson from Deon on how and why "*WEEEEEE* are one." We further explore the complexities of difference in this solidarity in chapter 4.

37 See Roseann Liu and Savannah Shange's "Toward Thick Solidarity." We also appreciate how they experiment with a "polyvocal *us*" in the essay Shange and Liu, "Solidarity-as-Debt," inviting readers to step in and out of their linked yet distinct subject positions.

38 Karen Fields's "What One Cannot Remember Mistakenly," written with her grandmother Mamie Garvin Fields, is a model of precisely the kinds of intergenerational and extra-academic modes of analysis and expertise that we are valuing and centering through our practice of collective authorship in this book.

39 Kaba and Hassan, *Fumbling towards Repair*, 67.

40 See the Born in Flames Living Archive collection of sources at the conclusion of this book, and explore the archive online at borninflames.com. Excerpts from the Born in Flames Living Archive are included in each chapter in the porch talks, life history interviews, speeches, and writings that we quote at length, as well as in the photographs and flyers that are woven throughout. See chapter 5 for a deeper discussion of the theory and method of the living archive's assemblage.

41 Harney and Moten, *Undercommons*, 98.

42 Katherine McKittrick's "On Plantations, Prisons, and a Black Sense of Place" is a model for us in tracing systems of violence without reproducing the analytical terms of our current order.

43 Ruth Wilson Gilmore's "Fatal Couplings of Power and Difference" guides our theorization of nurturing life-giving connections and severing fatal ones, as well as our insistence that by centering communities most vulnerable to the racial capitalism playbook, we can develop new strategies for organizing for liberation, our counter-playbook.

44 McTighe, with Women With A Vision, "Theory on the Ground."

45 "Grounded theory" is an inductive research methodology widely practiced in the social sciences. First developed by Barney Glaser and Anselm Strauss (*Discovery of Grounded Theory*, 1967), grounded theory prescribes a dynamic and cyclical process of conducting research, coding data, developing conceptual categories, and generating theory.

46 This dual commitment grounds Beth Richie's *Arrested Justice* (127–28). We also take inspiration from the Combahee River Collective, "The Combahee River Collective Statement"; Moraga and Anzaldúa, *This Bridge Called My Back*; Crenshaw, "Mapping the Margins"; Collins, *Black Feminist Thought*; Higginbotham, "African-American Women's History and the Metalanguage of Race."

47 Our work is unapologetically aligned with the politics of Black women's studies. As Akasha (Gloria T.) Hull and Barbara Smith write in their introduction to *But Some of Us Are Brave*, "Black women's studies must consider as primary the knowledge that will save Black women's lives." In this commitment, they distinguish Black women's studies from what they describe

as the reification of white male thought: "coldly 'objective' scholarship that changes nothing" (xxv). The pages of *But Some of Us Are Brave* gather essays, bibliographies, and syllabi of Black feminist thought, showing precisely what these foremothers mean when they insist that "research/criticism is not an academic/intellectual game," but rather "a pursuit with social meanings rooted in the 'real world'" in which the personal is political and the scholarly stance is engaged (193). See Hull, Bell-Scott, and Smith, eds., *All the Women Are White, All the Blacks Are Men, But Some of Us Are Brave*.

We also have many touchstones in the story-driven methods of our research as survival. Patricia J. Williams's autobiographical *The Alchemy of Race and Rights* has long been a model for illuminating the intersections of race, gender, and class through personal reflection. Likewise, Katherine McKittrick's *Dear Science and Other Stories* centers Black storytelling and stories as strategies of invention and collaboration for living outside prevailing knowledge systems. We also take inspiration from the participatory action research done by and for abolitionist organizers, including Young Women's Empowerment Project's *Girls Do What They Have to Do to Survive* and BreakOUT!'s *We Deserve Better*.

48 McKittrick, "Mathematics Black Life," 18.

49 Our thinking on intimacies has developed in conversation with Lisa Lowe's *Intimacies on Four Continents* and Micol Seigel's *Violence Work*.

50 Thomas, *Exceptional Violence*, 230–38.

51 In tracing these intimate registers of organized resistance, we are thinking of Cedric J. Robinson's short chapter "The Nature of the Black Radical Tradition" in *Black Marxism*, especially his discussion of landed struggle and spiritual imaginaries.

52 As Saidiya Hartman writes in *Lose Your Mother*, "If the ghost of slavery still haunts our present, it is because we are still looking for an exit from the prison" (133).

53 See A. Davis, "Reflections on the Black Woman's Role in the Community of Slaves"; and Haley, *No Mercy Here*, chapter 5.

54 This labor also calls to mind Judith Casselberry's concept of "spiritual labor" in *Labors of Faith*, her ethnography of Black women in the Church of Our Lord Jesus Christ of the Apostolic Faith Inc. in Harlem, which helpfully reorients our well-worn attention to agency in the study of Black religion. It further recalls Marla F. Frederick's *Between Sundays*, a careful study of "spirituality" in the lives of Black religious women in the rural South as the space through which social conditions are understood, interpreted, and reshaped.

55 McKittrick, *Demonic Grounds*, xxvi.

56 In conceptualizing time in this way, we are indebted to Deborah Thomas's "Time and the Otherwise," in which she describes time as "neither as linear

nor cyclical, but as simultaneous, where the future, past, and present are mutually constitutive and have the potential to be coincidentally influential" (177).

57 Alexander, *Pedagogies of Crossing*, 14.

58 Walker, *In Search of Our Mothers' Gardens*, xi. We are grateful to Judith Weisenfeld for reflecting to us this connection with Walker's definition.

59 Woods, "Katrina's World," 430.

60 Thomas, "Time and the Otherwise."

61 Our work here builds on that of Shana M. griffin and other members of the INCITE! New Orleans chapter, who organized tirelessly after the storm to ensure that any community plan for rebuilding had a gender analysis and a demand for community accountability. See Bierria, Liebenthal, and INCITE! Women of Color Against Violence, "To Render Ourselves Visible"; griffin, "An Unfragmented Movement"; griffin, "The Women of New Orleans after Katrina"; and griffin, "The Politics of Reproductive Violence." We also stand in solidarity with New Orleans education activists like Ashana Bigard, who taught everyone in our movements during her July 18, 2015, testimony at the African American Policy Forum's "Breaking the Silence" town hall: "To buy into the narrative of the [charter school] experiment, you need to buy into the idea that Black women are complicit in the under-education of Black children."

62 Campt, *Listening to Images*, 17. The idea of "prefigurative politics," as well as the term itself, has its roots in the anarchist and antiauthoritarian traditions, first gaining visibility with the revolutionary social movements that blossomed after 1968 and then again with the post-1999 movements opposing neoliberal globalization.

63 We return to #MyExistenceIsPolitical as core WWAV theory on the ground in chapter 5.

64 Gumbs, "Are You Afraid of Black Feminists?"

65 In realizing this method on the page, Aimee Meredith Cox's *Shapeshifters* has been an uncompromising model.

66 The term "misogynoir" was coined by Moya Bailey in 2010 to name the particular intersection of anti-Black racism and misogyny in Black cisgender and transgender women's lives, especially in digital culture spaces. In her 2021 book *Misogynoir Transformed*, Bailey explores this groundbreaking concept, as well as the world-building work of Black women's digital resistance.

67 Indigenous Action Media, "Accomplices Not Allies."

68 Audra Simpson's *Mohawk Interruptus* has helped shape a decade of scholarship on "the politics of refusal." We are especially moved by our friend and comrade Savannah Shange's work of refusal in "Black Girl Ordinary."

69 Essential works for us include Ashon Crawley's *Blackpentecostal Breath* and the *Otherwise Worlds* volume coedited by Tiffany Lethabo King, Jenell Navarro,

and Andrea Smith. Laura did foundational work on this concept in the "An Otherwise Anthropology" collection she coedited and coconvened with Megan Raschig.

70 Crawley, "Otherwise, Ferguson," emphasis in original.

71 On this incitement to "worldmaking," see Dorinne K. Kondo's *Worldmaking*; and Adom Getachew's *Worldmaking after Empire*.

72 See, for example, Weisenfeld, *New World A-Coming*. In thinking about sound in this way, we emphasize the ethics of listening and refuse long-standing post-Enlightenment sensory preoccupations that elevated sight as the sense of domination and degraded hearing as a site of submission (e.g., to be filled with sound). See Hirschkind, *Ethical Soundscape*.

73 Bambara, "What It Is I Think I'm Doing Anyhow."

74 Our respect for concealment and refusal of visibility here aligns with what Édouard Glissant has called "the right to opacity." See Glissant, *Poetics of Relation*.

75 Elizabeth Povinelli's *The Cunning of Recognition* attunes us to the ways in which the modern project of liberal multiculturalism extends colonial legacies of power by demanding that Black and Indigenous people identify with and perform impossible standards of so-called authentic traditional culture in order to gain state recognition. In McTighe and Haywood, "Front Porch Revolution," Laura and Deon examine this "cunning of recognition" through the post-Katrina commodification and parading of Black New Orleanian culture amid the organized abandonment of the city's Black geographies and Black people. See also Thomas, *Desire and Disaster in New Orleans*.

76 See borninflames.com.

77 In *Time and the Other*, Johannes Fabian explores the denial of coevalness, which he terms "allochronism," to illuminate how anthropologists create a temporal distance between the observer and the observed, between the West and the rest, thereby naturalizing the time of the West as now/real, and the time of the rest as past/primitive.

78 We use "provincializing" as a critical method developed by postcolonial scholars such as Dipesh Chakrabarty (*Provincializing Europe*) and Talal Asad (*Genealogies of Religion*) to call attention to the ways in which settler colonial understandings (in our case, of the new New Orleans) are generalized as universal theories in ways that "other" the experiences of the colonized.

Chapter 1: Front Porch Strategy

Portions of this chapter originally appeared in Laura McTighe, with Deon Haywood, "Front Porch Revolution: Resilience Space, Demonic Grounds, and the Horizons of a Black Feminist Otherwise," *Signs: Journal of Women in Culture and Society* 44, no. 1 (2018): 25–52, https://doi.org/10.1086/698276.

1   WWAV friend and NO Justice Project legal team member Bill Quigley has put together an annual "Katrina Pain Index" to illustrate who has benefited and who continues to suffer after the storm (see guides.wpunj.edu/pain_index). These figures are from the 2016 index, which emphasized the widening race and class gap in New Orleans.

2   Deon explained this during her speech at the 2013 Solidarity Rally for Trayvon Martin in New Orleans. Her words echoed ones offered by Kwame Ture during his 1971 "From Black Power to Pan-Africanism" lecture at Whittier College: "When you see people call themselves revolutionary always talking about destroying, destroying, destroying but never talking about building or creating, they're not revolutionary. They do not understand the first thing about revolution. It's creating." See Deon Haywood, "This Day, We Use Our Energy for Revolution"; Speeches, Presentations, and Writings in the Born in Flames Living Archive.

3   This criticism is not absent in the literature and has driven studies of community resilience, including among public health and mental health researchers after Katrina (e.g., Norris, Stevens, and Pfefferbaum, "Community Resilience"). Nonetheless, this literature still often fails to account for, much less prescribe interventions against, interlocking systems of oppression. A notable exception is Black feminist medical anthropology on resilience, within which Leith Mullings and Alaka Wali's *Stress and Resilience* remains a foundational text.

4   Richie, *Arrested Justice*, 133.

5   This foundational theory on the ground is the focus of chapter 2.

6   Our attention to Black women's premature deaths here builds on Ruth Wilson Gilmore's definition of racism from *Golden Gulag*: "the state-sanctioned or extralegal production and exploitation of group-differentiated vulnerability to premature death" (261). We work closely with her definition in chapter 2.

7   We have been grateful to many accomplices over the years for underlining this truth and helping us imagine beyond it. Katherine McKittrick and Clyde Woods's *Black Geographies* has been an important touchstone for us.

8   Woods, "Do You Know What It Means to Miss New Orleans?," 1005. See also Woods, *Development Drowned and Reborn*; Katz, "Bad Elements."

9   Deon Haywood et al., "Front Porch Strategy: Organizing for Black Women's Lives at the Intersection of Service, Activism, and Research"; Speeches, Presentations, and Writings in the Born in Flames Living Archive.

10 McKittrick, *Demonic Grounds*, 144.

11 McKittrick, *Demonic Grounds*, 44–52.

12 Tuck and Yang, "Decolonization Is Not a Metaphor."

13 Here, we follow Cindi Katz's "Bad Elements" in affirming that "sedimentations are not just the effects of direct environmental engagement, of course, but the outcomes of material and social practices on all scales" (17).

14 In spoken and written conversation at WWAV, "Lord" is replaced with the last name of Black feminist poet and activist Audre Lorde.

15 See "Resilience"; Collective Storytelling Sessions in the Born in Flames Living Archive.

16 This porch talk was recorded before WWAV developed the critique of allyship that grounds our discussion of accompliceship in the introduction. We have retained the use of the word *ally* here as recorded.

17 The phrase "white tears" puts a point on the racist logics that make the tears that white women shed when being called out for racism more important than the scars that Black people and other people of color bear for surviving racist violence. "White mediocrity" is another facet of these logics. Abigail Fisher, the plaintiff in *Fisher v. University of Texas Austin et al.*, claimed she had been denied admission to University of Texas Austin because she was white, and not because of her poor academic record. Comments from Justice Antonin Scalia made explicit Fisher's claim about affirmative action and Black intellectual "inferiority." During a 2016 lecture at the University of Southern California Gould School of Law, Mary Frances Berry argued that the *Fisher* case and Justice Scalia's opinion were rooted in the logics of the Dred Scott decision.

18 Klein, *Shock Doctrine*, 17, 21.

19 Woods's *Development Drowned and Reborn* is a "Blues geography" of New Orleans, which brings into focus the long Black freedom struggle in the region, as well as its unfinished business. Woods traces the organized abandonment of New Orleans beginning in 1690 under French colonial rule and considers how various expressions of this "Bourbonism" managed to reconstitute themselves at numerous historical junctures, from Jim Crow to the present day.

20 Gilmore, "Abolition Geography and the Problem of Innocence," 266. On the simultaneity of past, present, and future in WWAV's own temporality, see Thomas, "Time and the Otherwise."

21 See Berry and Blassingame, *Long Memory*.

22 Saulny, "Clamoring to Come Home to New Orleans Projects."

23 Rivlin, "Mogul Who Would Rebuild New Orleans."

24 The fight to preserve public housing in New Orleans in the wake of Katrina was carefully documented by Jordan Flaherty in his book *Floodlines*.

25 In part, the story here is about numbers. In destroying public housing, New Orleans adopted a policy defined by deconcentration and privatization through Housing and Urban Development (HUD) vouchers, which went up

from 64 percent of affordable housing access to 91 percent ten years after the storm. This meant that people entitled to affordable housing no longer had access to dedicated public housing units; they now had to join the renters' market and find a landlord willing to accept the HUD reimbursement rate while rents were ballooning citywide. There is also a much longer history of deconcentration at work here. Within the post-Katrina literature, Alecia P. Long's "Poverty Is the New Prostitution" offers a poignant reframing of policing space and vice in New Orleans history. For an intersectional analysis of housing after the storm see Luft and griffin, "Status Report on Housing in New Orleans after Katrina."

26 Mustafa, "Ongoing Colonization of New Orleans and Palestine."

27 Shana M. griffin recounted the story of "How New Orleans Has Lost One-Third of Its Black Population," with attention to these policies of erasure, to Dani McCain on the tenth anniversary of Hurricane Katrina.

28 Thomas, *Desire and Disaster in New Orleans*. In his 2016 *New York Times* op-ed "The End of Black Harlem," Michael Henry Adams references the Tremé in New Orleans, among other Black geographies, when comparing gentrification to colonialism: "Gentrification in Harlem might well be likened to the progress of the British Raj, where the most that 'civilizing' interlopers could muster was a patronizing interest in token elements of local culture. Thus: Yes to the hip Afro-fusion restaurant, but complaints to 311 over Sundae Sermon dances, barbecues and ball games in parks or church choir rehearsals."

29 Desiree and Laura spent a lot of time on the road together the summer of 2013, talking about the speed with which New Orleans was being remade, their respective graduate educations at Columbia University, and their shared commitments to oral history.

30 In *The National Uncanny*, Renée L. Bergland makes a similar argument about the United States settler colonial project, showing how the concept of American nationhood was deliberately constructed as haunted by the spectral presence of Indigenous people, thereby forcing Native Americans to become sharers in a national imagination that turns their genocide and forced removal into stories of glory and national pride.

31 See Povinelli, *Cunning of Recognition*, on the affective work of state recognition and right to land.

32 In the essay "Still Submerged," Bench Ansfield argues for understanding urban redevelopment as a racial project in which spatial and bodily purification is a far more appropriate conceptual frame than the market logics of gentrification (128). This frame helps render visible how the making of the new New Orleans white resilience space has been a covertly religious process of boundary setting. A tremendous amount of everyday ritual activity has been dedicated to creating and maintaining boundaries—that is, to deter-

mining what is (and is not) sacred, and to ensuring that matter never falls out of place. See Wuthnow, *Restructuring of Religion in America*; Durkheim, *Elementary Forms of Religious Life*; Douglas, *Purity and Danger*; and Eliade, *Sacred and the Profane*.

33 While Desiree was speaking about the breadth of WWAV's work, she was also specifically naming how the arson attack on WWAV happened exactly two months after our legal team secured the federal ruling against the state of Louisiana in the "Crime Against Nature by Solicitation" fight. The organizing process of WWAV's NO Justice Project and the generations-honed Black feminist analysis of criminalization that undergirded it are the focus of chapter 3.

34 McKittrick, *Demonic Grounds*, xxiv. In our other published work, we have explored front porch strategy through the concept of "the demonic" in Black feminist Caribbean, geographic, and critical prison studies. See McTighe, with Haywood, "Front Porch Revolution."

35 We invoke the term "cypher" here as it is used by the Nation of Gods and Earths or Five-Percenters and adopted by hip-hop MCs (e.g., "building the cypher") when forming a circle around a speaker sharing knowledge.

36 Dent, Schechner, and Moses, *Free Southern Theater, by the Free Southern Theater*; Gilroy, *Black Atlantic*.

37 In *Demonic Grounds*, McKittrick emphasizes how the idea of Black women's "absented presence" opens up new directions for geographic thought: "a new place to go" (xxvi). Of particular concern to McKittrick is that this absence not be reduced to a category of analysis for mapping domination. Rather, Black women's absence exposes the unfinished possibilities of a geographic story, thereby making possible more just conceptualizations of place. Here, McKittrick is working most closely with Jamaican writer and cultural theorist Sylvia Wynter's analysis of Black feminism in "Beyond Miranda's Meanings," through which Wynter excavates what she calls the "ontological absence" (361) of Caliban's potential mate to suggest that Black female life is not only missing but is so far outside the boundaries of reason as to be incomprehensible. McKittrick, extending Wynter's work, asks a provocative question that helps us approach the transformative presence asserted and conjured on the front porch: "What would happen to our understanding and conception of race and humanness if Black women legitimately inhabited our world and made their needs known?" (xxv).

38 See Cox, *Shapeshifters*; Shange, "Unapologetically Black?"

39 Here, we are thinking, for example, of Hortense Spillers's theorization of the interstice as the absented presence of the Black female subject in discursive formations: "the missing word—the interstice—both as that which allows us to speak about and that which enables us to speak at all" (77). See Spillers, "Interstices: A Small Drama of Words."

40 We invoke the image of the crossroads deliberately in order to conjure the history and power of liminal spaces in Black religion, rootwork, and the blues. See Raboteau, *Slave Religion*; Chireau, *Black Magic*; Alexander, *Pedagogies of Crossing*. See also Gore, *Radicalism at the Crossroads*.

41 See National Harm Reduction Coalition, "Principles of Harm Reduction," for discussion of the practical strategies to reduce the harms associated with drug use, as well as the vision for social justice that undergirds the movement. We return to WWAV's harm reduction work in chapter 2.

42 We understand our foremothers' care work in the tradition of Black women's household care turned organized community care, which Jacqueline Leavitt and Susan Saegert so powerfully document in 1980s Harlem in *From Abandonment to Hope*.

43 Public housing demolition began *before* Hurricane Katrina, which is why it could be completed in record time after the storm. As early as 2001, developers had designs on the Iberville Projects in the Tremé. In January 2004, the Fischer Projects high-rise buildings were demolished and replaced with low-rise rainbow models.

44 For the tenth anniversary of Hurricane Katrina, the *Times-Picayune* produced an interactive map showing the locations of the city's former housing projects, the mixed-income units erected on their grounds, and the disparity in number of units available. The transformation of C. J. Peete into Harmony Oaks is detailed in "The Long Road from C. J. Peete to Harmony Oaks" report by Katy Reckdahl.

45 Mindy Fullilove's *Root Shock* is a touchstone of ours for understanding the profound traumatic stress of surviving the demolition of one's neighborhood home.

46 Reckdahl, "New C. J. Peete Complex Is Solid, Shiny—but Not as Social, Some Residents Say"; Mock, "Beyoncé's Simple but Radical Porch-Front Politics."

47 Chakrabarty, *Provincializing Europe*.

48 Hartman, *Lose Your Mother*, 6.

49 Raboteau, *Slave Religion*. See also Woods, *Development Drowned and Reborn*, especially chapter 1.

50 On November 8–9, 2019, hundreds of reenactors retraced the path of the German Coast Uprising, embodying this history of resistance, freedom, and revolutionary action. See *Slave Rebellion Reenactment*. Assistant producer Shana M. griffin compiled an "Un-Bibliography" of texts, films, museums, and community resources for reading groups and classroom syllabi. For the first substantial history of the revolt, see Thrasher, *On to New Orleans!*

51 A. Davis, "Reflections on the Black Woman's Role in the Community of Slaves."

52 On marronage in Louisiana, see Diouf, *Slavery's Exiles*; and Housea, "A Land Called Louisiana."

53 On "otherwise possibilities," see Crawley, *Blackpentecostal Breath*. See also Deborah Thomas's coda to *Exceptional Violence*, in which she critiques reading the horizon of postcolonial struggle as empty and argues "that new futures are constantly being imagined and emplotted, but we will not see them if our vision is oriented only towards . . . mass-based revolutionary movements" (230).

54 Mock, "In Baton Rouge, Your Front Yard Is No Sanctuary from Police."

55 Protesters used social media to share live videos taken as the Baton Rouge police started to storm Batiste's lawn and front porch. One was archived as part of Terry L. Jones's coverage of the protest in the *Advocate*, "Video: Intense Scene at Alton Sterling Protest in Baton Rouge as Officers Charge Protesters in Woman's Front Lawn."

56 Allen and Jones, "'Disturbing' Turn at Alton Sterling Protest Sunday on Government Street."

57 Reed, "Baton Rouge Cops Barge into Woman's Yard to Arrest Black Lives Matter Protesters She Invited."

58 McTighe, "Southern Front Porches Are Revolutionary, Sacred Spaces."

59 Mock, "In Baton Rouge, Your Front Yard Is No Sanctuary from Police." This was a follow-up to his article "Beyoncé's Simple but Radical Porch-Front Politics," which features a still from Beyoncé's visual album *Lemonade* at about fifty-three minutes in, when Beyoncé sits surrounded by a group of women on a wooden porch.

60 See Collective Storytelling Sessions in the Born in Flames Living Archive, as well as the images that fill this and future chapters.

61 WWAV hosted our first public #BlackFeministPorchTalk on February 16, 2016, as a conversation on "#Formation, Activism and the Importance of Black [Southern] Women's Narratives," which was inspired by Beyoncé's "Formation." The month of May included two more porch talks. On May 4, WWAV hosted "Lemons: Black Women and Representation," following the release of Beyoncé's visual album *Lemonade*. On May 24, WWAV hosted "State Violence against Black Women and Girls," which was a part of our organizing for the national #SayHerName day of action. See Collective Storytelling Sessions in the Born in Flames Living Archive. WWAV's #SayHerName organizing is explored in depth in chapter 4.

62 See "Marley Dias, Founder #1000BlackGirlBooks, and Director Ava DuVernay"; Collective Storytelling Sessions in the Born in Flames Living Archive.

63 This more extensive collection of our porch talks, porch sits, and porch poses is available at borninflames.com.

Chapter 2: Doing the Work

Portions of this chapter originally appeared in: Laura McTighe, with Women With A Vision, "Theory on the Ground: Ethnography, Religio-Racial Study, and the Spiritual Work of Building Otherwise," *Journal of the American Academy of Religion* 88, no. 2 (2020): 407–39, https://doi.org/10.1093/jaarel/lfaa014; and Laura McTighe, Catherine Haywood, Deon Haywood, and Danita Muse, Women With A Vision, "Keep the South Dirty and Our Needles Clean," *Southern Cultures* 27, no. 3 (2021): 120–29, http://doi.org/10.1353/scu.2021.0048.

1   Studies (e.g., Betancourt et al., "Adolescents with and without Gestational Cocaine Exposure") have consistently shown that there is no difference in long-term physical and emotional development between babies who had been exposed to crack and those who had not; the actual factor that affects development is structural: poverty. In 2018, the *New York Times* ran a series of reporting on "Slandering the Unborn" to acknowledge its role in fueling the "moral panic" that "expanded the war on drugs into the womb." For a rich exploration of how these racist stereotypes invisibilize Black women's lives as they are lived, see Williamson, *Scandalize My Name*.

2   The breadth of scholarship by Black women has shaped a generation's political consciousness about America's systemic abuse of Black women's bodies and the unapologetic, intersectional, Black feminist agenda that anchors contemporary organizing. Dorothy Roberts's *Killing the Black Body* and Cathy Cohen's *Boundaries of Blackness* are foundational texts for us on Black women's reproductive lives and the Black AIDS epidemic, respectively.

3   Gilmore, *Golden Gulag*, 28.

4   Gilmore, "Abolition Geography and the Problem of Innocence," 226–27.

5   We are grateful to Susan L. Smith for tracing this genealogy of Black women's health activism from late nineteenth century to present day in *Sick and Tired of Being Sick and Tired*.

6   Shakespeare, *Tempest*, act 2, scene 1.

7   This quote is part of Audre Lorde's address "Learning from the 60s," which she delivered in February 1982 as part of the celebration of the Malcolm X weekend at Harvard University.

8   Interview for WWAV's 30th-anniversary report; see McTighe, Ritchie, and Women With A Vision, *Our Existence Is Political: 30 Years of Black Feminist Struggle*; Speeches, Presentations, and Writings in the Born in Flames Living Archive.

9   Catherine Haywood, interview, July 29, 2013; Life History Interviews in the Born in Flames Living Archive.

10 National Council of Negro Women, *Legacy of Mary Beth McCune*. See also Rebecca Tuuri's *Strategic Sisterhood*.

11 Danita Muse, interview, July 26, 2013; Life History Interviews in the Born in Flames Living Archive.

12 Muse, interview, July 26, 2013.

13 Later in her life history interview, Danita explained how she needed a job with security ("my check would come every month") and protection ("they'd have to go through civil service to get rid of me") when they started WWAV.

14 Muse, interview, July 26, 2013.

15 Muse, interview, July 26, 2013.

16 The Magnolia and Calliope Projects were among those targeted for demolition in the wake of Hurricane Katrina, despite unrelenting protests from residents.

17 Sweet, "A Vanished New Orleans Captured on 'Straight from the Projects.'" We return to this location later in this chapter during the collective storytelling session.

18 A quote from Danita during the collective storytelling session at this chapter's end. See "Strategic Planning Retreat Listening Session with WWAV Foremothers Catherine Haywood and Danita Muse"; Collective Storytelling Sessions in the Born in Flames Living Archive.

19 See the Born in Flames Living Archive collection of sources at the conclusion of this book, and explore the archive online at borninflames.com.

20 This recalls Robin D. G. Kelley's distinction between "why" and "how" questions, as discussed in the introduction.

21 Russo, "Why We Fight."

22 In his 2021 article "On Epidemiology as Racial-Capitalist (Re)Colonization and Epistemic Violence," Ryan J. Petteway explores how the persistent structural racism embedded within epidemiology research must be addressed to advance antiracist public health futures.

23 This mathematics was reminiscent of the so-called three-fifths compromise in the US Constitution, in which slaveholding states were allowed to "count" enslaved people in order to increase their political power without bestowing on them any of the rights of citizenship.

24 Haywood, interview, July 29, 2013.

25 Haywood, interview, July 29, 2013.

26 Haywood, interview, July 29, 2013.

27 In May 2021, Tom Farley was the center of a public reckoning around the voraciousness of anti-Black violence surrounding the 1985 MOVE bombing, when the City of Philadelphia had dropped explosives on the Black liberation group's West Philadelphia headquarters, killing eleven people (six adults and five children) and destroying more than sixty homes. It came to light that remains from victims of the bombing had been in the possession of the

City of Philadelphia and the University of Pennsylvania, unbeknownst to the MOVE family. The remains had also been passed between the University of Pennsylvania and Princeton University, treated like lab specimens in yet another episode in the long history of grave robbing and medical experimentation that dates back to before the Civil War. As Philadelphia health commissioner, Farley admitted to discovering, cremating, and disposing of remains from victims of the MOVE bombing in 2017, without ever notifying their surviving family members. He was forced to resign from his position. McCrystal, Whelan, and Goodin-Smith, "Philly Health Commissioner Resigns."

28 Haywood, interview, July 29, 2013.

29 Haywood, interview, July 29, 2013.

30 In his seminal work on the two-ness, the double-consciousness, of being Black in America, W. E. B. Du Bois observed in *The Souls of Black Folk* that "between me and the other world there is ever an unasked question: . . . *How does it feel to be a problem?*" (2, emphasis ours). The inflection of Catherine's voice when she said "I BELONG" was an implicit refusal of this question.

31 See Woods, *Development Arrested*; and Woods, "Katrina's World."

32 Harm Reduction Coalition, "Evolution of the Movement." See Nelson, *Body and Soul*; Fernández, *Young Lords*; Lloyd, *Health Rights Are Civil Rights*; Boston Women's Health Book Collective, *Our Bodies, Ourselves*; Taylor, *How We Get Free*; Thuma, *All Our Trials*; Schulman, *Let the Record Show*; ACE Program of the Bedford Hills Correctional Facility, *Breaking the Walls of Silence*.

33 Muse, interview, July 26, 2013.

34 In WWAV's early years, Danita and Catherine used the term "risk reduction" interchangeably with "harm reduction." As WWAV became the southern anchor to the growing national harm reduction movement in the mid- to late 1990s, "harm reduction" became our official language. Throughout this book, thus, we use "harm reduction" except when quoting directly from WWAV's early slogans on T-shirts, pamphlets, and other outreach materials.

35 Muse, interview, July 26, 2013.

36 Ruth Wilson Gilmore has long taken up Raymond Williams's claim in *The Long Revolution* that each age has its own "structure of feeling" and has further developed the concept as "infrastructure of feeling" to name what underlies the constantly evolving accumulation of the long Black Radical Tradition. See Gilmore, "Abolition Geography and the Problem of Innocence," 236–37. We return to this concept in chapter 4.

37 On the "culture of poverty" thesis, see Lewis, "Culture of Poverty"; United States Department of Labor, *Negro Family* (commonly known as "The Moynihan Report"); Katz, *Undeserving Poor*. On the "underclass" debate, see Murray, *Losing Ground*; Mead, "Should Congress Respond?"; Wilson, *Truly Disadvan-*

taged. Within Black feminist anthropology, see Mullings and Wali, *Stress and Resilience*; D. Davis, *Battered Black Women and Welfare Reform*; Rodriguez, "Invoking Fannie Lou Hamer"; and Mullings, "Households Headed by Women."

38 Within Black feminist historiography, see Berry, *My Face Is Black Is True*; Williams, *Politics of Public Housing*; Nadasen, *Welfare Warriors*; and *Haley, No Mercy Here*. We discuss more of the key texts and authors in WWAV's Black Feminist Library in chapter 4.

39 On Black girls and their "choreography of citizenship," see Cox, *Shapeshifters*.

40 On this regulatory, moralizing gaze, we draw on the work of many thinkers, including Foucault, "Body/Power" in *Power/Knowledge* and "Right of Death and Power over Life" in *The History of Sexuality*; Hall et al., *Policing the Crisis*; Arendt, *On Revolution*; Povinelli, *Cunning of Recognition*.

41 Muse, interview, July 26, 2013.

42 Danita's framing of how she and Catherine told people they were wrong provides an important counterpoint to scholarly work on community formation and boundary setting, which tends to analyze systems of social purification from the vantage point of those setting the boundaries, not those who are expelled. See Durkheim, *Elementary Forms*; Douglas, *Purity and Danger*; and Douglas's further discussion of the problem of evil in *Natural Symbols*.

43 The interview was completed as part of a video feature made about Deon's receipt of a Ms. Foundation "Gloria Award." See Ms. Foundation for Women, *Women of Vision Honoree Deon Haywood (Women With A Vision) #GloriaAwards 2019*; Video Recordings in the Born in Flames Living Archive.

44 Quoted in Ms. Foundation, *Women of Vision Honoree Deon Haywood*.

45 These words were offered by WWAV participant turned staff member Zina Mitchell during her life history interview. As she explained, "I knew when I walked in these doors I was Zina Mitchell, the outreach worker and harm reductionist." See Zina Mitchell, interview, August 21, 2013; Life History Interviews in the Born in Flames Living Archive.

46 Ms. Foundation, *Women of Vision Honoree Deon Haywood*.

47 Arundhati Roy, speech at the 2005 World Social Forum in Porto Alegre, Brazil.

48 See, especially, the interviews conducted in July–August 2013 with WWAV's cofounders, Danita Muse and Catherine Haywood, and with individuals who worked at WWAV in the organization's early years, including Robert Ellis, Sharon Peterson, Angelita Bolden, and Oscar Salinas; Life History Interviews in the Born in Flames Living Archive.

49 See, e.g., Weisenfeld, *New World A-Coming*.

50 Haywood, interview, July 29, 2013. "Hope is a discipline" is a practice we have learned from Mariame Kaba. In *We Do This 'til We Free Us*, Kaba explains how she learned it from a Catholic nun.

51 Muse, interview, July 26, 2013.

52 "Strategic Planning Retreat Listening Session with WWAV Foremothers Catherine Haywood and Danita Muse"; Collective Storytelling Sessions in the Born in Flames Living Archive.

53 *Saving Our Own Lives* is the title of Shira Hassan's book on a liberatory practice of harm reduction.

54 We are grateful to Eric A. Stanley for naming this incommensurability so pointedly in *Atmospheres of Violence*, and also for underlining that "ungovernability not only refuses the state; it also figures the ease of living now" (123).

55 All quotes that follow are part of "Strategic Planning Retreat Listening Session with WWAV Foremothers Catherine Haywood and Danita Muse."

56 This was a favorite phrase of Danita's, which she had already had staff laughing about after several in-house trainings on harm reduction, burnout, and boundaries.

57 "Strategic Planning Retreat Listening Session with WWAV Foremothers Catherine Haywood and Danita Muse."

58 "Strategic Planning Retreat Listening Session with WWAV Foremothers Catherine Haywood and Danita Muse."

59 "Strategic Planning Retreat Listening Session with WWAV Foremothers Catherine Haywood and Danita Muse."

60 "Strategic Planning Retreat Listening Session with WWAV Foremothers Catherine Haywood and Danita Muse."

61 We use the word "experimentation" in the spirit that Mariame Kaba did amid the summer 2020 global uprising to #DefundthePolice when she tweeted, "We need a million experiments. A bunch will fail. That's good because we'll have learned a lot that we can apply to the next ones." See also "One Million Experiments" website and podcast.

62 "Strategic Planning Retreat Listening Session with WWAV Foremothers Catherine Haywood and Danita Muse."

63 Negotiating condom use is a major risk for sex workers. The need to stay out of view of the police also puts sex workers out of each other's sight lines. Clients can use this isolation to pressure them into accepting riskier terms. Thus, learning how to "cheek a condom" has been a lifesaving strategy for managing risk. See Shannon et al., "Structural and Environmental Barriers to Condom Use."

64 "Strategic Planning Retreat Listening Session with WWAV Foremothers Catherine Haywood and Danita Muse."

65 Checks are especially meaningless forms of currency to many people living on the streets, because you need to have an ID to get a check cashed, or you need to have a bank account to deposit it into.

66 "Strategic Planning Retreat Listening Session with WWAV Foremothers Catherine Haywood and Danita Muse."

67 "Strategic Planning Retreat Listening Session with WWAV Foremothers Catherine Haywood and Danita Muse."

68 See, e.g., Richie, *Arrested Justice*, 133.

69 This mantra and its attendant refusal of Christian white supremacist categories of "victimhood" are discussed in depth in chapter 4.

70 "Strategic Planning Retreat Listening Session with WWAV Foremothers Catherine Haywood and Danita Muse."

71 What this conspiracy theory speaks truth to is the fact that the AIDS crisis in Black communities was produced through government indifference, organized abandonment, and mass criminalization.

72 "Strategic Planning Retreat Listening Session with WWAV Foremothers Catherine Haywood and Danita Muse."

73 "Strategic Planning Retreat Listening Session with WWAV Foremothers Catherine Haywood and Danita Muse."

74 "Strategic Planning Retreat Listening Session with WWAV Foremothers Catherine Haywood and Danita Muse."

75 Here, we are echoing Ruth Wilson Gilmore, Mariame Kaba, and other abolitionists' point that abolition is both a vision and a practice: it is a vision of a world without prisons, and the practice of how we build that world together.

76 Ms. Foundation for Women, *Women of Vision Honoree Deon Haywood (Women With A Vision) #GloriaAwards 2019*.

77 Speaking for Change, "Beyond Pipelines and Prisons—a Dialogue between Ruth Wilson Gilmore and Winona LaDuke." See also Maynard and Simpson, *Rehearsals for Living*.

78 Gumbs, "Are You Afraid of Black Feminists?"

Chapter 3: We Spoke Our Truths

Portions of this chapter appear in Laura McTighe, with Deon Haywood, "'There Is NO Justice in Louisiana': Crimes Against Nature and the Spirit of Black Feminist Resistance," *Souls: A Critical Journal of Black Culture, Politics and Society* 19, no. 3 (2017): 261–85, https://doi.org/10.1080/10999949.2017.1389584; and Laura McTighe, "'And Still We Rise': Moral Panics, Dark Sousveillance, and Politics Otherwise in the New New Orleans," in *Panic, Transnational Cultural Studies, and the Affective Contours of Power*, ed. Micol Seigel (New York: Routledge, 2018), 275–97.

1 "Small but mighty" is one of Desiree's descriptions of WWAV, coined the summer after the fire.

2 See the introduction for background on all of our people at WWAV, including executive director Deon Haywood, cofounders Catherine Haywood and Danita Muse, and our participants.

3 See *Doe v. Jindal*, Complaint, 851 F.Supp.2d 995 (E.D. La. 2012) (No. 11-CV-388); and Women With A Vision, "Just a Talking Crime." Copies of the *Doe v. Jindal* Complaint and other CANS case files are available through the Center for Constitutional Rights's "Crime Against Nature by Solicitation (CANS) Litigation" online archive; our NO Justice Project policy brief "Just a Talking Crime" is part of the Born in Flames Living Archive. We will return to the research process for creating this statistic later in this chapter. Throughout the chapter, we always name both cisgender and transgender women to underline that the NO Justice Project was organized by and for *all* women and femmes.

4 Statement made by one of the first WWAV participants forcibly placed on the sex offender registry.

5 *Doe v. Jindal*, Complaint.

6 Deon Haywood, "OUR WIN"; Speeches, Presentations, and Writings in the Born in Flames Living Archive.

7 Zina Mitchell, interview, August 21, 2013; Life History Interviews in the Born in Flames Living Archive.

8 Mitchell, interview, August 21, 2013.

9 We use the word "witness" here, first, to underline the responsibility of witnesses, which as James Baldwin taught us "was to move as largely and as freely as possible to write the story and to get it out" (see Peck, *I Am Not Your Negro*); and second, to call in the religious registers of witnessing as moral practice, which Rosetta E. Ross documented so powerfully in her study of Black women, religion, and civil rights, *Witnessing and Testifying*.

10 Deon Haywood et al., "Front Porch Strategy: Organizing for Black Women's Lives at the Intersection of Service, Activism, and Research"; Speeches, Presentations, and Writings in the Born in Flames Living Archive.

11 Haywood et al., "Front Porch Strategy."

12 We distinguish here WWAV's own organizational archive, which was destroyed in the arson attack, from the files that the members of the NO Justice legal team kept and remain intact, including their notes about the case, records of the stories that plaintiffs shared with them, and stories that were shared in the press.

13 E.g., Harney and Moten, *Undercommons*.

14 On the logic of evisceration, see Rodríguez, "Inhabiting the Impasse." On invisibilization and hypervisibilization in the contexts of the NO Justice Project, see Ritchie, *Invisible No More*.

15　In theorizing social death, we draw strongly on Orlando Patterson's *Slavery and Social Death* and Lisa Marie Cacho's *Social Death*.

16　In our chapter "And Still We Rise," we trace this theological and legal genealogy. See Jordan, *Invention of Sodomy in Christian Theology*, for a theological history on how God's sulphur rain in Sodom came to be understood as punishment for nonprocreative sex. See also McTighe, with Haywood, "There Is NO Justice in Louisiana."

17　Blackstone, "Chapter the Fifteenth," square brackets in original.

18　For an exploration of the prosecution of sex acts in colonial New Spain, see Tortorici, *Sins against Nature*.

19　Hood, "History and Development of the Louisiana Civil Code."

20　NO Justice attorneys Andrea Ritchie and Alexis Agathocleous led this massive undertaking on behalf of the whole legal team. The breadth of their research serves as the basis of the *Doe v. Jindal* Complaint. They also worked with us to distill this research into the "Just a Talking Crime" policy brief for community education and outreach, which included a side-by-side comparison of Louisiana's CANS and prostitution statutes, a timeline of the statute's history, and quotes from interviews with potential plaintiffs for the lawsuit to show its application. In the remainder of this section, we narrate this history with attention to the critical junctures in which the statute was revised, expanded, or changed, as well as the political contexts for doing so. See Women With A Vision, "Just a Talking Crime"; Speeches, Presentations, and Writings in the Born in Flames Living Archive.

21　Louisiana Acts chap. I, § 2. LA. REV. STAT. § 788.

22　For this history of race and religion, we draw on Sylvester Johnson's *The Myth of Ham in Nineteenth-Century American Christianity* and Curtis Evans's *The Burden of Black Religion*.

23　Acts of the State of Louisiana 1896, page 102, § 1, Act 69.

24　State v. Long, 133 La. 580 (1913).

25　Naquin, "Criminal Law—Miscegenation—Definition of 'Cohabitation.'"

26　La. Crim. Stat. Ann. § 43:89 (1943).

27　Bennett, "The Louisiana Criminal Code," 44 (emphasis ours).

28　Our "Just a Talking Crime" policy brief includes a timeline of Louisiana's Crime Against Nature Statute from 1805 to 2010, which lists the changes that were made to the statute in 1942 during the comprehensive revision of the Louisiana Criminal Code. It does not, however, include the proposal to add a Solicitation clause in 1942, nor the NOPD's role in advocating for this proposal. We uncovered this detail later, during our research on *State of Louisiana v. Michael Smith*.

29 We are grateful for Melinda Chateauvert's research in *Sex Workers Unite*, especially chapter 4.

30 Cited in Patton, *Sex and Germs*, 85.

31 A 1982 *Television/Radio Age* article confirmed that the premise of *Cruisin' the Streets* was entirely fabricated: a very young-looking college student was hired to pose as a male prostitute, and the reporters for the series claimed to be executives for a fake film in order to lure sex workers back to a French Quarter apartment with hidden cameras. In 1986, a lawsuit was brought by one person filmed without his consent. See Munson v. Gaylord Broadcasting Company, 496 So. 2d 335 (1986) (No. 86-CC-1799).

32 Georgia attorney general Gary Bowers bolstered the state's role in managing the country's mounting fears when he appealed the *Bowers v. Hardwick* criminal sodomy case all the way to the United States Supreme Court, insisting, "The *law* would help reduce the spread of AIDS." Cited in Chateauvert, *Sex Workers Unite*, 104 (emphasis ours).

33 A recording of the Louisiana House of Representatives Administration of Criminal Justice Committee discussing HB 853 is included as part of a CANS virtual museum by Matt Nadel and Joseph Fischel. See also Nadel, "Prostitution Was Already Illegal in Louisiana."

34 The NO Justice Project policy brief was called "Just a Talking Crime" for this reason. See also Terry and Ackerman, "Brief History of Major Sex Offender Laws."

35 Ritchie, "Crimes against Nature," 365. Here, Ritchie is thinking with and building on Cathy Cohen's field-defining essay "Punks, Bulldaggers, and Welfare Queens." Ritchie is also the author of *Invisible No More*; the coauthor, with Joey Mogul and Kay Whitlock, of *Queer (In)Justice*; the coauthor, with Kimberlé Williams Crenshaw, of the *Say Her Name* report; and the coauthor, with Mariame Kaba, of *No More Police*.

36 Louisiana State Sex Offender and Child Predator Registry, cited in Women With A Vision, "Just a Talking Crime." These statistics were produced by the NO Justice legal team through painstaking research. They went through every single record of every person on the registry and crunched the numbers to determine the precise gendered and racialized impacts.

37 United States Department of Justice, *Investigation of the New Orleans Police Department*. Again, this statistic, cited in Women With A Vision, "Just a Talking Crime," was the result of extensive research by the NO Justice legal team.

38 Quoted in Women With A Vision, "Just a Talking Crime." This quote and others in the NO Justice Project policy brief came from interviews the legal team conducted with potential plaintiffs for the lawsuit. Each of these components of sex offender registration that this person outlines became

standardized and tracked through the federal passage of the Adam Walsh Act in 2006.

39 Women With A Vision, "Just a Talking Crime."

40 Zina Mitchell emphasized this point during her life history interview. See Mitchell, interview, August 21, 2013.

41 In attention to the "everyday," we follow Saidiya Hartman in *Scenes of Subjection*, where she works to "illuminate the terror of the mundane and quotidian rather than exploit the shocking spectacle" (4). We also draw on Veena Das, *Life and Words*, especially chapter 4.

42 This analysis of invisibility and hypervisibility is central to the argument that our comrade and NO Justice attorney Andrea Ritchie advances in *Invisible No More*, which includes substantial discussion of these questions in reference to WWAV and the NO Justice Project. We also understand this Black feminist hermeneutic in the tradition of the Combahee River Collective; Crenshaw, "Demarginalizing the Intersection of Race and Sex"; Crenshaw, "Mapping the Margins"; Collins, *Black Feminist Thought*; Guy-Sheftall, *Words of Fire*; Higginbotham, "African-American Women's History and the Metalanguage of Race"; and Spillers, "Mama's Baby, Papa's Maybe."

43 As Hortense Spillers taught us in "Interstices," it is impossible to understand the contours of anti-Black violence in the United States without reckoning with how Black womanhood has been produced as a "paradox of non-being" (78).

44 Desiree offered this example from WWAV's work at the intersections of criminalization and intimate partner violence during our panel at the 2014 "Rethinking Mass Incarceration in the South" conference. See Deon Haywood et al., "Community Organizing Is a Reentry Program: How Formerly Incarcerated Women Are Decarcerating Their Communities in the Prison Capital of the World"; Speeches, Presentations, and Writings in the Born in Flames Living Archive.

45 Richie, *Arrested Justice*; Richie, *Invisible No More*; Kaba, *We Do This 'til We Free Us*; Kaba and Ritchie, *No More Police*; Roberts, *Killing the Black Body*; Carby, "Policing the Black Woman's Body in an Urban Context"; Hartman, *Wayward Lives*; Cohen, "Punks, Bulldaggers, and Welfare Queens"; Haley, *No Mercy Here*; Gilmore, *Golden Gulag*; and A. Davis, *Are Prisons Obsolete?* See also McDowell, Harold, and Battle, *Punitive Turn*, on the historical, political, economic, and sociocultural roots of "mass incarceration"; and Alexander, *New Jim Crow*, on how "mass incarceration" and post-prison restrictions created a racial caste in America.

46 "Jim Crow modernity" is a term coined by Sarah Haley in *No Mercy Here*. See also Talitha LeFlouria's *Chained in Silence*, which was the first major history of Black women's criminalization in the Jim Crow South. For examinations

of this intersection in Black women's worlds in turn-of-the-century northern cities, see Gross, *Colored Amazons*; and Hicks, *Talk with You Like a Woman*.

47 A. Davis, *Are Prisons Obsolete?*, chapter 4.

48 This fact was hardly a southern phenomenon. Jen Manion's groundbreaking *Liberty's Prisoners* traces how in early America, Black women were more heavily policed than other women, and often received much longer sentences for simple property and nuisance crimes. L. Mara Dodge documented similar disparities in *"Whores and Thieves of the Worst Kind,"* showing how in Illinois between 1890 and 1930, Black women averaged only 2.4 percent of the state's female population but represented two-thirds of the daily population at Joliet women's prison.

49 The convict lease system was a system of forced carceral labor that proliferated across the South after the abolition of slavery. Black people were criminalized en masse under newly passed "Black Codes" that rendered all dimensions of Black livingness criminal, and then leased to plantation owners, private mining corporations, and railways for the duration of their sentences. See LeFlouria, *Chained in Silence*; Oshinsky, *Worse than Slavery*; and Lichtenstein, *Twice the Work of Free Labor*.

50 Law, *Resistance behind Bars*, 161–62.

51 Haley, "Like I Was a Man."

52 See especially Alecia P. Long's study on sex, race, and respectability in New Orleans 1865–1920, *Great Southern Babylon*.

53 Curtin, *Black Prisoners and Their World*, 114–15. See also Simmons, *Crescent City Girls*, especially chapter 5.

54 Carby, "Policing the Black Woman's Body in an Urban Context," 739.

55 Carby, "Policing the Black Woman's Body in an Urban Context," 746.

56 Carby, "Policing the Black Woman's Body in an Urban Context," 739–40. See also Hartman, *Wayward Lives*.

57 WWAV is opposed to trafficking in all forms. We will discuss WWAV's analysis around the antitrafficking movement in more depth in chapter 4. Here, we only want to emphasize that the media frenzy generated by the antitrafficking movement about "victims of human trafficking" functions much like sensationalized stories of "crack babies" did in the 1980s. Both have been vehicles for massively expanding the criminalization of Black women. See Brown, "War on Sex Trafficking Is the New War on Drugs." See also WWAV's toolkit, developed by Women With A Vision and Sex Worker Advisory Committee, "Deep South Decrim: Towards Sex Work Decriminalization and Justice in Louisiana"; Speeches, Presentations, and Writings in the Born in Flames Living Archive.

58 Quoted in Women With A Vision, "Just a Talking Crime." Again, these quotes came from interviews the legal team conducted with potential plaintiffs for the lawsuit.

59 The haphazardness of what people were charged with—CANS, prostitution, or both—was actually central to the NO Justice legal team's argument in the case and to the court's ultimate decision that the sex offender registration was invalid.

60 A 2022 report by Cop Watch NOLA documents that nearly one in five New Orleans Police Department (NOPD) officers have been reported for sexual and/or intimate partner violence. See "Police Sexual Violence in New Orleans."

61 United States Department of Justice, "Fact Sheet: Department of Justice Law Enforcement Efforts in New Orleans, Louisiana." The federal resourcing of NOPD after the storm has been widely critiqued within the post-Katrina literature. See the 2009 *American Quarterly* special issue "In the Wake of Katrina," edited by Clyde Woods.

62 See Harris, Lobanov-Rostovsky, and Levenson, "Widening the Net."

63 See *Doe v. Jindal*, Complaint; and Women With A Vision, "Just a Talking Crime."

64 Rivlin, "Mogul Who Would Rebuild New Orleans."

65 Cohen, "Punks, Bulldaggers, and Welfare Queens," 444–45.

66 WWAV published stories on each of these projects. See Women With A Vision, "Join WWAV in Fighting Drug Testing for TANF Recipients" and "Micro-Enterprise, WWAV Style: Creating Beauty, Ending Poverty"; Speeches, Presentations, and Writings in the Born in Flames Living Archive.

67 Wendy Brown so powerfully expressed this sentiment in "Suffering the Paradoxes of Rights."

68 The term "empowerment" has been widely critiqued in revolutionary organizing circles because of its usage by people with power, who would claim to "empower" those with less without actually transforming the relationships of power. At WWAV, the term was used to underline members' own *self-empowerment* in the context of the NO Justice Project. No one can give another person power. As we discuss in depth in chapter 4, at WWAV, "we claim the power we were born with."

69 Deon asked Laura to work with her to reorganize the WWAV website so that the first thing people would see was a running newsreel of updates on the NO Justice Project. Once the structure was set, Deon contacted Laura whenever there was a new story that needed to get uploaded to the newsreel—about people impacted by CANS, a new facet of New Orleans policing that was exacerbating the criminalization crisis, or a milestone in WWAV's work to strike down the statute. Deon would talk; Laura would type; Deon would review text copy; Laura would incorporate her changes and make the post go live, sharing it across WWAV's social media platforms. These practices of collaboration were foundational to the Born in Flames Living Archive we built after the arson attack.

70 Louisiana earned the title "the world's prison capital" because it incarcerated more people per capita than any other US state. Chang, Threlkeld, and Smith, "Louisiana Incarcerated."

71 Ritchie tells this story in "Crimes Against Nature," 357, and in *Invisible No More*.

72 In his life history interview, attorney Bill Quigley explained how his practice of "social change lawyering" is modeled on the principles of legal aid during the Black freedom struggle. See William (Bill) Quigley, interview, August 15, 2013; Life History Interviews in the Born in Flames Living Archive. See also Quigley, "Ten Questions for Social Change Lawyers."

73 Andrea Ritchie and Alexis Agathocleous were the leads for the NO Justice Legal Team as a whole, with Alexis as CCR's lead counsel.

74 These claims are available at Center for Constitutional Rights, "Crime Against Nature by Solicitation (CANS) Litigation" under Case Files and are also linked to throughout the Case Timeline. Alexis Agathocleous and Andrea Ritchie both published law review articles that narrate the movement lawyering strategy for the NO Justice Project in detail. See Agathocleous, "When Power Yields to Justice"; and Ritchie, "Crimes against Nature."

75 *Doe v. Jindal*, Complaint.

76 Tatiana's statement and the statements by Deon Haywood, Andrea Ritchie, Shana M. griffin, and Rosana Cruz were transcribed by Rosana and published in *Bridging the Gulf*, "Grassroots Group Challenges Discriminatory Crime Against Nature Law." This story was reprinted with permission on the INCITE! blog.

77 Cruz, "Grassroots Group Challenges Discriminatory Crime Against Nature Law."

78 Cruz, "Grassroots Group Challenges Discriminatory Crime Against Nature Law."

79 Cruz, "Grassroots Group Challenges Discriminatory Crime Against Nature Law."

80 Cruz, "Grassroots Group Challenges Discriminatory Crime Against Nature Law."

81 See Quigley, interview, August 15, 2013.

82 While the legislative repeal of the CANS statute was building, two motions were filed to dismiss the federal lawsuit: one by the state of Louisiana on April 11, 2011, and the other by the city of New Orleans on May 17, 2011. On June 14, 2011, the NO Justice legal team filed an opposition to these motions and then, on June 23, filed an amicus brief in support of the lawsuit. On September 7, 2011, Judge Feldman ruled that the lawsuit would proceed. On October 31, 2011, the NO Justice legal team moved for summary judgment. See the Case Timeline at Center for Constitutional Rights, "Crime Against Nature by Solicitation (CANS) Litigation."

83 Krewe du Vieux was scheduled to roll on February 4, 2012, bringing all the "debaucheries between men" and "violations against nature" and "disordered desire" and "crimes of the flesh" out into the New Orleans streets. A majority white krewe, they played with a kind of politics of critique reminiscent of how Anthony Petro has analyzed the role of camp in ACT UP. See Petro, "Ray Navarro's Jesus Camp, AIDS Activist Video, and the 'New Anti-Catholicism.'" On Carnival in Africana traditions, see Aching, *Masking and Power*; Burton, *Afro-Creole*; and Stallybrass and White, *Politics and Poetics of Transgression*.

84 *Doe v. Jindal*, Order and Reasons, 851 F. Supp. 2d 995 (E.D. La. 2012) (No. 11-388).

85 Women With A Vision, "OUR WIN."

86 Judge Feldman granted summary judgment on March 29, 2012. On April 11, his formal judgment declared sex offender registration under Louisiana's CANS law unconstitutional and ordered that the state remove the nine NO Justice plaintiffs from the registry within thirty days. See *Doe v. Jindal*, Judgment, 851 F. Supp. 2d 995 (E.D. La. 2012) (No. 11-388). Alexis Agathocleous, CCR staff attorney, explained that when he called the people named in the lawsuit to share the details of the formal judgment, each person started to cry when he said, "A judge found that the state of Louisiana *violated your rights*."

87 Zina Mitchell emphasized this point in her life history interview; see Mitchell, interview, August 21, 2013.

88 Statement made to Deon Haywood in 2013, after the 2012 ruling was extended to all people with CANS convictions.

89 Women With A Vision, "Victory at Last! Louisiana Has Removed Hundreds of Individuals Unconstitutionally Placed on Sex Offender Registry"; Speeches, Presentations, and Writings in the Born in Flames Living Archive.

90 Women With a Vision, "OUR WIN."

91 Women With a Vision, "OUR WIN."

92 Kunzelman, "Louisiana Sex Law Violates Offenders' Rights, Federal Judge Rules."

93 Women With a Vision, "OUR WIN." Center for Constitutional Rights, "Judge Rules That Sex-Offender Registration for 'Crime Against Nature by Solicitation' Convictions Is Unconstitutional." See also Agathocleous, "When Power Yields to Justice" and "Building a Movement for Justice"; and Ritchie, "Crimes against Nature" and *Invisible No More*.

94 Because of the arson attack, the "We Spoke Our Truths" oral history project was never launched. Instead, our work to document the NO Justice victory became part of our research as survival after the fire and the Born in Flames Living Archive.

95 Women With A Vision, *Arson Destroys Women With A Vision Office—Please Help!*; Video Recordings in the Born in Flames Living Archive.

96 We are grateful to Mindy Fullilove for naming and tracing this in/as *Root Shock*.

97 See Doe v. Caldwell, Complaint, No. 12-1670, 2012 WL 6674415 (E.D. La. Jun. 27, 2012).

98 See Doe v. Caldwell, Stipulation of Settlement, No. 12-1670, 2012 WL 6674415 (E.D. La. Jun. 10, 2013)

Chapter 4: Working with Fire

Portions of this chapter appear in Laura McTighe, with Women With A Vision, "Theory on the Ground: Ethnography, Religio-Racial Study, and the Spiritual Work of Building Otherwise," *Journal of the American Academy of Religion* 88, no. 2 (2020): 407–39, https://doi.org/10.1093/jaarel/lfaa014.

1 Alexander, *Pedagogies of Crossing*, 266.

2 Shakur, *Assata*, 130.

3 Liu and Shange, "Toward Thick Solidarity."

4 That was why, as Ruth Wilson Gilmore has put it, "the racial in racial capitalism isn't secondary, nor did it originate in color or intercontinental conflict, but rather always group-differentiation to premature death." See Gilmore, "Abolition Geography and the Problem of Innocence," 240.

5 Shange and Liu, "Solidarity-as-Debt."

6 Iris Marion Young incisively critiques the universalizing violence of communalism, offering "city life" as a new normative, ideal social differentiation without exclusion in her work on "City Life and Difference."

7 In insisting on the right to complex, even contradictory, personhood for all in WWAV's network, we are thinking with Avery Gordon's observation in the first pages of *Ghostly Matters* of how, often, those who study domination withhold this right from the very people most impacted, preferring to script them as victims or superhuman agents.

8 Gilmore, *Golden Gulag*, 243. Here, she is building on Raymond Williams's claim in *The Long Revolution* that each age has its own "structure of feeling."

9 Gilmore, "Abolition Geography and the Problem of Innocence," 236–37.

10 In "Repairing La Memoria Rota," our *compa* Aurora Santiago Ortiz centers feminist oral histories as critical practices of memory recuperation and resistance.

11 First Grace United Methodist Church, "History." Building this union was described as a process of defying what Dr. Martin Luther King Jr. once referred to as "the most segregated hour in America" (see, e.g., Wishon, "New Orleans Church Defies 'Sunday Morning Segregation'").

12 "Front Porch Strategy: Organizing for Black Women's Lives at the Intersection of Service, Activism, and Research"; Speeches, Presentations, and Writings in the Born in Flames Living Archive.

13 WWAV distributes a whole range of harm reduction supplies to reduce the risk for transmitting HIV and hepatitis C, including clean syringes of a variety of sizes, small caps called "cookers" for reducing the drug into an injectable solution, cotton to filter the drug as it is pulled into the syringe, and tourniquets.

14 Women With A Vision, "WWAV Is an Organization without Walls!"; Speeches, Presentations, and Writings in the Born in Flames Living Archive.

15 Lorde, "Learning from the 60s."

16 Women With A Vision and SisterLove, "What's Up Down South? Perspectives on HIV and Its Challenges for Women in the Deep South in the U.S."; Speeches, Presentations, and Writings in the Born in Flames Living Archive.

17 Women With A Vision and SisterLove, "What's Up Down South?"

18 Women With A Vision and SisterLove, "What's Up Down South?"

19 Women With A Vision, "To Be a Human Rights Defender Is to Make a Choice"; Speeches, Presentations, and Writings in the Born in Flames Living Archive.

20 See, e.g., Hua, "Modern-Day Slavery."

21 Woods, "Antiblackness of 'Modern-Day Slavery' Abolitionism."

22 WWAV's "Deep South Decrim" toolkit helpfully distinguishes sex work done by choice or because of circumstance from coerced sexual labor, e.g., sex trafficking, through a "Spectrum of Choice" chart (10). The toolkit further distills the differences between sex work and sex trafficking. It also includes a discussion of how the criminalization of sex work has been proven to increase sex workers' vulnerability to trafficking and to increase violence against sex workers more broadly, especially at the hands of law enforcement (24–29). See Women With A Vision and Sex Worker Advisory Committee, *Deep South Decrim: Towards Sex Work Decriminialization and Justice in Louisiana*; Speeches, Presentations, and Writings in the Born in Flames Living Archive.

23 Here, we are thinking both of critical slavery studies like Annette Gordon-Reed's *Thomas Jefferson and Sally Hemings* and Stephanie Jones-Rogers's *They Were Her Property*, as well as Danielle McGuire's groundbreaking study of Black women, rape, and resistance in the civil rights era, *At the Dark End of the Street*.

24 See also Beloso, "Sex, Work, and the Feminist Erasure of Class," for an analysis of the contemporary feminist debate on prostitution.

25 For examples of mainstream media coverage, see Martin, "Former Sex Trafficking Victim Shines Light on Dark Underworld of Super Bowl"; and

Alpert, "Human Trafficking Draws Attention during Super Bowl, but It's a Year-Long, Worldwide Problem." For critiques of the mainstream media's role in producing this panic, see Martin and Hill, "Debunking the Myth of 'Super Bowl Sex Trafficking'"; and Hua, *Trafficking Women's Human Rights*.

26 The term "carceral feminism" was first coined by sociologist Elizabeth Bernstein in "Militarized Humanitarianism Meets Carceral Feminism." See also Victoria Law's "Against Carceral Feminism," for an analysis of this framework by abolition feminist movements.

27 The term "colonial feminism" was coined by Leila Ahmed in *Women and Gender in Islam*. It also undergirds anthropologist Lila Abu-Lughod's incisive critique of the Bush administration's branding of the so-called war on terror as a war to save women in her article "Do Muslim Women Really Need Saving?"

28 See Elizabeth Nolan Brown's distillation of why "The War on Sex Trafficking Is the New War on Drugs."

29 We use pseudonyms for all WWAV's participants in the "Diverting Diversion" section.

30 This leeway that people have to affect change within seemingly intractable systems is one of the principal terrains that WWAV works on when engaging with the bureaucracies that participants move through daily.

31 In "Abolition Geography and the Problem of Innocence," Ruth Wilson Gilmore analyzes how antiprison organizing predicated on innocence may achieve some measurable change, but usually does so in ways that harden the cages for everyone else (233–36). Survived and Punished New York's "Preserving Punishment Power" report revolutionizes this analysis into praxis through a six-part abolitionist screening tool for proposed criminal justice reforms, including "Does it create a division between 'deserving' and 'undeserving' people? Does it leave out especially marginalized groups (people with criminal records, undocumented people, etc.)? Does it cherry-pick particular people or groups as token public faces?" (3).

32 The Emerge program has been covered by Zenobia Jeffries Warfield, "What It Takes to Get Women Out of Prison—and Stay Out," and Kay Whitlock, "Endgame: How Bipartisan Criminal Justice Reform Institutionalizes a Right-Wing Neoliberal Agenda."

33 The language of "rescue" has long been used to describe the maternalist labors of white women, especially throughout the Progressive Era (e.g., Pascoe, *Relations of Rescue*). More recently, it has become especially popular among sex workers who get caught in and criminalized through the antitrafficking movement's efforts.

34 A. Davis, *Freedom Is a Constant Struggle*, 21.

35 A. Davis, *Freedom Is a Constant Struggle*, 118.

36 A. Davis, *Freedom Is a Constant Struggle*, 67.

37 Groundworks Mission Statement. Shared during Emerge Project, "Building Your Professional Brand"; Collective Storytelling Sessions in the Born in Flames Living Archive.

38 Emerge Project, "Building Your Professional Brand."

39 In using the word "dismember" here, we are thinking especially about the story of how Dana loses her arm in Octavia Butler's *Kindred*. When Dana time travels for the last time, returning to her California home in 1976 from the pre–Civil War Maryland plantation, she does so after stabbing the white enslaver Rufus, who had grabbed her while attempting to rape her. Surviving the physical and emotional violence of white supremacy is literally and permanently disfiguring for Dana.

40 For two compelling ethnographic accounts of moral rehabilitation in contemporary context, see Jared Zigon's "*HIV is God's Blessing*," and Angela Garcia's *The Pastoral Clinic*.

41 See the INCITE! "Critical Resistance Statement," which called movements to develop strategies and analysis around both state violence and violence against women.

42 Desiree offered this example during our panel at the "Rethinking Mass Incarceration in the South" conference. See Deon Haywood et al., "Community Organizing Is a Reentry Program: How Formerly Incarcerated Women Are Decarcerating Their Communities in the Prison Capital of the World"; Speeches, Presentations, and Writings in the Born in Flames Living Archive.

43 Michelle Jones's scholarship on the Indiana women's prison has illuminated how her state used "Magdalene societies," outside of the formal prison architecture, to discipline women arrested for prostitution. See Jones and Record, "Magdalene Laundries"; see also Onion, "Inmates at America's Oldest Women's Prison Are Writing a History of It—and Exploding the Myth of Its Benevolent Founders."

44 For a history of maternalistic rhetoric in this female reform tradition, see Mink, *Wages of Motherhood*.

45 On these technologies of gendered carceral control in early women's prisons, see Freedman, *Their Sisters' Keepers*; and Dodge, "*Whores and Thieves of the Worst Kind*."

46 Spaulding, "Results of Mental and Physical Examinations of Four Hundred Women Offenders," 716.

47 Prison Policy Initiative, "The Gender Divide: Tracking Women's State Prison Growth." See also Prison Policy Initiative, "Women's Mass Incarceration: The Whole Pie 2023."

48 The word "horrors" is a key coordinate of WWAV's southern Black feminist historical method, as it was in the title Ida B. Wells's 1892 pamphlet on lynching, *Southern Horrors*.

49 "Resilience"; Collective Storytelling Sessions in the Born in Flames Living Archive.

50 WWAV's Black Feminist Library includes biographies like Mary Frances Berry's *My Face Is Black Is True*; Jeanne Theoharis's *Rebellious Life of Miss Rosa Parks*; Barbara Ransby's *Ella Baker and the Black Freedom Movement*; and Pauli Murray's own *Autobiography of a Black Activist, Feminist, Lawyer, Priest, and Poet*; as well as anthologies like *Want to Start a Revolution?*, edited by Dayo F. Gore, Jeanne Theoharris, and Komozi Woodard; and *Toward an Intellectual History of Black Women*, edited by Mia Bay, Farah J. Griffin, Martha S. Jones, and Barbara D. Savage.

51 See, e.g., Albert Raboteau's *Slave Religion*. Foundational texts on Black women and religious activism were published in the 1990s and early 2000s, including Evelyn Higginbotham's *Righteous Discontent*, Anthea Butler's *Women in the Church of God in Christ*, and Judith Weisenfeld's *African American Women and Christian Activism*.

52 This literature on Black women and the carceral state grounds chapter 3. On Black women's organizing through labor movements and on public housing, see, e.g., Rhonda Williams's *Politics of Housing*; Felicia Kornbluh's *Battle for Welfare Rights*; Premilla Nadasen's *Welfare Warriors*; Nancy A. Naples's *Grassroots Warriors*; Lisa Levenstein's *Movement without Marches*; and Tomiko Brown-Nagin's *Courage to Dissent*.

53 By "legalized containment," we are thinking about processes that include segregation, the underdevelopment of "Black belts," the construction of public housing complexes, the forced migration of millions to prisons and jails, the policing of perimeters of Black neighborhoods with huge lights after dark, stop and frisk, "routine" stops while driving, and the use of security checkpoints, to name a few lethal policies from the racial capitalism playbook. We use the concept "slow death" to draw together processes including environmental devastation, illegal dumping, and medical neglect, which physically wear down groups of people and prefigure the premature death of entire communities. For a critical mapping of this concept in our liberatory fields of study, see Berlant, "Slow Death (Sovereignty, Obesity, Lateral Agency)."

54 Garza, "Love Letter to Black Folks."

55 Haywood, "This Day, We Use Our Energy for Revolution"; Speeches, Presentations, and Writings in the Born in Flames Living Archive.

56 Ross, "Understanding Reproductive Justice."

57 Katwiwa, "Violence, the Black Body & Reproductive Justice."

58 Calmes, "Advocates Shun 'Pro-choice' to Expand Message"; Laguens, "We're Fighting for Access, Not Choice."

59 Simpson, "Reproductive Justice and 'Choice.'" Planned Parenthood's president at the time, Cecile Richards, wrote "A Response to an Open Letter on Reproductive Justice and 'Choice,'" reflecting on the points in Simpson's letter and expressing her desire to meet with the leaders of national RJ groups and develop shared strategies.

60 See Turner et al., *We Always Resist*.

61 The question-and-answer period following the film was aggressively derailed by Melissa Flournoy, the white Louisiana state director of Planned Parenthood Gulf Coast. Kris Ford, a New Orleans native, queer Black femme, and member of WHJI (Women's Health and Justice Initiative) published an open letter the next morning which resulted in Flournoy's termination.

62 Trotter, "Citizens of New Orleans Hold a Moment of Silence for Michael Brown."

63 In their name, Wildseeds occupied grounds being opened nationally in Black women–led movement spaces, most especially through the Allied Media Conference workshops organized by adrienne maree brown and Walidah Imarisha, which resulted in the *Octavia's Brood* volume. They also claimed the "emergent strategy" principles for building otherwise, which were being developed in these same movement spaces and were curated in brown's *Emergent Strategy*, and which have now inspired hundreds of thousands organizers globally. See Wildseeds, "Wildseeds: The New Orleans Octavia Butler Emergent Strategy Collective."

64 Evans, "Well This Happened Today . . ."; Speeches, Presentations, and Writings in the Born in Flames Living Archive.

65 See "Photos: Protestors against Ferguson Killing."

66 Mwende Katwiwa, "On White People, Solidarity, and (Not) Marching for Mike Brown"; Speeches, Presentations, and Writings in the Born in Flames Living Archive.

67 Mwende Katwiwa, Facebook post, August 15, 2014; Speeches, Letters, and Writings in the Born in Flames Living Archive.

68 African American Policy Forum, #SayHerName; Fondren, "The 'Say Her Name' Movement Started for a Reason." WWAV was part of organizing the Breaking the Silence town hall in New Orleans in June 2015.

69 Harris, "Will Ferguson Be a Moment or a Movement?"

70 Pickens, "Ferguson."

71 Theoharis, "Arc of Justice Runs through Ferguson."

72 Taylor, *From #BlackLivesMatter to Black Liberation*.

73 Here, we are paraphrasing Gary Dorrien in *The New Abolition*: "King did not come from nowhere, and neither did the civil rights explosion of the 1950s" (10).

74 For example, in *Black Marxism*, Robinson argues that that the slave resistance was not predicated on Africans' experience of plantation life under slavery but rather on *a total rejection of their lot* (169). His refusal to script Black resistance as reactionary, episodic, or somehow secondarily reactive to oppressions shows us how racial capitalism operates through the contrary.

75 Robinson, *Black Marxism*, 307.

76 Gilmore, *Golden Gulag*, 243.

Chapter 5: The Grounds

1 "Smudging" is a ceremonial practice for cleansing a person or place from negative energies, which is common among many Indigenous peoples. Traditionally, smudging practices combine all four elements: a shell container (water), a sacred plant like sage (earth), the lighting of the sacred plant (fire), and the smoke produced (air). Within North America, smudging was among the Native religious practices criminalized under settler colonial rule. In recent years, the widespread appropriation and commercialization of smudging as whitewashed "spiritual" practice has been met with extensive critique by Indigenous communities and traditional healers. In the WWAV community, the practice of using sacred plants for cleansing honors the fugitive knowledges of the generations of Native Americans, Africans, Afro-Creoles, and African Americans that our work carries forward every day.

2 Michelle Wiley, interview, June 6, 2016; Life History Interviews in the Born in Flames Living Archive.

3 Christine Breland, interview, July 31, 2014; Life History Interviews in the Born in Flames Living Archive.

4 Gender structures the prison system and prisons are gendering institutions. People held captive are typically classified based on their sex assigned at birth, so the OPP women's pod could include cisgender women and transgender, gender-queer, and nonbinary people. See Stanley and Smith, eds., *Captive Genders*, for a landmark collection of essays on trans embodiment in the prison industrial complex.

5 "Kitchen Table: Women of Color Press" was an activist feminist press started in 1980 by Combahee River Collective cofounder Barbara Smith, at the suggestion of Audre Lorde.

6 Oscar Salinas, interview, August 7, 2013; Life History Interviews in the Born in Flames Living Archive.

7 See the Born in Flames Living Archive collection of sources at the conclusion of this book, and explore the archive online at borninflames.com.

8   Sharpe, *In the Wake*, 13. Here, we are indebted to liberatory works like Mary Frances Berry's *My Face Is Black Is True*; Saidiya Hartman's *Lose Your Mother*; Marisa Fuentes's *Dispossessed Lives*; Jessica Marie Johnson's *Wicked Flesh*; Michel-Rolph Trouillot's *Silencing the Past*; Aisha Finch's *Rethinking Slave Rebellion in Cuba*; and Sharon Luk's *Life of Paper*, among others.

9   Berry, "In Search of Callie House," 326.

10 Fuentes, *Dispossessed Lives*, 78. On "absented presence," see McKittrick, *Demonic Grounds*.

11 Hartman, "Venus in Two Acts," 11. On storying, see Young, *Grey Album*; and McKittrick, *Dear Science*.

12 Johnson, *Wicked Flesh*.

13 Sula Janet Evans is a self-described "Woman of Peace, Medicine Queen, Singer, Songwriter, Author, Entrepreneur, Artist, Birth Doula, and Akan Priestess," and a co-owner of King and Queen Emporium International in New Orleans. She is also a singer-songwriter with the world beat/reggae band Zion Trinity, who "salute the Orisha in song and give a pretty kicking Reggae show as well!," and the author and producer of *Spirit of the Orisha*, "a language and song preservation project in honor of the Yoruba People of Nigeria, West Africa."

14 Kelley, "We Are Not What We Seem," in *Race Rebels*, 78.

15 Central for us is the story of Callie House, a Tennessee washerwoman who organized hundreds of thousands of formerly enslaved people across the South at the start of the twentieth century to build locally rooted mutual aid societies, which then banded together to petition and sue the federal government in the first national case for reparations. Callie House's story had been lost for decades to any official record until historian and WWAV mentor Mary Frances Berry followed a lead from a union organizer who had spoken to an automotive worker who told him that there had once been a movement for reparations led by a woman. See Berry, *My Face Is Black Is True*.

16 Abu-Lughod, "Romance of Resistance," 53. This practice of letting resistance movements teach us about the complex interworkings of historically changing systems of power is related to, if almost the inverse of, the Black study practice of reading these historically changing systems of power from below for the clues they can provide to the challenges posed by resistance movements. Sarah Haley describes her methodological approach to studying gendered and racialized carceral control under Jim Crow in *No Mercy Here*, especially chapter 5. On Black study, see Harney and Moten, *Undercommons*.

17 This WWAV practice of being present and standing watch in largely white spaces maps onto the examples Simone Browne provides in *Dark Matters* for theorizing Black modes of countersurveillance—such as recording police interactions—as "dark sousveillance."

18 See Leigh Schmidt's *Consumer Rites*, especially chapter 3.

19 The analytical point comes into focus visually by juxtaposing Norman Rockwell's "rosy-cheeked white man" with the Netherlands' Zwarte Piet (or Black Pete).

20 Mwende Katwiwa, "Happy Holidays from #BlackFeministSanta"; Speeches, Presentations, and Writings in the Born in Flames Living Archive.

21 The term *nonreformist reform* was coined by André Gorz, "Strategies for Labor," in the context of anticapitalist organizing. The concept has been refined and expanded by prison industrial complex abolitionists to evaluate whether proposed reforms to the carceral state will undermine the existing system and support us in creating a police- and prison-free future in real time. Critical Resistance helpfully explicates the sorts of questions that abolitionists ask to distinguish "Reformist Reforms vs. Abolitionist Steps in Policing."

22 See A. Davis, *Freedom Is a Constant Struggle*, and chapter 4 for WWAV's work with the spatially and temporally expansive practices of study and struggle.

23 Allen's way of speaking of "the new" is reminiscent of Katherine McKittrick's description of the demonic as a working system that "can *only* unfold and produce an outcome when uncertainty, or (dis)organization, or something supernaturally demonic is integral to the methodology." McKittrick, *Demonic Grounds*, xxiv, emphasis added.

24 Haywood, "This Day, We Use Our Energy for Revolution"; Speeches, Presentations, and Writings in the Born in Flames Living Archive.

25 Ture, "From Black Power to Pan-Africanism."

26 Browne, *Dark Matters*.

27 "We specialize in the wholly impossible" was the motto of the National Training School for Women and Girls that Nannie Helen Burroughs founded in 1909.

28 A. Davis, Lecture at Southern Illinois University Carbondale, February 13, 2014.

29 Mwende was months away from launching their long-planned Young Women With A Vision (YWWAV) intergenerational mentoring program to connect school-aged girls with mothers and elders in the WWAV network. They had just left to go run an after-school poetry class.

30 "Mama Kat" was Raven Frederick's mom and a vital part of the WWAV family. She made her transition on July 18, 2022, but her spirit is always with us. Rest in Power.

31 We launched Front Porch Research Strategy as a dedicated research arm to honor WWAV's own history of starting as an idea thought up on a front porch in Central City, as well as the long legacy of southern women building

community, speaking truths, and crafting analysis in the interstices between street and home, between public and private. See Front Porch Research Strategy, "Home"; Speeches, Presentations, and Writings in the Born in Flames Living Archive.

32 Deon Haywood et al., "Front Porch Strategy: Organizing for Black Women's Lives at the Intersection of Service, Activism, and Research"; Speeches, Presentations, and Writings in the Born in Flames Living Archive.

33 United States Department of Justice, "Fact Sheet."

34 WWAV's framing that CANS put people at risk for HIV is rooted in our long-standing analysis of how racial capitalism, not individual behaviors, drives the HIV vulnerability of entire communities. Our analysis maps onto but also pushes deeper than public health frameworks around the structural drivers of disease and health.

35 While WWAV has always been inclusive of transgender and cisgender women, what Deon was drawing attention to in the early WWAV configuration was Black queer women and Black *straight* women working side by side.

36 Haywood et al., "Front Porch Strategy."

37 At other points, Shaquita has also talked about how, while studying for her MPH, she was assigned articles that were based on WWAV's work, but never cited the organization.

38 There are several explanations for this difficulty. One is a standard question that would be true across jurisdictions: Who has a right to have access to police data? The degree of secrecy in New Orleans has been exacerbated by the New Orleans Police Department and Orleans Parish Prison both being under consent decrees for racial profiling and inhumane conditions, respectively. Lack of access to data, especially pre-2005, can often be quite real, as so many records were destroyed in Hurricane Katrina. This can also be a cover used to prevent releasing potentially damaging local or state archives.

39 Shaquita is describing a classic tactic by state agencies, be that in court proceedings or Freedom of Information Act requests: when a request is made, bury people in reams of unindexed paperwork. This point also calls to mind a frustration that so many of us shared about the everyday violence of bureaucratic systems after the limits of the 2012 NO Justice court ruling became clear: If it was so easy to put women on the sex offender registry list, why is it so hard to get them off?

40 Haywood et al., "Front Porch Strategy."

41 This connection between religion and the law was so powerfully made by Ida B. Wells in her 1893 pamphlet *The Reason Why*, which she wrote and distributed at the World's Columbian Exposition in Chicago. In it, she distilled her careful observations of the convict lease system and the lynch law. She gave two interrelated explanations for these "twin infamies" deci-

mating Black life. First, "the religious, moral and philanthropic forces of the country—all the agencies which tend to uplift and reclaim the degraded and ignorant, are in the hands of the Anglo-Saxon." In word and deed, they believe that "to have Negro blood in the veins makes one unworthy of consideration, a social outcast, a leper, even in the church." Second, the judges, juries, and court officials "are white men who share these prejudices. They also make the laws." See Wells, *The Reason Why*. Shaquita and Laura discussed these dynamics around racism and religion at length while WWAV was conceptualizing a "Have Faith in RJ" program to mobilize faith-based communities for reproductive justice in the summer of 2015. See Women With A Vision, *Have Faith in Reproductive Justice*; Speeches, Presentations, and Writings in the Born in Flames Living Archive.

42 Haywood et al., "Front Porch Strategy."

43 See "#Formation, Activism, and the Importance of Black [Southern] Women's Narratives," "Lemons: Black Women and Representation," and "State Violence against Black Women and Girls"; Collective Storytelling Sessions in the Born in Flames Living Archive.

44 Haywood et al., "Front Porch Strategy."

45 "Strategic Planning Retreat Listening Session with WWAV Foremothers Catherine Haywood and Danita Muse"; Collective Storytelling Sessions in the Born in Flames Living Archive.

46 Haywood et al., "Front Porch Strategy."

47 Quoted in Farrag, "Role of Spirit in the #BlackLivesMatter Movement."

48 Kaba, "So You're Thinking about Becoming an Abolitionist."

49 This point is further developed in Laura's 2021 essay "Abolition Is Sacred Work."

50 See, e.g., Weisenfeld, *New World A-Coming*; Alexander, *Pedagogies of Crossing*; James, *Black Jacobins*; Roy, "Pandemic Is a Portal."

51 So ends a spell Octavia Butler cast for becoming a best-selling writer. See *Paris Review*, "So Be It, See to It."

Epilogue: Forward Ever

1 Laura McTighe, Andrea J. Ritchie, and Women With A Vision, *Our Existence Is Political: 30 Years of Black Feminist Struggle*; Speeches, Presentations, and Writings in the Born in Flames Living Archive; and Carol McDonald et al., *30 Years of WWAV*; Video Recordings in the Born in Flames Living Archive.

2 See Rhea, "Safe Sex Ed."

3 A. Davis, Lecture at Southern Illinois University Carbondale.

4 Women With A Vision and Sex Worker Advisory Committee, *Deep South Decrim: Towards Sex Work Decriminalization and Justice in Louisiana*; Speeches, Presentations, and Writings in the Born in Flames Living Archive.

5   Women With A Vision and Sex Worker Advisory Committee, *Deep South Decrim*, 10.

6   The "Safety and Love" collective visioning session is part of chapter 5. See "Safety and Love"; Collective Storytelling Sessions in the Born in Flames Living Archive.

7   Lorde, *Burst of Light*, 130.

8   McTighe, Ritchie, and Women With A Vision, *Our Existence Is Political*, 19.

9   For a report on WWAV's process of building community knowledge and consensus to develop a statewide EtE plan, see Women With A Vision, "Ending the Epidemic: Louisiana"; Speeches, Presentations, and Writings in the Born in Flames Living Archive. The core goals for this work are: (1) Eliminate Stigma; (2) Ensure Universal Access to Prevention Tools; (3) Ensure Universal Access to Health and Community Resources; (4) Improve Social Justice to Eliminate Health and Social Inequities; and (5) Achieve a More Coordinated Response to Ending the Epidemics.

10 HIV Racial Justice Now, "A Declaration of Liberation."

11 Women With A Vision, "BLACK WOMEN LEAD: The Meaning of a Reproductive Justice Framework"; Speeches, Letters, and Writings in the Born in Flames Living Archive.

12 Berry, *History Teaches Us to Resist*.

13 This phrase is the title of a poem by New Orleans poet Sunni Patterson written in the wake of Katrina. See Patterson, "We Know This Place" and *We Know This Place*.

14 Deon Haywood, "#BANSOFFOURBODIES"; Speeches, Presentations, and Writings in the Born in Flames Living Archive.

BORN IN FLAMES LIVING ARCHIVE

The Born in Flames Living Archive was launched in the immediate aftermath of the arson attack on the headquarters of Women With A Vision (WWAV), in New Orleans, on May 24, 2012. Knowing that the arsonists who firebombed and destroyed WWAV intended to erase our work once and for all, we began collecting every life-giving ember we could find. That included the handfuls of photographs, posters, and documents that had not gone up in flames, which are now preserved at our offices on Oretha Castle Haley Boulevard. It also extended to our research as survival to record our presence with one another and with our communities in new ways: life history interviews, collective storytelling sessions, and more.

Being present in these ways changed our understanding of what the Born in Flames Living Archive was and needed to be. We use the term *living archive* to center the relational practices through which our communities have shaped and passed down for generations what living freedom means amid constant surveillance. Our relationships hold all that we have imagined for ourselves and the world. Building this living archive, thus, has not simply been a matter of reconstructing the paper record that was destroyed by the fire. It has also meant honoring the relational caverns in which our thoughts, actions, and dreams have been kept safe for centuries. And it has meant organizing to ensure that all of us at WWAV have a place that can never be erased—neither from the geography of New Orleans, nor from history.

We share here a selection of the world-building knowledges held in our living archive, focusing on those that fill the pages of *Fire Dreams*. These resources and others will be made available at the borninflames.com website. WWAV welcomes contributions to this growing archive from all who have participated in our work or been touched by it.

Life History Interviews

We launched the oral history arm of our research as survival in the summer of 2013. Deon Haywood and Laura McTighe began by assembling a list of people to interview who had contributed to WWAV's work before Hurricane Katrina. That list soon expanded to include current staff; our longtime community partners in New Orleans; organizers who moved the vision forward locally, nationally, and internationally; and anyone else these people said we needed to talk to. We asked each interviewee about the whole of their life and work, not just the portions that related to WWAV, because we wanted our archive building to stay true to the ways that WWAV has always been in community. Our work to build this living record of the people who have made WWAV remains ongoing.

Interviews thus far have been conducted by Laura McTighe, in person, at locations in New Orleans, with the exception of one telephone interview, noted below.

Amy Wolfe, 2013–2014 Albert Schweitzer Fellow, WWAV. Interviewee's home, August 20, 2013.

Angelita Bolden, former Outreach Worker, WWAV. By telephone, August 5, 2013.

Catherine Haywood, Cofounder, WWAV. Home of Deon Haywood and Shaquita Borden, July 29, 2013.

Christine Breland Lobre, Public Health Intern and, later, Program Coordinator, WWAV. WWAV at ArtEgg, 1001 S. Broad Street, July 31, 2014.

Danita Muse, Cofounder, WWAV. Interviewee's home, July 26, 2013.

Dianne Jones, Harm Reduction Specialist, WWAV. Interviewee's home, August 6, 2015.

Don Evans, longtime Community Partner of WWAV; HIV Advocate. Home of Deon Haywood and Shaquita Borden, August 2, 2013.

Gwendolyn Richardson, longtime Community Partner of WWAV; Volunteer/Intern Program Coordinator, Ashé Cultural Arts Center. Ashé Cultural Arts Center, 1712 Oretha Castle Haley Boulevard, August 6, 2013.

Leslie Davis, Social Work Intern, WWAV. WWAV at ArtEgg, August 11, 2014.

Maryam Uloho, Participant, Summer 2013 Community Voices Sessions, WWAV; Founder, SisterHearts. Interviewee's home, August 2, 2013.

Michelle Wiley, Case Manager, WWAV. WWAV at 1226 N. Broad Street, June 6, 2016.

Mwende Katwiwa, VISTA Program Member and, later, Program Assistant, Executive Assistant, and Office Manager, WWAV. Interviewee's home, July 31, 2014, and June 3, 2016.

Nakita Shavers, Sexual and Reproductive Health Coordinator, WWAV. WWAV at 1226 N. Broad Street, June 6, 2016.

Nia Weeks, Policy Director, WWAV. WWAV at 1226 N. Broad Street, June 6, 2016.

Noel Twilbeck, CEO, CrescentCare Health Centers (formerly NO/AIDS Task Force). Interviewee's office, 2601 Tulane Avenue, August 8, 2013.

Oscar Salinas, former Staff Member, Mujeres Con Vision program, WWAV; Regional MAI Coordinator, Delta Region AIDS Education and Training Center. Interviewee's office, 2335 Poydras Street, August 7, 2013.

Raven Frederick, Community Outreach Specialist, WWAV. WWAV at 1226 N. Broad Street, June 6, 2016.

Rebecca Atkinson, Gender-Based Violence Program Coordinator, WWAV. WWAV at ArtEgg, August 5, 2014.

Robert Ellis, former Administrative Assistant, WWAV; Clinical Administrator, Bridge House. Interviewee's office, 4150 Earhart Boulevard, August 6, 2013.

Sharon Peterson, longtime Community Partner of WWAV and Organizer of WWAV Home Health Parties. Interviewee's home, August 9, 2013.

Timothy Craft, Social Work Intern and Emerge Program Manager, WWAV. WWAV at ArtEgg, August 4, 2014.

Wendi Cooper, Plaintiff in the NO Justice Project lawsuit, Coordinator of Girls With a Pearl, WWAV. WWAV at ArtEgg, August 2, 2014.

Wes Ware, longtime Community Partner of WWAV; Founding Director, Break-OUT! WWAV at ArtEgg, August 15, 2013.

William (Bill) Quigley, Core Member of the NO Justice Legal Team; Professor of Law, Director of the Law Clinic, and Director of the Gillis Long Poverty Law Center, Loyola University New Orleans. WWAV at ArtEgg, August 15, 2013.

Zina Mitchell, former Outreach Specialist, WWAV. Interviewee's home, August 21, 2013.

Collective Storytelling Sessions

Meaning at WWAV has always been made in community through collective storytelling sessions, often held on front porches. These sessions are how we turn everyday knowledge about the intimate and structural conditions that produce violence into a shared analysis of racial capitalism and a plan for coordinated action. They also bring us into communion with the wellsprings of dreams that have steadily been sheltered in these grounds for generations. Choosing to document our collective storytelling sessions after the fire enabled us to ascribe some permanence to this knowledge. But it is also important to state that the full breadth of our collective knowledge-making is not recorded here. We have intentionally chosen which facets of WWAV's work to render visible. Some things remain carefully concealed so that they may endure.

Collective storytelling sessions are listed here by title; some titles are official event or project names, while others are descriptive. Sessions took place in New Orleans unless otherwise noted.

"Black and Brown Sex Worker Second Line." March from WWAV, 1226 N. Broad Street, to "under the bridge" (under the Interstate 10 overpass along Claiborne Avenue), December 15, 2018.

"Black Feminist Santa." Photo Shoot. WWAV, 1226 N. Broad Street, December 11, 2015.

"Black Love Day Celebration." Hosted by WWAV's Black LGBTQ Action Coalition. Second Vine Wine, 4212 Magazine Street, February 14, 2016.

"Black Women's Reproductive Justice Convening." Dillard University, December 10, 2016.

"Black Women's Reproductive Justice Roundtable: Baton Rouge Session." HAART Clinic, 4550 North Boulevard #250, Baton Rouge, LA, June 4, 2016.

"Black Women's Reproductive Justice Roundtable: Lafayette Session." Arcadiana Cares, 809 Martin Luther King Jr. Drive, Lafayette, LA, July 9, 2016.

"Burnout Training." With foremother Danita Muse. WWAV, 1226 N. Broad Street, March 8, 2016.

Community Voices Project (2013). A series of community forums at the intersections of WWAV's core policy areas organized the first summer after the fire. Facilitated by Deon Haywood, Desiree Evans, Laura McTighe, and Shaquita Borden.

* "Never Going Back: Formerly Incarcerated Women Speak." RAE House, 1212 St. Bernard Avenue, July 25, 2013.
* "When Violence Hits Home: A Safe Space for Black Women Survivors." Community Book Center, 2523 Bayou Road, August 1, 2013.
* "Staying Alive: Harm Reduction & Overdose Prevention." RAE House, 1212 St. Bernard Avenue, August 15, 2013.
* "When Violence Hits Home: A Safe Space for LGBTQ Survivors." Rosa F. Keller Library, 4300 S. Broad Street, August 22, 2013.

"Dancers Speak OUT!: A Dancers' Safety Forum & Know Your Rights Conversation." WWAV, 1226 N. Broad Street, October 28, 2015.

"Driving Old Outreach Routes." With foremother Catherine Haywood and Laura McTighe. Various locations, January 30, 2016.

Emerge Project (2014–2015). A project to organize sex workers, launched in the wake of WWAV's victory against sex work criminalization through the NO Justice Project.

* WWAV Staff Program Development Session. With Timothy Craft, Christine Breland, and Leslie Davis. WWAV offices at ArtEgg, 1001 S. Broad Street, July 30, 2014.
* Emerge Sessions. With participants in the Crossroads Program. WWAV offices at ArtEgg, 2014–2015.
* "Building Your Professional Brand." Groundworks Training led by Emerge Graduates, WWAV offices at ArtEgg, March 27, 2015.

"Ending the Epidemic." Porch Talk. WWAV, 1226 N. Broad Street, March 25, 2019.

"Filing the NO Justice Lawsuit." "Tatiana," Deon Haywood, Shana M. griffin, Andrea Ritchie, and Rosana Cruz. Eastern District of Louisiana Court, February 15, 2011.

"#Formation, Activism, and the Importance of Black [Southern] Women's Narratives." Black Feminist Porch Talk. WWAV, 1226 N. Broad Street, February 16, 2016.
Have Faith in Reproductive Justice Project (2014). A faith-based organizing
project launched in the summer of 2014 amid targeted attacks on reproduc-
tive health in Louisiana and across the South.
  * WWAV Staff Weekly Planning Meetings. WWAV offices at ArtEgg, 1001 S.
    Broad Street, summer–fall 2014.
  * Focus Groups for African American Women of Faith. Rosa F. Keller Li-
    brary, 4300 S. Broad Street, July 31 and August 1, 2014.
  * Focus Groups at Churches in Louisiana and Mississippi. Locations confi-
    dential, summer–fall 2014,
"Housewarming and Open House." WWAV, 1226 N. Broad Street, December 9,
2015.
"Lemons: Black Women and Representation." Black Feminist Porch Talk.
WWAV, 1226 N. Broad Street, May 4, 2016.
"Marley Dias, Founder #1000BlackGirlBooks, and Director Ava DuVernay."
Black Feminist Porch Talk. WWAV, 1226 N. Broad Street, July 3, 2016.
"More than Collateral Consequences: Women, Incarceration, and the War on
Drugs." Hosted by WWAV. RAE House, 1212 St. Bernard Avenue, March 30,
2016.
"Our Voice, Our Time: Louisiana Black Women's Advocacy Day." Louisiana
State Capitol, Baton Rouge, April 26, 2017.
"Resilience." Porch Talk with WWAV Staff. WWAV, 1226 N. Broad Street, De-
cember 11, 2015.
"#SayHerName National Day of Action: A Conversation and Commemoration
for and in Support of Black Women, Girls, and Femmes." Hosted by WWAV,
BYP100, and other local organizations. Intersection, Ursulines and Clai-
borne Avenues, May 19, 2026.
"Safety and Love." Strategy Meeting and Porch Talk. WWAV, 1226 N. Broad
Street, March 24–25, 2016.
"Slow Your Roll: Research and Community Knowledge, a Reckoning" (2018). A
series of conversations led by Catherine Haywood and Laura McTighe with
core members of WWAV on the violences that WWAV and our communities have endured at the hands of researchers, and WWAV's own practices for
valuing community knowledge and developing community-driven research
projects.
  * Catherine Haywood and Laura McTighe, with Shaquita Borden. Home
    of Deon Haywood and Shaquita Borden, July 16, 2018.
  * Catherine Haywood and Laura McTighe, with Danita Muse. WWAV,
    1226 N. Broad Street, July 19, 2018.
  * Catherine Haywood, Laura McTighe, and Ashley Wennerstrom. Home
    of Ashley Wennerstrom, July 26, 2018.

* Catherine Haywood and Laura McTighe, with Ashley Wennerstrom, Danita Muse, Deon Haywood, and Shaquita Borden. WWAV, 1226 N. Broad Street, October 23, 2018.

"State Violence against Black Women and Girls." Black Feminist Porch Talk. WWAV, 1226 N. Broad Street, May 24, 2016.

"Strategic Planning Retreat Listening Session with WWAV Foremothers Catherine Haywood and Danita Muse." Destin, FL, May 11, 2016.

"30 Years at the Intersections: Justice, Action, and Black Feminist Struggle." A weeklong series of events with Deon Haywood and Shaquita Borden at Dartmouth College, Hanover, NH, culminating in a conversation with Deon Haywood and Laura McTighe, April 15–19, 2019.

"30+ Years of Black Feminist Struggle: A Central City Tour with Women With A Vision." American Studies Association Annual Meeting Program Committee Special Session, Tour with Deon Haywood, Shaquita Borden, Danita Muse, and Laura McTighe by bus through WWAV's old outreach routes in Central City New Orleans, November 5, 2022.

We Always Resist: Trust Black Women (2011, SisterSong: Trust Black Women; dir. Dionne Turner). Film screening, followed by a discussion with Deon Haywood and Paris Hatcher, 3300 S. Broad Street (outdoors), August 13, 2014.

"Where Do We Go from Here? A Conversation with WWAV Executive Director Deon Haywood, Mother of the Reproductive Justice Movement Loretta Ross, and Historian and Activist Mary Frances Berry." WWAV, 2028 Oretha Castle Haley Boulevard (also livestreamed), March 5, 2022.

"WWAV 25th Anniversary Party + Fundraiser." Mulate's Party Hall, 201 Julia Street, December 14, 2014.

"WWAV 30th Anniversary Gala." Latrobe's on Royal, 403 Royal Street, December 6, 2019.

"YWWAV Black Girls Brunch: A Meet-Up for Black Girls (13–18 years) Interested in the YWWAV Afterschool Program." WWAV, 1226 N. Broad Street, September 17, 2016.

Speeches, Presentations, and Writings

At WWAV, we have long understood that we need to tell our own stories about the histories we are making to audiences outside our communities. Over the years, that telling has taken on a lot of forms: speeches, presentations, open letters, toolkits, reports, blogs, social media posts, articles, and (now) books. The choice of medium is as much a function of the message being shared as it is of the person doing the sharing. We honor all of the Black feminist histories that have been created by WWAV, past, present, and future, as essential parts of this living archive. Our words, both spoken and written, testify to the complex ways in which southern Black women organizers have long navigated the chasm between the racial capitalism playbook and our own life-giving, liberatory work.

We include here a selection of speeches, presentations, and writings by members and accomplices of WWAV, focusing on those that are referenced or reproduced in *Fire Dreams*.

Evans, Desiree. "Well This Happened Today . . ." Email to WWAV staff after the National Moment of Silence vigil-turned-march in New Orleans, August 14, 2014.

Ford, Kris. "Bad Home Training: An Open Letter to Melissa Flournoy of Planned Parenthood Gulf Coast." *Women's Health and Justice Initiative Reproductive Justice Blog*, August 14, 2014. https://whjiblog.wordpress.com/2014 /08/14/open-letter-to-melissa-flournoy-of-planned-parenthood-gulf-coast/.

Front Porch Research Strategy. "Home." https://frontporchresearch.org/.

Haywood, Catherine. "Condom Social Marketing in the 'GHETTO.'" Unpublished manuscript, n.d. WWAV Archives, New Orleans.

Haywood, Deon. "Advancing Equity for Women and Girls of Color Summit." Conference presentation at the White House. Washington, DC, November 11, 2013.

Haywood, Deon. "#BANSOFFOURBODIES." Speech at protest. New Orleans, May 14, 2022.

Haywood, Deon. "Black Feminist Dreams in the American South: Strategizing for RJ Movement Building." Conference presentation at HIV PJA at Creating Change. Chicago, IL, February 22, 2016.

Haywood, Deon. "Ending Criminalization: Legal and Advocacy Strategies to Address and Repeal Discriminatory Laws." Keynote address at the XIX International AIDS Conference. Washington, DC, July 22–27, 2012.

Haywood, Deon. "Equality and Women Mapping the City: Atlanta, Detroit and New Orleans." Keynote address at the Faculty Inaugural Symposium, Spelman College. Atlanta, GA, April 8, 2016.

Haywood, Deon. "First Movement for Black Lives National Convening." Conference presentation at Cleveland State University. Cleveland, OH, July 24–26, 2015.

Haywood, Deon. "FREE HER Legislative Advocacy Conference." Conference presentation at the Charles Hamilton Houston Institute at Harvard Law School. Cambridge, MA, August 4–5, 2015.

Haywood, Deon. "Harm Reduction and Human Rights: Strategies on Expanding Harm Reduction through Human Rights." Panel at the Drug Policy Alliance webinar, May 12, 2015.

Haywood, Deon. "Marijuana, Racism, and the Future of Reform." Panel at "Facing Race: A National Conference." Dallas, TX, November 13–15, 2014.

Haywood, Deon. "Our Bodies, Our Lives, Our Voices: The State of Black Women & Reproductive Justice." Conference presentation at the National Press Club. Washington, DC, June 27, 2016.

Haywood, Deon. "OUR WIN—Letter from Women With A Vision Executive Director, Deon Haywood." *Women With A Vision*, March 30, 2012.

https://wwav-no.org/our-win-letter-from-executive-director-deon-haywood
/. Reposted at *Louisiana Justice Institute* (blog), March 30, 2012. http://
louisianajusticeinstitute.blogspot.com/2012/03/our-win-letter-from-women
-with-vision.html.

Haywood, Deon. "Racial Justice and HIV." Keynote address at the Cultural Con-
siderations of Healthcare Symposium. Student Union, University of Nevada
Reno, February 22, 2016.

Haywood, Deon. "Religion, Media, Markets and the Making of Black Sexualities." Plenary panel at "Are the Gods Afraid of Black Sexuality? Religion
and the Burdens of Black Sexual Politics," Institute for Research in African-
American Studies, Columbia University. New York, NY, October 23–24,
2014.

Haywood, Deon. "Reproductive Justice: Ethics in Human Services with Deon
Haywood and Dr. Willie Parker." Discussion at Tulane University. New Orleans, November 3, 2015.

Haywood, Deon. "The Sex Workers Rights Movement: Addressing Justice." Keynote address at the 6th National Desiree Alliance Conference. New Orleans,
July 10–15, 2016.

Haywood, Deon. "This Day, We Use Our Energy for Revolution." Speech at the
Solidarity Rally for Trayvon Martin, Washington Square, New Orleans,
July 14, 2013. Partial audio recording and transcript published at *Bridge the
Gulf,* https://bridgethegulfproject.org/blog/2013/day-we-use-our-energy
-revolution.

Haywood, Deon. "Southern Stories: Global and Domestic Drug Policy and
#NerdlandForever: Live with Melissa Harris-Perry." Presentation at the Mu-
seum of Drug Policy's pop-up cultural hub coinciding with the United Na-
tions General Assembly's Special Session on the World Drug Problem. New
York, NY, April 19, 2016.

Haywood, Deon. "Take Root: Red State Perspectives on Reproductive Justice."
Keynote address at the University of Oklahoma. Norman, OK, February 21–
22, 2014.

Haywood, Deon. "Theory on the Ground: Religion and Spirituality, Repressing
and Redeeming the Struggle for Justice." Panel at the Center for Religion and
Media, New York University. New York, NY, November 5, 2015.

Haywood, Deon. "This Day, We Use Our Energy for Revolution." Speech at solidarity rally for Trayvon Martin. Washington Square, New Orleans, July 14,
2013. https://bridgethegulfproject.org/blog/2013/day-we-use-our-energy
-revolution.

Haywood, Deon. "We Are Each Other's Keepers." *Abortion* (blog), *Women With
A Vision,* June 24, 2022. https://WWAV-no.org/abortion/.

Haywood, Deon. "When the War on Drugs Becomes a War on Women." Panel at
the International Drug Policy Reform Conference. Denver, CO, October 23–
26, 2013.

Haywood, Deon, Desiree Evans, Ashley Bernal, Shaquita Borden, and Laura Mc-
Tighe. "Community Organizing Is a Reentry Program: How Formerly Incarcerated Women Are Decarcerating Their Communities in the Prison Capital
of the World." Presentation at "Rethinking Mass Incarceration in the South,"
University of Mississippi. Oxford, MS, April 13–15, 2014.

Haywood, Deon, Mwende Katwiwa, Leslie Davis, Shaquita Borden, and Laura
McTighe. "'My Existence Is Political': Black Feminist Freedom Dreams in
the Prison Capital of the World." Presentation at "Rethinking Mass Incarceration in the South," Vanderbilt University. Nashville, TN, 2015.

Haywood, Deon, Mwende Katwiwa, Shaquita Borden, and Laura McTighe.
"Front Porch Strategy: Organizing for Black Women's Lives at the Intersections
of Service, Activism, and Research." Presentation at the Know Her Truths: Advancing Justice for Women and Girls of Color Conference. Anna Julia Cooper Center, Wake Forest University. Winston-Salem, NC, April 29, 2016.

Katwiwa, Mwende. Facebook post. August 15, 2014. https://www
.facebook.com/permalink.php?story_fbid=671934409562191&id
=100002369131532&substory_index=1.

Katwiwa, Mwende. "Happy Holidays from #BlackFeministSanta." *Women With
A Vision New Orleans*, December 17, 2015. https://myexistenceispolitical
.com/2015/12/17/happy-holidays-from-blackfeministsanta/.

Katwiwa, Mwende. "On White People, Solidarity and (Not) Marching for Mike
Brown." *FreeQuency Frequently Writes*, 2014. https://freeqthamighty.tumblr
.com/post/95573664816/on-white-people-solidarity-and-not-marching.

Katwiwa, Mwende. "Violence, the Black Body & Reproductive Justice." *Free-
Quency Frequently Writes*, 2014. https://freeqthamighty.tumblr.com/post
/94554773556/violence-the-black-body-reproductive-justice.

McTighe, Laura, Andrea J. Ritchie, and Women With A Vision. *Our Exis-
tence Is Political: 30 Years of Black Feminist Struggle*. New Orleans: Women
With A Vision, 2019. http://WWAV-no.org/wp-content/uploads/2019/12
/WomenWithAVision_2019Report_Print.pdf.

Muse, Danita. "NEEDLE EXCHANGE: Using the Existing Pharmacy System."
Unpublished manuscript, n.d. WWAV Archives, New Orleans.

Simpson, Monica. "Reproductive Justice and 'Choice': An Open Letter to
Planned Parenthood." *Rewire News Group*, August 5, 2014. https://
rewirenewsgroup.com/article/2014/08/05/reproductive-justice-choice
-open-letter-planned-parenthood/.

Women With A Vision. "BLACK WOMEN LEAD: The Meaning of a Reproductive Justice Framework." Flyer. June 29, 2020. https://myemail
.constantcontact.com/WE-WON.html?soid=1111872360833&aid
=pWF8hXP9r48.

Women With A Vision. "Ending the Epidemic: Louisiana." *Women With A
Vision*, n.d. https://WWAV-no.org/ete-louisiana/.

Women With A Vision. *Have Faith in Reproductive Justice*. Campaign toolkit.
New Orleans: Women With A Vision, 2015.

Women With A Vision. "An Intersectional Approach to Abortion Justice." *Women With A Vision*. May 2022. https://WWAV-no.org/wp-content /uploads/2022/05/WWAV-AbortionJustice.pdf.

Women With A Vision. "Join WWAV in Fighting Drug Testing for TANF Recipients." *Women With A Vision*, November 11, 2011. https://WWAV-no.org /drug-testing-for-tanf/.

Women With A Vision. "'Just a Talking Crime': A Policy Brief in Support of the Repeal of Louisiana's Solicitation of a Crime Against Nature (SCAN) Statute." 2011. https://wwav-no.org/wp-content/uploads/2019/09/Final _PolicyBrief_TalkingCrime.pdf.

Women With A Vision. "Micro-Enterprise, WWAV Style: Creating Beauty, Ending Poverty." *Women With A Vision*, January 13, 2012. https://WWAV-no.org /micro-enterprise-WWAV-style-creating-beauty-ending-poverty/.

Women With A Vision. "Rebuilding Our Archive." *Women With A Vision*, November 27, 2013. https://WWAV-no.org/rebuilding-our-archive-the -born-in-flames-oral-history-project-with-WWAV-board-member-laura -mctighe/.

Women With A Vision. "The Thrive Study." Report. *Women With A Vision*, December 2012. https://WWAV-no.org/wp-content/uploads/2022/12/Final -Thrive-Report-r2.pdf.

Women With A Vision. "To Be a Human Rights Defender Is to Make a Choice." *Women With A Vision*, October 14, 2013. https://WWAV-no.org/to-be-a -human-rights-defender-is-to-make-a-choice/.

Women With A Vision. "Victory at Last! Louisiana Has Removed Hundreds of Individuals Unconstitutionally Placed on Sex Offender Registry." *Women With A Vision*, October 28, 2013. http://WWAV-no.org/victory-at-last -louisiana-has-removed-hundreds-of-individuals-unconstitutionally-placed -on-sex-offender-registry/.

Women With A Vision. "WWAV Is an Organization without Walls!" *Women With A Vision*, March 12, 2013. http://WWAV-no.org/WWAV-is-an -organization-without-walls.

Women With A Vision. *Your Survival Guide to a Post-Roe Louisiana.* New Orleans: Women With A Vision, 2022. https://WWAV-no.org/wp-content /uploads/2022/11/Post-Roe-PDF.pdf.

Women With A Vision and BreakOUT! "Women With A Vision and Break-OUT! Respond to Times-Picayune's 'Uneasy Street.'" *Louisiana Justice Institute* (blog), August 12, 2013. http://louisianajusticeinstitute.blogspot.com /2013/08/women-with-vision-and-breakout-respond.html.

Women With A Vision and Sex Worker Advisory Committee. *Deep South Decrim: Towards Sex Work Decriminalization and Justice in Louisiana.* Toolkit. New Orleans: Women With A Vision, 2021. https://www.canva.com/design /DAEWosroygo/Pya5th_pl46ExUFfJoYZRw/view?website#4:cover.

Women With A Vision and SisterLove. "What's Up Down South? Perspectives on HIV and Its Challenges for Women in the Deep South in the U.S." Press release. July 23, 2012.

Video Recordings

WWAV started producing our own visual media the day after the 2012 arson attack with a short video titled *Arson Destroys Women With A Vision Office—Please Help!* We knew that we had to take control of the visual work of representing this violence against WWAV and framing why and how the work would continue to get done, no matter what. This video broke the story of the arson attack to thousands of people nationwide and rallied a groundswell of community support. It also inspired a series of "After the Fire" videos, created with WWAV staff and participants, and an "After the Fire" blog (since defunct), where we shared photographs and other forms of digital storytelling about the otherwise worlds we were making.

Listed below are some of the videos that we made or that were made with us and in our honor.

McDonald, Carol, Angélique Roché, Laura McTighe, and Andrea Ritchie. *30 Years of WWAV*. December 6, 2019. https://vimeo.com/377895341 ?embedded=true&source=vimeo_logo&owner=14178341.

Ms. Foundation for Women. *Women of Vision Honoree Deon Haywood (Women With A Vision) #GloriaAwards 2019*. https://www.youtube.com/watch?v =CBF57AjdHKM.

Women With A Vision. *After the Fire: Micro-Enterprise*. August 3, 2012. https:// www.youtube.com/watch?v=z24Rh9_Hvhw.

Women With A Vision. *After the Fire: Shaquita Borden*. June 29, 2012. https:// www.youtube.com/@WWAVnola87/videos.

Women With A Vision. *After the Fire: Zina Mitchell*. December 10, 2013. https:// www.youtube.com/watch?v=u8j3ivTw6HA&t=4s.

Women With A Vision. *Arson Destroys Women With A Vision Office—Please Help!* May 25, 2012. https://www.youtube.com/watch?v=Zp8lEEj1rc4.

Women With A Vision. *Vision House: Help Us Build the Vision*. December 3, 2013. https://www.youtube.com/watch?v=3duvwlald9Y.

Women With A Vision. *Women With A Vision 30th Anniversary Gala*. December 13, 2019. https://www.youtube.com/watch?v=g27B4-MOizc.

Please join us online at borninflames.com as we continue to grow this living archive and forge a path to freedom. *Forward Ever.*

BIBLIOGRAPHY

Abu-Lughod, Lila. "Do Muslim Women Really Need Saving? Anthropological Reflections on Cultural Relativism and Its Others." *American Anthropologist* 104, no. 3 (2002): 783–90. https://doi.org/10.1525/Aa.2002.104.3.783.

Abu-Lughod, Lila. "The Romance of Resistance: Tracing Transformations of Power through Bedouin Women." *American Ethnologist* 17, no. 1 (1990): 41–55. https://doi.org/10.1525/Ae.1990.17.1.02a00030.

ACE Program of the Bedford Hills Correctional Facility. *Breaking the Walls of Silence: AIDS and Women in a New York State Maximum Security Prison.* New York: Overlook, 1998.

Aching, Gerard. *Masking and Power: Carnival and Popular Culture in the Caribbean.* Minneapolis: University of Minnesota Press, 2002.

Adams, Michael Henry. "The End of Black Harlem." *New York Times*, May 27, 2016. https://www.nytimes.com/2016/05/29/opinion/sunday/the-end-of-black-harlem.html.

Adams, Vincanne. *Markets of Sorrow, Labors of Faith: New Orleans in the Wake of Katrina.* Durham, NC: Duke University Press, 2013.

African American Policy Forum. "Breaking the Silence." A National Town Hall Series on Women and Girls of Color. New Orleans, June 2015. Accessed July 17, 2021. https://www.aapf.org/btstownhall.

African American Policy Forum. "#SAYHERNAME." The African American Policy Forum. December 2014. Accessed July 17, 2021. https://www.aapf.org/sayhername.

Agathocleous, Alexis. "Building a Movement for Justice: *Doe v. Jindal* and the Campaign against Louisiana's Crime Against Nature Statute." In *The War on Sex*, edited by David M. Halperin and Hoppe Trevor, 429–53. Durham, NC: Duke University Press, 2017.

Agathocleous, Alexis. "When Power Yields to Justice: *Doe v. Jindal* and the Campaign to Dismantle Louisiana's Crime against Nature Statute." *Loyola Journal of Public Interest Law* 14, no. 2 (March 22, 2013): 331.

Ahmed, Leila. *Women and Gender in Islam*. New Haven, CT: Yale University Press, 1993.

Alexander, Michelle. *The New Jim Crow: Mass Incarceration in the Age of Colorblindness*. New York: New Press, 2012.

Alexander, M. Jacqui. *Pedagogies of Crossing: Meditations on Feminism, Sexual Politics, Memory, and the Sacred*. Durham, NC: Duke University Press, 2005.

Allen, Rebekah, and Terry L. Jones. "'Disturbing' Turn at Alton Sterling Protest Sunday on Government Street as Debris Hurled at Authorities; 50 Arrested." *Advocate*, July 10, 2016. https://www.theadvocate.com/baton_rouge/news/alton_sterling/article_455ad375-a8e1-585f-803f-d2c6f75da228.html.

Alpert, Bruce. "Human Trafficking Draws Attention during Super Bowl, but It's a Year-Long, Worldwide Problem." *Times-Picayune*, January 31, 2015. https://www.nola.com/news/politics/article_249c993e-9994-5d5f-983e-b91396cb3c28.html.

Ansfield, Bench. "Still Submerged: The Uninhabitability of Urban Redevelopment." In *Sylvia Wynter: On Being Human as Praxis*, edited by Katherine McKittrick, 124–41. Durham, NC: Duke University Press, 2020.

Anzaldúa, Gloria. *The Gloria Anzaldúa Reader*. Durham, NC: Duke University Press, 2009.

Arend, Orissa. *Showdown in Desire: The Black Panthers Take a Stand in New Orleans*. Fayetteville: University of Arkansas Press, 2009.

Arendt, Hannah. *On Revolution*. London: Penguin, 2006.

Asad, Talal. *Genealogies of Religion: Discipline and Reasons of Power in Christianity and Islam*. Baltimore: Johns Hopkins University Press, 1993.

Bacon-Blood, Littice. "The Largest Slave Revolt in US History Is Commemorated." *Times-Picayune*, January 4, 2011. https://www.nola.com/news/politics/article_cb0e4a53-718a-568a-8eb7-9ef1ce1e8b9a.html.

Bailey, Moya. *Misogynoir Transformed: Black Women's Digital Resistance*. New York: New York University Press, 2021.

Baldwin, James. *The Fire Next Time*. New York: Dial, 1963.

Bambara, Toni Cade. "What It Is I Think I'm Doing Anyhow." In *The Writer on Her Work*, edited by Janet Sternberg, 153–68. New York: W. W. Norton, 1980.

Battle, Juan, Claudrena N. Harold, and Deborah E. McDowell. *The Punitive Turn: New Approaches to Race and Incarceration*. Charlottesville: University of Virginia Press, 2013.

Bay, Mia E., Farah J. Griffin, Martha S. Jones, and Barbara D. Savage. *Toward an Intellectual History of Black Women*. Chapel Hill: University of North Carolina Press, 2015.

Beloso, Brooke Meredith. "Sex, Work, and the Feminist Erasure of Class." *Signs: Journal of Women in Culture and Society* 38, no. 1 (2012): 47–70. https://doi.org/10.1086/665808.

Bender, Courtney. "Practicing Religion." In *Cambridge Companion to Religious Studies*, edited by Robert Orsi, 273–95. Cambridge: Cambridge University Press, 2012.

Benjamin, Ruha. *Viral Justice: How We Grow the World We Want.* Princeton, NJ: Princeton University Press, 2022.

Ben-Moshe, Liat. *Decarcerating Disability: Deinstitutionalization and Prison Abolition.* Minneapolis: University of Minnesota Press, 2020.

Bennett, Dale E. "The Louisiana Criminal Code: A Comparison with Prior Louisiana Criminal Law." *Louisiana Law Review* 5, no. 1 (1942): 6–52.

Berger, Dan. *Stayed on Freedom: The Long History of Black Power through One Family's Journey.* New York: Basic Books, 2023.

Bergland, Renée. *The National Uncanny: Indian Ghosts and American Subjects.* Hanover, NH: University Press of New England, 2000.

Berlant, Lauren. "Slow Death (Sovereignty, Obesity, Lateral Agency)." *Critical Inquiry* 33, no. 4 (2007): 754–80. https://doi.org/10.1086/521568.

Bernstein, Elizabeth. "Militarized Humanitarianism Meets Carceral Feminism: The Politics of Sex, Rights, and Freedom in Contemporary Antitrafficking Campaigns." *Signs* 36, no. 1 (2010): 45–72. https://doi.org/10.1086/652918.

Bernstein, Elizabeth. "The Sexual Politics of the 'New Abolitionism.'" *Differences: A Journal of Feminist Cultural Studies* 18, no. 3 (2007): 128–51. https://doi.org/10.1215/10407391-2007-013.

Berry, Mary Frances. *History Teaches Us to Resist: How Progressive Movements Have Succeeded in Challenging Times.* Boston: Beacon, 2018.

Berry, Mary Frances. "In Search of Callie House and the Origins of the Modern Reparations Movement." *Journal of African American History* 91, no. 3 (2006): 323–27.

Berry, Mary Frances. *My Face Is Black Is True: Callie House and the Struggle for Ex-Slave Reparations.* New York: Alfred A. Knopf, 2005.

Berry, Mary Frances, and John W. Blassingame. *Long Memory: The Black Experience in America.* Oxford: Oxford University Press, 1982.

Best, Wallace D. *Passionately Human, No Less Divine: Religion and Culture in Black Chicago, 1915–1952.* Princeton, NJ: Princeton University Press, 2005.

Betancourt, Laura M., Wei Yang, Nancy L. Brodsky, Paul R. Gallagher, Elsa K. Malmud, Joan M. Giannetta, Martha J. Farah, and Hallam Hurt. "Adolescents with and without Gestational Cocaine Exposure: Longitudinal Analysis of Inhibitory Control, Memory and Receptive Language." *Neurotoxicology and Teratology* 33, no. 1 (2011): 36–46. https://doi.org/10.1016/j.ntt.2010.08.004.

Beyoncé. *Lemonade.* Parkwood Entertainment, 2016. www.beyonce.com/album/lemonade-visual-album/.

Bierria, Alisa, Jakeya Caruthers, and Brooke Lober, eds. *Abolition Feminisms Vol. 1: Organizing, Survival, and Transformative Practice.* Chicago: Haymarket, 2022.

Bierria, Alisa, Jakeya Caruthers, and Brooke Lober, eds. *Abolition Feminisms Vol. 2: Feminist Ruptures against the Carceral State.* Chicago: Haymarket, 2022.

Bierria, Alisa, Mayaba Liebenthal, and INCITE! Women of Color Against Violence. "To Render Ourselves Visible: Women of Color Organizing and Hurricane Katrina." In *What Lies Beneath: Katrina, Race, and the State of the Nation*, edited by The South End Press Collective, 31–47. Cambridge, MA: South End, 2007.

Blackstone, Sir William. "Chapter the Fifteenth: Of Offences against the Persons of Individuals." In *Commentaries on the Laws of England*. Accessed June 27, 2017. https://avalon.law.yale.edu/18th_century/blackstone_bk4ch15.asp.

Booker, Vaughn. *Lift Every Voice and Swing: Black Musicians and Religious Culture in the Jazz Century*. New York: New York University Press, 2020.

Boston Women's Health Book Collective. *Our Bodies, Ourselves.* [1st ed., 1970.] https://www.ourbodiesourselves.org/about-us/our-history/publications/our-bodies-ourselves-the-nine-u-s-editions/.

Bourdieu, Pierre. *The Logic of Practice*. Stanford: Stanford University Press, 1990.

Bourdieu, Pierre. *Outline of a Theory of Practice*. Cambridge Studies in Social Anthropology. Cambridge: Cambridge University Press, 1977.

BreakOUT! *We Deserve Better: A Report on Policing in New Orleans by and for Queer and Trans Youth of Color*. New Orleans: BreakOUT! 2014. https://issuu.com/youthbreakout/docs/we_deserve_better_report/1.

brown, adrienne maree. *Emergent Strategy Shaping Change, Changing Worlds*. Chico, CA: AK Press, 2017.

Brown, Elizabeth Nolan. "The War on Sex Trafficking Is the New War on Drugs: And the Results Will Be Just as Disastrous for 'Perpetrators' and 'Victims' Alike." *Reason*, November 2015. https://reason.com/2015/09/30/the-war-on-sex-trafficking-is/.

Brown, Ras Michael. *African-Atlantic Cultures and the South Carolina Lowcountry*. Cambridge Studies on the American South. Cambridge: Cambridge University Press, 2013.

Brown, Wendy. "Suffering the Paradoxes of Rights." In *Left Legalism, Left Critique*, edited by Wendy Brown and Janet Halley, 420–34. Durham, NC: Duke University Press, 2002.

Browne, Simone. *Dark Matters: On the Surveillance of Blackness*. Durham, NC: Duke University Press, 2015.

Brown-Nagin, Tomiko. *Courage to Dissent: Atlanta and the Long History of the Civil Rights Movement*. Oxford: Oxford University Press, 2012.

Burton, Richard D. E. *Afro-Creole: Power, Opposition, and Play in the Caribbean*. Ithaca, NY: Cornell University Press, 1997.

Butler, Anthea D. *Women in the Church of God in Christ: Making a Sanctified World*. Chapel Hill: University of North Carolina Press, 2007.

Butler, Octavia E. *Kindred*. Boston: Beacon, 2003.

Byrd, Rudolph P., Johnnetta Betsch Cole, and Beverly Guy-Sheftall, eds. *I Am Your Sister: Collected and Unpublished Writings of Audre Lorde*. Oxford: Oxford University Press, 2009.

Cacho, Lisa Marie. *Social Death: Racialized Rightlessness and the Criminalization of the Unprotected*. New York: New York University Press, 2012.

Calmes, Jackie. "Advocates Shun 'Pro-choice' to Expand Message." *New York Times*, July 29, 2014. https://www.nytimes.com/2014/07/29/us/politics/advocates-shun-pro-choice-to-expand-message.html.

Camp, Jordan T. "'We Know This Place': Neoliberal Racial Regimes and the Katrina Circumstance." *American Quarterly* 61, no. 3 (2009): 693–717.

Camp, Stephanie M. H. *Closer to Freedom: Enslaved Women and Everyday Resistance in the Plantation South*. Chapel Hill: University of North Carolina Press, 2004.

Campt, Tina. *Listening to Images*. Durham, NC: Duke University Press, 2017.

Carby, Hazel V. "Policing the Black Woman's Body in an Urban Context." *Critical Inquiry* 18 (1992): 738–55. https://doi.org/10.1086/448654.

Carmichael, Stokely. "From Black Power to Pan-Africanism." Whittier College, March 22, 1971. http://americanradioworks.publicradio.org/features/blackspeech/scarmichael-2.html.

Carroll, Rebecca. "The Charleston Shooter Killed Mostly Black Women. This Wasn't about 'Rape.'" *Guardian*, June 18, 2015. https://www.theguardian.com/commentisfree/2015/jun/18/charleston-shooter-black-women-white-women-rape.

Carter, Rebecca Louise. *Prayers for the People: Homicide and Humanity in the Crescent City*. Chicago: University of Chicago Press, 2019.

Casselberry, Judith. *The Labor of Faith: Gender and Power in Black Apostolic Pentecostalism*. Durham, NC: Duke University Press, 2017.

Castelli, Elizabeth Anne. *Martyrdom and Memory: Early Christian Culture Making*. New York: Columbia University Press, 2004.

Center for Constitutional Rights. "Crime Against Nature by Solicitation (CANS) Litigation." Last Modified March 7, 2023. https://ccrjustice.org/home/what-we-do/our-cases/crimes-against-nature-solicitation-cans-litigation.

Center for Constitutional Rights. "Judge Rules That Sex-Offender Registration for 'Crime Against Nature by Solicitation' Conviction Is Unconstitutional." March 30, 2012. https://ccrjustice.org/home/press-center/press-releases/judge-rules-sex-offender-registration-crime-against-nature.

Centers for Disease Control and Prevention. "Mortality Attributable to HIV Infection among Persons Aged 25–44 Years—United States, 1991 and 1992." *Morbidity and Mortality Weekly Report*, November 19, 1993. https://www.cdc.gov/mmwr/preview/mmwrhtml/00022174.htm.

Chakrabarty, Dipesh. *Provincializing Europe: Postcolonial Thought and Historical Difference*. Princeton, NJ: Princeton University Press, 2000.

Chang, Cindy, Scott Threlkeld, and Ryan Smith. "Louisiana Incarcerated: How We Built the World's Prison Capital—8-Part Series." *Times-Picayune*, May 13, 2012. https://www.nola.com/news/crime_police/article_8feef59a-1196-5988-9128-1e8e7c9aefda.html.

Chateauvert, Melinda. *Sex Workers Unite: A History of the Movement from Stonewall to Slut Walk*. Boston: Beacon, 2014.

Chidester, David. *Savage Systems: Colonialism and Comparative Religion in Southern Africa*. Charlottesville: University of Virginia Press, 1996.

Chireau, Yvonne Patricia. *Black Magic: Religion and the African American Conjuring Tradition*. Berkeley: University of California Press, 2003.

Cohen, Cathy J. *The Boundaries of Blackness: AIDS and the Breakdown of Black Politics*. Chicago: University of Chicago Press, 1999.

Cohen, Cathy J. *Democracy Remixed: Black Youth and the Future of American Politics*. Oxford: Oxford University Press, 2010.

Cohen, Cathy J. "Punks, Bulldaggers, and Welfare Queens: The Radical Potential of Queer Politics?" *Journal of Lesbian and Gay Studies* 1, no. 4 (1997): 437–65.

Collins, Patricia Hill. *Black Feminist Thought: Knowledge, Consciousness, and the Politics of Empowerment*. 2nd ed. New York: Routledge, 2004.

Combahee River Collective. "The Combahee River Collective Statement." [April 1977.] Accessed February 16, 2020. http://circuitous.org/scraps/combahee.html.

Conquergood, Dwight. *Cultural Struggles: Performance, Ethnography, Praxis*. Ann Arbor: University of Michigan Press, 2013.

Cooper, Anna J. *A Voice from the South: By a Black Woman of the South*. Chapel Hill: University of North Carolina at Chapel Hill Library, 2017.

Cop Watch NOLA. "Police Sexual Violence in New Orleans." 2022. https://copwatchnola.wordpress.com/data/.

Cox, Aimee Meredith. *Shapeshifters: Black Girls and the Choreography of Citizenship*. Durham, NC: Duke University Press, 2015.

Crawley, Ashon T. *Blackpentecostal Breath: The Aesthetics of Possibility*. New York: Fordham University Press, 2016.

Crawley, Ashon T. "Otherwise, Ferguson." *Interfictions Online* 4 (2013). http://interfictions.com/otherwise-fergusonashon-crawley/.

Crenshaw, Kimberlé. "Demarginalizing the Intersection of Race and Sex: A Black Feminist Critique of Antidiscrimination Doctrine, Feminist Theory and Antiracist Politics." *University of Chicago Legal Forum* 1989, no. 1 (1989): 139–68.

Crenshaw, Kimberlé. "Mapping the Margins: Intersectionality, Identity Politics, and Violence against Women of Color." *Stanford Law Review* 43, no. 6 (July 1, 1991): 1241–99. https://doi.org/10.2307/1229039.

Crenshaw, Kimberlé Williams, Andrea J. Ritchie, Rachel Anspach, Rachel Gilmer, and Luke Harris. *Say Her Name: Resisting Police Violence against Black Women*. New York: African American Policy Forum and the Center for Intersectionality and Social Policy Studies, 2015.

Critical Resistance. "Reformist Reforms vs. Abolitionist Steps in Policing." n.d. http://static1.squarespace.com/static/59ead8f9692ebee25b72f17f/t/5b65cd58758d46d34254f22c/1533398363539/CR_NoCops_reform_vs_abolition_CRside.pdf.

Cruz, Rosana. "Grassroots Group Challenges Discriminatory Crime Against Nature Law." *Bridge the Gulf*, February 18, 2011. https://bridgethegulfproject .org/node/262.

Curtin, Mary Ellen. *Black Prisoners and Their World, Alabama, 1865–1900*. Charlottesville: University Press of Virginia, 2000.

Das, Veena. *Life and Words: Violence and the Descent into the Ordinary*. Berkeley: University of California Press, 2007.

The Data Center. "Who Lives in New Orleans and Metro Parishes Now?" *Data Center*, June 30, 2017. https://www.datacenterresearch.org/data-resources /who-lives-in-new-orleans-now/.

Davis, Angela Y. *Are Prisons Obsolete?* New York: Seven Stories, 2011.

Davis, Angela Y. *Freedom Is a Constant Struggle: Ferguson, Palestine, and the Foundations of a Movement*. Chicago: Haymarket, 2016.

Davis, Angela Y. Lecture at Southern Illinois University Carbondale, February 13, 2014. https://www.youtube.com/watch?v=6s8QCucFADc.

Davis, Angela Y. "Reflections on the Black Woman's Role in the Community of Slaves." *Black Scholar* 3, no. 4 (1971): 2–15. https://doi.org/10.1080 /00064246.1981.11414214.

Davis, Angela, Gina Dent, Erica R. Meiners, and Beth E. Richie. *Abolition. Feminism. Now.* Chicago: Haymarket, 2022.

Davis, Dána-Ain. *Battered Black Women and Welfare Reform: Between a Rock and a Hard Place*. Albany: State University of New York Press, 2006.

Dawdy, Shannon Lee. *Building the Devil's Empire: French Colonial New Orleans*. Chicago: University of Chicago Press, 2008.

de Certeau, Michel. *The Practice of Everyday Life*. Berkeley: University of California Press, 1984.

Dean, Michelle. "'Black Women Unnamed': How Tanisha Anderson's Bad Day Turned into Her Last." *Guardian*, June 5, 2015. https://www.theguardian .com/us-news/2015/jun/05/black-women-police-killing-tanisha-anderson.

Dent, Thomas C., Richard Schechner, and Gilbert Moses, eds. *The Free Southern Theater, by the Free Southern Theater: A Documentary of the South's Radical Black Theater, with Journals, Letters, Poetry, Essays, and a Play Written by Those Who Built It*. Indianapolis: Bobbs-Merrill, 1969.

Didion, Joan. *We Tell Ourselves Stories in Order to Live*. New York: Knopf, 2006.

Diouf, Sylviane A. *Slavery's Exiles: The Story of the American Maroons*. New York: New York University Press, 2014.

Dodge, L. Mara. *"Whores and Thieves of the Worst Kind": A Study of Women, Crime, and Prisons, 1835–2000*. Dekalb: Northern Illinois University Press, 2006.

Dorrien, Gary J. *The New Abolition: W. E. B. Du Bois and the Black Social Gospel*. New Haven, CT: Yale University Press, 2015.

Douglas, Mary. *Natural Symbols: Explorations in Cosmology*. 3rd ed. London: Routledge, 1970.

Douglas, Mary. *Purity and Danger: An Analysis of Concepts of Pollution and Taboo*. London: Routledge, 1966.

Drake, Jamil. *To Know the Soul of a People: Religion, Race, and the Making of Southern Folk*. Oxford: Oxford University Press, 2022.

Du Bois, W. E. B. *Black Reconstruction in America, 1860–1880*. New York: Free Press, 1998.

Du Bois, W. E. B. *The Souls of Black Folk*. Boston: Bedford, 1997.

Dunbar-Ortiz, Roxanne. *An Indigenous Peoples' History of the United States*. Boston: Beacon, 2014.

Durkheim, Émile. *The Elementary Forms of Religious Life*. Translated by Karen E. Fields. New York: Free Press, 1912.

Eaves, LaToya E. "Black Geographic Possibilities: On a Queer Black South." *Southeastern Geographer* 57, no. 1 (2017): 80–95. https://doi.org/10.1353/Sgo.2017.0007.

Eliade, Mircea. *The Sacred and the Profane: The Nature of Religion*. New York: Harper and Row, 1961.

Elias, Norbert. *The Civilizing Process*. Oxford: Blackwell, 1994.

Evans, Curtis J. *The Burden of Black Religion*. Oxford: Oxford University Press, 2008.

Evans, Sula Janet. *Spirit of the Orisha*. 2022. https://www.sulaspirit.com/spirit-of-the-orisha.

Ewing, Eve. "Mariame Kaba: Everything Worthwhile Is Done with Other People." *Adi Magazine* 1 (Fall 2019). https://adimagazine.com/articles/mariame-kaba-everything-worthwhile-is-done-with-other-people/.

Fabian, Johannes. *Time and the Other: How Anthropology Makes Its Object*. New York: Columbia University Press, 1983.

Farrag, Hebah H. "The Role of Spirit in the #BlackLivesMatter Movement: A Conversation with Activist and Artist Patrisse Cullors." *Religion Dispatches*, June 24, 2015.

Fernández, Johanna. *The Young Lords: A Radical History*. Chapel Hill: University of North Carolina Press, 2020.

Fields, Karen. "What One Cannot Remember Mistakenly." In *History and Memory in African-American Culture*, edited by Robert O'Meally and Geneviéve Fabre, 150–63. New York: Oxford University Press, 1994.

Finch, Aisha K. *Rethinking Slave Rebellion in Cuba: La Escalera and the Insurgencies of 1841–1844*. Chapel Hill: University of North Carolina Press, 2015.

First Grace United Methodist Church. "History." n.d. Accessed June 27, 2017. http://firstgraceumc.org/history/.

Fischer, Anne Gray. *The Streets Belong to Us: Sex, Race, and Police Power from Segregation to Gentrification*. Chapel Hill: University of North Carolina Press, 2022.

FitzGerald, Susan. "'Crack Baby' Study Ends with Unexpected but Clear Result." *Philadelphia Inquirer*, July 21, 2013. https://www.inquirer.com/philly/health/20130721__Crack_baby__study_ends_with_unexpected_but_clear_result.html.

Flaherty, Jordan. *Floodlines: Community and Resistance from Katrina to the Jena Six*. Chicago: Haymarket, 2010.

Fondren, Precious. "The 'Say Her Name' Movement Started for a Reason: We Forget Black Women Killed by Police." *Teen Vogue*, June 11, 2020. https://www.teenvogue.com/story/say-her-name-origin.

Ford, Kris. "Bad Home Training: An Open Letter to Melissa Flournoy of Planned Parenthood Gulf Coast." *Women's Health and Justice Initiative: A Reproductive Justice Blog*, August 14, 2014. https://whjiblog.wordpress.com/2014/08/14/open-letter-to-melissa-flournoy-of-planned-parenthood-gulf-coast/.

Forret, Jeff. "Before Angola: Enslaved Prisoners in the Louisiana State Penitentiary." *Louisiana History: The Journal of the Louisiana Historical Association* 54, no. 2 (2013): 133–71.

Foster, Kimberly. "No One Showed Up to March for Rekia Boyd Last Night." *Harriet*, April 23, 2015. http://theculture.forharriet.com/2015/04/no-one-showed-up-to-rally-for-rekia.html.

Foucault, Michel. *Discipline and Punish: The Birth of the Prison*. New York: Vintage, 1995.

Foucault, Michel. *The History of Sexuality: An Introduction*. New York: Knopf Doubleday, 1990.

Foucault, Michel. *Power/Knowledge: Selected Interviews and Other Writings, 1972–1977*. New York: Pantheon, 1980.

Frederick, Marla F. *Between Sundays: Black Women and Everyday Struggles of Faith*. Berkeley: University of California Press, 2003.

Freedman, Estelle B. *Their Sisters' Keepers: Women's Prison Reform in America, 1830–1930*. Women and Culture Series. Ann Arbor: University of Michigan Press, 1981.

Fuentes, Marisa. *Dispossessed Lives: Enslaved Women, Violence, and the Archive*. Philadelphia: University of Pennsylvania Press, 2016.

Fullilove, Mindy Thompson. *Root Shock: How Tearing Up City Neighborhoods Hurts America, and What We Can Do about It*. New York: Ballantine, 2004.

Fullilove, Robert. "African Americans, Health Disparities and HIV/AIDS: Recommendations for Confronting the Epidemic in Black America." National Minority AIDS Council, 2006. https://repository.library.georgetown.edu/handle/10822/977043?show=full.

Gálvez, Alyshia. *Guadalupe in New York: Devotion and the Struggle for Citizenship Rights among Mexican Immigrants*. New York: New York University Press, 2010.

Garcia, Angela. *The Pastoral Clinic: Addiction and Dispossession along the Rio Grande*. Berkeley: University of California Press, 2010.

García Peña, Lorgia. *Community as Rebellion: A Syllabus for Surviving Academia as a Woman of Color*. Chicago: Haymarket, 2022.

Garza, Alicia. "Love Letter to Black People." Facebook, July 13, 2013.

Geertz, Clifford. *Interpretation of Cultures*. New York: Basic Books, 1973.

Getachew, Adom. *Worldmaking after Empire: The Rise and Fall of Self-Determination*. Princeton, NJ: Princeton University Press, 2019.

Gilmore, Glenda Elizabeth. *Gender and Jim Crow: Women and the Politics of White Supremacy in North Carolina, 1896–1920*. Chapel Hill: University of North Carolina Press, 1996.

Gilmore, Ruth Wilson. "Abolition Geography and the Problem of Innocence." In *Futures of Black Radicalism*, edited by Gaye Theresa Johnson and Alex Lubin, 224–50. New York: Verso, 2017.

Gilmore, Ruth Wilson. "Fatal Couplings of Power and Difference: Notes on Racism and Geography." *Professional Geographer* 54, no. 1 (February 1, 2002): 15–24. https://doi.org/10.1111/0033-0124.00310.

Gilmore, Ruth Wilson. *Golden Gulag: Prisons, Surplus, Crisis, and Opposition in Globalizing California*. Berkeley: University of California Press, 2007.

Gilroy, Paul. *The Black Atlantic: Modernity and Double Consciousness*. Cambridge, MA: Harvard University Press, 1995.

Glaser, Barney G., and Anselm L. Strauss. *The Discovery of Grounded Theory: Strategies for Qualitative Research*. New York: Aldine de Gruyter, 1967.

Glissant, Édouard. *Poetics of Relation*. Translated by Betsy Wing. Ann Arbor: University of Michigan Press, 1997.

Gordon, Avery. *Ghostly Matters: Haunting and the Sociological Imagination*. New edition. Minneapolis: University of Minnesota Press, 2008.

Gordon, Avery F. *The Hawthorn Archive: Letters from the Utopian Margins*. New York: Fordham University Press, 2017.

Gordon-Reed, Annette. *Thomas Jefferson and Sally Hemings: An American Controversy*. Richmond: University of Virginia Press, 1998.

Gore, Dayo. *Radicalism at the Crossroads: African American Women Activists in the Cold War*. New York: New York University Press, 2011.

Gore, Dayo F., Komozi Woodard, and Jeanne Theoharis. *Want to Start a Revolution? Radical Women in the Black Freedom Struggle*. New York: New York University Press, 2009.

Gorz, André. "Strategy for Labor." In *Theories of the Labor Movement*, edited by Simeon Larson and Bruce Nissen, 100–116. Detroit: Wayne State University Press, 1987.

Gottschalk, Marie. *The Prison and the Gallows: The Politics of Mass Incarceration in America*. New York: Cambridge University Press, 2006.

Graber, Jennifer. *The Furnace of Affliction: Prisons and Religion in Antebellum America*. Chapel Hill: University of North Carolina Press, 2011.

Graeber, David. "The New Anarchists." *New Left Review* 13, no. 6 (2002): 61–73.

Griffin, Farah Jasmine. *"Who Set You Flowin'?": The African-American Migration Narrative*. New York: Oxford University Press, 1995.

griffin, Shana M. "Policies That Make People Disappear." Interview by Dani McCain. *Public Eye*, November 11, 2015. https://www.politicalresearch.org/2015/11/02/policies-make-people-disappear.

griffin, Shana M. "Un-Bibliography." https://docs.google.com/document/d/e
/2PACX-1vS9IlSiHXPfThlG9TNCLc85hE4v96DesG3_YZ1g1Yelo_3RkbX4
7LpKn8NqMPGN4YEqx65OcO35kFjR/pub.

griffin, Shana M. "An Unfragmented Movement." Interview by Joanna Dubinsky.
NOLA Indymedia, January 2006. http://neworleans.indymedia.org/news
/2006/01/6740.php.

griffin, Shana M. "The Women of New Orleans after Katrina." Interview by Elena
Everett. *Counter Punch*, August 25, 2006. https://www.counterpunch.org
/2006/08/25/the-women-of-new-orleans-after-katrina/.

Griffith, Marie. *God's Daughter: Evangelical Women and the Power of Submission*.
Berkeley: University of California Press, 2000.

Gross, Kali N. *Colored Amazons: Crime, Violence, and Black Women in the City of
Brotherly Love, 1880–1910*. Durham, NC: Duke University Press, 2006.

Gumbs, Alexis Pauline. "Are You Afraid of Black Feminists? Or Just Your Own
Freedom?" *Indy Week*, October 1, 2019. https://indyweek.com/news/voices
/are-you-still-afraid-of-black-feminists/.

Gutiérrez, Gustavo. *Essential Writings*. Translated by James B. Nickoloff. Minneapolis: Fortress Press, 1996.

Guy-Sheftall, Beverly. *Words of Fire: An Anthology of African-American Feminist
Thought*. New York: New Press, 1995.

Guzmán, Joshua Javier. "Affect." In *Keywords for Gender and Sexuality Studies*, edited by The Keywords Feminist Editorial Collective, 13–16. New York:
New York University Press, 2021.

Haley, Sarah. "'Like I Was a Man': Chain Gangs, Gender, and the Domestic Carceral Sphere in Jim Crow Georgia." *Signs: Journal of Women in Culture and
Society* 39, no. 1 (2013): 55–56.

Haley, Sarah. *No Mercy Here: Gender, Punishment, and the Making of Jim Crow
Modernity*. Chapel Hill: The University of North Carolina Press, 2016.

Hall, Stuart, Chas Critcher, Tony Jefferson, John Clarke, and Brian Roberts. *Policing the Crisis: Mugging, the State, and Law and Order*. London: Macmillan,
1978.

Harm Reduction Coalition. "Evolution of the Movement." https://
harmreduction.org/movement/evolution/.

Hanhardt, Christina B. *Safe Space: Gay Neighborhood History and the Politics of
Violence*. Durham, NC: Duke University Press, 2013.

Harding, Rosemarie Freeney, and Rachel Elizabeth Harding. *Remnants: A Mem-
oir of Spirit, Activism, and Mothering*. 1st ed. Durham, NC: Duke University
Press, 2015.

Harney, Stefano, and Fred Moten. *The Undercommons: Fugitive Planning and
Black Study*. Wivenhoe, UK: Minor Compositions, 2013.

Harris, Andrew J., Christopher Lobanov-Rostovsky, and Jill S. Levenson. "Widening the Net: The Effects of Transitioning to the Adam Walsh Act's Feder-
ally Mandated Sex Offender Classification System." *Criminal Justice Behavior*
37, no. 5 (2010): 503–19. https://doi.org/10.1177/0093854810363889.

Harris, Frederick. "Will Ferguson Be a Moment or a Movement?" *Washington Post*, August 22, 2014. https://www.washingtonpost.com /opinions/will-ferguson-be-a-moment-or-a-movement/2014/08/22 /071d4a94–28a8–11e4–8593-da634b334390_story.html.

Harris-Perry, Melissa V. *Sister Citizen: Shame, Stereotypes, and Black Women in America*. New Haven, CT: Yale University Press, 2013.

Hartman, Saidiya. *Lose Your Mother: A Journey along the Atlantic Slave Route*. New York: Macmillan, 2007.

Hartman, Saidiya. *Scenes of Subjection: Terror, Slavery, and Self-Making in Nineteenth Century America*. New York: Oxford University Press, 1997.

Hartman, Saidiya. "Venus in Two Acts." *Small Axe: A Caribbean Journal of Criticism* 12, no. 2 (June 1, 2008): 1–14. https://doi.org/10.1215/-12-2-1.

Hartman, Saidiya. *Wayward Lives, Beautiful Experiments: Intimate Histories of Riotous Black Girls, Troublesome Women, and Queer Radicals*. New York: W. W. Norton, 2019.

Hassan, Shira. *Saving Our Own Lives: A Liberatory Practice of Harm Reduction*. Chicago: Haymarket, 2022.

Hayes, Kelly, and Mariame Kaba. *Let This Radicalize You*. Chicago: Haymarket, 2023.

Heatherton, Christina. *Arise! Global Radicalism in the Era of the Mexican Revolution*. Berkeley: University of California Press, 2022.

Hicks, Cheryl D. *Talk with You Like a Woman: African American Women, Justice, and Reform in New York, 1890–1935*. Gender and American Culture. Chapel Hill: University of North Carolina Press, 2010.

Higginbotham, Evelyn Brooks. "African-American Women's History and the Metalanguage of Race." *Signs* 17, no. 2 (January 1, 1992): 251–74. https://doi .org/10.1086/494730.

Higginbotham, Evelyn Brooks. *Righteous Discontent: The Women's Movement in the Black Baptist Church, 1880–1920*. Cambridge, MA: Harvard University Press, 1994.

Hirschkind, Charles. *The Ethical Soundscape: Cassette Sermons and Islamic Counterpublics*. Cultures of History. New York: Columbia University Press, 2006.

HIV Racial Justice Now. "A Declaration of Liberation: Building a Racially Just and Strategic Domestic HIV Movement." 2017. https://b7c725b6 -fb53–4792–9fe4-b563d0d7d42a.filesusr.com/ugd/13f2c1_e410e116a15044d 4a76a95899f670213.pdf.

Hobson, Janell, and Jessica Marie Johnson. "#Lemonade: A Black Feminist Resource List." *Black Perspectives*, May 12, 2016. https://www.aaihs.org /lemonade-a-black-feminist-resource-list/.

Hogue, James Keith. *Uncivil War: Five New Orleans Street Battles and the Rise and Fall of Radical Reconstruction*. Baton Rouge: Louisiana State University Press, 2006.

Hollandsworth, James G., Jr. *An Absolute Massacre: The New Orleans Race Riot of July 30, 1866*. Baton Rouge: Louisiana State University Press, 2001.

Hood, John. "The History and Development of the Louisiana Civil Code." *Louisiana Law Review* 19, no. 1 (1958). https://digitalcommons.law.lsu.edu/lalrev/vol19/iss1/14.

hooks, bell. *Reel to Real: Race, Class and Sex at the Movies.* New York: Routledge, 1996.

Horowitz, Andy. *Katrina: A History, 1915–2015.* Cambridge, MA: Harvard University Press, 2020.

Housea, M. G. "A Land Called Louisiana, Part II: Undermining Slavery from the Cypress Swamps." *Raging Pelican: Journal of Gulf Coast Resistance* 4. Accessed September 1, 2016. http://ragingpelican.com/a-land-called-louisiana-part-ii-undermining-slavery-from-the-cypress-swamps/.

Hua, Julietta. "Modern-Day Slavery: The Analogy Problem in Human Trafficking Reform." In *Panic, Transnational Cultural Studies, and the Affective Contours of Power,* edited by Micol Seigel, 244–63. London: Routledge, 2020.

Hua, Julietta. *Trafficking Women's Human Rights.* Minneapolis: University of Minnesota Press, 2011.

Hucks, Tracey E. *Yoruba Traditions and African American Religious Nationalism.* Religions of the Americas. Albuquerque: University of New Mexico Press, 2012.

Hull, Akasha (Gloria T.), Patricia Bell-Scott, and Barbara Smith, eds. *All the Women Are White, All the Blacks Are Men, But Some of Us Are Brave: Black Women's Studies.* 2nd ed. New York: Feminist Press, 2015.

Hunter, Tera W. *To 'Joy My Freedom: Southern Black Women's Lives and Labors after the Civil War.* Cambridge, MA: Harvard University Press, 1997.

Imarisha, Walidah, and adrienne maree brown, eds. *Octavia's Brood: Science Fiction Stories from Social Justice Movements.* Chico, CA: AK Press, 2015.

INCITE! "Critical Resistance Statement: Statement on Gender Violence and the Prison Industrial Complex." INCITE!, 2001. https://incite-national.org/incite-critical-resistance-statement/.

INCITE! Women of Color Against Violence. *The Revolution Will Not Be Funded: Beyond the Non-Profit Industrial Complex.* Cambridge, MA: South End, 2007.

Indigenous Action Media. "Accomplices Not Allies: Abolishing the Ally Industrial Complex." *Indigenous Action Media,* May 4, 2014. https://www.indigenousaction.org/accomplices-not-allies-abolishing-the-ally-industrial-complex/.

Jackson, John L., Jr. *Thin Description: Ethnography and the African Hebrew Israelites of Jerusalem.* Cambridge, MA: Harvard University Press, 2013.

James, Cyril Lionel Robert. *The Black Jacobins: Toussaint L'Ouverture and the San Domingo Revolution.* New York: Vintage, 1963.

James, Joy. *Shadowboxing: Representations of Black Feminist Politics.* New York: Palgrave Macmillan, 1999.

Johnson, Gaye Theresa, and Alex Lubin. *Futures of Black Radicalism.* New York: Verso, 2017.

Johnson, Jessica Marie. *Wicked Flesh: Black Women, Intimacy, and Freedom in the Atlantic World.* Philadelphia: University of Pennsylvania Press, 2020.

Johnson, Rashauna. *Slavery's Metropolis: Unfree Labor in New Orleans during the Age of Revolutions*. Cambridge: Cambridge University Press, 2016.

Johnson, Rucker C., and Steven Raphael. "The Effects of Male Incarceration Dynamics on Acquired Immune Deficiency Syndrome Infection Rates among African American Women and Men." *Journal of Law and Economics* 52, no. 2 (May 1, 2009): 251–93. https://doi.org/10.1086/597102.

Johnson, Sylvester. *The Myth of Ham in Nineteenth-Century American Christianity: Race, Heathens, and the People of God*. New York: Palgrave Macmillan, 2004.

Johnson, Walter. *Soul by Soul: Life inside the Antebellum Slave Market*. Cambridge, MA: Harvard University Press, 1999.

Jones, Alethia, Virginia Eubanks, and Barbara Smith. *Ain't Gonna Let Nobody Turn Me Around: Forty Years of Movement Building with Barbara Smith*. Albany: State University of New York Press, 2014.

Jones, Michelle, and Lori Record. "Magdalene Laundries: The First Prisons for Women in the United States." *Journal of the Indiana Academy of the Social Sciences* 17, no. 1 (2017). https://digitalcommons.butler.edu/jiass/vol17/iss1/12.

Jones, Terry L. "Video: Intense Scene at Alton Sterling Protest in Baton Rouge as Officers Charge Protesters in Woman's Front Lawn." *Advocate*, July 11, 2016. https://www.theadvocate.com/baton_rouge/news/alton_sterling/article _2a627377-f512-5368-aa1f-fc6ad14c6d97.html.

Jones-Rogers, Stephanie E. *They Were Her Property: White Women as Slave Owners in the American South*. New Haven, CT: Yale University Press, 2019.

Jordan, Mark D. *The Invention of Sodomy in Christian Theology*. The Chicago Series on Sexuality, History, and Society. Chicago: University of Chicago Press, 1997.

Kaba, Mariame. "So You're Thinking about Becoming an Abolitionist." *Level*, October 20, 2020. https://level.medium.com/so-youre-thinking-about -becoming-an-abolitionist-a436f8e31894.

Kaba, Mariame. *We Do This 'til We Free Us: Abolitionist Organizing and Transforming Justice*. Chicago: Haymarket, 2021.

Kaba, Mariame, and Shira Hassan. *Fumbling towards Repair: A Workbook for Community Accountability Facilitators*. Chicago: Project NIA/Just Practice, 2019.

Kaba, Mariame, and Andrea J. Ritchie. *No More Police: A Case for Abolition*. New York: New Press, 2022.

Katz, Cindi. "Bad Elements: Katrina and the Scoured Landscape of Social Reproduction." *Gender, Place & Culture* 15, no. 1 (2008): 15–29.

Katz, Michael B. *The Undeserving Poor: From the War on Poverty to the War on Welfare*. New York: Pantheon, 1990.

Kelley, Robin D. G. *Freedom Dreams: The Black Radical Imagination*. Boston: Beacon, 2003.

Kelley, Robin D. G. *Race Rebels: Culture, Politics, and the Black Working Class*. New York: Free Press, 1996.

King, Tiffany Lethabo, Jenell Navarro, and Andrea Smith, eds. *Otherwise Worlds: Against Settler Colonialism and Anti-Blackness*. Durham, NC: Duke University Press, 2020.

Klein, Naomi. *The Shock Doctrine: The Rise of Disaster Capitalism*. New York: Picador, 2008.

Kondo, Dorinne K. *Worldmaking: Race, Performance, and the Work of Creativity*. Durham, NC: Duke University Press, 2018.

Kornbluh, Felicia Ann. *The Battle for Welfare Rights: Politics and Poverty in Modern America*. Philadelphia: University of Pennsylvania Press, 2007.

Kunzelman, Michael. "Louisiana Sex Law Violates Offenders' Rights, Federal Judge Rules." *Times-Picayune*, March 29, 2012.

Laguens, Dawn. "We're Fighting for Access, Not Choice." *Huffington Post*, July 30, 2014. Updated September 29, 2014. https://www.huffpost.com/entry/were-fighting-for-access_b_5635999.

Landau, Emily Epstein. *Spectacular Wickedness: Sex, Race, and Memory in Storyville, New Orleans*. Baton Rouge: Louisiana State University Press, 2013.

Lane, Cassandra. *"Women With A Vision*'s Message Is Clear," *Louisiana Weekly* 75, no. 26, Week of March 19–25, 2001.

Latour, Bruno. *Reassembling the Social: An Introduction to Actor-Network-Theory*. Oxford: Oxford University Press, 2005.

Law, Victoria. "Against Carceral Feminism." *Jacobin*, October 17, 2014. https://jacobinmag.com/2014/10/against-carceral-feminism/.

Law, Victoria. *Resistance behind Bars: The Struggles of Incarcerated Women*. Oakland: PM Press, 2009.

Leavitt, Jacqueline, and Susan Saegert. *From Abandonment to Hope: Community-Households in Harlem*. New York: Columbia University Press, 1990.

Lefebvre, Henri. *The Production of Space*. Translated by Donald Nicholson-Smith. Oxford: Basil Blackwell, 1990.

LeFlouria, Talitha. *Chained in Silence: Black Women and Convict Labor in the New South*. Justice, Power, and Politics. Chapel Hill: University of North Carolina Press, 2015.

Levenstein, Lisa. *A Movement without Marches: African American Women and the Politics of Poverty in Postwar Philadelphia*. Chapel Hill: University of North Carolina Press, 2010.

Lewis, Oscar. "The Culture of Poverty." *Scientific American* 215, no. 4 (1966): 19–25.

Lichtenstein, Alexander C. *Twice the Work of Free Labor: The Political Economy of Convict Labor in the New South*. New York: Verso, 1996.

Litwack, Leon F. *Been in the Storm So Long: The Aftermath of Slavery*. New York: Vintage Books, 1980.

Liu, Roseann, and Savannah Shange. "Toward Thick Solidarity: Theorizing Empathy in Social Justice Movements." *Radical History Review* 1, no. 131 (2018): 189–98. https://doi.org/10.1215/01636545-4355341.

Long, Alecia P. *The Great Southern Babylon: Sex, Race, and Respectability in New Orleans, 1865–1920*. Baton Rouge: Louisiana State University Press, 2005.

Long, Alecia P. "Poverty Is the New Prostitution: Race, Poverty, and Public Housing in Post-Katrina New Orleans." *Journal of American History* 94, no. 3 (2007): 795–803.

Lopez, Patricia J., and Kathryn Gillespie. "A Love Story: For 'Buddy System' Research in the Academy." *Gender, Place & Culture* 23, no. 12 (2016): 1689–1700. https://doi.org/10.1080/0966369X.2016.1249354.

Lorde, Audre. *Burst of Light: And Other Essays*. Ithaca, NY: Firebrand, 1988.

Lorde, Audre. "Learning from the 60s." Lecture at Harvard University, February 1982. Accessed August 12, 2012. https://www.blackpast.org/african -american-history/1982-audre-lorde-learning-60s/.

Lorde, Audre. *Sister Outsider: Essays and Speeches*. Freedom, CA: Crossing Press, 1984.

Lowe, Lisa. *Intimacies on Four Continents*. Durham, NC: Duke University Press, 2015.

Loyd, Jenna M. *Health Rights Are Civil Rights: Peace and Justice Activism in Los Angeles, 1963–1978*. Minneapolis: University of Minnesota Press, 2014.

Loyd, Jenna M., Matt Mitchelson, and Andrew Burridge. *Beyond Walls and Cages: Prisons, Borders, and Global Crisis*. Athens: University of Georgia Press, 2013.

Luft, Rachel E. "Beyond Disaster Exceptionalism: Social Movement Developments in New Orleans after Hurricane Katrina." *American Quarterly* 61, no. 3 (2009): 499–527.

Luft, Rachel E. "Looking for Common Ground: Relief Work in Post-Katrina New Orleans as an American Parable of Race and Gender Violence." *NWSA Journal* 20, no. 3 (September 22, 2008): 5.

Luft, Rachel E., and Shana M. griffin. "A Status Report on Housing in New Orleans after Katrina: An Intersectional Analysis." In *Katrina and the Women of New Orleans*, edited by Beth Willinger, 50–53. New Orleans: Newcomb College Center for Research on Women, 2008.

Luk, Sharon. *The Life of Paper: Letters and a Poetics of Living beyond Captivity*. Berkeley: University of California Press, 2017.

Mahmood, Saba. *Politics of Piety: The Islamic Revival and the Feminist Subject*. Princeton, NJ: Princeton University Press, 2005.

Manigault-Bryant, LeRhonda S. "Remembering Octavia E. Butler (1947–2006)." *Black Perspectives*, February 19, 2016. https://www.aaihs.org/remembering -octavia-e-butler/.

Manigault-Bryant, LeRhonda S. *Talking to the Dead: Religion, Music, and Lived Memory among Gullah/Geechee Women*. Durham, NC: Duke University Press, 2014.

Manion, Jennifer. *Liberty's Prisoners: Carceral Culture in Early America*. Early American Studies. Philadelphia: University of Pennsylvania Press, 2019.

Martin, Lauren, and Annie Hill. "Debunking the Myth of 'Super Bowl Sex Trafficking': Media Hype or Evidenced-Based Coverage." *Anti-Trafficking*

Review no. 13 (September 26, 2019): 13–29. https://doi.org/10.14197/atr
.201219132.

Martin, Lerone. *Preaching on Wax: The Phonograph and the Making of Modern African American Religion*. New York: New York University Press, 2014.

Martin, Naomi. "Former Sex Trafficking Victim Shines Light on Dark Underworld of Super Bowl." NOLA.com, *Times-Picayune,* February 2, 2013. https://www.nola.com/news/crime_police/former-sex-trafficking-victim -shines-light-on-dark-underworld-of-super-bowl/article_e335d996-83e2 -513f-9956-2b089085311d.html.

Marx, Karl. *The Eighteenth Brumaire of Louis Bonaparte*. Beijing: Foreign Languages Press, 1978.

Maynard, Robyn, and Leanne Betasamosake Simpson. *Rehearsals for Living*. Chicago: Haymarket, 2022.

Mbembe, Achille. "Necropolitics." Translated by Libby Meintjes. *Public Culture* 15, no. 1 (2003): 11–40.

McCrystal, Laura, Aubrey Whelan, and Oona Goodin-Smith. "Philly Health Commissioner Resigns over Cremating MOVE Victims without Telling Family; Kenney Apologizes." *Philadelphia Inquirer*. Accessed June 12, 2021. https://www.inquirer.com/news/philadelphia/thomas-farley-resigns -philadelphia-health-commissioner-move-20210513.html.

McCutcheon, Russell T., ed. *The Insider/Outsider Problem in the Study of Religion: A Reader*. Controversies in the Study of Religion. London: Cassell, 1999.

McGuire, Danielle L. *At the Dark End of the Street: Black Women, Rape, and Resistance—a New History of the Civil Rights Movement from Rosa Parks to the Rise of Black Power*. New York: Vintage, 2010.

McKittrick, Katherine. *Dear Science and Other Stories*. Durham, NC: Duke University Press, 2021.

McKittrick, Katherine. *Demonic Grounds: Black Women and the Cartographies of Struggle*. Minneapolis: University of Minnesota Press, 2006.

McKittrick, Katherine. "Mathematics Black Life." *Black Scholar* 44, no. 2 (June 1, 2014): 16–28. https://doi.org/10.1080/00064246.2014.11413684.

McKittrick, Katherine. "On Plantations, Prisons, and a Black Sense of Place." *Social and Cultural Geography* 12, no. 8 (December 1, 2011): 947–63. https:// doi.org/10.1080/14649365.2011.624280.

McKittrick, Katherine. *Sylvia Wynter: On Being Human as Praxis*. Durham, NC: Duke University Press, 2015.

McKittrick, Katherine, and Clyde Woods. "No One Knows the Mysteries at the Bottom of the Ocean." In *Black Geographies and the Politics of Place*, 1–13. Cambridge: South End, 2007.

McTighe, Laura. "Abolition Is Sacred Work." In *The Immanent Frame*, January 28, 2021, coedited by Mona Oraby and Ahmad Greene-Hayes. https://tif .ssrc.org/2021/01/28/abolition-is-sacred-work/.

McTighe, Laura. "'And Still We Rise': Moral Panics, Dark Sousveillance, and Politics Otherwise in the New New Orleans." In *Panic, Transnational Cultural*

Studies, and the Affective Contours of Power, edited by Micol Seigel, 275–97. New York: Routledge, 2018.

McTighe, Laura. "Introduction: 'Religio-Racial Identity' as Challenge and Critique." *Journal of the American Academy of Religion* 88, no. 2 (May 23, 2020): 299–303. https://doi.org/10.1093/jaarel/lfaa015.

McTighe, Laura. "Our Relationships Carry the Movement." *Radical History Review* 140 (May 1, 2021): 186–96. https://doi.org/10.1215/01636545 -8841778.

McTighe, Laura. *Project UNSHACKLE—Confronting HIV and Mass Imprisonment: A Toolkit*. Brooklyn: Community HIV/AIDS Mobilization Project, December 2009.

McTighe, Laura. "Southern Front Porches Are Revolutionary, Sacred Spaces." Facebook, July 11, 2016. https://www.facebook.com/laura.e.mctighe/posts/ pfbido2ynp3A3EMFQAcAbfvKNJCyHCm6Lm8pExfjnDSpTWHccHd9DiJ 607Q567qZrJV8N8hl.

McTighe, Laura, with the Reverend Doris Green. "'To Instill Love for My People': Reassembling the Social in a Time of Mass Criminalization." In "Religion, Political Democracy, and the Specters of Race," edited by James Logan. Special issue, *CrossCurrents* 68, no. 1 (2019): 179–200. https://doi.org/10.1111 /cros.12306.

McTighe, Laura, with Deon Haywood. "Front Porch Revolution: Resilience Space, Demonic Grounds, and the Horizons of a Black Feminist Otherwise." *Signs: Journal of Women in Culture and Society* 44, no. 1 (2018): 25–52. https://doi.org/10.1086/698276.

McTighe, Laura, with Deon Haywood. "'There Is NO Justice in Louisiana': Crimes against Nature and the Spirit of Black Feminist Resistance." *Souls: A Critical Journal of Black Politics, Culture, and Society* 19, no. 3 (July 3, 2017): 261–85. https://doi.org/10.1080/10999949.2017.1389584.

McTighe, Laura, and Megan Raschig. "Introduction: An Otherwise Anthropology." Theorizing the Contemporary. *Fieldsights*, July 31, 2019. https:// culanth.org/fieldsights/introduction-an-otherwise-anthropology.

McTighe, Laura, Waheedah Shabazz-El, and Faghmeda Miller. "Refusing to Vanish: Muslim Women's AIDS Activism." *The Revealer: A Review of Religion and Media*, December 1, 2017. https://wp.nyu.edu/therevealer/2017/12/01 /refusing-to-vanish-muslim-womens-aids-activism/.

McTighe, Laura, with Women With A Vision. "Theory on the Ground: Ethnography, Religio-Racial Study, and the Spiritual Work of Building Otherwise." *Journal of the American Academy of Religion* 88, no. 2 (May 23, 2020): 407–39. https://doi.org/10.1093/jaarel/lfaa014.

Michna, Catherine. "Stories at the Center: Story Circles, Educational Organizing, and Fate of Neighborhood Public Schools in New Orleans." *American Quarterly* 61, no. 3 (2009): 529–55.

Mink, Gwendolyn. *The Wages of Motherhood: Inequality in the Welfare State, 1917–1942*. Ithaca, NY: Cornell University Press, 1995.

Mock, Brentin. "Beyoncé's Simple but Radical Porch-Front Politics." *CityLab*, April 27, 2016. https://www.bloomberg.com/news/articles/2016-04-27 /the-powerful-porch-front-politics-of-beyonce-s-lemonade.

Mock, Brentin. "In Baton Rouge, Your Front Yard Is No Sanctuary from Police." *CityLab*, July 11, 2016. https://www.bloomberg.com/news/articles/2016-07- 11/do-baton-rouge-residents-have-the-right-to-harbor-protesters-on-their -properties.

Mogul, Joey L., Andrea J. Ritchie, and Kay Whitlock. *Queer (In)Justice: The Criminalization of LGBT People in the United States.* Boston: Beacon, 2011.

Moore, Leonard N. *Black Rage in New Orleans: Police Brutality and African American Activism from World War II to Hurricane Katrina.* Baton Rouge: Louisiana State University Press, 2010.

Moraga, Cherríe, and Gloria Anzaldúa, eds. *This Bridge Called My Back: Writings by Radical Women of Color.* 2nd ed. New York, NY: Kitchen Table/Women of Color Press, 1983.

Moten, Fred. *In the Break: The Aesthetics of the Black Radical Tradition.* Electronic resource. Minneapolis: University of Minnesota Press, 2003.

Movement for Black Lives. "Reparations Now Toolkit." 2019. https://m4bl .org/wp-content/uploads/2020/05/Reparations-Now-Toolkit-FINAL .pdf.

Muhammad, Khalil Gibran. *The Condemnation of Blackness: Race, Crime, and the Making of Modern Urban America.* Cambridge, MA: Harvard University Press, 2010.

Mullings, Leith. "Households Headed by Women: The Politics of Class, Race, and Gender." In *New Poverty Studies: The Ethnography of Power, Politics and Impoverished People in the U.S.*, edited by Judith G. Goode and Jeff Maskovsky, 37–56. New York: New York University Press, 2001.

Mullings, Leith, and Alaka Wali. *Stress and Resilience: The Social Context of Reproduction in Central Harlem.* New York: Springer, 2001.

Murray, Charles A. *Losing Ground: American Social Policy, 1950–1980.* New York: Basic Books, 1984.

Murray, Pauli. *Pauli Murray: The Autobiography of a Black Activist, Feminist, Lawyer, Priest, and Poet.* Knoxville: University of Tennessee Press, 1987.

Mustafa, Tabitha. "The Ongoing Colonization of New Orleans and Palestine." *Pelican Bomb*, May 31, 2016. http://pelicanbomb.com/art-review/2016/the -ongoing-colonization-of-new-orleans-and-palestine.

Nadasen, Premilla. *Welfare Warriors: The Welfare Rights Movement in the United States.* New York: Routledge, 2004.

Nadel, Matt. "Prostitution Was Already Illegal in Louisiana. Then Republicans Crafted an Even More Damning Law Used to Target Trans Sex Workers." *Scalawag Magazine*, June 1, 2021. https://scalawagmagazine.org/2021/06 /trans-sex-worker-laws-new-orleans/.

National Council of Negro Women. *The Legacy of Mary McLeod Bethune.* https:// www.fordlibrarymuseum.gov/library/document/0126/39146853.pdf.

National Harm Reduction Coalition. "The Movement." Accessed May 1, 2022. https://harmreduction.org/movement/evolution/.

National Harm Reduction Coalition. "Principles of Harm Reduction." Accessed May 1, 2022. https://harmreduction.org/about-us/principles-of-harm -reduction/.

Naples, Nancy A. *Grassroots Warriors: Activist Mothering, Community Work, and the War on Poverty*. Perspectives on Gender. New York: Routledge, 1998.

Naquin, Maurice J., Jr. "Criminal Law—Miscegenation—Definition of 'Cohabitation.'" *Louisiana Law Review* 19, no. 3 (1959): 700–705.

Neale, Mark Anthony. "Left of Black S13 · E5 | Commemorating 'Freedom Dreams: The Black Radical Imagination' with Robin D. G. Kelley." Accessed March 31, 2023. https://www.newblackmaninexile.net/2022/11/left-of-black -s13-e5-commemorating.html.

Nelson, Alondra. *Body and Soul: The Black Panther Party and the Fight against Medical Discrimination*. Minneapolis: University of Minnesota Press, 2013.

New York Times Editorial Board. "Slandering the Unborn." *New York Times*, December 28, 2018. https://www.nytimes.com/interactive/2018/12/28/opinion /crack-babies-racism.html.

Norris, Fran H., Susan P. Stevens, Betty Pfefferbaum, Karen F. Wyche, and Rose L. Pfefferbaum. "Community Resilience as a Metaphor, Theory, Set of Capacities, and Strategy for Disaster Readiness." *American Journal of Community Psychology* 41, no. 1/2 (2008): 127–50. https://doi.org/10.1007 /s10464-007-9156-6.

One Million Experiments. Accessed July 27, 2021. https://millionexperiments.com.

Onion, Rebecca. "Inmates at America's Oldest Women's Prison Are Writing a History of It—and Exploding the Myth of Its Benevolent Founders." *Slate Magazine*, March 22, 2015. https://slate.com/news-and-politics/2015/03 /indiana-womens-prison-a-revisionist-history.html.

Orsi, Robert A. *History and Presence*. Cambridge, MA: The Belknap Press of Harvard University Press, 2016.

Orsi, Robert A. *Theorizing Closer to Home*. Vol. 1–2. Harvard Divinity Bulletin 38, 2010. https://bulletin-archive.hds.harvard.edu/articles/winterspring2010 /theorizing-closer-home.

Ortiz, Aurora Santiago. "Repairing La Memoria Rota: Feminist Oral Histories as Critical Memory Recuperation and Resistance." *Taller Electric Marronage*. https://www.electricmarronage.com/electricblog/2021/5/5/repairing-la -memoria-rota.

Oshinsky, David M. *Worse than Slavery: Parchman Farm and the Ordeal of Jim Crow Justice*. New York: Free Press, 1996.

Parenti, Christian. *Lockdown America*. London: Verso, 2008.

Paris Review. "So Be It, See to It: From the Archives of Octavia Butler." *Paris Review*, March 23, 2018. https://www.theparisreview.org/blog/2018/03/23/so -be-it-see-to-it-from-the-archives-of-octavia-butler/.

Pascoe, Peggy. *Relations of Rescue: The Search for Female Moral Authority in the American West, 1874–1939.* New York: Oxford University Press, 1993.

Patterson, Orlando. *Slavery and Social Death: A Comparative Study.* Cambridge, MA: Harvard University Press, 1982.

Patterson, Sunni. "We Know This Place." *American Quarterly* 61, no. 3 (2009): 719–21.

Patterson, Sunni. *We Know This Place.* New Orleans: University of New Orleans Press, 2022.

Patton, Cindy. *Sex and Germs: The Politics of AIDS.* Boston: South End, 1985.

Peck, Raoul, dir. *I Am Not Your Negro.* Magnolia Pictures, 2016.

Pelot-Hobbs, Lydia. "Organized Inside and Out: The Angola Special Civics Project and the Crisis of Mass Incarceration." *Souls: A Critical Journal of Black Politics, Culture, and Society* 15, no. 3 (2013): 199–217. https://doi.org/10.1080/10999949.2013.838860.

Pelot-Hobbs, Lydia. *Prison Capital: Mass Incarceration and Struggles for Abolition Democracy in Louisiana.* Chapel Hill: University of North Carolina Press, 2023.

Petro, Anthony M. *After the Wrath of God: AIDS, Sexuality, and American Religion.* Oxford: Oxford University Press, 2015.

Petro, Anthony M. "Ray Navarro's Jesus Camp, AIDS Activist Video, and the 'New Anti-Catholicism.'" *Journal of the American Academy of Religion* 85, no. 4 (December 30, 2017): 920–56. https://doi.org/10.1093/jaarel/lfx011.

Petteway, Ryan J. "On Epidemiology as Racial-Capitalist (Re)Colonization and Epistemic Violence." *Critical Public Health* 33, no. 1 (January 1, 2023): 5–12. https://doi.org/10.1080/09581596.2022.2107486.

"Photos: Protestors against Ferguson Killing." *Advocate,* September 20, 2014. nola.com/news/photos-protestors-against-ferguson-killing/article_7c2824ea-6ae4-5149-bb30-1abd20428527.html.

Pickens, Josie. "Ferguson: What's Respectability Got to Do with It?" EBONY, August 18, 2014. https://www.ebony.com/news/ferguson-whats-respectability-got-to-do-with-it-987/.

Polletta, Francesca. *It Was like a Fever: Storytelling in Protest and Politics.* Chicago: University of Chicago Press, 2006.

Povinelli, Elizabeth A. *The Cunning of Recognition: Indigenous Alterities and the Making of Australian Multiculturalism.* Durham, NC: Duke University Press, 2002.

Povinelli, Elizabeth A. *Economies of Abandonment: Social Belonging and Endurance in Late Liberalism.* Durham, NC: Duke University Press, 2011.

Povinelli, Elizabeth A. "The Will to Be Otherwise/The Effort of Endurance." *South Atlantic Quarterly* 111, no. 3 (Summer 2012): 453–75. https://doi.org/10.1215/00382876-1596236.

Powell, Lawrence N. *The Accidental City: Improvising New Orleans.* Cambridge, MA: Harvard University Press, 2013.

Prison Policy Initiative. "The Gender Divide: Tracking Women's State Prison Growth." January 9, 2018. https://www.prisonpolicy.org/reports/women_overtime.html.

Prison Policy Initiative. "Women's Mass Incarceration: The Whole Pie 2023." https://www.prisonpolicy.org/reports/pie2023.html.

Puar, Jasbir. *Terrorist Assemblages: Homonationalism in Queer Times*. Durham, NC: Duke University Press, 2007.

Quigley, William P. "Katrina Pain Index 2016: Race and Class Gap Widening." *Common Dreams*, August 22, 2016. https://www.commondreams.org/views/2016/08/22/katrina-pain-index-2016-numbers-race-and-class-gap-widening.

Quigley, William P. "Ten Questions for Social Change Lawyers." SSRN Scholarly Paper. Rochester, NY: Social Science Research Network, November 30, 2012. https://papers.ssrn.com/abstract=2272227.

Raboteau, Albert J. *Slave Religion: The "Invisible Institution" in the Antebellum South*. Oxford: Oxford University Press, 2004.

Ransby, Barbara. *Ella Baker and the Black Freedom Movement: A Radical Democratic Vision*. Chapel Hill: University of North Carolina Press, 2003.

Ransby, Barbara. *Eslanda: The Large and Unconventional Life of Mrs. Paul Robeson*. New Haven, CT: Yale University Press, 2013.

Reckdahl, Katy. "The Long Road from C. J. Peete to Harmony Oaks." *National Housing Institute Shelterforce Report*, 2013. https://shelterforce.org/wp-content/uploads/2014/01/Long_Road_to_Harmony_Oaks_final.pdf.

Reckdahl, Katy. "New C. J. Peete Complex Is Solid, Shiny—but Not as Social, Some Residents Say." *Times-Picayune*, August 11, 2011. https://www.nola.com/news/politics/article_1a918675-1b78-5759-9c91-d3081345e117.html.

Redmond, Shana L. *Anthem: Social Movements and the Sound of Solidarity in the African Diaspora*. New York: New York University Press, 2014.

Reed, Brad. "Baton Rouge Cops Barge into Woman's Yard to Arrest Black Lives Matter Protesters She Invited." *Raw Story*, July 11, 2016. https://www.rawstory.com/2016/07/baton-rouge-cops-barge-into-womans-yard-to-arrest-black-lives-matter-protesters-she-invited/.

Rhea, Shawn E. "Safe Sex Ed." *The Source: The Magazine of Hip-Hop Music, Culture, & Politics*, April 2001.

Richie, Beth E. *Arrested Justice: Black Women, Violence, and America's Prison Nation*. New York: New York University Press, 2012.

Ritchie, Andrea J. "Crimes against Nature: Challenging Criminalization of Queerness and Black Women's Sexuality." *Loyola Journal of Public Interest Law* 14, no. 2 (2013): 355–74.

Ritchie, Andrea J. *Invisible No More: Police Violence against Black Women and Women of Color*. Boston: Beacon Press, 2017.

Ritchie, Andrea J. *Practicing New Worlds: Abolition and Emergent Strategies*. Chico, CA: AK Press, 2023.

Rivlin, Gary. "A Mogul Who Would Rebuild New Orleans." *New York Times*, September 29, 2005. https://www.nytimes.com/2005/09/29/business/a-mogul-who-would-rebuild-new-orleans.html.

Roane, J. T. "On the Spiritual Geography of Black Working-Class Washington." *Black Perspectives*, June 20, 2017. https://www.aaihs.org/on-the-spiritual-geography-of-black-working-class-washington/.

Roberts, Dorothy E. *Killing the Black Body: Race, Reproduction, and the Meaning of Liberty.* New York: Vintage, 1999.

Robinson, Cedric J. *Black Marxism: The Making of the Black Radical Tradition.* Chapel Hill: University of North Carolina Press, 1983.

Rodney, Walter. *The Groundings with My Brothers.* Edited by Asha T. Rodney and Jesse J. Benjamin. With contributions from Carole Boyce Davies, Patricia Rodney, Verene Shepherd, Robin Small, Randall Robinson, and David Austin. New York: Verso, 2019.

Rodriguez, Cheryl. "Invoking Fannie Lou Hamer: Research, Ethnography and Activism in Low-Income Communities." *Urban Anthropology and Studies of Cultural Systems and World Economic Development* 32, no. 2 (July 1, 2003): 231–51.

Rodríguez, Dylan. "Inhabiting the Impasse: Racial/Racial-Colonial Power, Genocide Poetics, and the Logic of Evisceration." *Social Text* 33, no. 3 (2015): 19–44.

Rogers, Kim Lacy. *Righteous Lives: Narratives of the New Orleans Civil Rights Movement.* New York: New York University Press, 1993.

Ross, Loretta J. "Understanding Reproductive Justice." May 2006. https://d3n8a8pro7vhmx.cloudfront.net/rrfp/pages/33/attachments/original/1456425809/Understanding_RJ_Sistersong.pdf?1456425809.

Ross, Loretta J., and Rickie Solinger. *Reproductive Justice: An Introduction.* Berkeley: University of California Press, 2017.

Ross, Rosetta E. *Witnessing and Testifying: Black Women, Religion, and Civil Rights.* New York: Fortress, 2003.

Rouse, Carolyn Moxley. *Engaged Surrender: African American Women and Islam.* Berkeley: University of California Press, 2004.

Rousey, Dennis Charles. *Policing the Southern City: New Orleans, 1805–1889.* Baton Rouge: Louisiana State University Press, 1996.

Roy, Arundhati. "On a Quiet Day I Can Hear Another World Breathing," Speech. January 27, 2003, World Social Forum. Porto Alegre, Brazil. https://www.workersliberty.org/story/2017-07-26/world-social-forum-arundhati-roy.

Roy, Arundhati. "The Pandemic Is a Portal." *Financial Times*, April 3, 2020. https://www.ft.com/content/10d8f5e8-74eb-11ea-95fe-fcd274e920ca.

Russo, Vito. "Why We Fight." ACT UP Demonstration at the Department of Health and Human Services, Washington, DC, October 10, 1988. https://actupny.org/documents/whfight.html.

Sales, Ruby. "From My Front Porch." Facebook, April 30, 2017. https://www.facebook.com/ruby.sales.1/posts/1555241167843656.

Saulny, Susan. "Clamoring to Come Home to New Orleans Projects." *New York Times*, June 6, 2006. https://www.nytimes.com/2006/06/06/us/nationalspecial/06housing.html.

Savage, Barbara Dianne. *Your Spirits Walk beside Us: The Politics of Black Religion.* Cambridge, MA: Harvard University Press, 2008.

Schmidt, Leigh E. *Consumer Rites: The Buying and Selling of American Holidays.* Princeton, NJ: Princeton University Press, 1997.

Schulman, Sarah. "Israel and 'Pinkwashing.'" *New York Times*, November 23, 2011, sec. Opinion.

Schulman, Sarah. *Let the Record Show: A Political History of ACT UP New York, 1987–1993.* New York: Farrar, Straus and Giroux, 2021.

Scott, James C. *Domination and the Arts of Resistance: Hidden Transcripts.* New Haven, CT: Yale University Press, 1990.

Scott, Joan W. "Gender: A Useful Category of Historical Analysis." *The American Historical Review* 91, no. 5 (December 1986): 1053–75. https://doi.org/10.2307/1864376.

Seigel, Micol. *Violence Work: State Power and the Limits of Police.* Durham, NC: Duke University Press, 2018.

Shakespeare, William. *The Tempest.* Folger Shakespeare Library. https://www.folger.edu/tempest.

Shakur, Assata. *Assata: An Autobiography.* London: Zed Books, 2001.

Shames, Stephen, and Ericka Huggins. *Comrade Sisters: Women of the Black Panther Party.* New York: ACC Art Books, 2022.

Shange, Savannah. "Black Girl Ordinary: Flesh, Carcerality, and the Refusal of Ethnography." *Transforming Anthropology*, 27, no. 1 (April 2019): 3–21. https://doi.org/10.1111/traa.12143.

Shange, Savannah. *Progressive Dystopia: Abolition, Antiblackness, and Schooling in San Francisco.* Durham, NC: Duke University Press, 2019.

Shange, Savannah. "Unapologetically Black?" *Anthropology News* 57, no. 7 (July 18, 2016): 64–66. https://doi.org/10.1111/AN.41.

Shange, Savannah, and Roseann Liu. "Solidarity-as-Debt: Fugitive Publics and the Ethics of Multiracial Coalition." Theorizing the Contemporary. *Fieldsights,* July 31, 2019. https://culanth.org/fieldsights/solidarity-as-debt-fugitive-publics-and-the-ethics-of-multiracial-coalition.

Shannon, Kate, Steffanie A. Strathdee, Jean Shoveller, Melanie Rusch, Thomas Kerr, and Mark W. Tyndall. "Structural and Environmental Barriers to Condom Use Negotiation with Clients among Female Sex Workers: Implications for HIV-Prevention Strategies and Policy." *American Journal of Public Health* 99, no. 4 (April 2009): 659–65. https://doi.org/10.2105/AJPH.2007.129858.

Sharpe, Christina. *In the Wake: On Blackness and Being.* Durham, NC: Duke University Press, 2016.

Simmons, LaKisha Michelle. *Crescent City Girls: The Lives of Young Black Women in Segregated New Orleans.* Chapel Hill: University of North Carolina Press, 2015.

Simpson, Audra. *Mohawk Interruptus: Political Life across the Borders of Settler States.* Durham, NC: Duke University Press, 2014.

Simpson, Monica. "Reproductive Justice and 'Choice': An Open Letter to Planned Parenthood." *Rewire News Group*, August 5, 2014. https://

rewirenewsgroup.com/article/2014/08/05/reproductive-justice-choice
-open-letter-planned-parenthood/.

Slave Rebellion Reenactment. November 8–9, 2019. https://www.slave-revolt
.com/.

Smith, Barbara. "Black Feminism: A Movement of Our Own." In *Ain't Gonna
Let Nobody Turn Me Around: Forty Years of Movement Building with Barbara
Smith,* edited by Alethia Jones and Virginia Eubanks, 61–65. Albany: State
University of New York Press, 2014.

Smith, Barbara, and Loretta Ross. "Interview by Loretta Ross." Transcript of
video recording, May 7–8, 2003. Voices of Feminism Oral History Project.
Northampton, MA, Sophia Smith Collections, Smith College, 2003.

Smith, Michael. *Spirit World: Pattern in the Expressive Folk Culture of African-
American New Orleans.* New Orleans: Pelican, 1992.

Smith, Susan Lynn. *Sick and Tired of Being Sick and Tired: Black Women's Health
Activism in America, 1890–1950.* Philadelphia: University of Pennsylvania
Press, 1995.

Smith-Rosenberg, Carroll. *This Violent Empire: The Birth of an American National Identity.* Chapel Hill: University of North Carolina Press, 2010.

Solinger, Rickie, Paula C. Johnson, Martha L. Raimon, Tina Reynolds, and Ruby
Tapia. *Interrupted Life: Experiences of Incarcerated Women in the United
States.* Berkeley: University of California Press, 2010.

Sorett, Josef. "Secular Compared to What? Toward a History of the Trope of
Black Sacred/Secular Fluidity." In *Race and Secularism in America,* edited by
Jonathan Kahn and Vincent W. Lloyd, 43–73. New York: Columbia Univer-
sity Press, 2016.

Sorett, Josef. *Spirit in the Dark: A Religious History of Racial Aesthetics.* Oxford:
Oxford University Press, 2016.

Spade, Dean. *Normal Life: Administrative Violence, Critical Trans Politics, and the
Limits of Law.* Brooklyn: South End, 2011.

Spaulding, Edith R. "The Results of Mental and Physical Examinations of Four
Hundred Women Offenders with Particular Reference to Their Treatment
during Commitment." *Journal of Criminal Law & Criminology* 5, no. 5 (1915):
704–17.

Speaking for Change. "Episode 5: Beyond Pipelines and Prisons—a Dialogue
between Ruth Wilson Gilmore and Winona LaDuke." Accessed March 31,
2023. https://www.spreaker.com/user/cjru1280am/episode-5-beyond
-pipelines-and-prison-a-.

Spillers, Hortense J. "Interstices: A Small Drama of Words." In *Pleasure and Danger: Exploring Female Sexuality,* edited by Carole S. Vance, 73–100. Boston:
Routledge and Kegan Paul, 1984.

Spillers, Hortense J. "Mama's Baby, Papa's Maybe: An American Grammar
Book." *Diacritics,* Summer 1987, 65–81.

Stallybrass, Peter, and Allon White. *Politics and Poetics of Transgression.* Ithaca,
NY: Cornell University Press, 1986.

Stanley, Eric A. *Atmospheres of Violence: Structuring Antagonism and the Trans/Queer Ungovernable*. Durham, NC: Duke University Press, 2021.

Stanley, Eric A., and Nat Smith. *Captive Genders: Trans Embodiment and the Prison Industrial Complex, Revised Second Edition*. Oakland, CA: AK Press, 2015.

Stout, Jeffrey. *Blessed Are the Organized: Grassroots Democracy in America*. Princeton, NJ: Princeton University Press, 2010.

Sublette, Ned. *The World That Made New Orleans: From Spanish Silver to Congo Square*. Chicago: Lawrence Hill, 2008.

Sudbury, Julia, ed. *Global Lockdown: Race, Gender, and the Prison-Industrial Complex*. New York: Routledge, 2005.

Survived & Punished New York. "Preserving Punishment Power: A Grassroots Abolitionist Assessment of New York Reforms." 2020. https://www.survivedandpunishedny.org/wp-content/uploads/2020/04/SP-Preserving-Punishment-Power-report.pdf.

Sweet, Sam. "A Vanished New Orleans Captured on 'Straight from the Projects.'" *New Yorker*. Accessed June 5, 2021. https://www.newyorker.com/culture/culture-desk/a-vanished-new-orleans-captured-on-straight-from-the-projects.

Swenson, Dan. "Then and Now: Interactive Map of New Orleans Housing Developments." *Times-Picayune*, August 20, 2015. https://www.nola.com/news/article_d2cfa990-a749-5905-a051-d3aa0d792780.html.

Taylor, Keeanga-Yamahtta. *From #BlackLivesMatter to Black Liberation*. Chicago: Haymarket, 2016.

Taylor, Keeanga-Yamahtta, ed. *How We Get Free: Black Feminism and the Combahee River Collective*. Chicago: Haymarket, 2012.

Terry, Karen, and Alissa Ackerman. "A Brief History of Major Sex Offender Laws." In *Sex Offender Laws: Failed Policies and New Directions*, 2nd ed., edited by Richard G. Wright. New York: Springer, 2014.

Theoharis, Jeanne. "The Arc of Justice Runs through Ferguson." MSNBC, August 26, 2014. https://www.msnbc.com/msnbc/ferguson-and-the-legacy-the-civil-rights-movement-msna398741.

Theoharis, Jeanne. *The Rebellious Life of Mrs. Rosa Parks*. Boston: Beacon, 2013.

Thomas, Deborah A. *Exceptional Violence: Embodied Citizenship in Transnational Jamaica*. Durham, NC: Duke University Press, 2011.

Thomas, Deborah A. "Time and the Otherwise: Plantations, Garrisons and Being Human in the Caribbean." *Anthropological Theory* 16, no. 2–3 (June 1, 2016): 177–200.

Thomas, Lynnell L. *Desire and Disaster in New Orleans: Tourism, Race, and Historical Memory*. Durham, NC: Duke University Press, 2014.

Thomas, Todne. "When a Black Church Burns (but Not to the Ground): Views of Religion and Racism from Knoxville, Tennessee." *Anthropology News* 56, no. 9 (September 2015): 49–50. https://doi.org/10.1111/j.1556-3502.2015.560905.x.

Thompson, Robert Farris. *Flash of the Spirit: African and Afro-American Art and Philosophy*. New York: Random House, 1983.

Thornton, John K. "African Dimensions of the Stono Rebellion." *American Historical Review* 96, no. 4 (October 1, 1991): 1101–13.

Thrasher, Albert. *On to New Orleans! Louisiana's Heroic 1811 Slave Revolt.* New Orleans: Cypress, 1996.

Thuma, Emily. *All Our Trials: Prisons, Policing, and the Feminist Fight to End Violence.* Urbana: University of Illinois Press, 2016.

Tortorici, Zeb. *Sins against Nature: Sex and Archives in Colonial New Spain.* Durham, NC: Duke University Press, 2018.

Trotter, Darian. "Citizens of New Orleans Hold Moment of Silence for Michael Brown." WGNO, August 15, 2014. https://wgno.com/news/citizens-of-new -orleans-hold-moment-of-silence-for-michael-brown/.

Trouillot, Michel-Rolph. *Silencing the Past: Power and the Production of History.* Boston: Beacon, 1995.

Tuck, Eve, and K. Wayne Yang. "Decolonization Is Not a Metaphor." *Decolonization: Indigeneity, Education and Society* 1, no. 1 (2012): 1–40.

Ture, Kwame [Stokely Carmichael]. "From Black Power to Pan-Africanism." Whittier College, Whittier, CA, March 22, 1971. http://americanradioworks .publicradio.org/features/blackspeech/scarmichael-2.html.

Turner, Dionne, Loretta Ross, Jasmine Burnett, and Charles C. Stuart. *We Always Resist: Trust Black Wome*n. Atlanta, GA: SisterSong, 2011.

Turner, Nicole Myers. *Soul Liberty: The Evolution of Black Religious Politics in Postemancipation Virginia.* Chapel Hill: University of North Carolina Press, 2020.

Tuuri, Rebecca. *Strategic Sisterhood: The National Council of Negro Women in the Black Freedom Struggle.* Chapel Hill: University of North Carolina Press, 2018.

TV News and Public Affairs. "Audience Participation Newest Public Affairs Trend." *Television/Radio Age* 29, no. 24 (July 26, 1982). https:// worldradiohistory.com/Archive-TV-Radio-Age/80s/1982/TV-Radio-Age -1982-07-26.pdf.

United States Department of Justice. "Fact Sheet: Department of Justice Law Enforcement Efforts in New Orleans, Louisiana." August 21, 2006. https://www .justice.gov/archive/opa/pr/2006/August/06_opa_564.html.

United States Department of Justice. "Investigation of the New Orleans Police Department." Civil Rights Division, 2011. https://www.justice.gov/sites /default/files/crt/legacy/2011/03/17/nopd_report.pdf.

United States Department of Labor. *The Negro Family: The Case for National Action.* Washington, DC: United States Department of Labor, 1965. https:// www.dol.gov/general/aboutdol/history/webid-moynihan.

Walcott, Rinaldo. "After Ferguson: Defend the Dead." *rabble.ca*, November 26, 2014. https://rabble.ca/news/2014/11/after-ferguson-defend-dead.

Walker, Alice. *In Search of Our Mother's Gardens.* New York: Harcourt Brace Jovanovich, 1983.

Warfield, Zenobia Jeffries. "What It Takes to Get Women Out of Prison—and Stay Out." *Yes! Magazine*, January 12, 2017. https://www.yesmagazine.org

/issue/50-solutions/2017/01/12/what-it-takes-to-get-women-out-of-prison
-and-stay-out.

Weber, Max. *The Protestant Ethic and the Spirit of Capitalism.* Routledge Classics.
London: Routledge, 2001.

Weber, Max. "Science as a Vocation." 1918. Indianapolis: Hackett, 2004. https://
hscif.org/wp-content/uploads/2018/04/Max-Weber-Science-as-a-Vocation
.pdf.

Weisenfeld, Judith. *African American Women and Christian Activism: New York's
Black YWCA, 1905–1945.* Cambridge, MA: Harvard University Press, 1997.

Weisenfeld, Judith. *New World A-Coming: Black Religion and Racial Identity during the Great Migration.* New York: New York University Press, 2016.

Wells, Ida B. *The Reason Why the Colored American Is Not in the World's Columbian Exposition: The Afro-American's Contribution to Columbian Literature.*
Chicago: Miss Ida B. Wells, 1893. https://digital.library.upenn.edu/women
/wells/exposition/exposition.html.

Wells, Ida B. *Southern Horrors: Lynch Law in All Its Phases.* New York: The New
York Age Print, 1892. https://www.gutenberg.org/files/14975/14975-h
/14975-h.htm.

Wells-Barnett, Ida B. *Mob Rule in New Orleans: Robert Charles and His Fight to
the Death.* 1900. https://www.gutenberg.org/files/14976/14976-h/14976-h
.htm.

Wells-Oghoghomeh, Alexis S. *The Souls of Womenfolk: The Religious Cultures of
Enslaved Women in the Lower South.* Chapel Hill: University of North Carolina Press, 2021.

Whitlock, Kay. "Endgame: How Bipartisan Criminal Justice Reform Institutionalizes a Right-Wing Neoliberal Agenda." *Political Research Associates,* June 6,
2017. https://truthout.org/articles/how-bipartisan-criminal-justice-reform
-institutionalizes-a-right-wing-neoliberal-agenda/.

Wildseeds. "Wildseeds: The New Orleans Octavia Butler Emergent Strategy
Collective." Facebook. https://www.facebook.com/nolawildseeds.org/.

Williams, Patricia J. *The Alchemy of Race and Rights.* Cambridge, MA: Harvard
University Press, 1992.

Williams, Raymond. *The Long Revolution.* New York: Columbia University Press,
1961.

Williams, Rhonda. *The Politics of Public Housing: Black Women's Struggles against
Urban Inequality.* New York: Oxford University Press, 2004.

Williamson, Terrion L. *Scandalize My Name: Black Feminist Practice and the
Making of Black Social Life.* New York: Fordham University Press, 2016.

Wilson, William J. *The Truly Disadvantaged: The Inner City, the Underclass, and
Public Policy.* Chicago: University of Chicago Press, 1987.

Wishon, Jennifer. "New Orleans Church Defies 'Sunday Morning Segregation.'"
Charisma News, February 2, 2014. https://www.charismanews.com/us
/42727-new-orleans-church-defies-sunday-morning-segregation.

Woods, Clyde. *Development Arrested: The Blues and Plantation Power in the Mississippi Delta*. New York: Verso, 1998.

Woods, Clyde. "Do You Know What It Means to Miss New Orleans? Katrina, Trap Economics, and the Rebirth of the Blues." *American Quarterly* 57, no. 4 (2005): 1005–18.

Woods, Clyde, ed. "In the Wake of Katrina: New Paradigms and Social Visions." Special Issue, *American Quarterly* 61, no. 3 (2009).

Woods, Clyde. "Katrina's World: Blues, Bourbon, and the Return to the Source." *American Quarterly* 61, no. 3 (2009): 427–53.

Woods, Clyde, Jordan T. Camp, and Laura Pulido. *Development Drowned and Reborn: The Blues and Bourbon Restorations in Post-Katrina New Orleans*. Athens: University of Georgia Press, 2017.

Woods, Clyde, and Shana M. griffin. "The Politics of Reproductive Violence." *American Quarterly* 61, no. 3 (2009): 583–91.

Woods, Tyron P. "The Antiblackness of 'Modern-Day Slavery' Abolitionism." *Open Democracy*, October 10, 2014. https://www.opendemocracy.net/en/beyond-trafficking-and-slavery/antiblackness-of-modernday-slavery-abolitionism/.

Woodward, C. Vann. *Origins of the New South, 1877–1913*. Baton Rouge: Louisiana State University Press, 2009.

Wynter, Sylvia. "Beyond Miranda's Meaning: Un/Silencing the 'Demonic Ground' of Caliban's Women." In *Out of the Kumbla: Caribbean Women and Literature*, edited by Carole Boyce Davies and Elaine Savory Fido, 355–72. Trenton, NJ: Africa World Press, 1990.

Wynter, Sylvia. "Unsettling the Coloniality of Being/Truth/Freedom: Towards the Human, after Man, Its Overrepresentation—An Argument." *New Centennial Review* 3, no. 3 (2003): 257–337.

Wynter, Sylvia, and David Scott. "The Re-Enchantment of Humanism: An Interview with Sylvia Wynter." *Small Axe* 8 (2000): 119–207.

Young, Iris Marion. "City Life and Difference." In *Justice and the Politics of Difference*, 226–56. Princeton, NJ: Princeton University Press, 1990.

Young, Kevin. *The Grey Album: On the Blackness of Blackness*. Minneapolis: Graywolf, 2012.

Young Women's Empowerment Project. *Girls Do What They Have to Do to Survive: Illuminating Methods Used by Girls in the Sex Trade and Street Economy to Fight Back and Heal*. Chicago: Young Women's Empowerment Project, 2011. https://ywepchicago.files.wordpress.com/2011/06/girls-do-what-they-have-to-do-to-survive-a-study-of-resilience-and-resistance.pdf.

Zigon, Jarrett. *HIV Is God's Blessing: Rehabilitating Morality in Neoliberal Russia*. Berkeley: University of California Press, 2011.

INDEX

Page references in italics indicate illustrations.

abandonment, governmental, 157, 232n75; and the AIDS crisis in Black communities, 243n71; and population displacement, 7, 40–41, 58–59, 96, 112, 130–31, 137. *See also* HIV/AIDS; displacement

abolition feminism: and WWAV, 1, 10–11, 54, 107, 130, 143, 145, 150, 154, 216, 228n26. *See also* carceral feminism

abortion justice, 218–22. *See also* reproductive justice (RJ)

Abu-Lughod, Lila: on everyday resistance, 183; on the war on terror (and saving women), 254n27

academia: and erasure, 17, 20, 86; and the HIV epidemic, 62; institutional power of, 22; and research, 62–63, 66, 76, 83–85; and "resilience," 36

accompliceship, 12, 21–23, 25, 28, 32–33, 90, 120, 124, 127, 143, 150, 183, 213, 233n7; vs. allyship, 22, 170–71, 233n16. *See also* relationships

accumulation, 23; of the Black Radical Tradition, 241n36; of criminal charges (in the course of survival), 111–12, 148; of history, 85, 90; vs. linearity, 20; of stories, 171; of structures of feeling, 135; of theory on the ground, 74; of work (to get wins), 100

action: Black feminist call to, 141, 160–62, 201; collective, 69; and feeling, 135; from storytelling, 18, 20, 33, 53, 90, 106; vs. talk, 22. *See also* revolution

ACT UP, 61, 251n83. *See also* HIV/AIDS; Russo, Vito

Adams, Michael Henry: on gentrification, 235n28. *See also* gentrification

Adam Walsh Child Protection and Safety Act, 112, 247n38. *See also* Sex Offender Registry

Agathocleous, Alexis: and the NO Justice Project, 118–19, *120*, 130, 245n20, 250nn73–74, 251n86. *See also* NO Justice Project

agency: political (of poor Black women), 69, 195, 213. *See also* political

Ahmed, Leila: and "colonial feminism," 254n27

AIDS. *See* HIV/AIDS

Alexander, M. Jacqui: on entering fire, 132; on truth as antidote, 19. *See also* truth

All-African People's Revolutionary Party, 139, 160

Ansfield, Bench: on urban redevelopment, 235n32

anticriminalization. *See* decriminalization

Anzaldúa, Gloria: on relationships (as constellations), 14. *See also* relationships

apprenticeship: and WWAV, 12, 54, 75–76, 205

archive: Black feminist theories of, 178; Born in Flames Living Archive, 15–16, 26, 158, 228n32, 229n40, 250n69, 252n94, 265–75; "Crime Against Nature by Solicitation (CANS) Litigation" online archive, 245n3; ephemerality of Black archives, 59; front porch as, 49, 180; living, 16, 23, 60, 168, 177–78, 183; NO Justice Project living archive, 99, 116, 120, 124, 245n12, 250n69; relationships as, 178, 183; "We Spoke Our Truths" oral history project, 128, 252n94. *See also* Berry, Mary Frances; Fuentes, Marisa; Hartman, Saidiya; Johnson, Jessica Marie; McKittrick, Katherine

Arenas, Iván: and WWAV's 30th-anniversary report, *212*

arson attack on WWAV offices, 1–5, 10, 13, 15, 18–19, 21–22, 24, 26–27, 29, 34, 37, 41, 54, 60, 75, 99, 128–71, 173, 175–78, 181, 191, 205, 211, 221–22, 228n32, 236n33, 245n12. *See also* Born in Flames oral history project

authentic, so-called: in Aboriginal Australia, 232n75; in Black Harlem 235n28; in Black New Orleans, 36, 40–41

Bailey, Moya: on "misogynoir," 231n66. *See also* "misogynoir"

bail outs, 130, 211–12. *See also* incarceration

Baker, Ella, 158

Baker, Richard H.: on the post-Katrina "cleaning up" of New Orleans public housing, 39. *See also* public housing

Baldwin, James, 245n9; *The Fire Next Time*, 7. *See also* fire

Bambara, Toni Cade: on the power of words, 24. *See also* power; speaking

Batiste, Chanelle: and the protest of police murders of Black people, 165. *See also* police: murder; protests

Batiste, Lisa: and the protest over the police murder of Alton Sterling, 47–48, 237n55. *See also* front porch; police: murder

belonging, 63–65, 74–75, 134, 241n30; and shedding victimhood narratives, 155

Bergland, Renée L.: on settler colonialism, 235n30.

Bernstein, Elizabeth: on "carceral feminism," 255n26. *See also* carceral feminism

Berry, Mary Frances, 6, 138, 221, *222*; on *Fisher v. University of Texas Austin*, 234n17; *My Face Is Black Is True*, 260n8; and the story of Callie House, 260n15; and the threat of Black women organizers, 178. *See also* archive

Beyoncé: *Lemonade*, 206, 238n59, 238n61. *See also* front porch

Bigard, Ashana: on the charter school experiment, 231n61

Black and Brown Sex Worker Second Line, 214–15. *See also* sex workers

Black Codes, 101, 249n49

Black Feminist Future, 164. *See also* futurity; reproductive justice (RJ)

Black Feminist Library (WWAV's), 25, 158, 180, 226n13, 242n38, 257n50

Black Feminist Santa, 183–84, 186–89, 198, 206

Black Lives Matter. *See* Movement for Black Lives

Black Panther Party: and community survival programs, 66

Black Radical Tradition, 135, 162, 170–71, 182, 208, 241n36. *See also* feeling: infrastructure of

Blackstone, Sir William: and the term "Crime Against Nature," 101. *See also* CANS statute

Black study, 100, 198, 260n16

Black Youth Project 100, 219

blame, 3–4, 8, 17–18, 23, 25, 30–31, 36, 40, 42, 52, 56, 68–69, 83, 85, 93, 103, 107, 111, 133, 156; refusal to, 81, 83, 148, 157. *See also* racial capitalism playbook

blankness: as obscuring displacement/ erasure, 4, 39–41, 113, 159. *See also* displacement; erasure; new New Orleans

Blutcher, Dimitri, 2

bodies: controlling/managing/policing of Black, 62, 106–13, 212, 239n2; geographic, 32 invisibilization of Black women's, 62, 97–100, 104, 106–7, 111, 128, 156, 201–2, 239n1; and spatiality, 32, 42. *See also* criminalization; embodied

Bolden, Angelita, 58, 81–82, 88–89

Borden, Lizzie: *Born in Flames* (film), 228nn31–32. *See also* relationships

Borden, Shaquita (Quita), 1–2, 10–14, 22, 31, 47, 50, 71, 73, 93, 128, 138, 144, 158, 173, 179, 180, 186, 217, 262n37, 262n39, 262n41; on Canizaro, 193; on Catherine, 179; and the Community Voices Project, 139; and going on the road, 10, 27, 136, 140–45, 159, 170, 197–208; and the Know Her Truths conference, 197–207; and public health, 13, 202–4; and the "resilience" porch talk, 34; and the "Safety and Love" visioning session, 193–97

Born in Flames (Borden), 228nn31–32. *See also* relationships

Born in Flames Living Archive, 15–16, 26, 158, 228n32, 229n40, 250n69, 252n94, 265–75. *See also* arson attack; fire

Born in Flames oral history project, 10, 13, 53–54, 74, 99, 205, 228n32. *See also* arson attack; fire

Bowers, Gary: and the *Bowers v. Hardwick* criminal sodomy case, 247n32

BreakOUT!, 119, 229n47

breath: of another world a-coming, 74; catching one's (and freedom/ possibility), 114, 191; communal, 183; as release, 146; of relief, 177

Breland, Christine, 90, 173–75, 177, 192–95, 197, 217; and anticriminalization work, 75, 175, 189–90, 194–95, 211; on Canizaro, 193; and the "Safety and Love" visioning session, 192–97. *See also* criminalization

brown, adrienne maree: *Emergent Strategy*, 258n63; and organizing/ dreams, 7

Brown, Michael: police murder of (and resultant protests), 23, 164–69. *See also* police: murder; protests

Brown, Wendy: "Suffering the Paradoxes of Rights," 250n67

Browne, Simone: on "dark sousveillance," 260n17. *See also* "dark sousveillance"; surveillance

Burroughs, Nannie Helen: on specializing in the wholly impossible, 193, 261n27

Butler, Octavia, 263n51; *Kindred*, 256n39. *See also* dismemberment

Cacho, Lisa Marie: *Social Death*, 246n15

Campt, Tina: on the grammar of black feminist futurity, 20–21. *See also* futurity

Canizaro, Joseph, 193, 226n9; on postKatrina New Orleans, 39, 113

CANS statute, 9–10, 12, 95–131, 156–57, 199–203, 236n33, 246n20, 246n28, 250n69, 251n82, 252n86; and gender/race, 9, 104; and HIV/AIDS risk, 106, 140, 262n34; and photo-ID branding, 9, 12, 27, 96, 98, 105–6, 112, 117, 121–22, 199–200, 202; vs. prostitution charges, 103–4, 119, 123–24, 200, 203, 246n20, 250n59. *See also* criminalization; NO Justice Project; Sex Offender Registry; sex workers

Carby, Hazel V.: on invisibility/hypervisibility, 107; on the policing of Black women's bodies, 109–11

carceral feminism, 110, 143–45, 154–57, 159, 204, 214, 255n26. *See also* abolition feminism; incarceration care, 71, 119, 154; community, 98, 237n42; and front porches, 44; for histories of struggle, 158; as life-giving, 19; and solidarity, 93; of speech, 24

Casselberry, Judith: on spiritual labor, 230n54

Centers for Disease Control and Prevention: Diffusion of Effective Behavioral Interventions (DEBI) program, 83–85

Charbonnet, Judge Desiree: and WWAV, 147–48. *See also* Emerge program

Chateauvert, Melinda (Mindy), *50*, 138, *160*, 247n29

Chemis, *44*. *See also* front porch

Children's Pediatric AIDS Program, 55–56, 76. *See also* HIV/AIDS

Chisholm, Shirley, 158

civil rights movement, 125, 127–28, 168

Claiborne, William C. C.: and "crimes against nature," 101. *See also* CANS statute

Cohen, Cathy, 6, 107; *Boundaries of Blackness*, 239n2; "Punks, Bulldaggers, and Welfare Queens," 247n35; on transformation, 113. *See also* transformation

collectivity: and authorship, 22, 54, 206, 229n38; and knowledge, 42; and solidarity, 14, 127–28, 133–34, 162. *See also* community; solidarity

Combahee River Collective, 141, 229n47, 248n42, 259n5; and the phrase "interlocking systems of oppression," 227n18

communication: and sex work, 151; wordless (at WWAV), 8, 57, 76, 88–89, 185. *See also* relationships; speech

community: care, 98, 237n42; listening sessions, 16, 115–18, 139–40, 200; meaning of, 91; resilience, 233n3; and safety, 88–89; and spatiality, 16; working in, 9, 27, 31, 53, 62, 65–72, 74, 76–92, 98–99, 114–17, 119, 123, 131, 136–37, 139, 148, 161–62, 171, 179, 190, 193, 196, 198–99, 204, 223, 229n43, 264n9. *See also* relationships; solidarity

Community HIV/AIDS Mobilization Project, 12.

Community Voices Project, 139–40. *See also* community

condoms: "cheeking" of, 74, 83, 243n63; vs. criminalization of sex work, 142; distribution of, 8, 57–58, 76–77, 81, 83, 136–37; flavored, 81, 83; negotiation re: (as major risk for sex workers), 243n63. *See also* harm reduction; HIV/AIDS; safety; sex workers

congregation: historical limits on Black, 46. *See also* collectivity; front porch

conjuring: fire dreams, 50; the future, 24–25; revolution, 208

convict lease system, 108, 249n49, 262n41. *See also* incarceration

Cooper, Anna Julia, 98, 158, 197, 199, 225n3

Cooper, Wendi, *50*, 173. *See also* NO Justice Project

Cox, Aimee Meredith: *Shapeshifters*, 231n65

crack babies (as violent narrative), 8, 52, 239n1, 249n57. *See also* drug users; misinformation

Crawford, John: police murder of, 165. *See also* police: murder

Crawley, Ashon, 231n69; on the otherwise, 23–24. *See also* otherwise

Crenshaw, Kimberlé: on intersectionality, 227n18

criminalization, 3–5, 8–12, 17, 23, 25, 30, 40–42, 56–57, 59, 69, 83, 85, 93, 133, 144, 185, 204; of abortion, 222; of Blackness / Black women, 40–41, 52–53, 71–73, 100, 106–13, 118, 120–22, 125, 128–30, 142, 155–57, 161, 200–202, 211–12, 248n46, 249nn48–49, 249n57, 257n53; compounded, 98, 106; and gender, 72–73, 189; of sex work, 1, 5, 9–10, 12, 23, 27, 64, 83, 95–131, 141–42, 145–55, 191, 199–203, 212, 214–17, 254n22. *See also* CANS statute; decriminalization; police; racial capitalism playbook

Critical Resistance, 12

crossroads, 8, 43–44, 46, 227n21, 237n40; front porch as, 43, 46. *See also* Emerge project

Cruisin' the Streets (television series), 103, 247n31. *See also* misinformation; sex workers

Cruz, Rosana (R. Cielo), 2, 251n76; on the impacts of criminalization, 122–23; and the NO Justice Project, 119, 122–23. *See also* criminalization; NO Justice Project

Cullors, Patrisse: and #BlackLivesMatter, 159, 170; on the fight to save your life, 208. *See also* Movement for Black Lives

culture: as not an excuse for oppression, 36, 41

Curtin, Mary Ellen: on race and the image of the fallen woman in the South, 109

"dark sousveillance," 191, 260n17. *See also* vision; surveillance

Davis, Angela Y., 107, 226; and dreams, 7; on gender and the prison system, 108; on intersectionality, 149; on (radically) transforming the world, 132, 193–94, 213

Davis, Jaliyah, *221. See also* abortion justice; reproductive justice (RJ)

Davis, Leslie: and the Emerge/Groundworks programs, 150, 152, 173. *See also* Emerge program; Groundworks program

death: and Black women (HIV), 8, 52; premature 31, 53, 69–70, 73, 76, 168, 227n23, 233n6, 253n4, 257n53; slow, 158, 257n53; social, 100, 127, 158, 245n15

decriminalization, 1, 60, 75, 136, 138–39, 144, 174, 187, 215–17. *See also* criminalization; Deep South Decrim Project; NO Justice Project

Dee, Anita, *164. See also* protests

Deep South Decrim Project, 215–17, 254n22. *See also* criminalization; decriminalization

defacement: and the arson attack on WWAV's offices, 2, 128

Degree, Elyse: and sex worker justice, *215;* and voter engagement, 212. *See also* voter engagement; sex workers

destabilization, 2–4, 6, 8, 17, 23, 25, 30, 32, 40, 42, 52, 56, 59, 69, 71, 83, 85, 93, 107, 191, 201. *See also* racial capitalism playbook

deviance: narratives of sexual, 103–4, 109, 111

Diallo, Dazon Dixon: on the AIDS epidemic in the deep South, 141. *See also* HIV/AIDS epidemic; SisterLove

Dias, Marley: and WWAV's front porch, 49. *See also* front porch

difference: and relationships, 133–34; and theory on the ground, 155. *See also* relationships; theory on the ground

dismemberment, 154–55, 223, 256n39. *See also* racial capitalism playbook

displacement, 7, 30, 33, 36–37, 39–43, 45, 58–59, 71, 96, 110, 112, 130–31, 137, 235n27; and creativity, 36. *See also* erasure

dispossession, 157; of Black women, 55, 69, 97, 127, 143; of Black women's work, 163–64; of knowledge, 54, 59, 71, 84–86; and the racial capitalism playbook, 145, 215. *See also* CANS statute; taking

diversion: and WWAV 130, 132, 136, 145–55, 214. *See also* criminalization; Emerge program; incarceration

documentation, 60, 168; of Deon's journey to healing, 216; excess (as tactic), 262n39; as explanation (for those with CANS convictions), 117; lack of (in the early days of WWAV), 81–82, 90; and legitimacy, 203; and the NO Justice Project, 115–116, 120, 124, 126, 128, 252n94; of nontraditional forms of work, 147–54, 170; of porch talks / story circles, 35, 75–76, 82, 206. *See also* Born in Flames oral history project; Born in Flames Living Archive

Dodge, L. Mara: on the criminalization of Black women, 248n46. *See also* criminalization

Doe v. Jindal, 118–24, 130, 246n20. *See also* Jindal, Governor Bobby; NO Justice Project

Donelon, Jim: and the expansion of Louisiana's "Crime Against Nature" statute, 103. *See also* CANS statute

Dorrien, Gary: on King and the civil rights explosion of the 1950s, 259n73. *See also* civil rights movement; King, Dr. Martin Luther, Jr.

dreams, 7; and Black study, 100; and creation, 7, 19; dreaming with eyes wide open, 5–7, 14, 25, 192; fire, 6, 7, 16–18, 19, 33, 26, 27, 48, 50, 54, 60, 70, 74, 90, 108, 130, 131, 134–36, 178, 181, 183, 192, 208–9; and enchantment, 19; freedom, 227nn19–20; and front porches, 14, 26, 33, 46, 48, 49, 187; and infrastructure of feeling, 134–35, 208; and memory, 19; and otherwise, 7, 24; and prophets, 7; sheltered/protected, 25, 48–49, 65, 74, 100, 177–78, 181, 221; and surveillance, 25; and theory on the ground, 17–18; wellsprings of, 19, 43, 65. *See also* fire dreams; Kelley, Robin D. G.; Woods, Clyde

Drug Policy Alliance, 144–45

drug users: and HIV/AIDS, 61–62, 90; "nice people take drugs," 72; normalization of, 77–78; and WWAV, 3, 5, 9, 53–54, 56, 60, 62, 66, 72–74, 76–78, 82–83, 97, 104–5, 137–39, 141–43, 148. *See also* criminalization; war on drugs

Dublin Platform for Human Rights Defenders, 142–43

Du Bois, W. E. B., 241n30

DuVernay, Ava: and WWAV's front porch, 49. *See also* front porch

Ellis, Robert, 58

embodied: ethics, 75; practices, 23–24, 32, 43. *See also* bodies; front porch

Emerge program, 10–11, 14, 145–55, 170, 173–74, 191, 214. *See also* Groundworks program; NO Justice Project; sex workers

erasure, 3–8, 17–18, 23, 25, 30, 40, 52, 56, 69, 73–74, 83, 85, 93, 100, 107, 145, 159, 186; and academia, 17, 20, 86; of Black women's work, 21–22, 85–86, 159, 163–64, 168, 170, 177–78, 262n37; of community-based organizers, 84; and criminal justice reform, 255n31; "palatable" forms of, 159; post-Katrina, 4, 6–7, 30, 37, 42–43, 59, 64, 100, 131, 157, 235n27; and "progress," 20, 39; refusal of, 181, 183; and "resilience," 36, 39, 49, 59, 106, 131, 191–92; #StopErasing, 164. *See also* displacement; dispossession; invisibilization; racial capitalism playbook; taking

Evans, Desiree (Des), 31, *50*, 90, 93, 138, 144, *146*, *167*, *180*, *197*, *209*, 175, 228n27, 235n29, 248n44, 256n42; and "Black Feminist Santa," 183–84; and the Broad Street office, 173–74, 178–80, 185–86; and communications/programming, 75; and the Community Voices Project, 139; on the "Disneyfication of New Orleans," 40; and the protesting of police murder of Black people, 165–70; and the "resilience" porch talk, 34–38, 40–41; and the "Safety and Love" visioning session, 192–97; on WWAV, 244n1; and WWAV's Black Feminist Library, 158

Evans, Sula Janet, 179, 260n13

everyday: knowledge, 16–17; oppression, 182, 207; resistance, 183; surveillance, 27, 58, 65, 74, 100, 109–11, 113, 115, 145, 165, 178, 191, 201, 212; terror/violence, 12–13, 16–17, 33, 46, 65, 77, 86, 98, 100, 105–7, 110–13, 116–17, 119, 121–22, 142–43, 165, 202, 216–18

existence: as political, 21, *66*, 183–84, 211–12

exploitation: of difference, 133; of disaster, 39, 59, 71; of group-differentiated vulnerabilities (racism), 53, 227n23, 233n6

Fabian, Johannes: on "allochronism," 232n77. *See also* temporality

family: chosen, 12, 14; as put first, 218; and WWAV activism, 220–21; and WWAV outreach, 44, 214; and WWAV programming, 118–19

Farley, Tom, 82; and attempts to silence WWAV, 63; and the MOVE bombing, 240n27

Farrow, Kenyon, 12

fear: of Black women's freedom, 21, 94; and CANS convictions, 122; feeling (vs. expressing), 91; of going into the community, 62, 76, 91; of having a son, *164*; and respect, 80

feeling, 16; and action, 135; of entitlement (as needed), 193; of home, 201; infrastructure of, 68, 134–36, 170–71, 182, 208; and memory, 175–79; of WWAV, 175–78

Feinberg, Jonathan: and the NO Justice Project, 130. *See also* NO Justice Project

Feldman, Judge Martin: and the federal case against CANS, 96, 124, 127, 129, 251n82, 252n86. *See also* CANS statute; criminalization; sex workers

Ferrell, Jonathan: police murder of, 165. *See also* police: murder

Fields, Karen: "What One Cannot Remember Mistakenly," 229n38. *See also* collectivity: and authorship

Fields, Mamie Garvin: "What One Cannot Remember Mistakenly," 229n38. *See also* collectivity: and authorship

Finger, Davida: and the NO Justice Project, 118–19, *120*, 130. *See also* NO Justice Project

fire: and abolitionist organizing, 18; *The Fire Next Time* (Baldwin), 7; of Pentecost, 7; and rebirth, 7; and sodomy (historically), 101; and terror, 7, 18, 37, 134, 181; using your own, 210; *Words of Fire* (Guy-Sheftall), 7; working with, 132–71, 178, 220–22. *See also* Alexander, M. Jacqui; arson attack; fire dreams

fire dreams, 6, 7, 16–18, 19, 33, 26–27, 48, 50, 54, 60, 70, 74, 90, 108, 130–31, 134–36, 178, 181, 183, 192, 208–9; of Black southern women organizers, 50, 135, 178, 183; and Black study, 100; and enchantment, 19; and front porches, 14, 26, 33, 46, 48–49, 187; and infrastructure of feeling, 134–35, 208; and surveillance, 25; and theory on the ground, 17–18; and worldmaking, 7; of WWAV foremothers, 16, 50, 54, 60, 70, 90, 192. *See also* dreams; fire

First Grace United Methodist Church, 253n11; and WWAV (post-Katrina), 136–38

Fisher, Abigail, 39, 234n17

Flaherty, Jordan: *Floodlines*, 234n24. *See also* public housing

Flournoy, Melissa: termination of, 258n61. *See also* Planned Parenthood; reproductive justice

Floyd, George: police murder of, 216, 225n2. *See also* police: murder

Ford, Kris: and the termination of Melissa Flournoy, 258n61. *See also* Planned Parenthood

François, France: #TooManyToName, 165, *166*. *See also* Brown, Michael; police: murder; protests

Frederick, Marla F.: *Between Sundays*, 230n54

Frederick, Raven, 50, 77, 185–86, *209*, 215, 217, 261n30; and sex worker justice, *215*; and voter engagement, 75, 212; on working in community, 90–91

Free Southern Theater, 42. *See also* storytelling

Frimpong, Allen Kwabena, 261n23; and the "Safety and Love" visioning session, 190–97

Front Line Defenders, 142

front porch: as crossroads, 43, 46; and interstitiality, 43–45; and otherwise, 41–43; and outreach, 44–45; as place of rest/restoration, 11, 43, 45; as place of revolutionary things,

front porch (continued)
29–30, 33, 45, 48–49, 180–83,
198; policing of the, 45–49; poses,
49–50, 183–84, 196–97; and state
violence, 33; stories/talks, 14–16,
23–24, 26, 29–51, 71, 75, 130, 157,
180, 182–83, 186, 206, *219*, 238n61;
strategy, 26, 29–51, 54, 57, 179–208,
218–19, 236n34, 261n31; as undo-
mesticable, 41; and witnessing, 52
Front Porch Research Strategy institute,
197–98, 261n31. *See also* front porch;
research
Fuentes, Marisa: on reading along the
bias grain, 178. *See also* archive
fugitivity, 3, 22, 134; and Black women,
108, 112
Fullilove, Mindy: *Root Shock*, 237n45,
253n96
futurity: Black feminist, 19–21, 27, 51,
53, 73, 75–76, 134, 136, 149, 208; and
prefigurative politics, 25, 231n62;
and revolution, 238n53. *See also*
imagining otherwise; temporality;
world-building

Garner, Eric: police murder of, 165.
See also police: murder
Garza, Alicia: and the Black Lives
Matter movement, 159, 170. *See also*
Movement for Black Lives
gatekeepers: community, 45, 57–58,
63, 74, 79, 185; and health parties,
63, 74; at WWAV, 174–75. *See also*
community
gentrification: vs. colonialism, 235n28;
and population displacement, 7
geography/geographies, 17, 24, 41, 145,
180, 208; abolition, 172, 226n6,
234n20, 239n4, 255n31; Black, 18,
41, 43, 134, 233n7, 235n28; and Black
Radical Tradition, 182, 208, 241n36;
of Black women's bodies, 32, 42;
Black women's geographic knowledges, 33, 47, 49, 63, 65, 67, 70, 159,
198; blues, 234n19; front porch, 42–43,
50, 236n34; geographic story, 19, 33,
42, 49, 50, 236n37; New Orleans

19, 41, 73, 127, 134, 178, 183, 232n75;
and otherwise, 182; and scale, 26–27,
133, 136, 140, 142, 145, 180, 234n13.
See also crossroads; displacement;
front porch; Gilmore, Ruth Wilson;
grounds; McKittrick, Katherine;
place-making; space
German Coast Uprising, 46, 237n50
Gilmore, Ruth Wilson, 107, 229n43,
244n75; on abolition and innocence,
255n31; on freedom (as a place),
172; *Golden Gulag*, 227n23, 233n6,
253n8; on the infrastructure of feeling, 135, 171, 241n36, 253n8; on life
in rehearsal, 94; on racial capitalism,
225n6, 253n4; on racism as premature death, 52–53, 227n23, 233n6.
See also feeling: infrastructure of
Glaser, Barney: and "grounded theory,"
229n45
Glissant, Édouard: on the right to opacity, 232n74
Gordon, Avery: on the right to personhood (and the study of domination),
253n7
Gore, Dayo, 6
Gorz, André: and "nonreformist reform," 261n21
Great Migration, 100, 109, 158
griffin, Shana M., 2, 11–12, 231n61; and
the NO Justice Project, 118–19, *120*,
121–22; on post-Katrina erasure,
235n27. *See also* erasure; NO Justice
Project
grounds, 5, 11, 19, 33, 41–43, 45–49,
53, 58, 74–75, 90, 130, 172–209,
213, 237n44; demonic, 230n55,
236n34, 236n37, 261n23; hallowed,
47, 74, 134, 221. *See also* geography/
geographies
Groundworks program, 149–53, 207.
See also Emerge program; sex
workers
Gumbs, Alexis Pauline: on the threat
of Black women's freedom, 21, 94.
See also threat
Gusman, Sheriff Marlin: and incarceration, 110; on WWAV (as a reentry

program), 175. *See also* incarceration; Orleans Parish Prison

Guy-Sheftall, Beverly: *Words of Fire*, 7. *See also* fire

Guzmán, Joshua Javier: on the film *Born in Flames*, 228n31. *See also* relationships

Haley, Oretha Castle, 158

Haley, Sarah, 6; on invisibility/hypervisibility, 107–8; on Jim Crow modernity, 18, 107, 248n46; *No Mercy Here*, 248n46, 260n16

Hamer, Fannie Lou, 53, 158

harm reduction: and holding difference, 133; movement, 9, 58, 66–67, 139, 190, 237n41, 241n34; National Harm Reduction Conference, 66–67; Southern Harm Reduction Conference, *146*; and WWAV, 9, 50, 54, 65–68, 70–71, 76–90, 97, 114, 136–37, 139, 145, 148, 199, 210, 212, 214–15, 241n34, 254n13

Harris-Perry, Melissa: and the Know Her Truths conference, 198–99

Hartman, Saidiya, 107; on the afterlife of slavery, 46, 226n8, 230n52; on critical fabulation, 178; on the terror of the mundane/quotidian, 248n41. *See also* archive; slavery

Hassan, Shira: on relationships, 15; *Saving Our Own Lives*, 243n53. *See also* harm reduction; relationships

Hatcher, Paris: and Black RJ, 164. *See also* reproductive justice (RJ)

having another's back, 16, 88–89, 151–52, 179. *See also* community; safety

Haywood, Bailey (Bunny), 2, 179, *180, 220*

Haywood, Brandon, 2, 71

Haywood, Catherine (Lady), 2, 10, 14, 22, 53–66, 71–77, 89–94, 114, 142–43, 154, 159, *184*, 185, 211, *212, 217*, 242n42; and belonging, 63–65, 74–75, 134, 241n30; as cook, 173, 176–77, 182, 196; on Deon, 64–65; on *doing the work*, 60, 64, 70, 77, 94, 171; on front porches, 44–46;

and harm-reduction work, 9, 65–70, 77–85, 97, 139, 241n34; and the origins of WWAV, 8–9, 44, 55–60; on relationships, 133, 181; as ungovernable, 93; as unwavering, 55, 73, 94

Haywood, Charles: and the Ending the HIV Epidemic (EtE) project, 218–219. *See also* HIV/AIDS

Haywood, Cynthia, 2, 71, 142

Haywood, Deon, 1–3, 9–14, 22–23, *31*, 34, 47, 49, *50*, 53–55, 58–59, 64, 70–76, 79, 81–82, 84–95, 97, 106, *124*, 135, 138, 147–49, 154–58, 173–77, *184, 209*, 210–13, *217*, 222, 228n36, 242n43, 250n69, 262n35; and the All-African People's Revolutionary Party, 139, 160; on allyship, 35; on being a human rights defender, 143; on being tired (yet undeterred), 73, 86; and the Black Feminist Library at WWAV, 158; as "Black Feminist Santa," 183–84, 186–89; as cancer survivor, 216–19; on Catherine, 179; and the Community Voices Project, 139; on continuity and change in WWAV, 71–72; and the Emerge project, 147–48; on fire and terror/rebirth, 7, 130, 132–33; on First Grace church, 137; on front porches and revolutionary things, 29–30, 33, 183; "Front Porch Revolution," 232n75; and going on the road, 10, 12, 27, 98, 136, 140–45, 159, 162–63, 170, 197–208; on the invisibilization of Black women, 104, 201–2, 218; on Katrina, 32; and the Know Her Truths conference, 197–207; on Michelle Wiley, 173–74; and the NO Justice Project, 113–18, 121, 123–30, 154, 159, 168; and the origins of WWAV, 9–10; and the presence of history, 134; on the racial capitalism playbook, 185; on racism, 149; and reproductive justice, 162–64; and the "resilience" porch talk, 34–38; and the "Safety and Love" visioning session, 192–97; and the Solidarity Rally for Trayvon Martin, 159–62, 168, 191, 232n2; on

Haywood, Deon (continued)
the South, 141; and UNSHACKLE
convention, 11–12; on "victimhood,"
86–87, 154–57, 204, 207; and working across movement, 139–40, 143;
on WWAV after the arson attack, 34,
129–30, 139, 171, 185
Haywood, (Little) Brandon, 71, *214*
health, 54; care, 11–12, 141, 216–18;
education, 4, 57, 66, 85–87, 150,
218; New Orleans Women's Health
Clinic, 11; parties, 62–63, 74, 85–87,
176–177; vs. survival, 141; Women's
Health & Justice Initiative, 11,
118–19
Henry VIII: and the criminalization of
sodomy, 101. *See also* CANS statute
Hill, Ashley, 210
HIV/AIDS: ACT UP, 61, 252n83; and
Black communities, 5, 8, 52, 54, 56–57,
61–63, 98, 106, 141–42, 228n29,
239n2, 244n71; and the CANS statute, 106, 140, 262n34; Children's
Pediatric AIDS Program, 8, 55; and
criminalization, 11–12, 228n29,
244n71; and drug users, 61–62, 90;
Ending the HIV Epidemic (EtE),
218–19, 264n9; and government
neglect, 6, 61; International AIDS
Conference, 140–42; perception
of as "gay" disease (and effect on
Black communities), 8, 56, 76, 98;
and "respectable victims," 73; and
sex workers, 61, 98, 103, 141–42; and
sodomy law, 247n32; United States
Conference on HIV/AIDS, 12; and
WWAV, 3–5, 8–9, 11–12, 54, 61–62,
65–67, 71, 73, 78–79, 83–85, 93, 114,
139–41, 144–45, 199, 203–4, 210–14,
218–19. *See also* Centers for Disease
Control and Prevention; condoms;
needle exchanges; UNSHACKLE
convention
Holl, Jenny: and the Ending the HIV
Epidemic (EtE) project, 218–219.
See also HIV/AIDS
hooks, bell: on one's power, 1. *See also*
power

House, Callie, 158, 260n15
Hull, Akashi (Gloria T.), 229–30n47
Hunter, Tera: *To 'Joy My Freedom*, 158
Hurricane Katrina: and displacement, 7,
40–41, 58–59, 96, 112, 130–31, 137;
and erasure, 4, 6–7, 30, 37, 42–43,
59, 64, 100, 131, 157, 235n27; as a
manmade disaster, 32, 37, 41, 157,
201; and narratives of "resilience," 26,
30–41, 49, 59, 71, 100, 132, 158, 191,
194, 198, 205–6, 233n3, 235n32; and
sex workers, 96, 105, 109–10. *See also*
displacement; erasure; resilience
hypervisibility: of Black (cisgender and
transgender) women, 100, 106–7,
112–13; and invisibility (simultaneously), 106–7, 116, 137, 143; and
survival sex work, 108–9. *See also*
invisibilization

imagining otherwise, 4–7, 13–14, 17,
19–22, 28, 32, 46, 51–52, 60, 70, 73–77,
90, 94, 100, 113–14, 120, 134–36,
149, 154, 158–59, 162, 170–71, 178,
181–83, 191–92, 208, 213, 238n53.
See also futurity; world-building
Imarisha, Walidah, 258n63; and organiz-
ing/dreams, 7
incarceration: capital of the world
(Louisiana), 117, 122, 126, 148, 211,
250n70; carceral feminism, 110,
143–45, 154–57, 159; and gender,
106–11, 143–45, 154–57, 159, 173–75,
256n43, 259n4; and health, 11–12,
228n29; after Katrina, 30; "mass,"
107, 248n45; National Council for
Currently and Formerly Incarcerated Women and Girls, 145; and racism (in the South), 107–9. *See also*
Orleans Parish Prison; prison industrial complex
INCITE!, 11, 118, 231n61, 256n41
Indigenous Action Media: on accomplices vs. allies, 22. *See also*
accompliceship
International Day to End Violence
Against Sex Workers, 214–15.
See also sex workers

intimacy: and the NO Justice Project, 100; and pedagogy/training, 185; and relationships/solidarity, 85–87, 99; of violence, 129, 142–43, 216; of world-building, 213. *See also* community; relationships; solidarity

invisibilization: of Black (cisgender and transgender) women's bodies, 62, 97–100, 104, 106–7, 111, 128, 156, 201–2, 238n1; of Black women's work, 21–22, 187; and hypervisibility (simultaneously), 106–7, 116, 137, 143; of WWAV (as attempted by arsonists), 129. *See also* dispossession; erasure; hypervisibility

isolation, 23, 25, 30, 40, 42, 69; of Black women's organizing, 168; into categories, 133; and infrastructure, 135; and risk (for sex workers), 243n63; from social services/information/ resources, 2, 8, 52, 56, 62, 76–78, 92–93, 107, 121–22; from those "studied," 17–18, 85. *See also* racial capitalism playbook

James, Andrea: and the National Council for Currently and Formerly Incarcerated Women and Girls, 145. *See also* incarceration

Jindal, Governor Bobby, 128; failures of, 124; as a Grinch, 186, *189*. *See also* CANS statute; *Doe v. Jindal*

Johnson, Jessica Marie, 178, 226n7. *See also* archive

Johnson, Rashauna, 226n7

Jones, Dianne, *209*, *217*; and harm-reduction work, 212. *See also* harm reduction

Jones, Michelle: on the Indiana women's prisons and "Magdalene societies," 256n43. *See also* incarceration

Kaba, Mariame, 6, 244n75; on experimentation (and learning), 243n61; on hope (as a discipline), 242n50; imagining otherwise, 208; on invisibility/ hypervisibility, 107; on relationships, 14–15. *See also* relationships

Katrina, Hurricane. *See* Hurricane Katrina

Katwiwa, Mwende, *31*, *50*, 157, *164*, *167*, 185, 194, *209*, *217*; and "Black Feminist Santa," 183–84, 186–89; and the Know Her Truths conference, 197–207; "On White People, Solidarity, and (Not) Marching for Mike Brown," 167–68; and protesting the murder of Black people, 163–70; and reproductive justice, 163–64; and the "resilience" porch talk, 34–38, 40; on WWAV, 178–79, 199–201; and WWAV's Black Feminist Library, 158; and Young Women With A Vision, 34, 75, 261n29. *See also* protests

Katz, Cindi: on sedimentations, 234n13. *See also* Hurricane Katrina

Kelley, Blair: on Deon Haywood, 199

Kelley, Robin D. G., 6–7; on dreaming with one's eyes open, 7; on *how* vs. *why* questions, 6, 181, 240n20

King, Dr. Martin Luther, Jr. 168, 253n11, 259n73

Kitchen Table: Women of Color Press, 259n5

Klein, Naomi: on the shock doctrine, 39

Know Her Truths conference, 98, 197–208. *See also* truth

knowledge: ancestral, 158, 170, 208; dispossession, 54, 59, 71, 84–86; everyday, 16–17; fugitive, 258n1; geographic, 33, 49, 63, 65, 70, 159; as guide, 10–12, 16, 115–18, 139–40, 149, 264n9; #KnowYourHistory, 164; leveraging of, 73; and liberation, 5, 12–13, 33, 59–60, 72, 74–75, 83–85, 99, 145, 198, 209, 213; of one's worth, 75, 94; production of, 9–10, 12–13, 17, 20, 23, 33, 42, 49, 53–55, 59–60, 62, 70, 72, 74–75, 83–85, 99, 128, 145, 178, 183, 198, 209, 213; revolutionization of, 5, 209; sharing, 12, 53–54, 129, 170, 213, 236n35; storytelling as, 18–19; world-building, 208. *See also* research

Kreimer, Seth: and the NO Justice Project, 130. *See also* NO Justice Project

Krewe du Vieux, 124, 252n83

Lalani, Samai, *164. See also* protests

leadership: Black women's, 5, 21, 75, 94, 108, 205, 207–8, 216, 218–20; sex workers', 214–15. *See also* threat

Leavitt, Jacqueline: *From Abandonment to Hope*, 237n42

LeFlouria, Talitha: *Chained in Silence*, 248n46

life-giving: care as, 19; storytelling as, 15; WWAV as, 23, 145–149, 182. *See also* care; storytelling

linearity: refusal of, 19–20, 32, 39, 51, 133–34, 230n56. *See also* progress; temporality

Liu, Roseann: on empathy, 133; and solidarity, 229n38

Lorde, Audre, 34, 158, 216, 234n14, 239n7, 259n5; on the idea of a "single-issue struggle," 54, 139; on the power of the erotic, 13, 228n31; on using your own fire, 210. *See also* power: of the erotic

Manion, Jen: on the criminalization of Black women, 248n46. *See also* criminalization

Marchand-Stiaes, Charmaine: and HB 141, 123. *See also* CANS statute; NO Justice Project

Martin, Trayvon: murder of (and resultant protests), 159–65, 169, 191. *See also* Movement for Black Lives; protests

McBride, Renisha: murder of, 165

McCune, Mary Beth, 239n10. *See also* National Council of Negro Women

McDonald, Carol, 211

McKittrick, Katherine: *Black Geographies*, 233n7; on Black women's "absented presence," 236n37; on Black women's bodies (as geographic), 32; *Dear Science*, 229n47; *Demonic Grounds*, 236n37, 261n23; on entering into space, 41–42; and storying, 178, 229n47

McTighe, Laura (Tiggy), 1–2, 10–14, *31*, 47–48, 128, 138, 142, 144, 173, 177, *180*, 211–12, 235n29, 250n69, 262n41;

as accomplice, 12, 22, 93; and the Community Voices Project, 139–40; and the Emerge/Groundworks programs, 150–51, 153–54; "Front Porch Revolution," 232n75; and HIV/criminalization, 11–12, 204; and the Know Her Truths conference, 197–207; and the otherwise, 231n69; and the "resilience" porch talk, 34; and the "Safety and Love" visioning session, 192–97; and sex worker justice, 10, 114–16, 118; and storytelling/narrative, 12–13. *See also* narrative; storytelling

memory, 19; and feeling, 175–79; and oral history, 253n10; as under attack, 39

mentorship, 34, 199, 213, 221, 260n15; and the Community Voices Project, 139; and Young Women With A Vision, 34, 75, 261n29

miscegenation, 102, 108

misinformation, 77, 103, 133, 247n31; in education, 39; and the police, 3–4

"misogynoir," 21–22, 231n66

Mitchell, Zina, *146*, 242n45, 248n40; on the (successful) challenge to the CANS statute, 97, 129. *See also* CANS statute; criminalization; sex workers

Mock, Brentin: on Black front porch politics, 49. *See also* front porch

Morrison, Toni, 158

MOVE bombing, 240n27

movement: as analytical tool, 109–10; restriction of, 140–41; of space, 174

Movement for Black Lives, 47–48, 159, 167; #AllBlackLivesMatter, 169; #BlackLivesMatter, 159, 167–69, 187, *189*, 208

Mujeres Con Vision, 58, 74, 176–77

Mullings, Leith: *Stress and Resilience*, 233n3. *See also* resilience

Murray, Pauli, 158

Muse, Danita, 2, 10, 14, 22, 53–66, 71–77, 94, 114, 134, 143, 154, 159, 171, 174, 211, *212*, 217, 242n42, 243n56; on the drug user and sex worker communities, 56, 69, 104; and front porches, 44–45; and harm-reduction work, 9, 54, 65–70, 77–90, 97, 139, *176*, 177, 241n34; and the origins of WWAV, 8–9, 44, 55–60, 179, 240n13; as unapologetic, 56, 94; as ungovernable, 93; on WWAV staff members (and trust), 93

mutual aid, 4, 54, 106, 158, 260n15; and reparations work, 182, 198, 226n13

names: speaking, 19, 158, 165, 168–69, 183, 206, 238n61

narrative: to avoid imprisonment, 110–11; framing/amplifying the, 10, 12–14, 47–49, 114–15, 124–25, 128, 147–54, 170; *re*framing/correcting the, 4, 69; violent, 8, 52, 238n1, 249n57. *See also* communication; storytelling

National Bail Out collective, 211. *See also* bail outs

National Council for Currently and Formerly Incarcerated Women and Girls, 145. *See also* criminalization; incarceration; James, Andrea

National Council of Negro Women, 55

Nation of Gods and Earths, 236n35. *See also* storytelling: cypher

needle exchanges, 136–37; underground/barroom, 23, 45, 58, 64–65, 78–79, 90, 199. *See also* harm reduction; outreach

new new New Orleans, 195

new New Orleans, 92–93, 157; and "resilience" narratives, 26, 30–41, 49, 59, 71, 100, 132, 158, 191, 194, 198, 205–6, 233n3, 235n32. *See also* Hurricane Katrina; racial capitalism playbook; resilience

New Orleans Abortion Fund. *See also* reproductive justice (RJ)

New Orleans Baby Dolls, 210

New Orleans Hospitality Alliance, 219

New Orleans People's Assembly, 218–19

New Orleans Workers' Center for Racial Justice, 218

NO Justice Project, 10, 12–13, 23, 27, 73, 96–97, 99–101, 104, 106, 113–31,

141–42, 144, 147–48, 150, 157, 159, 167, 189, 191, 200, 214, 219, 236n33, 245n3, 247nn36–38, 250nn68–69; expansion of, 138–39; guiding principles of, 115, 119; and legal tactics, 118–31, 227n24, 245n12, 246n20, 247nn36–37, 248n42, 249nn58–59, 251nn73–74, 251n82, 262n39; No Justice coalition, 115–18. *See also* CANS statute; criminalization; Emerge program; Sex Offender Registry; sex workers

normalization: of condom use, 77; of drug use / needle exchange, 77–78

Nun, Nijme Rinaldi, *79*

Obama, Barack: and the "travel ban," 140–41

objectification: of Black people, 69

objectivity: as myth, 17, 85. *See also* academia

obscenity: and the law, 102–3

occupying: as protest, 165–67, 170

open-endedness, 16, 60

openness: to new ways of doing things, 54, 59, 71–72, 90–91, 97, 201–3. *See also* transformation

organizing: and Black women in the South, 5–6, 14–17, 50, 69, 73, 75, 88–89, 115–16, 125, 135, 165–69, 178, 182–83, 198, 205, 208, 214; and dreams, 7, 50

Orleans Parish Prison (OPP), 110, 259n4; conditions at, 175, 262n38; Reform Coalition, 161; and WWAV, 130, 174–75, 189–91. *See also* incarceration; prison industrial complex

Ortiz, Aurora Santiago: on feminist oral histories, 253n10

otherwise, 21, 23–25, 32–33, 70; analysis, 16, 127, 130; doing, 46; front porches as, 41–43; as *here*, 226n20; imagining, 4–7, 13–14, 17, 19–22, 28, 32, 46, 51–52, 60, 70, 73–77, 90, 94, 100, 113–14, 120, 134–36, 149, 154, 158–59, 162, 170–71, 178, 181–83, 191–92, 208, 213, 238n53; living, 6; making, 42–43, 48–49; space, 41

Our Existence Is Political (WWAV's 30th-anniversary report), 211–12. *See also* political

outreach: and safety, 85–89; and trust, 62, 83; and WWAV, 4, 8, 12, 15, 58, 62–71, 76–92, 100, 114–17, 123, 136–37, 139, 149–50, 159, 173, 181, 185, 207–8, 212. *See also* community; NO Justice Project

Parks, Rosa, 158
Patel, Sunita: and the NO Justice Project, 118–19, 130. *See also* NO Justice Project
Patterson, Orlando: *Slavery and Social Death*, 245n15
Patterson, Sunni: "We Know This Place," 222, 264n13
Peterson, Sharon, 58
Petro, Anthony, 252n83
Petteway, Ryan J.: on racism and public health, 240n22
Pinettes, 210
pity: refusal of, 73, 207
place-making: and front porches 46, 49, 51; and racial capitalism, 33, 39, 41, 49, 53, 159, 170, 225n6
Planned Parenthood, 258n61; and the erasure of Black RJ, 163
Plessy v. Ferguson, 102. *See also* segregation
police: alternatives to calling, 50, 66; and the CANS solicitation clause, 103–4; data (and access), 262n38; and the front porch, 45–49; increased, 30, 112, 136, 144, 250n61; and misinformation, 3–4; movement to defund, 216, 243n61; murder, 23, 47–48, 164–69, 216, 225n2; overcharging (to press for guilty pleas), 111; predatory/violent, 2, 11, 40, 99–100, 107, 115, 120–22, 162, 164–69, 200–202, 249n60, 257n53, 262n38; recording, 260n17; and sexual abuse, 111, 122, 249n60. *See also* criminalization
political: existence as, 21, *66*, 183–84, 211–12; poverty and the, 69, 195, 213; sex work as, *215*

porch. *See* front porch
Positive Women's Network–USA, 11
Povinelli, Elizabeth: *The Cunning of Recognition*, 232n75
power: building, 123, 195, 213; claiming/standing in one's, 87, 132, 134, 147, 154, 156, 158, 181, 194–95, 213, 250n68; of the community, 87, 137, 143, 147; of the erotic, 13–14, 19, 228n31; of fire dreams, 130; of front porch strategy, 51; imbalances (in knowledge-production), 84; institutional (of academia), 22; naming/speaking as, 10, 13, 24–25, 63, 127, 187, 191–92; of New Orleans, 194; of the police (as in need of unraveling), 212; and resistance, 260n16; self-empowerment, 250n68; threat of one's, 1; of words, 24, 195; of WWAV, 149, 154, 156, 158
Price, Ursula, 211
prison industrial complex, 61, 189, 259n4. *See also* incarceration
privacy: gained (at WWAV's Broad St. office), 173; lost (due to CANS conviction), 105. *See also* CANS statute
progress: narratives of, 20, 25, 30–32, 39, 158, 159. *See also* linearity
prostitution, 130, 156; vs. CANS charge, 103–4, 119, 123–24, 200, 203, 246n20, 250n59; male, 103–4, 247n31. *See also* diversion; sex workers
protests: over the acquittal of George Zimmerman, 159–65, 169; over the drug war as a war on women, 146; over the police murder of Michael Brown, 164–65, 168–69; over the police murder of Alton Sterling, 47–48. *See also* Movement for Black Lives; police: murder
public housing, 57, 257n53; post-Katrina, 39–40, 96, 234nn24–25, 237n44, 240n16; pre-Katrina, 237n43
public transportation: post-Katrina, 39
purification: aural, 74; bodily (and urban redevelopment), 235n32; social (and ideas of community formation), 242n42

Quigley, Bill, 251n72; and the "Katrina Pain Index," 232n78; and the NO Justice Project, 118–19, *120*, 123, 130.

racial capitalism playbook, 3–5, 8–10, 13, 16–25, 30–33, 39–41, 46–47, 49, 52–54, 56, 60, 63, 65, 69–71, 74, 83, 85, 92–93, 96–97, 101, 106–7, 109–13, 127, 133–34, 142–45, 155–59, 162–63, 168–71, 178, 181–82, 185, 187, 190, 204, 208–9, 223, 225n6, 226n7, 229n43, 257n53, 259n74
Radical Reconstruction, 101
Ransby, Barbara, 6
Raschig, Megan: and the otherwise, 231n69. *See also* otherwise
recognition: cunning of, 232n75, 235n31, 242n40; as not required (at WWAV), 25
refusal, 21–23, 32–33, 73, 127, 231n68; of academic knowledge-production, 20; of the arson attack on WWAV's office, 145; to blame, 81, 83, 148, 157; of carceral feminism, 214; of complicity, 94, 231n61; of the dispossession of Black women, 55; of erasure, 181, 183; of the grammar of "progress," 25, 31; of linearity, 19–20, 32, 39, 51, 133–34, 230n56; of normative politics, 198; of official post-Katrina narratives, 33; of pity, 73, 207; of premature death, 76; of (the violence of) the present, 4, 14, 22, 52, 77, 93, 113, 128; of the racial capitalism playbook, 17–19, 21–25, 33, 43, 46, 60, 69–70, 83, 97, 127, 163, 169–71, 181–82, 187, 190, 209; of "single-issue" lives, 163; storytelling and, 23; of surveillance, 27; of victimhood, 86–87, 154–57, 181, 207; of visibility, 232n74. *See also* Simpson, Audra
relationships: as archive, 178, 183; and deep communication, 76, 88–89; and difference, 133–34; as living archive, 178; as method, 13–15; and patience, 91; and survival, 12; and WWAV, 4, 6, 8–16, 18, 23–24, 43–45, 60, 62, 64–65, 68, 76–91, 98–99,

113–16, 120, 124, 127, 133–36, 143, 149, 154–55, 161–62, 170–71, 178, 181–82, 213, 218. *See also* community
reparations, 22, 69
repetition: for emphasis, 79; of history, 161; of instructive questions, 21; of mantras/slogans, 21, 186; and meaning-loss ("resilience"), 36; of stories, 20, 74
reproductive justice (RJ), 50, 73, 75, 138, 145, 175, 185, 213, 218–22; Black, 136, 162–64, 170, 210–11; and religion, 262n41
research: academic (as harmful), 62–63, 66, 76, 83–85; Front Porch Research Strategy institute, 197–98, 261n31; lack of (in the early days), 81; and policy, 200; as study, 206; as survival, 4–6, 13, 15–17, 21–22, 60, 178, 198–200, 203–5, 211, 226n12, 252n94. *See also* knowledge
resilience: as academic fodder, 36; of Black people, 35, 39; and erasure, 36, 39, 49, 59, 106, 131, 191–92; narratives of (surrounding the "new New Orleans"), 26, 30–41, 49, 59, 71, 106, 158, 162, 191, 194, 198, 205–6, 235n32
respect: and fear, 80; getting/earning, 90. *See also* community; relationships
rest/restoration: Black women's need for, 74; porches as places of, 11, 43, 45
revolution: calls to, 160–62; and creating, 191, 233n2; and futurity, 237n53; as having a plan, 30, 161, 187, 191, 198;
Richie, Beth, 229n46; on Deon Haywood, 73; on invisibility/hypervisibility, 107; on the violence matrix, 31, 225n5
risk reduction. *See* harm reduction
Ritchie, Andrea, 6, 211–12, 247n35; on the CANS statute, 104; on invisibility/hypervisibility, 107; and the NO Justice Project, 118–19, *120*, 130, 246n20, 248n42, 251nn73–74. *See also* CANS statute; NO Justice Project

Rivers, Whitney: and WWAV's 30th-anniversary report, *212*

Roberts, Dorothy: on invisibility/hypervisibility, 107; *Killing the Black Body*, 239n2

Robinson, Cedric, 230n51; and "racial capitalism," 225n6; on the realization of new theory, 169–70; on slave resistance, 259n74. *See also* racial capitalism playbook

Roché, Angélique, 211

Rodney, Walter: on knowledge and liberation, 5. *See also* knowledge

Rose Tavern, 58, 64, 78–79, 90, 179; closing of, 71

Ross, Loretta, 163, 221, *222*. *See also* reproductive justice (RJ)

Ross, Rosetta E.: *Witnessing and Testifying*, 245n9. *See also* witnessing

Roy, Arundhati: on the coming of another world, 74

Rudovsky, David: and the NO Justice Project, 130. *See also* NO Justice Project

Russo, Vito: on HIV and government neglect, 61. *See also* ACT UP; HIV/AIDS

sacred, 181, 208, 235n32; abolition and the, 263n49; Black women's lives and the, 158; southern front porches and the, 48, 238n58; WWAV as, 73, 181, 208–9. *See also* conjuring; smudging

Saegert, Susan: *From Abandonment to Hope*, 237n42

safety: and community, 88–89; and love, 191–98, 216; and outreach work, 85–89; and sex work, 81–83; and success, 216. *See also* condoms; having another's back

Sales, Ruby, 29. *See also* storytelling

Salinas, Oscar, 58, *92*, 176–77

#SayHerName, 50, 168–69, 238n61, 258n68. *See also* names; speaking

Scott, Eisa, 58, 81, 88–89

segregation, 55, 60, 102

settler colonialism, 23, 50, 232n78, 235n30; and criminalization, 97, 259n1; and the racial capitalism playbook, 3, 33, 39, 134, 158. *See also* racial capitalism playbook

Sex Offender Registry, 9–10, 12, 27, 96–97, 103–6, 111–13, 115, 116–17, 119, 121–24, 129–30, 199–200, 245n4, 247n36, 247n38, 252n86, 262n39. *See also* CANS statute; criminalization; NO Justice Project; sex workers

sex trafficking, 156, 249n57; conflated with sex work, 110–11, 143–45, 148, 156, 215, 254n22, 255n33. *See also* sex workers

sex workers: criminalization of, 1, 5, 9–10, 12, 23, 27, 64, 83, 95–131, 141–42, 145–55, 191, 199–203, 212, 214–17, 254n22; and decriminalization efforts, 1, 50, 113–131, 191, 212, 214–17; and education, 74; and health parties, 62–63, 74, 85–87, 176–177; and Hurricane Katrina, 96, 105, 109–10; and safety, 81–83; and sex trafficking conflation, 110–11, 143–45, 148, 156, 215, 254n22, 255n33; and surveillance, 98, 106, 108–11, 121, 146, 202, 207, 254n22; and survival, 98, 106, 108–11, 121, 146, 202, 207, 254n22; and WWAV, 1, 9, 23, 50, 53–54, 60, 66, 72–74, 76–77, 80–85, 95–131, 136–39, 141–43, 145–55, 191, 212, 214–16. *See also* CANS statute; criminalization; Emerge program; NO Justice Project; prostitution

Shabazz-El, Waheedah, 11–12

Shakur, Assata: on getting one's freedom, 95; on love, 133

Shange, Savannah: "Black Girl Ordinary," 231n68; on empathy, 133; and solidarity, 229n38

Sharpe, Christina: *In the Wake*, 226n12, 260n8. *See also* undisciplined

Shavers, Nakita, *31*, *50*, 185; and reproductive justice work, 75; and the "resilience" porch talk, 34–35

Shelton, Ashley, 210–11

silence: of elected officials, 61; national moment of, 165–68, 170; sitting with, 99; in WWAV's archive, 178

Simmons, LaKisha Michelle, 249n53

Simpson, Audra: and the politics of refusal, 231n68. *See also* refusal

Simpson, Monica: on Planned Parenthood and the erasure of Black RJ, 163, 170. *See also* reproductive justice (RJ)

SisterLove, 141

SisterSong, 163–64. *See also* reproductive justice (RJ)

slavery, 23, 46, 50, 240n23, 259n74; and criminalization, 97, 143; "modern-day" (sex trafficking), 143–44, 156; and the racial capitalism playbook, 3, 33, 39, 134, 158. *See also* racial capitalism playbook

Smith, Barbara, 229–30n47, 259n5. *See also* Combahee River Collective

Smith, Susan L.: *Sick and Tired of Being Sick and Tired*, 239n5

smudging, 172, 259n1

social change lawyering, 118, 251n72. *See also* NO Justice Project; Quigley, Bill

solidarity, 14, 70–71, 86–87, 93, 104, 116, 147, 162, 207, 209, 228n36; and care, 93; and collectivity, 14, 127–28, 133–34, 162; Solidarity Rally for Trayvon Martin, 159–65, 191, 233n2; thick, 133–34. *See also* collectivity; community; relationships

Southerners on New Ground, 211. *See also* bail outs

space: holding, 47, 96, 133, 136–39, 142, 164; making/having/taking/claiming, 4, 11, 33, 42, 51, 64, 70–71, 73, 133, 136–39, 149, 165, 174, 181; movement of, 174. *See also* front porch; spatiality

SPARK Reproductive Justice NOW, 164. *See also* reproductive justice (RJ)

spatiality: and "authentic Blackness," 40; and the Black body, 32, 42; and community, 16; and flow, 174; and intersectionality, 149. *See also* space

speaking: into being/existence (generative), 11, 20–21, 24–25, 32–33, 74, 130, 136, 138, 146–47, 153, 159, 162, 183; and the interstice, 236n39;

knowledge, 53, 170; names, 19, 158, 165, 168–69, 183, 206, 238n61; one's truth, 4, 63, 70, 72, 83, 94, 97, 125–28, 143, 155, 183, 206–7, 242n42, 261n31; one's vision, 220; and place, 42; as power, 10, 13, 24–25, 63, 127, 187, 191–92; unbridled, 63, 70, 72, 83, 94, 242n42. *See also* communication

speech. *See* speaking

Spillers, Hortense: on the Black female subject, 236n39, 248n43

spirituality, 179, 208; and the Black Radical Tradition, 230n51; and building otherwise, 238, 252. *See also* Casselberry, Judith

Stanley, Eric A.: on ungovernability, 243n54. *See also* ungovernable

Sterling, Alton: police murder of (and resultant protests), 47–48. *See also* police: murder; protests

Stiaes, Shelley, 2

storytelling, 12–13, 15–16, 26–27, 70, 94, 105, 139–40, 154, 193, 205, 229n47; becoming action, 18, 20, 33, 53, 90, 106; cypher, 42, 83, 90, 236n35; and front porches, 15–16, 42, 49–50, 75, 130, 206; and home, 177–79; and imagining otherwise, 178; as knowledge, 18–19; as life-giving, 15; as method/theory, 201; and the NO Justice Project, 115–17; as pedagogy, 54, 75, 150, 185; and refusal, 23; and repetition, 20, 74; and sight, 191; story circles, 23, 42, 65, 75–94; storying, 178, 229n47; and survival, 18–19, 134; and trust, 142; and truth, 200–201; through vision boards, 146–47; and world-making, 74. *See also* front porch; narrative

Strauss, Anselm: and "grounded theory," 229n45

surveillance, 16; community-based, 147; "dark sousveillance," 191, 260n17; epidemiological, 62; everyday, 27, 58, 65, 74, 100, 109–11, 113, 115, 145, 165, 178, 191, 201, 212; as violence, 11, 25, 74, 145, 162 survival: affective labor and, 40; front porches and, 45; vs. health, 141; and relationships, 12; research as, 4–6, 13, 15–17, 21–22, 60, 178, 198–200, 203–5, 211, 226n12, 252n94; sex work and, 98, 106, 108–11, 121, 146, 202, 207, 254n22; and storytelling, 18–19, 134; thriving vs. mere, 6, 11, 17, 19, 37, 183, 209, 218

Survived and Punished New York, 255n31

taking, 23, 25, 30, 56, 69, 83, 93, 107; of connections, 155; of credit, 82–86, 186–87; of data/methods, 15, 66, 83–86; of knowledge, 54, 59, 71, 84–86; of land/housing, 3–4, 8, 39–43; of stories, 205. *See also* dispossession; racial capitalism playbook

temporality: and "allochronism," 232n77; and "authentic Blackness," 40; and front porch strategy, 26, 33, 39, 42–43; and (in)justice, 18–19; and intersectionality, 149; simultaneity of past, present, and future, 19, 134, 234n20; and WWAV's fire dreams, 18–19, 27–28, 134–36, 155, 170–71. *See also* futurity; linearity; Thomas, Deborah; time

Thanos, Nikki: and the NO Justice Project, *120*, 129–30.

theory on the ground, 17–19, 23, 25–26, 31, 33, 41–45, 49, 67, 70–71, 74, 77, 84, 97, 100, 107, 110–11, 123, 133, 155, 170–71, 183, 190, 205, 213

"They ain't gotta like you" (slogan), 54, 70, 80, 93–94

"They ain't ready" (slogan), 21, 38–39, 42–43, 80, 186

Thomas, Deborah: on futurity and revolution, 238n53; on time (as simultaneous), 230n56. *See also* temporality

threat: of Black womanhood, 109; of Black women's freedom, 21, 94; of Black women's leadership, 5, 21, 75, 94, 108, 205, 207–8; of Black women's organizing, 178; of one's power, 1

Thuma, Emily, 6

time, 7, 14, 18, 46, 134–35, 144; "allochronism," 40, 232n77; and dispossession, 5, 84, 134, 222; making, 149; simultaneity of past/present/future, 19, 39, 230n56, 234n20; in space/relationship, 16, 19, 135, 149, 154–55, 168, 170, 182, 187. *See also* dispossession; futurity; linearity; progress; temporality

Tometi, Opal: and #BlackLivesMatter, 159, 170. *See also* Movement for Black Lives

tourism: and New Orleans, 40, 55

trafficking. *See* sex trafficking

transformation, 113–14, 126, 129, 136, 149, 198; of the world, 132, 193–94, 213. *See also* openness

Treen, Governor Dave: and the CANS statute, 103.

Trotter, Darian, 165

trust, 93; and outreach, 62, 83; and storytelling, 142; #TrustBlackWomen, 21, 136, 168, 216; "We Always Resist: Trust Black Women," 164

truth: as antidote, 19; community (as centered in the NO Justice Project), 114–17; of enchantment, 208; and history, 180; Know Her Truths conference, 98, 197–208; about Santa, 186–87; speaking one's, 4, 63, 70, 72, 83, 94, 97, 125–28, 143, 155, 183, 206–7, 242n42, 261n31; in stories, 200–201; "We Spoke Our Truths," 128, 252n94

Truth, Sojourner, 29, 158

Tubman, Harriet, 158

Tuck, Eve: on decolonialization, 32

Ture, Kwame: on revolution as about creating, 191, 233n2

undisciplined: WWAV as, 5, 11, 23, 54, 178. *See also* Sharpe, Christina

ungovernable, 76, 93, 100, 154, 243n54

United States HIV Racial Justice Now network, 218.

UNSHACKLE, 11–12, 118

Vera Institute: and the NO Justice Project, 119.

victimhood, 159, 204; refusal of 86–87, 154–57, 181, 207. *See also* carceral feminism

violence: of abstraction, 125, 127; of communalism, 253n6; domestic, 107, 122, 156, 172, 248n44, 250n60; everyday/structural, 12–13, 16–17, 33, 46, 65, 77, 86, 98, 100, 105–7, 110–13, 116–17, 119, 121–22, 142–43, 165, 202, 216–18; gender-based, 33, 54, 141; and intimacy, 129, 142–43, 216; matrix, 31, 86, 110, 225n5; of official narratives, 33, 133; and recovery, 31; state, 33, 142–43, 206, 216; of white tears, 38, 234n17

vision, 114; into action, 192; boarding, 146–47, 191–96; "dark sousveillance," 191, 260n17; of the hidden (in plain sight), 178, 213; session ("Safety and Love"), 191–98; vs. sound, 232n72. *See also* imagining otherwise

Voice of the Experienced (VOTE), 119

voter engagement, 72, 75, 212

Wali, Alaka: *Stress and Resilience*, 233n3. *See also* resilience

Walker, Alice: on a "Womanist," 19

Ware, Wes: and the NO Justice Project, 119, *120.*

war on drugs, 3–5, 31, 52, 63–64, 144–46, 239n1. *See also* drug users

Weeks, Nia, *31, 50,* 185, *209, 217*; and policy work, 75, 189, 192–97; and the "resilience" porch talk, 34–38; and the "Safety and Love" visioning session, 192–97

Weisenfeld, Judith, 231n58

welfare queens (as violent narrative), 8, 52

Wells, Ida B., 158, 199, 257n48, 262n41

Wildmon, Donald: lobbying efforts of (against sex workers), 103. *See also* sex workers

Wildseeds, 165, 258n63

Wiley, Michelle, *50,* 75, 126, 173–74, 179, *180,* 185, *197, 209,* 212, *214, 217. See also* Emerge program

Williams, Erica, 2

Williams, Patricia J.: *The Alchemy of Race and Rights*, 229n47

Williams, Raymond: "structure of feeling," 241n36, 253n8. *See also* feeling

Wilson, Darren: and the murder of Michael Brown, 164. *See also* police: murder; protests

witnessing, 52, 55; responsibility of, 245n9; and storytelling, 18

Women of African Descent for Reproductive Justice, 163. *See also* reproductive justice (RJ)

Women's Health & Justice Initiative, 11, 258n61

women's health movement, 66

Women With A Vision (WWAV): and abolition feminism, 1, 10–11, 54, 107, 130, 143, 145, 150, 154, 216, 228n26; arson attack, 1–5, 10, 13, 15, 18–19, 21–22, 24, 26–27, 29, 34, 37, 41, 54, 60, 75, 99, 128–71, 173, 175–78, 181, 191, 205, 211, 221–22, 228n32, 235n33, 245n12; ArtEgg office, 137–38, 145–46, 157–58, 172–74, 178–79, 185; Black Feminist Library of, 25, 158, 180, 226n13, 242n38, 257n50; Black Feminist Porch Talks, 49–50, 206, 238n61; Born in Flames Living Archive, 15–16, 26, 158, 228n32, 229n40, 250n69, 252n94, 265–75; Born in Flames oral history project, 10, 13, 53–54, 74, 99, 205, 228n32; Broad Street office, 29–51, 171–73, 178–80, 183–85, 187, 189, 198–98, *209,* 213, *219*; Community Voices Project, 139–40; and the Deep South Decrim Project, 215–17, 254n22; and drug users, 3, 5, 9, 53–54, 56, 60, 62, 66, 72–74, 76–78, 82–83, 97, 104–5, 137–39, 141–43, 148; and the Emerge program, 10–11, 14, 145–55, 170, 173–74, 191, 214; and First Grace United Methodist Church, 136–38; and fresh flowers, 185; front porch strategy, 26, 29–51, 54, 57, 179–208, 218–19, 261n31, 236n34; and harm reduction, 9, 50,

Women With A Vision (continued)
54, 65–68, 70–71, 76–90, 97, 114,
136–37, 139, 145, 148, 199, 210, 212,
214–15, 241n34, 254n13; and HIV/
AIDS, 3–5, 8–9, 11–12, 54, 61–62,
65–67, 71, 73, 78–79, 83–85, 93, 114,
139–41, 144–45, 199, 203–4, 210–14,
218–19; homecoming of (after arson
attack), 27–31, 34, 171–80; and the
impossible, 193; intersectionality of,
53, 155, 162, 200–201, 208, 210–11,
216, 218–19, 248n44; legacy of (as
in place), 92–93; as life-giving, 23,
145–149, 182; and the NO Justice
Project, 10, 12–13, 23, 27, 73, 96–97,
99–101, 104, 106, 113–31, 141–42,
144, 147–48, 150, 157, 159, 167, 189,
191, 200, 214, 219, 236n33, 245n3,
247nn36–38, 250nn68–69; Norman C. Francis Parkway office, 2, 95,
174, 177, 225n1; origins of, 3–4, 8–11,
30, 44, 55–60, 213; and the Orleans
Parish Prison (OPP), 130, 174–75,
189–91; *Our Existence Is Political*
(30th-anniversary report), 211–12;
and outreach, 4, 8, 12, 15, 58, 62–71,
76–92, 100, 114–17, 123, 136–37, 139,
149–50, 159, 173, 181, 185, 207–8,
212; and policy work, 72, 75, 98,
173–74, 185, 189–97, 211–12, 214;
power of, 149, 154, 156, 158; rebirth
of (after arson attack), 128–71;; and
relationships, 4, 6, 8–16, 18, 23–24,
43–45, 60, 62, 64–65, 68, 76–91,
98–99, 113–16, 120, 124, 127, 133–36,
143, 149, 154–55, 161–62, 170–71,
178, 181–82, 213, 218; and reproductive justice, 162–64, 175, 211; and
the sacred, 73, 181, 208–9; and sex
workers, 1, 9, 23, 50, 53–54, 60, 66,
72–74, 76–77, 80–85, 95–131, 136–39,

141–43, 145–55, 191, 212, 214–16;
theory on the ground, 17–19, 23,
25–26, 31, 33, 41–45, 49, 67, 70–71,
74, 77, 84, 97, 100, 107, 110–11, 123,
133, 155, 170–71, 183, 190, 205, 213;
as undisciplined, 5, 11, 23, 54, 178;
as vision and practice, 93; and voter
engagement, 72, 75, 212; and working in community, 9, 27, 31, 53, 62,
65–72, 74, 76–92, 98–99, 114–17,
119, 123, 131, 136–37, 139, 148, 161–62,
171, 179, 190, 193, 196, 198–99, 204,
223, 229n43, 264n9; and working
across scales, 27, 140–42, 144–45,
180, 220; Young Women With A
Vision (YWWAV), 34, 261n29
Woods, Clyde, 226n7, 233n7, 234n19; on
the Blues and Bourbon restorations,
39; on post-Katrina New Orleans,
32, 65
world-building, 4–5, 7, 9, 13–14, 17–19,
21, 23–27, 33, 51–53, 65, 70, 73–77,
93, 132, 135–36, 154, 158–59, 162,
182–83, 191–92, 198, 208, 213, 223,
244n75. *See also* futurity; imagining
otherwise; speaking
writing: and organizing/theorizing, 14
WWAV. *See* Women With A Vision
Wynter, Sylvia: on absented presence
and the demonic, 236n37

Yang, K. Wayne: on decolonialization, 32
Young, Iris Marion: on city life, 253n6
Young Lords: and community survival
programs, 66
Young Women's Empowerment Project,
229n47

Zimmerman, George: acquittal of (and
resultant protests), 159–65, 169, 191
Zion Trinity, 260n13